Lecture Notes in Computer Science 12227

More information about this series at http://www.springer.com/series/7408

Ivan Lanese · Mariusz Rawski (Eds.)

Reversible Computation

12th International Conference, RC 2020
Oslo, Norway, July 9–10, 2020
Proceedings

 Springer

Editors
Ivan Lanese 🆔
University of Bologna
Bologna, Italy

Mariusz Rawski 🆔
University of Warsaw
Warsaw, Poland

ISSN 0302-9743   ISSN 1611-3349   (electronic)
Lecture Notes in Computer Science
ISBN 978-3-030-52481-4   ISBN 978-3-030-52482-1   (eBook)
https://doi.org/10.1007/978-3-030-52482-1

LNCS Sublibrary: SL2 – Programming and Software Engineering

This Springer imprint is published by the registered company Springer Nature Switzerland AG
The registered company address is: Gewerbestrasse 11, 6330 Cham, Switzerland

Preface

This volume contains the papers presented at the 12th Conference on Reversible Computation (RC 2020), held during July 9–10, 2020, online due to the COVID-19 pandemic, while initially expected to take place virtually in Oslo, Norway, hosted by the Institute for Informatics, University of Oslo.

The RC conference brings together researchers from computer science, mathematics, engineering, and physics to discuss new developments and directions for future research in the emerging area of Reversible Computation. This includes, for example, reversible formal models, reversible programming languages, reversible circuits, and quantum computing.

The conference received 23 submissions with authors from 16 countries. All papers were reviewed by at least three members of the Program Committee. After careful deliberations, the Program Committee selected 17 papers for presentation. In addition to these papers, this volume contains the abstracts of the two invited talks: "Problems and Prospects for Bidirectional Transformations" by Perdita Stevens (University of Edinburgh, UK) and "Inverse Problems, Constraint Satisfaction, Reversible Logic, Invertible Logic and Grover Quantum Oracles for Practical Problems" by Marek Perkowski (Portland State University, USA).

Of course the COVID-19 pandemic had a strong impact on the conference, as well as on research and the society in general. This was the first edition of RC to be held online, similar to other conference scheduled for this time. This is of course a difficulty, since in-person presence makes interaction much easier, but also a challenge and an occasion. Indeed, an online conference stimulates larger participation, in particular from persons whose budget or constraints may not allow in-person participation, not even under normal circumstances.

The conference would not be possible without the enthusiasm of the members of the Program Committee; their professionalism and their helpfulness was exemplary. For the work of the Program Committee and the compilation of the proceedings, the extremely useful EasyChair conference managment system was employed. Finally, we would like to thank all the authors for their submissions, their willingness to continue improving their papers, and their wonderful presentations during RC 2020.

April 2020

Ivan Lanese
Mariusz Rawski

Organization

Program Committee

Gerhard Dueck	University of New Brunswick, Canada
Robert Glück	University of Copenhagen, Denmark
Jarkko Kari	University of Turku, Finland
Jean Krivine	CNRS, France
Ivan Lanese	University of Bologna, Italy, and INRIA, France
Martin Lukac	Nazarbayev University, Kazakhstan
Kazutaka Matsuda	Tohoku University, Japan
Claudio Antares Mezzina	Università di Urbino, Italy
Lukasz Mikulski	Nicolaus Copernicus University, Poland
Torben Ægidius Mogensen	University of Copenhagen, Denmark
Claudio Moraga	TU Dortmund, Germany
Iain Phillips	Imperial College London, UK
Krzysztof Podlaski	University of Lodz, Poland
Mariusz Rawski	Warsaw University of Technology, Poland
Markus Schordan	Lawrence Livermore National Laboratory, USA
Peter Selinger	Dalhousie University, Canada
Mathias Soeken	École Polytechnique Fédérale de Lausanne, Switzerland
Milena Stankovic	University of Nis, Serbia
Himanshu Thapliyal	University of Kentucky, USA
Irek Ulidowski	University of Leicester, UK
German Vidal	MiST, VRAIN, Universitat Politecnica de Valencia, Spain
Robert Wille	Johannes Kepler University Linz, Austria
Tetsuo Yokoyama	Nanzan University, Japan

Additional Reviewers

Gogolinska, Anna
Hoey, James
Kirkeby, Maja
Mróz, Andrzej
Varacca, Daniele

Abstracts of Invited Talks

Problems and Prospects For Bidirectional Transformations

Perdita Stevens

School of Informatics, University of Edinburgh

Abstract. Bidirectional transformations maintain consistency between two, or more, sources of information. These information sources can be code, documents, database views, etc.: the general term "model" covers them all. I will explain why I think bidirectional transformations have the potential to transform software development and help solve the "capacity crisis", in which the demand for software engineering outstrips the supply of people able to do it. In order to bring this to fruition we need to solve many problems; for example I have recently been working on how to manage networks of many models, not just two. It turns out that reversibility – whose relationship with bidirectionality is, in general, not as obvious as we might think at first sight – is relevant to some outstanding problems. I will describe progress and indicate some possible directions for future work.

Inverse Problems, Constraint Satisfaction, Reversible Logic, Invertible Logic and Grover Quantum Oracles for Practical Problems

Marek Perkowski

Department of Electrical and Computer Engineering, Portland State University,
Portland, OR 97207, USA
mperkows@ee.pdx.edu

Abstract. It is well-known that the "Unsorted Database" quantum algorithm by Grover gives quadratic speedup to several important combinatorial and enumerative problems, such as: SAT, Graph Coloring, Maximum Cliques, Travelling Salesman and many others. Recently, quantum programming languages such as Quipper start to be used to design, verify and simulate practical quantum algorithms for important problems in Quantum Machine Learning. So far, however, no methodologies have been created to program Grover Oracles for particular classes of problems. In contrast, such methodologies have been already created for classical Constraint Satisfaction Problems. The goal of this invited talk is to show results of some initial research towards creating systematic methodologies to program quantum computers that solve search problems in Artificial Intelligence, Logic Design and Machine Learning. Our methods are based on unified oracle blocks for such problem representations as set partition algebra, cube calculus and optimal mappings. For instance, several important problems in CAD and Machine Learning can be solved using only two basic operations on set partitions; $\Pi_1 \leq \Pi_2$ and $\Pi_1 \Pi_2$. Moreover, building oracles is the fundamental concept in the new approach to solve CSP proposed here and based on Invertible Logic introduced recently by Supriyo Datta and his team.

Contents

Circuit Synthesis

Tools and Applications

Invited Talks

Inverse Problems, Constraint Satisfaction, Reversible Logic, Invertible Logic and Grover Quantum Oracles for Practical Problems

Marek Perkowski[✉]

Department of Electrical and Computer Engineering, Portland State University,
Portland, OR 97207, USA
mperkows@ee.pdx.edu

Abstract. It is well-known that the "Unsorted Database" quantum algorithm by Grover gives quadratic speedup to several important combinatorial and enumerative problems, such as: SAT, Graph Coloring, Maximum Cliques, Travelling Salesman and many others. Recently, quantum programming languages such as Quipper start to be used to design, verify and simulate practical quantum algorithms for important problems in Quantum Machine Learning. So far, however, no methodologies have been created to program Grover Oracles for particular classes of problems. In contrast, such methodologies have been already created for classical Constraint Satisfaction Problems. The goal of this invited talk is to show results of some initial research towards creating systematic methodologies to program quantum computers that solve search problems in Artificial Intelligence, Logic Design and Machine Learning. Our methods are based on unified oracle blocks for such problem representations as set partition algebra, cube calculus and optimal mappings. For instance, several important problems in CAD and Machine Learning can be solved using only two basic operations on set partitions; $\Pi_1 \leq \Pi_2$ and $\Pi_1 \cdot \Pi_2$. Moreover, building oracles is the fundamental concept in the new approach to solve CSP proposed here and based on Invertible Logic introduced recently by Supriyo Datta and his team.

Keywords: Inverse problems · Oracles · Grover algorithm · Invertible logic

1 Introduction

There are two important and large classes of problems: Constraint Satisfaction Problems (CSP) and optimization problems. CSP problems are specified just by a set of constraints that the solution has to satisfy. To solve a CSP problem we want to find a solution that satisfies all the constraints (like for a robot passing a labyrinth without bouncing any wall). In optimization problems we want to find the solution that optimizes some cost function (like a robot driving from room A to room B in the labyrinth using minimum energy from its battery). Mathematical problem formulations such as Graph Coloring or Shortest Path are abstractions of many problems from real life. Mathematical optimization problems can be reduced to repeated applications of constraint satisfaction problems. Every next problem in the sequence is solved with added and modified constraints.

© Springer Nature Switzerland AG 2020
I. Lanese and M. Rawski (Eds.): RC 2020, LNCS 12227, pp. 3–32, 2020.
https://doi.org/10.1007/978-3-030-52482-1_1

For instance, the Node Coloring Problem in a graph can be formulated as a problem of coloring nodes with some restricted number of colors such that every two nodes n_i and n_j that share the same edge $e_{ij} = (n_i, n_j)$ obtain different colors. The chromatic number of the graph is the minimum number of colors used to color this graph. When we want to find the chromatic number of the graph (and the respective actual coloring) we can proceed as follows. We set some number K for which a correct coloring exists, this can be the number of nodes in the worst case. Next we exactly solve the constraint satisfaction problem for this graph, assuming that the graph is K-colorable. When we are able to color the graph with K colors, we guess that we can color the graph with K-1 colors. If we were able to do this, then we repeat coloring again as a new constraint satisfaction problem with K-2 colors, and so on. If we were not able to color the graph with K-2 colors but we were able to color it with K-1 colors then K-1 is the chromatic number of the graph. This simple principle of "reducing optimization problem to the repeated constraint satisfaction problem with some changed constraints" is applicable to very many, if not all, optimization problems. The key idea here is to formulate the problem as the Constraint Satisfaction Problem and next to generate the Oracle for this problem. If this oracle is realized in hardware as a circuit built especially for every problem instance, the solution can be very fast. Oracle can be realized as a quantum reversible circuit and used in Grover Algorithm. Here we will show that the oracle can be also built in standard binary logic or in the recently proposed Invertible Logic [5, 17]. To exercise Oracle in classical and quantum logic we need also a Generator that creates combinations to be verified by the Oracle. We call that the Oracle is exercised by the Generator.

This paper presents the universality and power of systematic creation of oracles that are next mapped to one of the three types of oracles: classical, quantum and invertible. Section 2 formulates the general idea of formulating oracles for CSP problems, used to solve both the decision and optimization problems. Section 3 presents how to solve this class of problems using classical Boolean logic. The oracle model introduced in this section is universal for quantum and Invertible Logic circuits. Section 4 explains briefly Grover Algorithm and reversible oracles for it. We illustrate how to modify the oracle in a succession of Grover Algorithm runs. Section 5 discusses how to modify or design the oracles realized in Invertible logic for this class of problems. In Sect. 6 we present how the logic programming language Prolog is used to design and verify oracles and especially the Invertible Logic oracles. Section 7 gives conclusions on this new approach to solve a large class of practical problems.

2 Classical Grover Oracles Versus Invertible Logic Oracles

Because optimization problems are reducible to CSP, let us concentrate on the Constraint Satisfaction Problem, which has by itself very many applications in logic design, logic, cryptography, robotics, Machine Learning and control. There is also some evidence that animals, and even bacteria, solve the constraint satisfaction problems by blind probabilistic mechanisms just to survive [29]. Let us present some simple CSP examples.

Graph coloring is a simple constraint satisfaction problem formulated as follows: Given is graph G with N nodes and E edges, edges being pairs of nodes $e_{ij} = (n_i, n_j)$. Nodes are colored with function COLOR: $N \to C$ where C is a set with K elements called colors. COLOR(n_1) = *red* means coloring node n_1 with color *red*. For every edge $e_{ij} = (n_i, n_j)$ the constraint COLOR(n_i) $\neq$ COLOR (n_j) which means that every two adjacent (neighbor) nodes have different colors. Correct coloring is one that the constraint is satisfied for every edge. Find a solution to the following problem:

Is it possible to correctly color graph G with K colors? If yes, graph G is K-colorable, its chromatic number is K or less. The CSP algorithm constructively demonstrates the correct coloring and the user can easily verify the correctness of the coloring found. Note, that the above formulation is a decision version of graph coloring, not the optimization version. The answer is of type Yes/No.

Another CSP problem is **Satisfiability** or SAT Problem. Given is a formula F in some logic (possibly Boolean logic) and we ask *"is this formula satisfiable?"* Which means, *"can we find a specific value for every variable that the formula F = 1?"*. For instance, formula $F(a, b) = (a + b) * (a' + b) * (a + b') * (a' + b')$ in Boolean logic is not satisfiable. But this formula is 3-satisfiable, which means that when we remove any single one of the four OR-terms from the product F(a, b) above, the formula would be satisfiable. For instance, formula $F_1(a, b) = (a + b) * (a' + b) * (a + b') = (a + bb')$ $(a' + b) = a(a' + b) = ab$, thus for a = 1 and b = 1 the formula is satisfied. This fundamental problem has hundreds applications in real life engineering problems that can be reduced to it. Problems such as optimizing digital designs, and also practical life problems such as finding the best escape routes from some territory after Nuclear Plant disaster.

SAT Problem can be also reduced to CSP. Similarly, CSP problems can be reduced to SAT. One more problem of CSP type is a **crypto arithmetic problem:** SEND + MORE = MONEY in which we have to substitute digits 0–9 for letters S, E, N, D, M, O, R, Y in an unique mapping (a mapping function) such that the symbolic equation above is converted to a valid arithmetic addition on digits. This toy problem is a simplification of similar problems in cryptography, a research area with huge military and security impacts. The same way as the SAT Problem, graph coloring, or any CSP problem, this problem can be solved using an oracle, in our case a hardware oracle. For this kind of problems, the oracle is built from logic gates AND, OR, NOT, logic blocks such as predicates (A = B) or (A > C) and arithmetic blocks such as adders and multipliers.

Building oracles in reversible logic is the fundament of quantum Grover algorithm. The oracle is problem-dependent and even problem-instance dependent. Quantum algorithms are circuits from quantum gates. A quantum oracle is the heart of Grover circuit, other gates in this circuit are always the same, easy and well-known. Practically, applying Grover Algorithm to a new problem means to design an oracle for the constraint satisfaction problem to be solved. When we know how to build the oracle in Boolean Logic and using standard arithmetic, we can convert the Boolean circuit of the oracle to a quantum oracle in reversible logic just by a conversion of Boolean gates and blocks to equivalent reversible logic gates such as Toffoli, Fredkin and Feynman and "reversible blocks" such as a quantum adder.

Reversible functions are mathematical functions which are one-to-one mappings of input vectors to output vectors and vice versa. If a function to be mapped is not reversible, which is frequently the case in oracles, it can be mapped to reversible gates and blocks but it requires ancilla qubits. Most Boolean Functions (single or multiple-output) are not reversible, but building quantum oracles we want to realize them with quantum gates that are reversible. This means that we need to add ancilla qubits initialized to 0 or 1, to be able to perform this mapping. Therefore, what we call "reversible gates" and "reversible blocks" are not reversible functions in mathematical sense because many of them require ancilla qubits. Thus they may correspond to mathematical Boolean functions that are not reversible, but allow the designer familiar with classical digital design of combinational circuit to use immediately his knowledge to build optimized and tricky quantum oracles [11, 15].

Let us make a strong point here, that the very idea of hardware oracle is much more than a Grover Oracle and quantum circuits. One can build a Boolean circuit of the oracle in FPGA [2, 26, 44] and find as the solution to this hardware oracle the input vectors which lead to satisfaction F = 1 observed on oracle's output. Oracles are thus hardware devices to solve the inverse function problem that is known in many areas of mathematics and practical applications. Very little is published about using oracles in hardware with logic circuits that are different than quantum reversible oracles. Grover Algorithm [9] uses oracles built from various quantum reversible gates, plus blocks such as quantum adders or quantum comparators built from quantum gates. Grover algorithm gives a quadratic speedup over classical exhaustive search algorithms for the same problem. Although other quantum algorithms such as the Shor Algorithm [19] give exponential speedup, Grover Algorithm is very important because very many problems of big practical importance can be reformulated for Grover, and not that many problems can be reduced to Shor Algorithm. Several publications of various authors found solutions to important problems based on Grover Algorithm but the authors usually do not build these oracles from gates so that they cannot evaluate their practical complexity. They just show that this can be done by formulating for instance circuits as unitary matrices. In contrast, work of our PSU team designs the oracles in detail, bottom-up and using practical and experimentally verified "truly quantum gates" [23] or "quantum reversible" gates and blocks [3, 8, 11, 12, 15, 16, 21–24, 29, 32, 45].

When one realizes that the fundamental, most important idea in Grover Algorithm is to find the inverse function, one can realize that quantum is not the only technology in which we can build efficient oracles and obtain speedup of algorithms when compared to classical circuits, classical algorithms or parallel algorithms. One naive method would be to build the oracle in classical Boolean logic with standard Boolean gates and logical/arithmetical blocks. Next this oracle could be exercised (exhaustively or randomly) from input to output. Whenever the output equal value 1 is found, the state of the binary input vector gives the solution to the constraint satisfaction problem described by the oracle. Although this method was used in several designs [2, 26, 44], it is harmed by the very slow speed when solving problems of practical size, like those SAT problems encountered in industrial CAD applications. This is because for the Boolean function of n variables in the worst case the oracle needs to be evaluated 2^n times (for each of its minterms representing the Boolean function that corresponds to this oracle). Minterms for a Boolean function of n variables are products of all n literals of this function. True minterms are those for which value of the function is 1. Circuits with quantum oracles are better that classical Boolean circuits because they operate using quantum parallelism and quantum superposition - on all vectors being potential solutions at the same time (all minterms). Thus quantum oracle iterated sufficiently many times as part of the "Grover Loop" highly increases the probability of finding one of the solutions in a single measurement of all input qubits together with the output qubit of the Boolean function realized in the oracle. Grover Algorithm implemented in quantum circuits gives a quadratic speedup when compared to exhaustive classical circuit (algorithm) for the same problem.

Recently a new and very powerful concept was found in the area of recursive Deep Neural Networks (DNN) and this is the idea of Invertible Logic [5, 6, 17, 18, 20, 27]. This logic can be realized with magnetic spins [6], but it can be also emulated using FPGAs (sacrifying speed, FPGAs used mainly for verification). So far very few applications of this idea were published and they are reduced to adders, multipliers, number factorization [14] and one class of neural networks [10]. In contrast, here we present a unified methodology to solve CSP and optimization problems by building and exercising oracles that can be realized very similarly in Quantum and Invertible Logic.

Let us compare **three types of logic realized in circuits**:

1. Classical Boolean combinational logic
2. Reversible (permutative) logic as used in quantum oracles
3. Invertible Logic of Supriyo Datta et al.

Classical Boolean logic propagates signals from inputs to outputs. In <u>inverse problems</u> we want to find the input vectors with the given output value (like $F = 1$ here). Thus if we want to find solutions to non-trivial inverse problems about which we have no additional information (the proverbial "Unsorted Database" in Grover case) we have to go through all or many input combinations before we find the input vector for which $F = 1$. Creating the binary input vectors, the solution candidates for this procedure can be done with a sequential counter or with a random number generator (RNG) such as LFSR on the input to the oracle circuit.

For a motivating example, let us assume that the oracle circuit of function F2 is just a tree of two-input AND gates with 64 inputs in total, but the function (or its circuit) is not known to the observer. To find this function, the oracle in classical logic would be evaluated 2^{64} number of times, which is an astronomical number. Grover Algorithm would evaluate the oracle "only" $2^{\wedge} (64/2) = 2^{32}$ times which may be also not practical. However, in Invertible logic in which one propagates the signals from output to inputs, the Invertible Logic method would need only one evaluation of the oracle realized with invertible gates. The main principle is that the **Invertible Logic Gates** can propagate signals in any direction. In Invertible Logic a two-input $C = AND(A, B)$ gate with output fixed to $C = 1$ creates the input value "1" on both its inputs: $A = 1$, $B = 1$. Therefore in we start from output $F2 = 1$ in the above 64-input tree of AND gates, value 1 will be propagated from the function F2 output to previous levels of the tree and ultimately will create values 1 on all 64 inputs without backtracking and in one value propagation process. If one gives value 0 to the output of two-input AND invertible gate, on inputs the sequence $(A, B) = (0, 0), (0, 1)$ and $(1, 0)$ appears in random order, because the values $(A, B) = (0, 0), (0, 1), (1, 0)$ all create a 0 on the output of classical AND gate. Thus if one gives value 0 on the function F2 output in this example, the circuit realized in Invertible Logic will create sequentially (randomly and with repetitions) all $2^{64} - 1$ primary input that produce F2 = 0. Concluding, Invertible Logic allows to find solutions to all kinds of CSP problems and for some of them it can find a solution faster than the quantum algorithm of Grover. Active research is on technologies in which this logic can be practically realized [1, 4–6, 17, 20, 25]. Next section will relate classical Boolean Oracles, Quantum and Invertible Logic oracles, and how to design them in an uniform way, methodologically and efficiently.

3 Classical Boolean Oracles

3.1 Cryptoarithmetic Example and Discussion of TWO + TWO = FOUR Oracle

Our first larger example is to build classical Boolean Logic Oracle [2, 44]. To evaluate the standard FPGA realization of a classical Boolean Logic Oracle we used the crypto-arithmetic problem TWO + TWO = FOUR. Each letter of this symbolic equation can be substituted with values 0–9. The purpose of our oracle is to find all possible solutions to this problem. In other words, we look for all binary input combinations to this oracle that satisfy all partial constraints. The research problems are: (1) is how to build such oracle, (2) how to exercise this oracle from a Generator, (3) how to build the Generator, (4) How to select the best overall design of the Generator-Verifier system that would minimize the cost and maximize the speed.

Let us discuss few strategies how to solve this problem. Mathematically this problem can be formulated as follows. Given are sets L = {T, W, O, F, U, R} and D = {0, 1, 2, 3, 4, 5, 6, 7, 8, 9}. Find a mapping L → D such that $\forall\, l_1, l_2 \in$ L [MAP(l_1) ≠ MAP(l_2)] and all arithmetic constraints of addition TWO + TWO = FOUR are satisfied. The naive solution dictated directly by the problem formulation is this. We create a tree [49] with all 10 combinations for node with letter T in first tree level, next for every node of the second level we create all 10 combinations for letter W, next the same is done for letter O and so on. The tree will have 6 levels and the branching factor for every level is 10. Thus we will have to check 10^6 = 1,000,000 cases for arithmetic correctness in the Oracle. A better idea is to observe that in standard notation for addition formulas the value of F cannot be a 0. Moreover, it is obvious that it must be a 1. Therefore we have now not 6 letters but only 5 letters T, W, O, F, U, R for substitutions. We also know that F = 1, so now our tree will have 5 levels, with branching factor 9 where we select for every letter one of {0, 2, 3, 4, 5, 6, 7, 8, 9}. This leads to 59,049 cases of leafs of the tree, they are the mappings to be verified with use of arithmetic constraints in the Oracle. This simple common sense trick gave us a big gain in the size of the solution space, from = 1,000,000 to 59,049. Next observation is that while in the first level we branch for 9 letters, in the next level we should branch for 8, next for 7, etc. So in total the number of leaves of the tree will be 9·8·7·6·5·4·3·2 = 15,120. Further reduction. In this case the trick was trivial, but in general it can be much more sophisticated. Our design goal for any type of oracle is to reformulate the problem in order to build a better generator and a better Oracle to decrease the size of the solution space as much as possible. After this redesign, the tree would still generate solutions with more than one digit assignment for letters, a large redundancy. Thus, instead of generating Cartesian Product $\{0, 2, 3, 4, 5, 6, 7, 8, 9\}^5 = \{0, 2, 3, 4, 5, 6, 7, 8, 9\} \times \{0, 2, 3, 4, 5, 6, 7, 8, 9\} \times \{0, 2, 3, 4, 5, 6, 7, 8, 9\} \times \{0, 2, 3, 4, 5, 6, 7, 8, 9\} \times \{0, 2, 3, 4, 5, 6, 7, 8, 9\}$ we generate combinations without repetitions of five out of nine, which is $9!/(9 - 5)! = 15,120$. A more sophisticated reasoning can lead in this particular problem to finding a solution without much search that can be done "by hand". This reasoning leads for instance to solution $734 + 734 = 1468$, which means T = 7, O = 4, W = 6, R = 8. If we want however to create a general method for solving ALL this kind of puzzles, we reason differently. Our goal is to create a generator for the binary oracle that will create systematically all possible "*combinations without repetitions of five out of nine*" for letters T, W, O, U, R. (Pay attention that F is already mapped to 1 so it does not appear in the set of letters). As usually, the entire problem is solved by the Generator and the Oracle (Verifier). In this case the Selector and the Permuter (plus generator of carries C1 and C2) are the Generator Part and the Arithmetic Checker is the Oracle (combinational circuit). Observe that in general the boundary between generation and verification is not fixed and some parts can be shifted from generator to verifier, the trick that is used in quantum oracles and Invertible Logic Oracles.

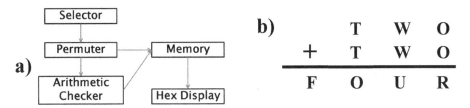

Fig. 1. (a) Schematics of the TWO + TWO = FOUR Generator (Selector and Permuter) and Oracle (Arithmetic Checker). Additional blocks Memory and HexDisplay are also shown from FPGA realization. The answers for the problem are displayed on a LCD display. (b) The representation of the TWO + TWO = FOUR problem that helps to create equations for the oracle of this problem.

The purpose of the oracle is to select a value for every letter from set {T, W, O, U, R}. In numerical terms, this means we verify all candidates that are "*five out of nine combinations without repetitions*" of digits 0, 2, 3, 4, 5, 6, 7, 8, 9 assigned to vector <T, W, O, U, R>. All candidates for mapping like this: <T, W, O, U, R> = <0, 2, 3, 4, 5>, <T, W, O, U, R> = <0, 2, 3, 5, 4> ,..., <T, W, O, U, R> = <5, 6, 7, 8, 9>. The generation of all candidate solutions for the Oracle can be done by selecting subset of five letters (binary codes of letters) out of nine and then doing all their permutations. There is still a problem remaining how to generate the set of all solutions based on combinations of five out of nine without repetitions. This must be done in the most efficient way, possibly with one solution candidate at every clock cycle of the counter (Generator), a requirement of optimality formulated in [26]. Schematic of our oracle is shown in Fig. 1. There are three major blocks in our oracle: the **Selector**, the

Permuter, and the Arithmetic Checker (Oracle). In the practical FPGA design, there are also smaller circuits in order to store and display the combinations: the RAM (memory) module, the RAM counter, and the LCD display module. This generator/oracle combination is an improved, optimized version of our previous oracle-based designs for this and similar problems (SEND + MORE = MONEY). Optimization is the result of a redesign aimed at reducing the size of the space of all potential solutions. This limits the search, as explained in our "methodology" in Sect. 3.2. The space reduction explained here is equally applicable to quantum and Invertible Logic oracles.

To follow the above presented idea, the **Selector** from Fig. 1 is decomposed to two blocks: the (sequential) **Counter** and the (combinational) **Multiplexers.** The counter gives its outputs to the multiplexers (see Fig. 4). The Counter block of the Selector simply counts up in the given modulo. The Counter block is decomposed to five **Small Counters** (shown schematically as rectangles at the top of Fig. 4). Each of the small counters has three outputs. In the problem of TWO + TWO = FOUR, since there are five unique letters, the counter counts modulo 5 and the largest vector for every Small Counter is 4 (selection states are 000, 001, 010, 011, and 100). Figure 2 shows the beginning of the sample count sequence generated by the Counter to be used by the **Multiplexers** inside the **Selector** block.

Time (t)	Output Combination
T = 0	00000
T = 1	10000
T = 2	11000
T = 3	11100
T = 4	11110
T = 5	11111
T = 6	20000

Fig. 2. Sample count sequence for the selector counter. In the actual circuit, the output signal is 3 bits, so that a value of 2 (in T = 6) is actually 010. Thus in time T = 6 the sequence generated on output of selector has 5 * 3 = 15 bits and is 010 000 000 000 000.

The outputs of each **Small Counter** (Fig. 5) are then directly connected to control the corresponding multiplexer located at the bottom of Fig. 4. Each multiplexer has only five data inputs coming from top of the counter. The particular inputs to every multiplexer are selected for it in different way. The multiplexers are controlled with three bits each, coming from the left of MUX schematics. These signals come from respective Small Counters from the top. Figure 3 shows initial steps of the resulting output sequence generated by the entire Selector circuit.

Time (t)	Output Combination
T = 0	56789
T = 1	46789
T = 2	45789
T = 3	45689
T = 4	45679
T = 5	45678
T = 6s	36789

Fig. 3. Sample beginning of the sequence of combinations of five out of nine without repetitions, generated by the Selector circuit. Each digit has 4 bits. For instance, 9 = 1001, 5 = 0101, 0 = 0000. Thus the output of the Selector has 5 * 4 = 20 bits, as shown on bottom of Fig. 4.

The purpose of the **Permuter** (Fig. 6) is to permute in all possible ways the values given by the **Selector** from Fig. 4. This allows for all possible number to letter combinations to be tested (as the selector does not repeat any set of numbers). Much like we discussed for the **Selector**, in **Permuter** there are the **Counter1** and **Multiplexer1** blocks. (This follows a general principle of designing advanced Generators). The **Counter1** consists of 5 normal counters which select which of the inputs to use. The **Multiplexer1** contains the inputs of each of the numbers selected (from **Selector**). It then goes through a $_4C_5$, $_3C_4$, and $_2C_3$ to gradually lessen the input for each further multiplexer. Figure 7 explains how signals C2, C1, C0 that control MUXes to select input data in Fig. 6 are generated. Recall that C3 = F so C3 is not used as input variable in the oracle. Figure 8 shows part of the sequence generated by the **Permuter**.

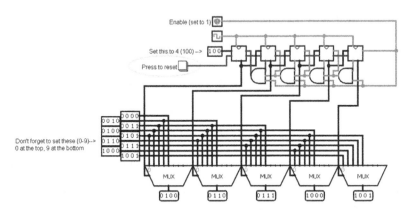

Fig. 4. Schematics of Selector composed of the Counter and Multiplexers circuits. The first from left MUX selects between values 5, 4, 3, 2, 0. The second from left MUX selects between values 6, 5, 4, 3, 2. The third from left MUX selects between values 7, 6, 5, 4, 3. The fourth from left MUX selects between values 8, 7, 6, 5, 4. The right MUX selects between values 9, 8, 7, 6, 5. The binary sequence on output of the selector has 5 * 4 = 20 bits. Above the sequence 0100 0110 0111 1000 1001 = 4 6 7 8 9 is shown.

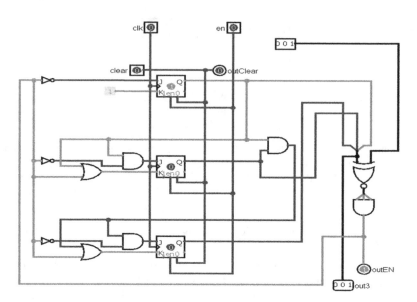

Fig. 5. A single Small Counter out of five shown on top of Fig. 4. It counts in code 000, 001, 010, 011, 100. Its three-bit output out3 goes to respective multiplexer in block Multiplexers.

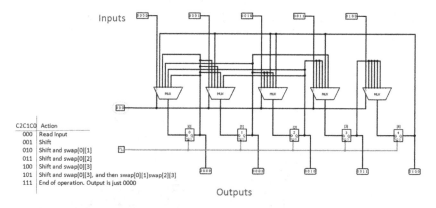

Fig. 6. Internals of the Permuter block. This circuit generates all permutations of data received on inputs. The inputs on top come from the Selector. The outputs at the bottom go to the Arithmetic Checker block from Fig. 10. Each of the five MUXes has 5 data inputs, 4 bits each. These MUXes are controlled but the 3-bit control C2, C1, C0. On bottom we see 5 small rectangles which represent counters, 4 bits each. At the left of Fig. 6 we see the encoded controls C2, C1, C0 and the corresponding actions of this Permuter that is the so-called "Generalized Register" type of "Micro-controlled Processor". Above we show the case of controlling MUXes with C2C1C0 = 000.

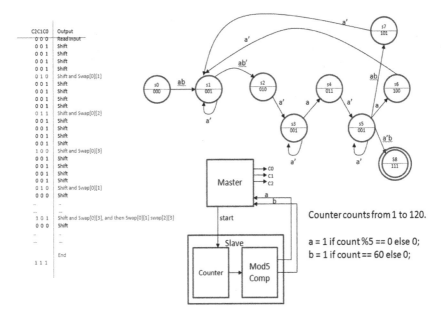

C2C1C0	Output
0 0 0	Read input
0 0 1	Shift
0 0 1	Shift
0 0 1	Shift
0 0 1	Shift
0 1 0	Shift and Swap[0][1]
0 0 1	Shift
0 0 1	Shift
0 0 1	Shift
0 0 1	Shift
0 1 1	Shift and Swap[0][2]
0 0 1	Shift
0 0 1	Shift
0 0 1	Shift
0 0 1	Shift
1 0 0	Shift and Swap[0][3]
0 0 1	Shift
0 0 1	Shift
0 0 1	Shift
0 0 1	Shift
0 1 0	Shift and Swap[0][1]
0 0 0	Shift
..	..
1 0 1	Shift and Swap[0][3], and then Swap[0][1] swap[2][3]
0 0 0	Shift
..	..
	End
1 1 1	

Master — C0, C1, C2, a, b, start
Slave
Counter — Mod5 Comp

Counter counts from 1 to 120.

a = 1 if count %5 == 0 else 0;
b = 1 if count == 60 else 0;

Fig. 7. Explanation of the Finite State Machine Master to generate control variables C2, C1, C0. C1 and C0 are also used as inputs to Oracle.

Time (t)	Output Combination
T = 0	12345
T = 1	12354
T = 2	12435
T = 3	12453
T = 4	12534
T = 5	12543
T = 6	13245

Fig. 8. Part of the sequence of all permutations of set {1, 2, 3, 4, 5} generated by the **Permuter**.

The purpose of the **Arithmetic Checker** is to check the arithmetic validity of the solution proposed by the Generator using the outputs of the Permuter. The arithmetic checker was designed just by converting arithmetic equations derived from the TWO + TWO = FOUR problem. Figure 9 shows the derived equations.

$$2(O) = 10(C_1) + R$$
$$C_1 + 2(W) = 10(C_2) + U$$
$$C_2 + 2(T) = 10(C_3) + O$$
$$C_3 = F$$

Fig. 9. Equations derived from the TWO + TWO = FOUR problem.

The equations shown in Fig. 9 come from each column for the TWO + TWO = FOUR problem (Fig. 1b). In this problem, it is assumed that F has to equal 1, not 0. This is because if the value was 0, there is no need for a letter. It is also noticed that carry positions were added, similar to the handwritten method of addition. The Arithmetic Checker (Fig. 10) strictly follows the equations, by replacing the '+', '*', and '=' operators with their respective arithmetic and predicate blocks.

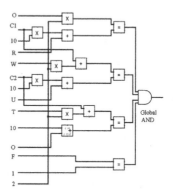

Fig. 10. Complete Arithmetic Checker Oracle circuit. The inputs are binary encodings of letters T, W, O, F, U, R, the constants 1, 2 and 10 and intermediate binary variables C1 and C2 (not discussed in more detail). This oracle is far from minimal logical design but it explains the general method to create oracles from arithmetic/Boolean equations. It can be optimized using methods from logic synthesis and digital design.

The RAM Module. Although when the circuits described above can make a complete oracle, there is no way for a user to know what the successful combinations are. In order to show what the combinations are, there first needs to be any type of memory to store the successful combinations. This is done on the FPGA by utilizing its RAM (Random Access Memory). The circuit used for the RAM of the FPGA is based on the concept of vectors. In a vector, information can be inserted, as well as removed according to a reference number. The circuit first stores the successful combinations (combinations with an Arithmetic Checker output of 1) into the vector. In the post-processing stage, the combinations in the vector can be displayed to the user by the **RAM Counter**.

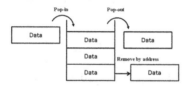

Fig. 11. Concept of a vector used for memory in the TWO + TWO = FOUR oracle.

The RAM Counter. In order to cycle through all of the solutions to the problem, a counter is required. The counter used to do the task is very similar to a normal counter, incrementing its value by 1, but it has an adjustable limit. This limit is imposed on the counter such that the counter won't go to empty cells in the vector, leaving the counter only counting the solutions.

The LCD Display. The LCD Display is required in order to display the solutions. Without it, the user will not be able to see what the calculated answers are. The circuit for the LCD is fairly simple; the output from the RAM is displayed on the LCD. Only the initialization of special ports (to turn on the backlight and other functions) is required.

3.2   Experimental Results for the TWO + TWO = FOUR Problem

The experiment of the *"TWO + TWO = FOUR Problem"* is a comparison between two methods: a hardware optimized implementation of the oracle, and a software implementation of an arbitrary oracle. The hardware implementation is run on a Terasic DE2-115 board, while the software implementation is run on a laptop with an Intel Core i5 CPU clocked at 2.40 GHz. These methods are compared for speed, or in this case, the time it takes to find all solutions for the same given problem. Counters are implemented in both the hardware and software oracles, yielding for more accurate results. The answers of the hardware program are verified by the software program. The solutions are: $938 + 938 = 1876$, $928 + 928 = 1856$, $867 + 867 = 1734$, $846 + 846 = 1692$, $836 + 836 = 1672$, $765 + 765 = 1530$, $734 + 734 = 1468$. Since the Selector, Permuter, and Arithmetic Checker operate under one clock pulse, theoretically stating, without glitches in the circuit, it would take n clock pulses to go through n combinations. The circuit has to go through $_9C_5$ combinations, and from that number of combinations, it has to go through $_5P_5$ permutations. Solving it would figure out how many clock pulses it would take in order to complete. Let us derive the number of clock pulses required to solve the problem: $(_9C_5)(_5P_5) = (126)(120) = 15,120$. The number of clock pulses is then converted into time. 1 MHz is equivalent to 1000 kHz. Since the clock on the DE2-115 is 50 MHz, it is equivalent to $50(1000) = 50,000$ kHz. There is a formula of $1/(KHz)$ which converts Kilohertz to milliseconds. Substituting 50,000 into the equation, $1/50,000$ is the result, the number of milliseconds per cycle. The number of cycles, 15120, is multiplied to the factor, receiving 0.3024 as an answer, stating that the computational time is 0.3024 ms. Theoretical predictions were perfectly verified in experiments [2].

Table 1. Comparison of an oracle for hardware and software in terms of computational time for TWO + TWO = FOUR.

	Hardware (predicated) *in milliseconds*	Hardware (actual) *in milliseconds*	Software *in milliseconds*
Trial 1	0.3024	0.3024	1105886
Trial 2	0.3024	0.3024	1136322
Trial 3	0.3024	0.3024	1136897
Average	0.3024	0.3024	1126368

From the data shown in Table 1, it can be concluded that the software computational speed was significantly slower than that of both hardware times. Also, the hardware computational times were equivalent, therefore showing no signs of error in calculation. In the average computational time comparison, the software took 1126368 ms to calculate, while the hardware only took a small fraction of 0.3024 ms. Thus, from the data, the hardware has **around 3724762 speed up time**.

In conclusion of the TWO + TWO = FOUR experiment, the hardware implementation of the oracle performed significantly faster than the software implementation in terms of computational time. For all trials tested, the hardware performed over three million times faster than the software equivalent. The results of the predicted hardware time and the actual hardware time were the same. Each trial always took exactly 0.3024 ms to calculate. This is because the circuits implemented in the FPGA operate on every clock pulse, and it is very rare for the clock pulse to have a glitch. Thus, the computational time of the FPGA can be proven by hand. There were no sources of error while taking data, as the timers were implemented on the respective systems. However, there can be lots of improvements to the experiment that could be made. First of all, the software tested is for an arbitrary amount of problems, meaning that it is very inefficient. Therefore, in order to have more accurate data, a specific oracle for the TWO + TWO = FOUR problem needs to be made. Also, the clocks of both systems are different (50 MHz on the FPGA versus 2.4 GHz on the computer). If one were to measure the ratio of FPGA speed-up, the clocks would have to be equivalent.

We can observe that this problem can be solved differently without creating carry variables C_1, C_2, C_3 in Fig. 9. In the second variant the decimal adder can be designed with binary-encoded digits and with internal binary carry signals that are not considered as input variables to the oracle. The oracle is not created as in Fig. 10 based on equations from Fig. 9, but is just the adder with two inputs (T1, W1, O1) and (T2, W2, O2) and outputs (F, O3, U, R). This adder realizes equation (T1, W1, O1) + (T2, W2, O2) = (F, O3, U, R). But now in this second variant additional constraints are needed: T1 = T2, W1 = W2, O1 = O2 = O3. This is a common tradeoff when designing Generator-Oracle systems. While we call the first variant of oracle as shown here the *"Oracle with Control of Intermediate Signals"*, the second type of the oracle we call the *"Oracle without Control of Intermediate Signals"*, in this case carries C_1, C_2 and C_3 are these intermediate signals. Observe that in this variant we do not use sequential generator. All knowledge is in combinational oracle, which makes it a good candidate for Grover oracle and for Invertible Logic Oracle. Both oracle types can have some advantages and disadvantages, depending on the problem. These two design types of oracles illustrate again the tradeoff that we deal with when designing efficient oracles.

3.3 Concluding on Boolean Oracles and Their Relation to Quantum Oracles and Invertible Logic Oracles

Boolean Oracles realized in FPGAs are useful for problems for which the designer has no information and no heuristics to solve the problem. There exists also no other than exhaustive algorithm for these types of problems (in some problems dynamic programming may be better, so there is in these cases no reason to create our type of "unsorted database" approach based on generators and oracles). Under these conditions classical hardware oracles are better than software programs for small problems. However, in case of large problems these oracles cannot be used because of the size of hardware to exercise systematically and exhaustively all possible input combinations. In software some efficient search algorithm can be used that will execute cuts in tree branches early and can backtrack efficiently. For problems that have many solutions, good design of the oracle plus good design of the generator help to solve problems [2] that are difficult to solve otherwise, but still not too large in size. Tricks as those illustrated in Sect. 3.1 are therefore used. Other good solution that may be helpful for some problems is to design generators as special counters that count in advanced codes that correspond to depth-first or breadth-first searches. Any sequences of binary vectors can be simply created by adding large ROMs at outputs of standard counters. Concluding, there is some combination of the problem size and problem type for which hardware oracles based on classical logic are practical, realistic solutions. They may be realized in ASIC, FPGA or any new nano-technology such as memristors.

Please note that designing classical generator/oracle systems is fundamental to our general methodology. This is because the oracle concept is the base of our "*CSP methodology of problem-solving in hardware*". It is only a technical aspect to translate Boolean oracles to reversible logic used in quantum computing or to invertible logic used in magnetic spins. These are the two technologies that will prove useful to solve these problems in future when the number of reliable qubits in quantum computers will increase, and when larger Invertible Logic circuits with magnetic spins will be built. At this time the ideas presented in this paper will become useful not only to better solve toy problems as used for illustration here, but also to solve quickly practical problems of large size.

The theoretical base to create quantum and Invertible Logic oracles already exists. Actually, the literature presents many solutions to reversible/quantum arithmetic blocks such as adders, multipliers, shifters, code converters, comparators and others. Thus converting classical logic/arithmetic blocks to reversible blocks for Grover or other Quantum Algorithm can be automated. General Boolean functions that can appear in some oracles are more difficult to convert because in quantum the EXOR-based circuits are better while in classical design the OR-based circuits are better. However, there are many methods to convert SOP-based logic to EXOR-based logic such as Exclusive-Or-Sum-of-Products (ESOP) [13]. Observe also that converting combinational Boolean circuit to Invertible Logic is theoretically trivial because Hamiltonians are known for every two-input binary gate ([4] and many papers by Biamonte), and Hamiltonians are also known for many other gates and blocks such as adders and multipliers. There exist also methods to realize arbitrary Hamiltonians built from smaller Hamiltonians.

3.4 General Methodology for Oracle Design

While designing a binary oracle the designer has to ask himself first – "*what is the problem type that I want to solve?*" Knowledge of these problem types and blocks used to solve them is very helpful. Let us explain the essence of this question. For any realization of the oracle, especially quantum and classical, we need some generator that would create a set of input vectors to exercise the oracle. In Grover Algorithm the vector of Hadamard gates serves as this generator of all possible binary strings being solution candidates. We want to reduce the size of the input vectors in order to reduce (often dramatically) the size of the entire solution space and the cost and operation time of the oracle. Knowing the type of the problem helps to find good encoding of data and as the result helps to reduce the cost and increase the speed. Below we discuss this problem.

Observe that starting from $|0\rangle$ the Hadamard gate creates superposition of $|0\rangle$ and $|1\rangle$. Two Hadamard gates working in parallel create a superposition of $|00\rangle$, $|01\rangle$, $|10\rangle$ and $|11\rangle$, in another variant of Dirac's notation $|0\rangle$, $|1\rangle$, $|2\rangle$ and $|3\rangle$. Therefore n Hadamard gates working in parallel generate all binary numbers from 0 to 2^{n-1}. We can see that the parallel vector of Hadamard gates is a "quantum generator" of all numbers from 0 to 2^{n-1}. But also, assuming that the individual bits of these numbers represent presence or absence of an item in the set of n elements, these numbers represent all possible subsets of the set with n elements. For two-element set, like this: $|00\rangle$ = empty set {}, $|10\rangle$ = {a}, $|01\rangle$ = {b}, $|11\rangle$ = {a, b}. Therefore, as also known from Grover and quantum algorithms, the vector of Hadamard gates is a quantum generator of all subsets of a set. This is used in Grover Oracles and also in other quantum algorithms such as Bernstein–Vazirani. This property of Hadamard operator leads to natural design of oracles in which we look for a solution being a subset of the set [2, 49]. For instance, when the designer wants to find the best partition of a set to two subsets X and Y, every binary vector represents a subset of bits with value 1 as subset X and a subset of elements with value 0 as subset Y. The oracle evaluates if this separation to two subsets satisfies all constraints. The same method can be used to design oracles which look for a mapping from a set to a set. Several algebraic systems, such as the "*Partition Calculus*" [12, 15, 16, 47] and "*Cube Calculus*" [46] are based hierarchically on set operations and relations. Therefore these algebraic systems can use the natural Hadamard-based encoding of solution candidates that are verified by constraints [21, 22, 30]. For instance, several important problems in CAD and Machine Learning can be solved using only two basic operations on set partitions from Partition Calculus; operator $\Pi_1 \cdot \Pi_2$ which finds the product of partitions, and relation (predicate) $\Pi_1 \leq \Pi_2$. These problems include Ashenhurst-Curtis Decomposition [12], Bi-Decomposition, State Minimization, Concurrent State Minimization and Encoding, ROM-based design and other.

In addition to algebraic models, it is important how the variables (symbols) are encoded in various binary codes. Some problems may require other than standard methods of information encoding, for instance using "*one-hot encoding*" or "*thermometer encoding*" of numbers (data). Therefore, the first question is this: "*what is my problem type and how should I encode the data*". As an example, when we solve the graph theory problems we may encode nodes while treating edges as pairs of nodes. Or we can encode edges as bits in a set-theoretical representation with as many qubits as edges in our graph. We can also encode a graph as a binary incidence matrix. Permutation problems such as Traveling Salesman or Generalized Traveling Salesman would require to deal with permutations. Few standard ways of dealing with permutations have been created [8, 15, 31]. One method is to treat the binary input vector of numbers as a single permutation of natural numbers with k successive bits for a number and to use constraints that will not allow the repeated numbers to be considered as solution candidates [31]. Other method to solve permutation problems with oracles is to create inside the oracle, just at its input, a large encoder that converts the set of all subsets to the set of all permutations [15]. As done usually in AI and ML, the problem is solved by a combination of a "generator" and "verifier". A simple generator creates too many candidates so that most of them are next disqualified by the "verifier" (all the constraints in the oracle). A more advanced generator creates only reasonable candidates that would require less constraints checking, but creating such a generator may be more difficult. The most natural generator in quantum is the "generator of all subsets of a set". Observe that in the case of quantum oracles the "initial counter" coming from vector of Hadamards generates always a set of subsets, which may be converted by a special circuit to another type of combinational objects similarly as it was done in Sect. 3.1 [49].

The proposed methodology for designing oracles and especially Grover Oracles is the following:

1. We ask ourselves – *"what kind of problem are we solving?"*. Is this a *"subset of set"* problem, a mapping problem, a *"combination with repetitions"* problem, a permutation problem, a spectral transform problem [11], etc.? The answers to this problem and the respective data encoding have huge influence on the final oracle design (as illustrated in cryptoarithmetic puzzles).
2. Next question – how the data for this problem should be encoded? Can we use one of the well-known encoding methods like natural number encoding, one-hot-encoding, thermometer encoding, Gray Code Encoding, etc.? Answers to question 1 and question 2 are related.
3. Next question, assuming the type of problem and the type of encoding, we ask *"what are the blocks to be designed for the oracle and how they are combined?"*. There can be standard blocks such as shifters, arithmetic operators or predicates. Comparators and combinational counters, such as variants of "counter of ones" are often used. Some blocks must be designed from scratch and then in case of quantum oracles the methods of logic synthesis for reversible circuits should be used [13]. In case of quantum circuits these blocks can be designed on the level of binary reversible logic [13] or, better, on the level of truly quantum primitives such as Control-V and Control-V^+, Pauli rotations, etc. [23, 39, 41].
4. The blocks are taken from library of standard or quantum blocks. In case of non-standard reversible blocks they are designed using methods from "reversible logic synthesis". Next the blocks are combined to larger blocks and subsystems. The final output AND-gate (Multi-input Toffoli gate in quantum case) is added to combine together binary answers from all partial constraints.
5. If an optimization problem is solved (see Sect. 4) we have to create a part of the oracle that is modified in every repeated CSP problem solved by calling the successive Grover algorithm. The same is true for our Invertible Logic oracle-based method of problem-solving.

4 Grover Quantum Oracles

4.1 Minimum Set of Support Problem

As an example of bottom-up systematic design of Grover Oracle for optimization problem, we present here a new approach to find the minimum set of support for binary switching functions. Next, the essential part of this algorithm, *"POS → SOP conversion for unate functions"* is sped up by Grover quantum search algorithm that brings a quadratic speedup. We present below in detail how to build the Grover oracle. Our quantum algorithm can be easily adapted to solve other important but similar problems. There is a large body of literature on the Minimum Set of Support Problem, because this problem finds many important applications such as: minimization of Boolean functions (SOP, POS, PLA, FPGA, etc.) [34, 37], Ashenhurst-Curtis Decomposition and other functional decomposition methods for binary and multi-valued functions [35] and information systems [33], cryptography, data mining and Machine Learning, large databases, rule and expert systems [36], index generation functions [38], complementation of Boolean Functions, rough set problems, minimizing Petrick functions (prime covering in SOP), etc. This problem is also known as the "attribute reduction problem" and "unate covering problem".

A. What is the problem?

Given a Boolean function f: $\{0, 1\}^n \rightarrow \{0, 1, x\}$ of n variables (the function is completely specified, or mostly likely, incompletely specified in case of ML problems) the minimum set of support is the minimum number of variables required to express the function as an equation or set of rules. This method is useful to reduce the unnecessarily large representation of functions (for instance using ON and OFF sets for binary functions) to all representations that include minimum numbers of variables. Using the minimum set of support variables simplifies the logic synthesis or Machine Learning methods. Several methods have been proposed for reduction of features (variables, attributes) in Machine Learning and knowing all the minimal sets of attributes has an importance in those applications where learned rules on less features are easier to understand and do not lead to overfitting.

B. Classical approach to find Minimum Set of Support for Boolean function

The new procedure for finding Minimum set of support is as follows:

1. List all the OFF-minterms row-wise and ON-minterms column-wise in a rectangular table and perform bitwise Exclusive-OR operation between all possible pairs of binary strings of OFF-minterms with ON-minterms. Write the resultant binary strings as the Boolean OR of the corresponding variables. In every intersection of row and column we have the sum of variables which separate the given ON-minterm from the column and the respective OFF-minterm from the row.
2. After completing the entire table, create a POS formula being the AND of all OR terms from the intersection cells in point-1 above.
3. Convert the above POS formula to an equivalent minimal SOP formula. This can be done, for instance, by a step-by-step Boolean Multiplication together with

absorption of products created in every step. In the final SOP formula each product corresponds to a minimum set of support of variables. This step is solved using Grover Algorithm.

Comment 1. There are several methods how to convert POS to SOP. The case here is simpler as our POS is a unate function. All these methods can be used at this step to create a quantum oracle, but our interest in this paper is restricted to unate functions.

Comment 2. The user may verify the correctness of results of this algorithm by folding Karnaugh maps with respect to all combinations of variables that are not present in every minimum set of support. For instance, for a function of five variables f (a, b, c, d, e) the correctness of the minimum set of support {a, b} is verified by sequentially folding according to variables c, d and e, without encountering contradictions and thus creating function $f_1(a, b) = f(a, b, c, d, e)$.

A useful pre-processing method is to simplify initial POS (in point 2) by using repeatedly the Boolean laws; $A \cdot A = A$; $A \cdot (A + B) = A$ and $(A + B) \cdot (A + B + C) = A + B$. Therefore, we start the simplification from the shortest OR terms and we remove the OR terms containing them. The minimum set of support problem is an NP problem [34], thus all exact algorithms for classical computers can be applied only to relatively small problems. For larger problems, the classical algorithms are heuristic and take large time and space complexity to find only some minima or approximate minima. In this section, we illustrate our methodology by presenting a hybrid classical/quantum algorithm to solve **exactly** the minimum set of support problem for k-valued switching functions. It provides a quadratic speedup with respective to its classical counterpart algorithm for the stage of POS to SOP exact conversion of a unate Boolean function.

4.2   Example of Finding the Minimum Set of Support for a Binary Function

We illustrate our algorithm from Sect. 4.1.B step by step.

Consider a Boolean function represented in a Karnaugh map as shown in Fig. 12.

ab\cd	00	01	11	10
00	x	x	1	x
01	1	x	x	1
11	x	x	0	x
10	0	x	x	0

Fig. 12. The Karnaugh map of an incompletely specified Boolean function.

Step 1. The possible values of the Boolean function are 0 (OFF) and 1 (ON). The cells on the intersection of OFF-minterms and ON-minterms are created by bitwise EXOR. For instance, bitwise EXORing of OFF-minterm 1111 with ON-minterm 0011 the binary string 1100 is obtained which is written as $a + b$.

OFF\ON	0011	0100	0110
1111	$a+b$	$a+c+d$	$a+d$
1000	$a+c+d$	$a+b$	$a+b+c$
1010	$a+d$	$a+b+c$	$a+b$

Fig. 13. Illustration of the method to find all separating variables for every pair of true and false minterms of a Boolean function from Fig. 9. True minterm 1111 and false minterm 0011 are separated with variable a or variable b, this is the formula $a + b$ seen at the intersection of row 1111 and column 0011.

Step 2. A POS formula is created being the AND of all the terms from cells in Fig. 13, which becomes the product of sums as represented as below, $\equiv (a + b) \cdot (a + c + d) \cdot (a + d) \cdot (a + c + d) \cdot (a + b) \cdot (a + b + c) \cdot (a + d) \cdot (a + b + c) \cdot (a + b)$

Step 3. Using laws from the algorithm, the expression gets reduced to $(a + b) \cdot (a + d)$. Transforming this POS to a minimum SOP is in general a difficult problem. In this particular didactic case, the transformation is trivial and based on Boolean algebra $(a + b) \cdot (a + d) \equiv a + ab + ad + bd \equiv a + bd$

We found in the last formula that the Boolean function from Fig. 12 depends on only a single variable $\{a\}$ or it depends on two variables $\{b, d\}$. The function has exactly two minimum sets of support – $\{a\}$ and $\{b, d\}$. For large functions the above "POS to minimum SOP" transformation is a complicated NP problem and thus we apply Grover Algorithm to solve this step.

4.3 Grover Algorithm

Grover algorithm is one of the few most famous quantum algorithms. Grover algorithm performs searching on a "black box," an unsorted database, in order to find an element that satisfies the oracle [9]. The oracle is built specifically for the given problem instance. The idea of Grover's algorithm is to place the qubits representing entire search space of size N in a superposition state. Then the phase of the states marked by oracle is inverted, followed by an inversion about the mean operation, which is also known as the diffusion operation. Diffusion operation amplifies the amplitude of the marked states to increase probability that this state will be a result of measurement performed on a vector of input qubits. Oracle followed by diffusion is called the Grover Loop. After $O \sqrt{N}$ iterations of Grover Loop, the probability of measuring the target solution approaches to 1 (in case of a single solution) [9, 39, 40].

4.4   Oracle for Minimum Set of Support

A. Oracle circuit for Grover Algorithm

To build a Grover's algorithm to find the minimum set of support for function from Fig. 12 an Oracle for this specific problem is built in such a way that it checks if the input satisfies the following three constraints: (A) that the POS is satisfied, (B) that it is a new solution and not one found already previously, (C) that the number of variables in solution is equal to a constant *Threshold* given on the input. The first thing to build the Grover oracle is to encode the input and output of the problem in binary. For our oracle, the search space is a collection of all potential solutions. Potential solutions are all subsets of the set variables {a, b, c, d}. Some of these subsets are the searched Minimum Sets of Support for this function.

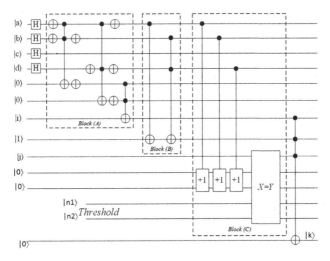

Fig. 14. Part of Oracle to find all Minimum Sets of Support for the binary function from Fig. 12 with the minimum set of support {{a}, {b, d}}. POS = (a + b) · (a + d) = 1 ⊕ (a′b′)′ · (a′d′)′ is realized in Block (A). The Hadamard gates at top left do not belong to the oracle and are explained in point 2 of the algorithm. They are drawn here for didactic reasons as they serve as a generator of all subsets of set {a, b, c, d} by creating the superposition of all numbers from 0 to 15.

The block diagram of the proposed quantum oracle is shown in Fig. 14. It consists of three major blocks; (A), (B) and (C). The inverse circuit corresponds to blocks (A), (B) and (C) in reverse order must be designed respectively, to restore all the modified qubits to their original values. This is done in the "Mirror Part" of the oracle composed from mirror of C, followed by mirror of B and followed by mirror of A. This mirror part is not shown in Fig. 14 due to space limitations. Qubit |k⟩ is the solution of the oracle. It marks that all constraints of the oracle (A), (B) and (C) are satisfied.

Block (A) is a Boolean satisfiability function in POS form. Qubit $|i\rangle$ is initialized to $|1\rangle$ to realize POS $(a + b) \cdot (a + d)$ based on DeMorgan theorem from Toffoli gates and inverters. This qubit recognizes <u>every solution of this POS</u> from the superposition of inputs. It is given as one of three AND-ed inputs to the far right Toffoli gate that creates the solution to the entire oracle. Block (B) does not exist in the first run of Grover and will be discussed later on. This block represents modification of constraints in subsequent runs of Grover Algorithm typical for the optimization problems, which we already discussed.

Block (C) contains three counters and the equality comparator. The three counters count together the number of input variables required to satisfy the POS function. Each counter adds a 1 if the corresponding variable controlling it has value 1. The Comparator $X = Y$ compares the output from the counters with the threshold value given as a constant values $|n1\rangle$ and $|n2\rangle$ of *Threshold* on input to Grover Algorithm. Then a Toffoli gate is applied on ancilla qubit $|k\rangle$ controlled by $|i\rangle$, $|1\rangle$ and $|j\rangle$. If the conditions are met, ancilla bit k will be flipped. It changes the solution phase so that the solutions that satisfy both conditions can be marked.

B. Finding all solutions to the minimum set of support problem

In this section we will explain how the Grover Algorithm is used multiple times with modified oracles to find all exact minimum solutions to our problem. The first run of the Grover uses the oracle without block (B). Qubit $|i\rangle$ gives all solutions that satisfy POS $(a + b) \cdot (a + d)$. In general, we start from the lowest bound of the solution cost and we go up. In this case, we optimistically assume that there exists a single variable that satisfies the POS. Thus the value of *Threshold* is set to 1 and all solutions with single input variables are checked with counters and the comparator. The solution a is found. Now block (B) is compiled to the oracle by the pre-processing standard computer that controls the quantum computer. Block (B) includes now the representation of the first solution a which is subtracted (inhibition operator $X \cdot Y'$ realized as part of the large Toffoli gate at right). Therefore, all possible solution sets that include variable a are being excluded. These are all products of literals included in cube a. No solution with one variable is found by subsequent runs of Grover with this modified oracle. Now we look for solutions with two variables. We set the value of *Threshold* to value 2. A new solution bd is found. It is next added to the ESOP realized in the output qubit from block (B), marking the solution bd as already used. So now the block (B) is $a \oplus bd$ as shown in Fig. 10. (Let us remind that in our encoding solution a is represented as 1000 and solution bd as 0101, so that solutions are <u>disjoint</u> minterms for which OR-ing is the same as EXOR-ing, based on the rule $A + B = A \oplus B \oplus AB$. Therefore, the logic sum of all previous solutions in block B can be stored as their EXOR). This method of creating a sequence of oracles is general and we applied it to design sequences of Grover oracles for various problems.

With the full oracle as in Fig. 11 the Grover algorithm finds no more solutions. But it is still unclear if there are solutions with three or four variables? In this case, because of properties of unate symmetric functions all solutions with three variables are cancelled by solution a (1101, 1110, 1011) or cancelled by solution bd (0111, 1101). So there are no other solutions. In general, one has to keep increasing the value of threshold if he attempts to find all minimum sets of support. To confirm that there are no any solutions besides those that we already found, the oracle can be also run by Grover with blocks (A) and (B) but without (C). Our hybrid Algorithm finds that there is no solution to this function, thus no more solutions exist at all. Every binary vector $|a, b, c, d\rangle$ of a solution can be verified on block (A) of the oracle run outside of the Grover Algorithm. In one more variant of our approach, the number of remaining solutions can be found using the Quantum Counting Algorithm that returns the number of values 1 in the function.

4.5   Remarks on This Design

As an example of the methodology proposed in Sects. 2, 3 and 4 of this paper we presented a hybrid algorithm in which pre-processing, i.e. creating the POS formula, is done in a standard computer. Only solving of the NP problem of *"POS → SOP conversion for a positive unate function and with finding all prime implicants"* is solved by our hybrid algorithm based on a sequence of calls of Grover with modified oracles. We presented the detailed design of the oracle from reversible gates and blocks. More details of the blocks used here and a discussion can be found in [12]. Other typical blocks are presented in other cited here papers of the PSU team. This Sect. 4 illustrated some elements of our methodology: (1) selection of encoding, (2) problem representation, (3) combining of constraints, (4) hybrid design and role of the standard computer that supervises the quantum computer, (5) repetition of Grover with modified oracles to solve the optimization problem.

Very similar Grover oracles can be built for other fundamental CAD problems: function complementation, binate covering, unate covering, and prime implicant generation for SOP minimization. Moreover, these problems can be solved by our approach for multiple-valued functions as well. The method presented in this section is very similar when applied to binary or multiple-valued functions from ML [30], and their quantum component is exactly the same. Similarly to the oracle example from Sect. 3, this oracle can be also converted to Invertible Logic Oracle and solved with Invertible Logic methods explained in Sect. 5. All these oracles can be simulated with the logic programming CSP software outlined in Sect. 6.

5   Invertible Logic Oracles

First, to convince the reader about power of invertible logic let us give few more simple examples.

1. A circuit is a tree of three AND gates as in Fig. 15. Because for the 2-input-AND gate for the value 1 on output is the combination (1, 1) on inputs, the backward (output to input) propagation of signals is represented as in Fig. 15 and the oracle requires only one evaluation. Classical circuit would require in the worst case $2^4 = 16$ evaluations and the quantum Grover oracle would require $(16)^{(1/2)} = 4$ evaluations because of its quadratic speedup.

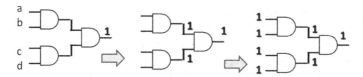

Fig. 15. Propagation from output to inputs in a single oracle evaluation for function a · b · c · d

2. A circuit is a tree of Boolean Gates $F_2 = (ab) \oplus (cd)$ as in Fig. 16. The snapshots show the propagation of signals backward with fast finding of one solution. EXOR is a better combining gate than the OR gate, because for output 1 it has only two not three input combinations (0, 1) and (1, 0).

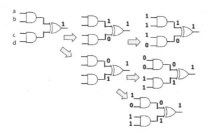

Fig. 16. Propagation from output to inputs in a single oracle evaluation for function a · b ⊕ c · d (only some solutions shown)

3. Suppose we have a graph with three nodes as in Fig. 17. In Fig. 17a the graph is 1-colorable, the graphs from Figs. 17b and 17c are 2-colorable and the graph from Fig. 17d has a chromatic number of 3. The oracle for the graph from Fig. 17d in ternary-input binary-output logic is shown in Fig. 17e. Here outputs of all three inequality comparators are equal 1, which means that all partial constraints are satisfied. Let us analyze how Invertible Logic works. Let us say the top comparator is satisfied by coloring node 1 with color *a* and node 2 with color *b*. Now color *b* is propagated to upper input of the middle comparator. If this comparator selects color *a* on its second input, it will propagate 1 to output. But the bottom comparator will be not satisfied as it will have color *a* on both inputs. Thus if the middle comparator will select color c on lower input it will produce output 1 but also the bottom comparator will be satisfied as it will get various colors *a* and *c* on its inputs. The coloring with only colors *a* and *b* is not possible, which is illustrated for one coloring case in Fig. 17d. The inequality comparator for edge (1, 2) produces a zero on output, but inequality comparators for edges (1, 3) and (2, 3) produce a 1 on their outputs so the circuit is not satisfiable (not 3-satisfiable) but the circuit is 2-satisfiable. This example shows the close relation between the graph coloring, SAT and MAX-SAT problems. Similarly, every oracle can be in theory transformed to a SAT problem, because oracle is a Boolean function and every Boolean function can be realized in a POS (CNF) form.

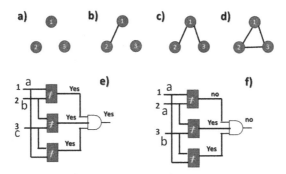

Fig. 17. Graph Coloring in network of constraints realized in Invertible Logic, (a) one-colorable graph, (b) two-colorable graph, (c) two-colorable graph, (d) three-colorable graph, (e) good coloring of graph from d with colors a, b and c, (f) bad coloring of graph from d with two colors, constraint for nodes 1 and 2 is not satisfied because these neighbor nodes have the same color a.

Now that we appreciate the power of Invertible Logic, let us observe that every oracle is basically a kind of SAT-solver that solves a non-standard type of SAT using Boolean gates and blocks, and not only the classical POS-SAT formula. Thus every classical logic oracle [2, 26] or every reversible logic oracle [3, 8, 11, 12, 15, 16, 21, 22, 24, 28, 30, 31] can be easily converted to the Invertible Logic oracle and simulated in software, emulated and verified using an FPGA. Most importantly, Invertible Logic Oracle can be realized using the real hardware nano-technology such as magnetic spins. The only question that remains when we want to use standard FPGA or one of nano-technologies is this: "how to design the inside of logic gates and blocks that externally are standard Boolean circuits?" Several methods have been proposed [1, 4–7, 10, 14, 17, 18, 20, 43].

Any hardware realization of an Oracle is in essence a Boolean Function (it can be extended to multi-valued functions), so the theory of such functions, as well as their synthesis methods, can and should be used to build oracles. For instance, oracles from [8] make use of the theory of symmetric Boolean problems, because of symmetries found in problem data such as 3 Missionaires and 3 Cannibals from the known puzzle.

In addition, internally the blocks of Invertible Logic oracles are like neural nets or other systems based on Hamiltonian Dynamics. Therefore, when the entire circuit is built from blocks, the blocks are externally Boolean (or multi-valued) but their internal design is based on methods typical for Neural Networks design and Adiabatic Quantum Computing design. Theoretically, every oracle can be built from AND gates and Inverter gates, or from some larger set of gates and blocks, but a better method is to create new types of blocks corresponding to relations that can be satisfied (1) or not satisfied (0), based on their characteristic functions. For instance, in case of the graph coloring problem we can create a network of comparators of inequality, one comparator for every edge of the graph. The inputs to these comparators are encoded data for colors of their corresponding nodes. Finally, a large AND gate is used to combine answers from partial constraints on all edges of the graph (the inequality comparators). However, another approach would be to create a relation for every node of the graph that would operate on this principle – *"If my color is different from all colors of my neighbors I will keep my color. If my color is in a disagreement with any color of my neighbor, I will change my color randomly"*. A Hamiltonian can be calculated for such rules. Thus the number of blocks in the oracle is the number of nodes. When all nodes are happy with colors of their neighbor nodes the minimum energy is reached and thus the solution to the graph coloring problem with K colors is found. In case that we want to solve the optimization variant of graph coloring, the successful oracle for K1 colors is repeated with a smaller number of colors K1 < K (see Sect. 2 and [12, 31]). This means in a special case that the oracle blocks for constraint $COLOR(n_i) \leq K$ are replaced in the repeated oracle with blocks $COLOR(n_i) \leq K - 1$.

How to design the internals of the blocks? In case of Invertible Logic analog circuit design methods are used when building gates with nano-magnets. Hamiltonian design methods and stochastic system based methods are used when emulating with FPGAs. A standard approach is to follow this line of transformations:

$Circuit \rightarrow TruthTable \rightarrow CharacteristicFunction \rightarrow$ **Linear Programming** $\rightarrow Hamiltonian \rightarrow Invertible\ Logic\ Block$

Many problems require arithmetic, so how are the arithmetic operators implemented? Even the AND gate implemented as a Hopfield Network internally needs arithmetic – adders and constant multipliers - as well as some non-linear threshold or similar operators typically used in Neural Nets. Various number systems can be used to design the Hamiltonian-based internals of relations that specify the problem. For example such number systems as SNR – Stochastic Number Systems [1, 20] or Frequency Number Representation [43].

6 Prolog Oracle Simulator

Currently, simulating a correctness of a quantum circuit and in particular a Grover-based algorithm with a complex oracle is difficult because of the small number of qubits that can be used by the contemporary quantum circuit simulators [12, 41]. However, the designer of an oracle of any kind (Boolean, Quantum or Invertible) wants usually to verify correctness of his design and the density of solutions in the solution space. In quantum case this is because the entire Grover Algorithm is known to be correct and the non-oracle components of Grover Algorithm hardware are easy. This is also true for other quantum algorithms such as Shor, Bernstein-Vazirani or Quantum Walk. Let us observe that we do not need a quantum simulator to achieve this *"quantum circuit built from permutative gates"* verification goal. Instead of simulating the oracle being a part of Grover Loop inside the iterated Grover Algorithm it is often sufficient just to simulate the oracle itself as an invertible logic circuit, even before converting to reversible logic with ancillae qubits (reversible gates are described by permutative matrices). Simulation of oracles can be done in hardware description languages such as VHDL or System Verilog, but it is better to use a logic programming languages such as Prolog, because of their natural capability to simulate CSP systems based on mechanisms such as backtracking and matching. While Verilog cannot simulate directly the Invertible Logic circuits, Prolog and CSP Languages can do this.

A program in Prolog [42] can easily simulate an oracle just be defining all gates and blocks as their truth tables (characteristic functions) or as blocks (sub-systems) composed hierarchically from lower level gates and blocks. Next, oracles built from these blocks can be exercised from inputs to outputs, from outputs to inputs or in any possible direction by fixing subsets of inputs and outputs and finding values of all remaining signals such that all constraints (relations) are satisfied. The designer can create variants such as the "*Oracle with Control of Intermediate Signals*", and the "*Oracle without Control of Intermediate Signals*" and set intermediate signals to some heuristically assumed values.

The Prolog simulator is composed from two types of blocks: the Oracle and the Generator [42]. Generator creates inputs to Oracle in case of classical input-to-output simulation. In case of output-to-input simulation the "*hidden generator*" creates combinations of inputs/outputs for individual gates but the simulations start from outputs assigned to constant values. For instance, an adder with two-bit arguments **input1** and **input2** and result **output** is defined as **adder[input1, input2, output]**. It works as follows: **adder[1, 2, X]** produces **X = 3**. But also: **adder[X, 2, 3]** produces **X = 1.** In addition, **adder[X, Y, 3]** will give: **X = 0, Y = 3,** next will produce **X = 1, Y = 2,** next **X = 2, Y = 1,** next **X = 3, Y = 0.** The order of generating the pairs of inputs **X** and **Y** will depend on the "*Generator*".

Therefore, if the user just describes the oracle as a composition of any type of gates, classical or invertible, or reversible, or Hamiltonian gates and blocks, our simulator in Prolog would be able to verify correctness of his/her design. Moreover, various directions of simulating gates, blocks or subsystems are possible that can help the designer when he considers various architectures for complex oracles. Also, in some problems we do not know how many solutions a given problem instance has. In case that we want to find ALL solutions to our problem we use the Quantum Counting algorithm [28] in addition to Grover Algorithm. If we want to verify the correctness of our entire quantum algorithm composed of Quantum Counting Algorithm and Grover Algorithm, it is useful to know how many solutions our problem instance has (how many "true minterms" or "minterms with value 1" the oracle function has). Again, the Prolog simulator helps in this respect. Therefore, the Prolog simulator becomes a universal simulator of oracles, regardless if we want to use these oracles for classical Boolean logic as in Sect. 3, for reversible logic in Grover Algorithm as in Sect. 4, or for Invertible Logic as in Sect. 5. Prolog Simulator can be also used to verify any reversible logic circuits (with Ancillae) used in quantum algorithms such as Shor Algorithm and similar, as well as several Quantum Random Walk Algorithms.

7 Conclusions

Solving optimization problems can be reduced to the repeated solving of decision problems such as CSP with oracles modified at every CSP round. CSP problems can be solved by exercising oracles. These oracles can be exercised from inputs to output sequentially as in classical Boolean logic. In quantum they are exercised in parallel thanks to superposition and quantum parallelism used in the Grover Algorithm. Based on an observation that both these formerly known approaches solve the inverse function and that the Invertible Logic can be used to solve the inverse functions, in this paper we propose a general methodology to solve optimization and CSP problems based on designing oracles bottom–up from a hierarchy of blocks. These oracles can be exercised in Prolog from outputs to inputs. Next, as the first method, these oracles can be converted to reversible logic and used in Grover Algorithm (with adding ancillae qubits). As the second method, these classical logic oracles can be converted to Invertible Logic [5, 6, 17, 18, 20, 27] and realized with nano-magnetic spins. As the third method, Invertible Logic oracles can be emulated using standard FPGAs using stochastic number representations. Various number systems, radices and operators can be used to operate on numbers and encoded symbolic data in these oracles [1, 7]. Please observe that there are many systems to represent numbers and arithmetic operators executed on them [1, 2, 5, 20]. Some of these number systems may be better when used inside the gates and blocks of invertible logic. This is an area of current research. (It is very likely that some day FPGAs based on magnetic spin technology will be invented and fabricated). As the fourth method, the oracles can be exercised sequentially (but only from input to output) in standard Boolean Logic and realized in standard FPGAs. Finally, as the fifth method a complete quantum circuit can be built for a quantum neural network built as a composition of small quantum networks. The top network is an oracle, the small networks are gates and blocks.

Concluding, the very general "oracle-based" methodology for solving CSP and optimization problems outlined in this paper can be applied to many important problems from Design Automation, Logistics, Optimization, Control, Artificial Intelligence, Machine Learning and Robotics. The methodology will become even more practical with the appearance of: (1) quantum computers that will have more qubits, (2) magnetic spin technologies with higher number os gates, (3) standard FPGAs with very-high-quality hardware random number generators. It is also an open problem how well these quantum oracles will work in Noisy Intermediate Scale Quantum (NISQ) computers [48] without error correction.

References

1. Ardakani, A., Leduc-Primeau, F., Onizawa, N., Hanyu, T., Gross, W.J.: VLSI implementation of deep neural network using integral stochastic computing. IEEE Trans. Very Large Scale Integr. (VLSI) Syst. **25**(10), 2588–2599 (2017)
2. Cheng, A., Tsai, E., Perkowski, M.: Methodology to create hardware oracles for solving constraint satisfaction problems. In: 22nd International Workshop on Post-Binary ULSI Systems, pp. 36–43. Toyama International Conference Center, Toyama (2013)
3. Dhawan, S., Perkowski, M.: Comparison of influence of two data-encoding methods for grover algorithm on quantum costs. In: ISMVL, pp. 176–181 (2011). https://doi.org/10.1109/ismvl.2011.29
4. Biamonte, J.D.: Non-perturbative k-body to two-body commuting conversion Hamiltonians and embedding problem instances into Ising spins. Phys. Rev. A **77**, 052331 (2008)
5. Camsari, K., Faria, R., Sutton, B., Datta, S.: Stochastic p-bits for invertible logic. Phys. Rev. X **7**, 031014 (2017)

6. Debashis, P., Faria, R., Camsari, K.Y., Appenzeller, J., Datta, S., Chen, Z.: Experimental demonstration of nanomagnet networks as hardware for Ising computing. In: IEEE International Electron Devices Meeting (IEDM), pp. 34.3.1–34.3.4 (2016)
7. Gaines, B.R.: Stochastic computing systems. In: Tou, J.T. (ed.) Advances in Information Systems Science. Advances in Information Systems Science, pp. 37–172. Springer, Boston (1969). https://doi.org/10.1007/978-1-4899-5841-9_2
8. Gao, P., Li, Y., Perkowski, M., Song, X.: Realization of quantum oracles using symmetries of Boolean functions. Quantum Inf. Comput. **20**(5&6), 0417–0446 (2020)
9. Grover, L.K.: A fast quantum mechanical algorithm for database search. In: 28th Annual ACM Symposium on Theory of Computing, pp. 212–219 (1996)
10. Hinton, G.E., Sejnowski, T.J., Ackley, D.H.: Boltzmann machines: constraint satisfaction networks that learn. Department of Computer Science, Carnegie-Mellon University, Technical report CMUCS-84-119 (1984)
11. Lee, B., Perkowski, M.: Quantum machine learning based on minimizing Kronecker-Reed-Muller forms and Grover search algorithm with hybrid oracles. In: 2016 Euromicro Conference on Digital System Design (DSD), pp. 413–422 (2016)
12. Li, Y., Tsai, Y., Perkowski, M., Song, X.: Grover-based Ashenhurst-Curtis decomposition using quantum language quipper. Quantum Inf. Comput. **19**(1&2), 0035–0066 (2019)
13. Mishchenko, A., Perkowski, M.: Fast heuristic minimization of exclusive sums-of-products. In: RM 2001 Workshop (2001)
14. Monaco, J.V., Vindiola, M.M.: Factoring integers with a brain-inspired computer. IEEE Trans. Circuits Syst. I Regul. Pap. **65**(3), 1051–1062 (2018)
15. Perkowski, M.: Methodology to design oracles for Grover algorithm, poster presentation. In: Workshop on Design Automation for Quantum Computers, IEEE 2017 International Conference On Computer Aided Design, Marriott Hotel, Irvine, CA (2017)
16. Luba, T., Selvaraj, H.: A general approach to Boolean function decomposition and its application in FPGA based synthesis. VLSI Des. **3**(3–4), 289–300 (1995)
17. Pervaiz, A.Z., Ghantasala, L.A., Camsari, K., Datta, S.: Hardware emulation of stochastic p-bits for invertible logic. Sci. Rep. **7** (2017). Article No. 10994
18. Pervaiz, A.Z., Sutton, B.M., Ghantasala, L.A., Camsari, K.Y.: Weighted p-bits for FPGA implementation of probabilistic circuits. arXiv e-prints (2017)
19. Shor, P.W.: Polynomial-time algorithms for prime factorization and discrete logarithms on a quantum computer. SIAM J. Comput. **26**, 1484–1509 (1997)
20. Smithson, S.C., Onizawa, N., Meyer, B.H., Gross, W.J., Hanyu, T.: Efficient CMOS invertible logic using stochastic computing. IEEE Trans. Circuits Syst. I Regul. Pap. **66**(6), 2263–2274 (2019)
21. Tsai, E., Perkowski, M.: A quantum algorithm for automata encoding. Facta Universitatis. Ser. Electron. Energ. **33**, 169–215 (2020)
22. Tsai, E., Perkowski, M.: Towards the Development of Quantum Design Automation Tools: A Methodology for Construction of Oracles to Solve Constraint Satisfaction Problems using Grover's Algorithm (2020, Submitted)
23. Tsai, E., Perkowski, M.: Realization of Arbitrary Symmetric Functions in Quantum Logic Using Two-Qubit Gate (2020, Submitted)
24. Wang, Y., Perkowski, M.: Improved complexity of quantum oracles for ternary Grover algorithm for graph coloring. In: ISMVL, pp. 294–301 (2011). https://doi.org/10.1109/ismvl.2011.42
25. Whitfield, J.D., Faccin, M., Biamonte, J.D.: Ground-state spin logic. Europhys. Lett. **99**(5), 57004 (2012)
26. Butler, J.T., Sasao, T.: Combinational computing. One object per clock. In: Reed-Muller Symposium, Toyama, Japan (2013)

27. Sutton, B., Camsari, K.Y., Behin-Aein, B., Datta, S.: Intrinsic optimization using stochastic nanomagnets. Sci. Rep. **7**(1), 1–9 (2017)
28. Brassard, G., HØyer, P., Tapp, A.: Quantum counting. In: Larsen, K.G., Skyum, S., Winskel, G. (eds.) ICALP 1998. LNCS, vol. 1443, pp. 820–831. Springer, Heidelberg (1998). https://doi.org/10.1007/BFb0055105
29. Venkatachalapathy, R.: Systems isomorphisms in stochastic dynamic systems. PSU, Systems Science, Ph.D. Dissertation (2019)
30. Sivakumar, S., Li, Y., Perkowski, M.: Grover Algorithm for Minimum Set of Support Problem of Multi-Valued Functions (2020, Submitted)
31. Zhang, W.: Quantum Algorithms for Two-Arm robot and generalization to Travelling Salesman Problem (2020, in Preparation)
32. Hou, W., Perkowski, M.: Quantum Algorithm for Knapsack problem (2020, Submitted)
33. Rawski, M., Jóźwiak, L., Luba, T.: Functional decomposition with an efficient input support selection for sub-functions based on information relationship measures. J. Syst. Architect. **47**, 137–155 (2001)
34. Konieczny, P.A., Jóźwiak, L.: Minimal input support problem and algorithms to solve it, vol. 95-E-289. Eindhoven University of Technology Report E, Faculty of Electrical Engineering, Eindhoven, 01 January 1995
35. Mishchenko, A., Files, C., Perkowski, M., Steinbach, B., Dorotska, C.: Implicit algorithms for multi-valued input support manipulation. In: 4th International Workshop on Boolean Problems (2000)
36. Kiran, R.U., Reddy, P.K.: An improved multiple minimum support based approach to mine rare association rules. IEEE (2009). 978-1-4244-2765-9/09
37. Łuba, T., Rybnik, J.: Algorithmic approach to discernibility function with respect to attributes and objects reduction. Found. Comput. Decis. Sci. **18**(3–4), 241–258 (1993)
38. Sasao, T., Fumishi, I., Iguchi, Y.: On an exact minimization of variables for incompletely specified index generation functions using SAT. Note Multiple-Valued Logic Jpn. **38**, 1–8 (2015)
39. Nielsen, M.A., Chuang, I.L.: Quantum Computation and Quantum Information. Cambridge University Press, Cambridge (2000)
40. Boyer, M., Brassard, G., Høyer, P., Tapp, A.: Tight bounds on quantum searching. Fortschr. Phys. **46**, 493 (1998)
41. Cross, A.: The IBM Q experience and QISKit open-source quantum computing software. APS March Meeting (2018). Abstract id L58.003. Bibcode 2018 APS .. MARL58003C
42. Al-Bayaty, A., Perkowski, M.: Simulating Boolean, Quantum and Invertible Logic Oracles using a Prolog-based system. Report PSU (2020, in Preparation)
43. Taha, M.M.A., Perkowski, M.: Realization of arithmetic operators based on stochastic number frequency signal representation. In: ISMVL 2018, pp. 215–220 (2018)
44. Cheng, A.: Designing FPGA Oracles for Cryptography Problems. PSU report (2013)
45. Li, Y.: Quantum Oracles for Graph Coloring and Maximum Clique. PSU report in preparation (2020)
46. Perkowski, M., Foote, D., Chen, Q., Al-Rabadi, A., Jozwiak, L.: Learning hardware using multiple-valued logic – Part 2: cube calculus and architecture. IEEE Micro Chips Syst. Softw. Appl. **22**(3), 52–61 (2002)
47. Kohavi, Z.: Switching and Finite Automata Theory. McGraw-Hill, New York (1978)
48. Preskill, J.: Quantum computing in the NISQ era and beyond. arXiv:1801.00862v3 [quant-ph], 31 July 2018
49. Perkowski, M., Liu, J., Brown, J.: Quick software prototyping: CAD design of digital CAD algorithms. In: Zobrist, G. (ed.) Progress in Computer Aided VLSI Design, vol. 1, pp. 353–401. Ablex Publishing Corp, New York (1989)

Foundations

Reversible Occurrence Nets and Causal Reversible Prime Event Structures

Hernán Melgratti[1], Claudio Antares Mezzina[2], Iain Phillips[3],
G. Michele Pinna[4(✉)], and Irek Ulidowski[5]

[1] ICC - Universidad de Buenos Aires - Conicet, Buenos Aires, Argentina
[2] Dipartimento di Scienze Pure e Applicate, Università di Urbino, Urbino, Italy
[3] Imperial College London, London, England
[4] Università di Cagliari, Cagliari, Italy
gmpinna@unica.it
[5] University of Leicester, Leicester, England

Abstract. One of the well-known results in concurrency theory concerns the relationship between event structures and occurrence nets: an occurrence net can be associated with a prime event structure, and vice versa. More generally, the relationships between various forms of event structures and suitable forms of nets have been long established. Good examples are the close relationship between inhibitor event structures and inhibitor occurrence nets, or between asymmetric event structures and asymmetric occurrence nets. Several forms of event structures suited for the modelling of reversible computation have recently been developed; also a method for reversing occurrence nets has been proposed. This paper bridges the gap between reversible event structures and reversible nets. We introduce the notion of reversible occurrence net, which is a generalisation of the notion of reversible unfolding. We show that reversible occurrence nets correspond precisely to a subclass of reversible prime event structures, the causal reversible prime event structures.

Keywords: Event structures · Causality · Reversibility · Petri nets

1 Introduction

Event structures and nets are closely related. Since the seminal papers by Nielsen, Plotkin and Winskel [21] and Winskel [29], the relationship among nets and event structures has been considered as a pivotal characteristic of concurrent

The authors were partially supported by COST Action IC1405 on Reversible Computation - Extending Horizons of Computing.
H. Melgratti—Partially supported by the EU H2020 RISE programme under the Marie Skłodowska-Curie grant agreement 778233, by the UBACyT projects 20020170 100544BA and 20020170100086BA, and by the PIP project 11220130100148CO.
C. A. Mezzina—Partially supported by the project DCore ANR-18-CE25-0007 and the INdAM–GNCS project Reversible Concurrent Systems: from Models to Languages.
G. M. Pinna—Partially supported by RAS Project SardCoin, CUP: F72F16003030002.

© Springer Nature Switzerland AG 2020
I. Lanese and M. Rawski (Eds.): RC 2020, LNCS 12227, pp. 35–53, 2020.
https://doi.org/10.1007/978-3-030-52482-1_2

systems. The ingredients of an event structure are a set of events and a number of relations that are used to express which events can be part of a configuration (the snapshot of a concurrent system), modelling a consistency predicate, and how events can be added to reach another configuration, modelling the dependencies among the events. On the net side, the ingredients boil down to constraints on how transitions may be executed, and usually have a structural flavour.

Since the introduction of event structures there has been a flourish of investigations into the possible relations among events, giving rise to a number of different definitions of event structures. We first mention the classical *prime* event structures [29] where the dependency between events, called *causality*, is given by a partial order and the consistency is determined by a *conflict* relation. *Flow* event structures [6] drop the requirement that the dependency should be a partial order, and *bundle* event structures [18] are able to represent OR-causality by allowing each event to be caused by a member of a bundle of events. *Asymmetric* event structures [3] introduce the notion of weak causality that can model asymmetric conflicts. *Inhibitor* event structures [2] are able to faithfully capture the dependencies among events which arise in the presence of read and inhibitor arcs. In [4] event structures, where the causality relation may be circular, are investigated, and in [1] the notion of dynamic causality is considered. Finally, we mention the quite general approach presented in [27], where there is a unique relation, akin to a *deduction relation*. To each of the aforementioned event structures a particular class of nets corresponds. To prime event structures we have *occurrence* nets, to flow event structures we have *flow* nets, to bundle event structures we have *unravel* nets [7], to asymmetric and inhibitor event structures we have *contextual* nets [2,3], to event structures with circular causality we have *lending* nets [4], to those with dynamic causality we have *inhibitor unravel* nets [8] and finally to the ones presented in [27] *1-occurrence* nets are associated.

Recently a new type of event structure tailored to model *reversible* computation has been proposed [24,26]. In particular, in [24], *reversible* prime event structures have been introduced. In this kind of event structure two relations are added: the *reverse causality* relation and the *prevention relation*. The first one is a standard dependency relation: in order to reverse an event some other events must be present. The second relation, on the contrary, identifies those events whose presence *prevents* the event being reversed. This kind of event structure is able to model both causal-consistent reversibility [9,15,23] and out-of-causal-order reversibility [13,25]. Causal-consistent reversibility relates reversibility with causality: an event can be undone provided that all of its effects have been undone first. This allows the system to get back to a past state, which was possible to reach by just the normal (forward) computation. This notion of reversibility is natural in reliable distributed systems since when an error occurs the system tries to go back to a past consistent state. Examples of application of causal-consistent reversibility to model reliable systems include transactions [10,14] and rollback protocols [28]. Also, there are applications in program analysis and debugging [12,17]. The out-of-causal-order reversibility does not preserve causes, and this feature makes it suitable to model biochemical reactions where, for example, a bond can be undone 'out-of-order' thus leading to a new state that was not present before.

Reversibility in Petri nets has been studied in [19,22] with two different approaches. In [22] reversibility in an acyclic Petri net is obtained by adding a new kind of tokens, called bonds, that keep track of the execution history. Bonds are rich enough to permit modelling of both the causal-consistent and out-of-causal order reversibility. In [19] a notion of *unfolding* of a P/T (place/transition) net, where all the transitions can be reversed, has been proposed. By resorting to standard notions of the Petri net theory [19] provides a causal-consistent reversible semantics for P/T nets. This exploits the well-known unfolding of P/T nets into occurrence nets [29], and is done by adding for each transition its reversible counterpart. We also note that a problem of making a Petri net reversible (meaning every computation is able to reach back to the initial state) has been solved by showing how to add a minimal number of additional transitions [5].

In this paper we study what kind of nets can be associated with reversible prime event structures. To this aim we introduce *reversible occurrence* nets, which are occurrence nets enriched with additional transitions (called *reversing* transitions) that undo the effects of executing the ordinary transitions.

Each reversing transition (event in the occurrence net dialect) is associated with a unique transition that produces the effects that the reversing transition undoes. A reversing event associated with an event e can be executed in a reversible occurrence net only when all the events caused by e have been previously reversed. If this is not possible then the reversing event cannot be executed. This means that some events in a reversible event structure may *prevent* the occurrence of a reversing event. A reversible occurrence net where the reversing events have been removed is just an occurrence net. This discussion suggests a natural way of relating reversible occurrence nets and reversible prime event structures: the causality relation is the one induced by the occurrence net while the prevention relation is induced by the inverse of causality: a reversing event associated with e is prevented by any event that causally depends on e. In this way we associate a reversible occurrence net with a *causal* reversible prime event structure [24,26], which is a subclass of reversible prime event structures.

We also show how to obtain a reversible occurrence net from a causal reversible prime event structure. The ingredients that are used are just the causality relation and the set of reversible events. We prove that the two formalisms have the same configurations. Hence, this gives us the precise correspondence between causal reversible prime event structures and reversible occurrence nets. We do not consider non-causal reversible prime event structures here; however, we hint at how this can be done in Sect. 5.

Structure of the Paper. Section 2 reviews some preliminary notions for nets and event structures, including reversible prime event structures. Section 3 recalls the well-known relationship between prime event structures and occurrence nets. The core of the paper is Sect. 4 where we first introduce reversible occurrence nets and then we show how to obtain a reversible occurrence net from an occurrence net. We then show how to associate a causal reversible prime event structure with a reversible occurrence net, and vice versa. Section 5 concludes the paper.

2 Preliminaries

We denote with $\mathbb{N}$ the set of natural numbers. Let A be a set, a *multiset* of A is a function $m : A \to \mathbb{N}$. The set of multisets of A is denoted by μA. We assume the usual operations on multisets such as union $+$ and difference $-$, and $k \cdot m$ stands for the scalar multiplication of m by k, i.e., $(k \cdot m)(a) = k \cdot m(a)$ for all $a \in A$. We write $m \subseteq m'$ if $m(a) \leq m'(a)$ for all $a \in A$. For $m \in \mu A$, we denote with $\llbracket m \rrbracket$ the multiset defined as $\llbracket m \rrbracket(a) = 1$ if $m(a) > 0$ and $\llbracket m \rrbracket(a) = 0$ otherwise. When a multiset m of A is a set, i.e. $m = \llbracket m \rrbracket$, we write $a \in m$ to denote that $m(a) \neq 0$, and often confuse the multiset m with the set $\{a \in A \mid m(a) \neq 0\}$. Furthermore we use the standard set operations like $\cap$, $\cup$ or $\setminus$. Given a set A and a relation $< \subseteq A \times A$, we say that $<$ is an *irreflexive partial order* whenever it is irreflexive and transitive. We shall write $\leq$ for the reflexive closure of a partial order $<$.

2.1 Petri Nets

We review the notion of Petri net along with some auxiliary notions.

Definition 1. *A* Petri net *is a 4-tuple* $N = \langle S, T, F, \mathsf{m} \rangle$*, where* S *is a set of* places *and* T *is a set of* transitions *(with* $S \cap T = \emptyset$*),* $F \subseteq (S \times T) \cup (T \times S)$ *is the* flow *relation, and* $\mathsf{m} \in \mu S$ *is called the* initial marking*.*

Given a net $N = \langle S, T, F, \mathsf{m} \rangle$ and $x \in S \cup T$, we define the following sets: $^\bullet x = \{y \mid (y, x) \in F\}$ and $x^\bullet = \{y \mid (x, y) \in F\}$, which can be viewed as multisets. If $x \in S$ then $^\bullet x \in \mu T$ and $x^\bullet \in \mu T$; analogously, if $x \in T$ then $^\bullet x \in \mu S$ and $x^\bullet \in \mu S$. A multiset of transitions $A \in \mu T$, called *step*, is enabled at a marking $m \in \mu S$, denoted by $m \, [A\rangle$, whenever $^\bullet A \subseteq m$, where $^\bullet A = \sum_{x \in \llbracket A \rrbracket} A(x) \cdot {}^\bullet x$. A step A enabled at a marking m can *fire* and its firing produces the marking $m' = m - {}^\bullet A + A^\bullet$, where $A^\bullet = \sum_{x \in \llbracket A \rrbracket} A(x) \cdot x^\bullet$. The firing of A at a marking m is denoted by $m \, [A\rangle \, m'$. We assume that each transition t of a net N is such that $^\bullet t \neq \emptyset$, meaning that no transition may fire *spontaneously*. Given a generic marking m (not necessarily the initial one), a (step) *firing sequence* (shortened as fs) of $N = \langle S, T, F, \mathsf{m} \rangle$ starting at m is defined as: (*i*) m is a firing sequence (of length 0), and (*ii*) if $m \, [A_1\rangle \, m_1 \, \cdots \, m_{n-1} \, [A_n\rangle \, m_n$ is a firing sequence and $m_n \, [A\rangle \, m'$, then also $m \, [A_1\rangle \, m_1 \, \cdots \, m_{n-1} \, [A_n\rangle \, m_n \, [A\rangle \, m'$ is a firing sequence. Let us note that each step A such that $|A| = n$ can be written as $A_1 + \cdots + A_n$ where for each $1 \leq i \leq n$ it holds that $A_i = \llbracket A_i \rrbracket$ and $|A_i| = 1$, and $m \, [A\rangle \, m'$ then, for each decomposition of A in $A_1 + \cdots + A_n$, we have that $m \, [A_1\rangle \, m_1 \ldots m_{n-1} \, [A_n\rangle \, m_n = m'$. When A is a singleton, i.e. $A = \{t\}$, we write $m \, [t\rangle \, m'$. The set of firing sequences of a net N starting at a marking m is denoted by $\mathcal{R}_m^N$ and it is ranged over by σ. Given an fs $\sigma = m \, [A_1\rangle \, \sigma' \, [A_n\rangle \, m_n$, we denote with $start(\sigma)$ the marking m, with $lead(\sigma)$ the marking m_n and with $tail(\sigma)$ the fs $\sigma'\,[A_n\rangle\, m_n$. $tail(\sigma)$ is defined only when σ has length greater than 0. Given a net $N = \langle S, T, F, \mathsf{m}\rangle$, a marking m is *reachable* iff there exists an fs $\sigma \in \mathcal{R}_m^N$ such that $lead(\sigma)$ is m. The set of reachable markings of N is $\mathcal{M}_N = \{lead(\sigma) \mid \sigma \in \mathcal{R}_m^N\}$. Given an fs $\sigma = m\,[A_1\rangle\, m_1 \cdots m_{n-1}\,[A_n\rangle\, m'$, we write $X_\sigma = \sum_{i=1}^n A_i$ for the multiset of transitions associated to fs. We call X_σ a *state* of the net and write $\mathsf{St}(N) = \{X_\sigma \in \mu T \mid \sigma \in \mathcal{R}_m^N\}$ for the set of states of N.

Definition 2. *A net $N = \langle S, T, F, \mathsf{m}\rangle$ is said to be* safe *if each marking $m \in \mathcal{M}_N$ is such that $m = [\![m]\!]$.*

In this paper we consider safe nets $N = \langle S, T, F, \mathsf{m}\rangle$ where each transition can be fired, i.e. $\forall t \in T\ \exists m \in \mathcal{M}_N.\ m\,[t\rangle$, and every place is reachable (i.e., marked in at least one reachable marking).

2.2   Prime Event Structures

We now recall the notion of prime event structure [29].

Definition 3. *A* prime event structure (PES) *is a triple $P = (E, <, \#)$, where*

- E *is a countable set of* events,
- $< \,\subseteq E \times E$ *is an irreflexive partial order called the* causality relation, *such that $\forall e \in E.\ \{e' \in E \mid e' < e\}$ is finite, and*
- $\# \,\subseteq E \times E$ *is the* conflict relation, *which is irreflexive, symmetric and hereditary with respect to $<$: if $e\ \#\ e' < e''$, then $e\ \#\ e''$ for all $e, e', e'' \in E$.*

Intuitively, $e < e'$ models that e' can occur only after e, while $e\ \#\ e'$ indicates that e and e' are mutually exclusive. Given an event $e \in E$, $\lfloor e \rfloor$ denotes the set $\{e' \in E \mid e' \leq e\}$. A set of events $X \subseteq E$ is left-closed if $\forall e \in X.\lfloor e \rfloor \subseteq X$. Given a set $X \subseteq E$ of events, we say that X is *conflict free*, written $\mathsf{CF}(X)$, iff for all $e, e' \in X$ it holds that $e \neq e' \Rightarrow \neg(e\ \#\ e')$. Given $X \subseteq E$ such that $\mathsf{CF}(X)$ and $Y \subseteq X$, then also $\mathsf{CF}(Y)$. When adding reversibility to PESes, conflict heredity may not hold. Therefore, we rely on a weaker form of PES by following the approach in [24].

Definition 4. *A* pre-PES (pPES) *is a triple $P = (E, <, \#)$, where*

- E *is a set of* events,
- $\# \,\subseteq E \times E$ *is an irreflexive and symmetric relation,*
- $< \,\subseteq E \times E$ *is an irreflexive partial order such that for every $e \in E.\ \{e' \in E \mid e' < e\}$ is finite and conflict free, and*
- $\forall e, e' \in E.$ *if $e < e'$ then not $e\ \#\ e'$.*

A pPES is a prime event structure in which conflict heredity does not hold, and since every PES is also a pPES the notions and results stated below for pPESes also apply to PESes.

Definition 5. *Let $P = (E, <, \#)$ be a pPES and $X \subseteq E$ such that $\mathsf{CF}(X)$. For $A \subseteq E$, we say that A is enabled at X if $A \cap X = \emptyset$ and $\mathsf{CF}(X \cup A)$, and $\forall e \in A$. if $e' < e$ then $e' \in X$. If A is enabled at X, then X can reach $Y = X \cup A$, and is written as $X \xrightarrow{A} Y$.*

Definition 6. *Let $P = (E, <, \#)$ be a pPES and $X \subseteq E$ such that $\mathsf{CF}(X)$. X is a* forwards reachable configuration *if there exists a sequence $A_1, \ldots, A_n$, such that $X_i \xrightarrow{A_i} X_{i+1}$ for all i, and $X_1 = \emptyset$ and $X_{n+1} = X$. We write $\mathsf{Conf}_{p\mathrm{PES}}(P)$ for the set of all (forwards reachable) configurations of P.*

When a pPES is a PES we shall write $\mathsf{Conf}_{\mathrm{PES}}(P)$ instead of $\mathsf{Conf}_{p\mathrm{PES}}(P)$, with $\mathsf{Conf}_{\mathrm{PES}}(P) = \mathsf{Conf}_{p\mathrm{PES}}(P)$ holding. A PES can be obtained from a pPES.

Definition 7. *Let $P = (E, <, \#)$ be a pPES. Then $\mathsf{hc}(P) = (E, <, \natural)$ is the* hereditary closure *of P, where $\natural$ is derived by using the following rules*

$$\frac{e \# e'}{e \natural e'} \quad \frac{e \natural e'}{e \natural e''} \quad \frac{e' < e'' \quad e' \natural e}{e \natural e''}$$

The following proposition relates pPES to PES [24].

Proposition 1. *Let $P = (E, <, \#)$ be a pPES. Then*

- *$\mathsf{hc}(P) = (E, \leq, \natural)$ is a PES,*
- *if P is a PES, then $\mathsf{hc}(P) = P$, and*
- *$\mathsf{Conf}_{p\mathrm{PES}}(P) = \mathsf{Conf}_{\mathrm{PES}}(\mathsf{hc}(P))$.*

2.3   Reversible Prime Event Structures

We now focus on the notion of *reversible prime event structure*. The definitions and the results in this subsection are drawn from [24]. In reversible event structures some events are categorised as *reversible*. In addition to the usual causality and conflict relations, reversible event structures incorporate two new ones that relate events and those representing the *actual* undoing of the reversible events. The undoing of events is represented by *removing* them (from a configuration), which is achieved by *executing* the appropriate *reversing* events.

Definition 8. *A reversible prime event structure (rPES) is the tuple $\mathsf{P} = (E, U, <, \#, \prec, \rhd)$ where $(E, <, \#)$ is a pPES, $U \subseteq E$ are the reversible/undoable events (with reverse events being denoted by $\underline{U} = \{\underline{u} \mid u \in U\}$ and disjoint from E, i.e., $\underline{U} \cap E = \emptyset$) and*

- *$\rhd \subseteq E \times \underline{U}$ is the* prevention *relation,*
- *$\prec \subseteq E \times \underline{U}$ is the* reverse causality *relation and it is such that $u \prec \underline{u}$ for each $u \in U$ and $\{e \in E \mid e \prec \underline{u}\}$ is finite and conflict-free for every $u \in U$,*
- *if $e \prec \underline{u}$ then not $e \rhd \underline{u}$,*
- *the* sustained causation *$\ll$ is a transitive relation defined such that $e \ll e'$ if $e < e'$ and $e \in U$, then $e' \rhd \underline{e}$, and*

- $\#$ *is hereditary with respect to* $\ll$*: if* $e \# e' \ll e''$*, then* $e \# e''$*.*

The ingredients of an rPES partly overlap with those of a PES: there is a causality relation ($<$) and a conflict one ($\#$) and the two are related by the *sustained causation* relation $\ll$. The new ingredients are the *prevention* relation and the *reverse causality* relation. The prevention relation states that certain events should be absent when trying to reverse an event, e.g., $e \rhd \underline{u}$ states that e should be absent when reversing u. The reverse causality relation $e \prec \underline{u}$ says that $\underline{u}$ can be executed only when e is present.

Example 1. Let $\mathsf{P} = (E, U, <, \#, \prec, \rhd)$ where $E = U = \{a, b, c\}$, $a < b$ and $a \prec \underline{a}$, $b \prec \underline{b}$, $c \prec \underline{c}$, $c \prec \underline{a}$ with $b \rhd \underline{a}$ and no conflict. Then $a \ll b$ because $a < b$ and $b \rhd \underline{a}$. P states that b causally depends on a and that c is concurrent w.r.t. both a and b. Note that every event is reversible in P because $U = E$. As expected, the reverse causality relation $\prec$ is defined such that every reverse event requires the presence of the corresponding reversible event, i.e., $e \prec \underline{e}$ for all $e \in E$. Additionally, it also requires $c \prec \underline{a}$, i.e., a can be reversed only when c is present. The prevention relation states that a cannot be reversed when b is present, i.e., $b \rhd \underline{a}$.

Definition 9. *Let* $\mathsf{P} = (E, U, <, \#, \prec, \rhd)$ *be an* rPES *and* $X \subseteq yE$ *be a set of events such that* $\mathsf{CF}(X)$*. For* $A \subseteq E$ *and* $B \subseteq U$*, we say that* $A \cup \underline{B}$ *is enabled at* X *if*

- $A \cap X = \emptyset$, $B \subseteq X$ *and* $\mathsf{CF}(X \cup A)$,
- $\forall e \in A, e' \in E.$ *if* $e' < e$ *then* $e' \in X \setminus B$,
- $\forall e \in B, e' \in E.$ *if* $e' \prec \underline{e}$ *then* $e' \in X \setminus (B \setminus \{e\})$,
- $\forall e \in B, e' \in E.$ *if* $e' \rhd \underline{e}$ *then* $e' \notin X \cup A$.

If $A \cup \underline{B}$ *is enabled at* X *then* $X \xrightarrow{A \cup \underline{B}} Y$ *where* $Y = (X \setminus B) \cup A$.

Example 2. Consider the rPES in Example 1. We have, e.g., $\emptyset \xrightarrow{\{a,c\}} \{a, c\} \xrightarrow{\{\underline{a}\}}$ $\{c\}$ and $\emptyset \xrightarrow{\{a\}} \{a\} \xrightarrow{\{b\}} \{a, b\} \xrightarrow{\{c, b\}} \{a, c\} \xrightarrow{\{b\}} \{a, b, c\}$. While $\emptyset \xrightarrow{\{a\}} \{a\}$ holds, $\emptyset \xrightarrow{\{a\}} \{a\} \xrightarrow{\{\underline{a}\}} \{\}$ does not hold; this is because $a \prec \underline{a}$ and $c \prec \underline{a}$ require that a and c are in the configuration ($\{a\}$) for $\{\underline{a}\}$ to be enabled. Also $\emptyset \xrightarrow{\{a,c\}} \{a, c\} \xrightarrow{\{b\}} \{a, c, b\}$ holds but $\{a, c, b\} \xrightarrow{\{\underline{a}\}} \{b, c\}$ does not hold since, given $b \rhd \underline{a}$, the presence of b prevents the execution of $\underline{a}$.

Reachable configurations are sets of events that can be reached from the empty set by performing events or undoing previously performed events.

Definition 10. *Let* $\mathsf{P} = (E, U, <, \#, \prec, \rhd)$ *be an* rPES *and let* $X \subseteq E$ *be a set of events such that* $\mathsf{CF}(X)$*. We say that* X *is a* (reachable) configuration *if there exist two sequences of sets* A_i *and* B_i*, for* $i = 1, \ldots, n$*, such that*

- $A_i \subseteq E$ *and* $B_i \subseteq U$ *for all* i*, and*
- $X_i \xrightarrow{A_i \cup B_i} X_{i+1}$ *for all* i *with* $X_1 = \emptyset$ *and* $X_{n+1} = X$.

The set of configurations of P *is denoted by* $\mathsf{Conf}_{rPES}(P)$.

Example 3. The set of configurations of P defined in Example 1 is $\mathsf{Conf}_{rPES}(P) = \{\emptyset, \{a\}, \{c\}, \{a, b\}, \{a, c\}, \{a, b, c\}\}$ as illustrated by the sequences shown in Example 2.

As discussed in Sect. 1, rPESes accommodate different flavours of reversibility. Henceforth, we focus on causal-consistent reversibility [9,16], which is one of the most common models of reversibility in distributed systems, in which an event can be reversed only when all the events it has caused have already been reversed. In the setting of rPESes we consider these two forms of causal-consistent reversibility.

Definition 11. *Let* $P = (E, U, <, \#, \prec, \rhd)$ *be an* rPES. *Then* P *is* cause-respecting *if for any* $e, e' \in E$, *if* $e < e'$ *then* $e \ll e'$. P *is* causal *if for any* $e \in E$ *and* $u \in U$ *the following holds:* $e \prec \underline{u}$ *iff* $e = u$, *and* $e \rhd \underline{u}$ *iff* $u < e$.

Example 4. The rPES P in Example 1 is a cause-respecting rPES. However P is not causal because of $c \prec \underline{a}$, which means that c has to be present for a to be reversed even if c does not causally depend on a. If we remove $c \prec \underline{a}$ then we obtain a causal rPES.

Example 5. An example of out-of-causal order reversibility can be obtained from the definition of the rPES P in Example 1 by replacing $b \rhd \underline{a}$ by $a \rhd \underline{b}$. Then, we have $\emptyset \xrightarrow{\{a\}} \{a\} \xrightarrow{\{b,c\}} \{a, b, c\} \xrightarrow{\{a\}} \{b, c\}$. Note that a can be reversed even in the presence of the event b, which causally depends on a.

Cause-respecting and causal rPESes enjoy the following useful properties [24].

Proposition 2. *Let* $P = (E, U, <, \#, \prec, \rhd)$ *be an* rPES. *Let* X *be a left-closed and conflict-free set of events in* E *and let* $A, B \subseteq U$. *Then*

- *if* P *is cause-respecting and* $X \xrightarrow{A \cup B} X'$, *then* X' *is also left-closed,*
- *if* P *is cause-respecting and* $X \xrightarrow{B} X'$, *then* $X' \xrightarrow{B} X$,
- *if* P *is causal and* $X \xrightarrow{A \cup B} X'$, *then* $X' \xrightarrow{B \cup A} X$.

Example 6. The above properties do not hold when an rPES is not cause-respecting or not causal. Consider the rPES in Example 5. We have that $\{a, b, c\} \xrightarrow{\{a\}} \{b, c\}$ but $\{b, c\}$ is not left-closed.

A particular rôle will be played by the configurations that can be reached without executing any reversible event.

Definition 12. *Let* $P = (E, U, <, \#, \prec, \rhd)$ *be an* rPES *and* $X \in \mathsf{Conf}_{rPES}(P)$ *be a configuration.* X *is* forwards reachable *if there exists a sequence of sets* $A_i \subseteq E$, *for* $i = 1, \ldots, n$, *such that* $X_i \xrightarrow{A_i} X_{i+1}$ *for all* i, *with* $X_1 = \emptyset$ *and* $X_{n+1} = X$.

The set $\{b, c\}$ in Example 6 is a reachable configuration which is not forwards reachable. The configurations of a cause-respecting rPES are forwards reachable (see [24]).

Proposition 3. *Let* $P = (E, U, <, \#, \prec, \rhd)$ *be a cause-respecting* rPES, *and let* X *be a configuration of* P. *Then* X *is forwards reachable.*

3   Occurrence Nets and Prime Event Structures

We review the notion of occurrence nets [21,29]. Given a net $N = \langle S, T, F, \mathsf{m} \rangle$, we write $<_N$ for the transitive closure of F, and $\leq_N$ for the reflexive closure of $<_N$. We say N is *acyclic* if $\leq_N$ is a partial order. For occurrence nets, we adopt the usual convention and refer to places and transitions respectively as *conditions* and *events*, and correspondingly use B and E for the sets of conditions and events [29]. We will often confuse conditions with places and events with transitions.

Definition 13. *An* occurrence net *(ON)* $C = \langle B, E, F, \mathsf{c} \rangle$ *is an acyclic, safe net satisfying the following restrictions:*

- $\forall b \in B.\ ^\bullet b$ *is either empty or a singleton, and* $\forall b \in \mathsf{c}.\ ^\bullet b = \emptyset$,
- $\forall b \in B.\ \exists b' \in \mathsf{c}$ *such that* $b' \leq_C b$,
- *for all* $e \in E$ *the set* $\lfloor e \rfloor = \{ e' \in E \mid e' \leq_C e \}$ *is finite, and*
- $\# \subseteq E \times E$ *defined as* $e \ \#_0\ e'$ *iff* $e, e' \in E$, $e \neq e'$ *and* $^\bullet e \cap\ ^\bullet e' \neq \emptyset$, $x \ \# \ x'$ *iff* $\exists y, y' \in E$ *such that* $y \ \#_0\ y'$ *and* $y \leq_C x$ *and* $y' \leq_C x'$, *is an irreflexive and symmetric relation.*

The intuition behind occurrence nets is the following: each condition b represents the occurrence of a token, which is produced by the *unique* event in $^\bullet b$, unless b belongs to the initial marking, and it is used by only one transition (hence if $e, e' \in b^\bullet$, then $e \ \# \ e'$). On an occurrence net C it is natural to define a notion of *causality* among elements of the net: we say that x is *causally dependent* on y iff $y \leq_C x$. Occurrence nets are often the result of the *unfolding* of a (safe) net. In this perspective an occurrence net is meant to describe precisely the non-sequential semantics of a net (a semantics where concurrency is faithfully represented), and each reachable marking of the occurrence net corresponds to a reachable marking in the net to be unfolded. Here we focus purely on occurrence nets and not on the nets they are unfoldings of.

Definition 14. *Let* $C = \langle B, E, F, \mathsf{c} \rangle$ *be a* ON *and* $X \subseteq E$ *be a set of events. Then X is a* configuration *of C whenever* $\mathsf{CF}(X)$ *and* $\forall e \in X.\ \lfloor e \rfloor \subseteq X$. *The set of configurations of the occurrence net C is denoted by* $\mathsf{Conf}_{\mathrm{ON}}(C)$.

Given an occurrence net $C = \langle B, E, F, \mathsf{c} \rangle$ and a state $X \in \mathsf{St}(C)$, it is easy to see that it is *conflict free*, i.e. $\forall e, e' \in X.\ e \neq e' \Rightarrow \neg(e \ \# \ e')$, and *left closed*, i.e. $\forall e \in X.\ \{ e' \in E \mid e' \leq_C e \} \subseteq X$.

The following propositions make clear the relations between prime event structures, occurrence nets, states of the occurrence nets and configurations of the prime event structures. Proofs are standard and can be found in papers investigating prime event structures and occurrence nets.

Proposition 4. *Let* $C = \langle B, E, F, \mathsf{c} \rangle$ *be an occurrence net and* $X \in \mathsf{St}(C)$. *Then* $X \in \mathsf{Conf}_{\mathrm{ON}}(C)$.

Occurrence nets and prime event structures are connected as follows [29].

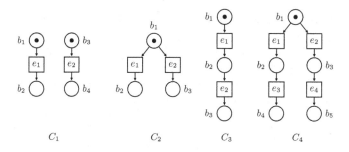

Fig. 1. Some occurrence nets

Proposition 5. *Let* $C = \langle B, E, F, \mathsf{c} \rangle$ *be an occurrence net. Then* $\mathcal{P}(C) = (E, \leq_C, \#)$ *is a* PES, *and* $\mathsf{Conf}_{\mathrm{ON}}(C) = \mathsf{Conf}_{\mathrm{PES}}(\mathcal{P}(C))$.

Example 7. Figure 1 illustrates some (finite) occurrence nets (nets are depicted as usual). We can associate PESes to them as follows. The net C_1 has two concurrent events, which are neither causally ordered nor in conflict; hence $<$ and $\#$ are empty. The events e_1 and e_2 in C_2 are in conflict, i.e., $e_1 \# e_2$, while they are causally ordered in C_3, namely $e_1 < e_2$, but not in conflict. Finally, in C_4 we have $e_1 < e_3$ and $e_2 < e_4$ and $e_1 \# e_2$. Additionally, conflict inheritance give us $e_1 \# e_4$, $e_2 \# e_3$ and $e_3 \# e_4$.

Conversely, every PES can be associated with an occurrence net. With $\#(A)$ we denote the set of events A such that $\forall e, e' \in A.\ e \neq e' \Rightarrow e \# e'$.

Proposition 6. *Let* $P = (E, <, \#)$ *be a* PES *and let* $\bot \notin E$ *be a new symbol. Then* $\mathcal{E}(P) = \langle B, E, F, \mathsf{c} \rangle$ *defined as follows*

- $B = \{(a, A) \mid a \in E \cup \{\bot\} \wedge A \subseteq E \wedge \#(A) \wedge (a \neq \bot \Rightarrow \forall e \in A.\ a < e)\}$,
- $F = \{(b, e) \mid b = (a, A) \wedge e \in A\} \cup \{(e, b) \mid b = (e, A)\}$, *and*
- $\mathsf{c} = \{(a, A) \mid (a, A) \in B \wedge a = \bot\}$.

is an occurrence net, and $\mathsf{Conf}_{\mathrm{PES}}(P) = \mathsf{Conf}_{\mathrm{ON}}(\mathcal{E}(P))$.

4   Reversible Occurrence Nets and Causal Reversible Prime Event Structures

We now introduce the notion of *reversible occurrence nets*. A similar notion has been proposed in [19] for adding causal-consistent reversibility to Petri nets by making reversible every event in the unfolding of the net. In this work we deal with a generalised version of reversible occurrence nets in which transitions may be irreversible, i.e., we do not require every transition of a net to be undoable. The intuition behind reversible occurrence nets is the following: we add special transitions (events in the classical occurrence net terminology) to an occurrence net which, when executed, *undo* the execution of other (standard) transitions. When we remove these special transitions from a reversible causal net we obtain a standard occurrence net.

Definition 15. *A* reversible occurrence net *(*RON*) is a tuple* $R = \langle B, E, U, F, \mathsf{c} \rangle$ *where* $\langle B, E, F, \mathsf{c} \rangle$ *is a safe net such that*

- $U \subseteq E$ *and* $\forall u \in U.\ \exists!\ e \in E \setminus U$ *such that* $^\bullet u = e^\bullet$ *and* $u^\bullet = {}^\bullet e$,
- $\forall e, e' \in E.\ {}^\bullet e = {}^\bullet e' \wedge e^\bullet = e'^\bullet \Rightarrow e = e'$,
- $\bigcup_{e \in E}({}^\bullet e \cup e^\bullet) = B$, *and*
- $C_{E \setminus U} = \langle B, E \setminus U, F', \mathsf{c} \rangle$ *is an occurrence net, where* F' *is the restriction of* F *to the transitions in* $E \setminus U$.

The events in U are the reversing ones and we often say that a reversible occurrence net R is reversible *with respect to* U. We write $\overline{E}$ for the set of events $E \setminus U$ and $C_{\overline{E}}$ instead of $C_{E \setminus U}$. The first condition in Definition 15 implies that each reversing event $u \in U$ is associated with a unique event e that causes the effects that u is intended to *undo*; hence e here is a *reversible* event. Moreover, the second condition ensures that there is an injective mapping $h : U \to E$ that associates each event $u \in U$ with a different event $e \in E$ such that $^\bullet e = u^\bullet$ and $e^\bullet = {}^\bullet u$, in other words, each reversible event has exactly one reversing event. The third requirement guarantees that all conditions (places) of the net appear at least in the pre or the postset of some event (transition), i.e., there are no isolated conditions. The last condition ensures that the net obtained by deleting all reversing events is an occurrence net.

Example 8. We present some reversible occurrence nets in Fig. 2. The reversing events are drawn in red, and their names are underlined. The events e_1 and e_2 in R_1 are both reversible, while e_1 is the only reversible event in R_2. In R_3 the events e_1, e_3 and e_4 are the reversible ones.

We prove that the set of reachable markings of a reversible occurrence net is not influenced by performing reversing events.

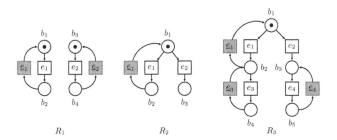

Fig. 2. Some reversible occurrence nets

Proposition 7. *Let $R = \langle B, E, U, F, c \rangle$ be an* RON. *Then* $\mathcal{M}_R = \mathcal{M}_{C_{\overline{E}}}$.

Proof. One direction is trivial, namely $\mathcal{M}_{C_{\overline{E}}} \subseteq \mathcal{M}_R$. For the other direction, we first observe that $\neg(c \, [e\rangle)$ holds for all $e \in U$. This is because $C_{\overline{E}}$ is an occurrence net, and this implies that $\forall b \in c$. ${}^\bullet b$ is either $\emptyset$ or it contains elements in E^r, and $\forall e \in U$. ${}^\bullet e \cap b^\bullet = \emptyset$. Now we show that if an event $u \in U$ is executed then the corresponding event $h(u)$ has been executed before. W.l.o.g. we assume that all the events executed before u are the events in $E \setminus U$. Consider the fs $\sigma \, [u\rangle \, \sigma'$, then we have $lead(\sigma) \, [u\rangle$, which means that ${}^\bullet u \subseteq lead(\sigma)$, but the conditions ${}^\bullet u$ have been produced by the execution of a unique event, namely $h(u)$. Now we prove that $\sigma \, [u\rangle \, m$ can be reached without executing both u and $h(u)$. Consider the marking $lead(\sigma)$, as $\sigma \, [u\rangle$ we know that $h(u)^\bullet \subseteq lead(\sigma)$. Now σ can be rewritten as $\sigma'' \, [h(u)\rangle \, \sigma'''$ and $h(u)$ is concurrent with all the events in σ''', which means that σ can be rewritten as $\hat{\sigma} \, [h(u)\rangle \, lead(\sigma)$. Now we have $m = lead(\hat{\sigma})$ which implies that each reachable marking can be reached executing the events in $E \setminus U$ only, hence $\mathcal{M}_R \subseteq \mathcal{M}_{C_{\overline{E}}}$.

A consequence of the above proposition is the following corollary, which establishes that each marking can be reached by using just *forward events*.

Corollary 1. *Let $C = \langle B, E, U, F, c \rangle$ be an* RON *and σ be an* fs. *Then, there exists an* fs σ' *such that $X_{\sigma'} \subseteq \overline{E}$ and $lead(\sigma) = lead(\sigma')$.*

Definition 16. *Let $R = \langle B, E, U, F, c \rangle$ be an* RON, *and $X \subseteq \overline{E}$ be a set of forward events. Then, X is a configuration of R whenever* $\mathsf{CF}(X)$ *and $\forall e \in X$. $\lfloor e \rfloor \cap \overline{E} \subseteq X$. The set of configurations of R is usually denoted with* $\mathsf{Conf}_{\mathrm{RON}}(R)$.

A configuration of a reversible occurrence net R with respect to U is a subset of $E \setminus U$; consequently, the reversing events (i.e., the ones in U) that may have been executed to reach a particular marking are not considered as part of the configuration. Observe that, differently from occurrence nets, $\mathsf{St}(R) \neq \mathsf{Conf}_{\mathrm{RON}}(R)$ because the former may contain also reversing events. However, as a consequence of Corollary 1, there is no loss of information.

Proposition 8. *Let $R = \langle B, E, U, F, c \rangle$ be an* RON. *Then $X \in \mathsf{Conf}_{\mathrm{RON}}(R)$ iff $X \in \mathsf{Conf}_{\mathrm{ON}}(C_{\overline{E}})$.*

We show how to construct a reversible occurrence net from an occurrence net, once we have identified the events to be *reversed*.

Definition 17. *Let $C = \langle B, E, F, c \rangle$ be an occurrence net and $U \subseteq E$ be the set of reversible events. Define $\mathsf{R}(C) = \langle B, \hat{E}, U \times \{r\}, \hat{F}, c \rangle$ be the net where $\hat{E}$ and $\hat{F}$ are defined as follows:*

- $\hat{E} = E \times \{\mathsf{f}\} \cup U \times \{\mathsf{r}\}$, *and*
- $\hat{F} = \{(b, (e, \mathsf{f})) \mid (b, e) \in F\} \cup \{((e, \mathsf{f}), b) \mid (e, b) \in F\} \cup \{(b, (e, \mathsf{r})) \mid (e, b) \in F\} \cup \{((e, \mathsf{r}), b) \mid (b, e) \in F\}.$

The mapping $h : U \times \{\mathsf{r}\} \to E \times \{\mathsf{f}\}$ is defined as $h(e, \mathsf{r}) = (e, \mathsf{f})$.

The construction above simply adds as many events (transitions) as those to be reversed. The preset of each added event is the postset of the corresponding event to be reversed, and its postset is defined as the preset of the event to be reversed. The events in $U \times \{\mathbf{r}\}$ are the reversing events.

Proposition 9. *Let $C = \langle B, E, F, \mathsf{c} \rangle$ be an occurrence net, $U \subseteq E$ be the set of reversible events, and $\mathsf{R}(C) = \langle B, \hat{E}, U \times \{\mathbf{r}\}, \hat{F}, \mathsf{c} \rangle$ be the net in Definition 17. Then, $\mathsf{R}(C)$ is a reversible occurrence net with respect to $U \times \{\mathbf{r}\}$.*

Proof. We just have to prove that $\mathsf{R}(C)$ is a safe net; the other conditions are satisfied by construction. First we observe that if $b \notin \mathsf{c}$ and ${}^{\bullet}b$ is not a singleton in $\mathsf{R}(C)$ then ${}^{\bullet}b$ contains at most one event of the form $(e, \mathbf{f})$, and it contains at least one of the form $(e', \mathbf{r})$, and these are originated by the events in $b^{\bullet}$ in C. In the case $b \in \mathsf{c}$ and ${}^{\bullet}b$ is not empty, then again ${}^{\bullet}b$ contains only events of the form $(e', \mathbf{r})$, and these are originated by the events in $b^{\bullet}$ in C. Assume it is not, and assume that $b \in B$ is the condition which receives a token when it is already marked. As C is an occurrence net, if the condition is marked then the event $e \in E$ such that $b \in e^{\bullet}$ has been executed and none of the events $e' \in E$ such that $e' \in b^{\bullet}$ (if any) have yet been executed. Thus in $\mathsf{R}(C)$ the event $(e, \mathbf{f})$ has been executed and none of the events $(e', \mathbf{f}) \in b^{\bullet}$ has been executed yet. To be marked again an event of the form $(e'', \mathbf{r}) \in {}^{\bullet}b$ should have occurred, but this is impossible as none of the events $(e', \mathbf{f}) \in b^{\bullet}$ have been executed, and among these also $(e'', \mathbf{f})$, contradicting the fact that the condition b is marked again.

Example 9. Consider the occurrence net C_1 in Fig. 1, and assume that both events are reversible. The net R_1 in Fig. 2 is $\mathsf{R}(C_1)$ (after renaming events with the convention that $(e, \mathbf{f})$ is named as e and $(e, \mathbf{r})$ as $\underline{e}$). The RON R_3 in Fig. 2 is $\mathsf{R}(C_4)$, with C_4 in Fig. 1 and the set of reversible events $U = \{e_1, e_2, e_4\}$.

From RON *to* rPES: As is usually done for occurrence nets, we now associate each reversible occurrence net with a reversible prime event structure. Given an RON $R = \langle B, E, U, F, \mathsf{c} \rangle$, we denote the set of events $\{e' \mid e <_R e'\}$ by $\lceil e \rceil$. Observe that this set is not necessarily conflict-free.

Proposition 10. *Let $R = \langle B, E, U, F, \mathsf{c} \rangle$ be a reversible occurrence net with respect to U, then $\mathcal{C}_r(R) = (E', U', <, \#, \prec, \rhd)$ is its associated rPES, where*

- *$E' = \overline{E}$ and $U' = h(U)$,*
- *$<$ is $<_{C_{\overline{E}}}$, and $\#$ is the conflict relation defined on the occurrence net $C_{\overline{E}}$,*
- *$e \rhd \underline{e}'$ whenever $e \in \lceil e' \rceil$, $e \prec \underline{e}'$ whenever $e = e'$, and $\ll = <$.*

Proof. First of all it is quite clear that $(E', <, \#)$ is a pPES (if we close $<$ reflexively we get indeed a PES), as it is obtained by $C_{\overline{E}}$. The relation $\prec \subseteq E' \times U'$ satisfies the requirement that $e \prec \underline{e}$ and that $\{e' \mid e' \prec \underline{e}\}$ is finite for each $e \in U'$ as it contains just e. If $e \prec \underline{e}$ then not $e \rhd \underline{e}$ as $e \notin \lceil e \rceil$. The sustained causation relation $\ll$ coincides with the relation $<$ and so the conflict relation is inherited along this relation. Furthermore, for $e \in U'$, if $e < e'$ for some e', then we have that $e' \rhd \underline{e}$, as required. We can then conclude that $\mathcal{C}_r(R)$ is an rPES.

Example 10. Consider the reversible occurrence net R_3 in Fig. 2. The associated rPES has the events $\{e_1, e_2, e_3, e_4\}$ and the reversible events $\{e_1, e_3, e_4\}$. The causality relation of the associated pPES is $e_1 < e_3$, $e_2 < e_4$, the conflict relation is *generated* by $e_1 \# e_2$, and it is inherited along $\ll$, which coincides with $<$. The reverse causality stipulates that $e_1 \prec \underline{e_1}$, $e_3 \prec \underline{e_3}$ and $e_4 \prec \underline{e_4}$ and finally $e_3 \rhd \underline{e_1}$, as to be allowed to undo e_1 it is necessary to undo e_3 first.

The following result states that the rPES associated to a reversible occurrence net is causal, hence cause-respecting.

Proposition 11. *Let $R = \langle B, E, U, F, \mathsf{c} \rangle$ be a reversible occurrence net with respect to U and $\mathcal{C}_r(R) = (E', U', <, \#, \prec, \rhd)$ be the associated rPES. Then $\mathcal{C}_r(R)$ is a causal rPES.*

Proof. Easy inspection of the construction in Proposition 10. The sustained causality $\ll$ clearly coincides with $<$. If $e \prec \underline{e'}$ then $e' = e$ and by construction if $e \rhd \underline{e'}$ then $e' < e$ as $e \in \lceil e' \rceil$.

We show that each configuration of an RON is a configuration of the corresponding rPES, and vice versa.

Theorem 1. *Let $R = \langle B, E, U, F, \mathsf{c} \rangle$ be a reversible occurrence net with respect to U and $\mathcal{C}_r(R) = (E', U', <, \#, \prec, \rhd)$ be the associated rPES. Then $X \subseteq E'$ is a configuration of R iff X is a configuration of $\mathcal{C}_r(R)$.*

Proof. As $\mathcal{C}_r(R)$ is a cause-respecting and causal rPES we have that each configuration is forward reachable, and the forward reachable configurations are precisely those conflict-free and left-closed of the pPES $\mathcal{C}_r(R) = (E', <, \#)$, which correspond to the configurations of the occurrence net $R_{\overline{E}}$.

We stress that a reversing event in a reversible occurrence net is enabled at a marking when the conditions in the postset of the event to be reversed are marked. This may happen only when all the events that causally depend on the event to be reversed have either been executed and reversed or have not been executed at all. Thus every RON enjoys *causally consistent* reversibility [9, 15], and consequently cannot implement the so called *out-of-causal order* reversibility [13]. In contrast, rPESes are able to model *out-of-causal order* reversibility (as illustrated in Example 5).

Proposition 12 below formalises what are called *mixed-reverse* transitions in [11], namely a correspondence between the steps in a reversible occurrence net and the sequences of reachable configurations of the associated rPES. We now introduce some auxiliary notation. Let $R = \langle B, E, U, F, \mathsf{c} \rangle$ be an RON, and $X \subseteq E$ be a configuration of R, we write $\mathsf{mark}(X)$ to denote the marking reached after executing the events in X; this marking can be expressed as $(\mathsf{c} \cup X^\bullet) \setminus {}^\bullet X$.

Proposition 12. *Let $R = \langle B, E, U, F, \mathsf{c} \rangle$ be a reversible occurrence net and $\mathcal{C}_r(R) = (E', U', <, \#, \prec, \rhd)$ be its associated rPES. Let $X \in \mathsf{Conf}_{\mathrm{RON}}(R)$ and $A \subseteq E$ be a set of events such that $\mathsf{mark}(X) [A\rangle$. Then $\hat{A} \cup \underline{B}$ is enabled at X in $\mathcal{C}_r(R)$, where $\hat{A} = \{e \in A \mid e \notin U\}$ and $\underline{B} = \{e \in A \mid e \in U\}$.*

Proof. By Theorem 1 we know that $X \in \mathsf{Conf}_{rPES}(\mathcal{C}_r(R))$. We have to check that $\hat{A} \cup \underline{B}$ is enabled at X. As $\mathsf{mark}(X)\,[A\rangle$ we know that ${}^\bullet A \subseteq \mathsf{mark}(X)$, hence $A \cap X$ should be equal to $\emptyset$. Furthermore for any $e \in A \cap U$, as $\mathsf{mark}(X)\,[\{e\}\rangle$, we have that $h(e) \in X$ (otherwise the conditions enabling e would not have been produced), and then we have that $B = \{h(e) \mid e \in \underline{B}\} \subseteq X$. Finally, as $\mathsf{mark}(X)\,[A\rangle$, we have that $\mathsf{CF}(X \cup \hat{A})$ holds. Consider now $e \in \hat{A}$, and $e' < e$. Clearly $e' \in X \setminus B$. Assume the contrary, then $e' \in B$ and there exists an $\underline{e'} \in A \cap U$ such that $h(\underline{e'}) = e'$, but then we have that $\neg\mathsf{mark}(X)\,[A\rangle$. Consider now $e \in B$ (which means that $\underline{e} \in A \cap U$) and $e' \prec \underline{e}$. As $\mathcal{C}_r(R)$ is a causal rPES, we know that $e' = e$ and $e \in X \setminus (B \setminus \{e\})$. Take now $e \in B$ and $e' \rhd \underline{e}$. This means that $e' \in \lceil e \rceil$ which implies that $e \notin X$, and also that $e \notin \hat{A}$. By Definition 9 we can conclude that $\hat{A} \cup \underline{B}$ is enabled at X. Finally we observe that $\mathsf{mark}(Y) = c'$ where $\mathsf{mark}(X)\,[A\rangle\,c'$ and $X \xrightarrow{\hat{A} \cup \underline{B}} Y$.

From rPES *to* RON: Correspondingly to what is usually done when relating nets to event structures, we show that if we focus on causal rPESes then we can relate them to reversible occurrence nets. The construction is indeed quite standard (see [4, 29] among many others), but we do need a further observation on causal rPES.

Proposition 13. *Let* $\mathsf{P} = (E, U, <, \#, \prec, \rhd)$ *be a causal rPES. Then, $\#$ is inherited along $<$, i.e. $e \mathbin{\#} e' < e'' \Rightarrow e \mathbin{\#} e''$.*

Proof. In general we have that, given an rPES, $(E, \ll, \#)$ is a PES [24]. But in a causal rPES we have that $\ll$ is indeed the transitive closure of $<$.

A consequence of this proposition is that the conflict relation is fully characterized by the causality relation.

The same intuition underlying the introduction of reversible occurrence net can be used in associating a net to a causal rPES like the one used to associate an occurrence net to a PES.

Definition 18. *Let* $\mathsf{P} = (E, U, <, \#, \prec, \rhd)$ *be a causal rPES, and* $\bot \notin E$ *be a new symbol. Define* $\mathcal{E}_r(\mathsf{P})$ *as the Petri net* $\langle B, \hat{E}, F, \mathsf{c} \rangle$ *where*

- $B = \{(a, A) \mid a \in E \cup \{\bot\} \wedge A \subseteq E \wedge \#(A) \wedge a \neq \bot \Rightarrow \forall e \in A.\ a \ll e\}$,
- $\hat{E} = E \times \{\mathtt{f}\} \cup U \times \{\mathtt{r}\}$,
- $F = \{(b, (e, \mathtt{f})) \mid b = (a, A) \wedge e \in A\} \cup \{((e, \mathtt{f}), b) \mid b = (e, A)\} \cup \{(b, (e, \mathtt{r})) \mid b = (e, A)\} \cup \{((e, \mathtt{r}), b) \mid b = (a, A) \wedge e \in A\}$, *and*
- $\mathsf{c} = \{(a, A) \mid (a, A) \in B \wedge a = \bot\}$.

In essence the construction above takes the PES associated to an rPES and constructs the associated occurrence net, which is then *enriched* with the reversing events (transitions). The result is a reversible occurrence net.

Proposition 14. *Let* $\mathsf{P} = (E, U, <, \#, \prec, \rhd)$ *be a causal rPES. Then* $\mathcal{E}_r(\mathsf{P}) = \langle B, \hat{E}, U \times \{\mathtt{r}\}, F, \mathsf{c} \rangle$ *as defined in Definition 18 is a reversible occurrence net with respect to* $U \times \{\mathtt{r}\}$.

Proof. By construction $\mathcal{E}_r(\mathsf{P})_{E\times\{\mathbf{f}\}}$ is a occurrence net. The other requirements can be easily checked. For each $(e, \mathbf{r})$ there exists a unique event $(e, \mathbf{f})$, and if two events share the same preset and postset they are clearly the same event. Each condition $b \in B$ is clearly related to an event in $E \times \{\mathbf{f}\}$ hence in $\hat{E} \setminus (E' \times \{\mathbf{r}\})$.

Theorem 2. *Let* P *be a causal* rPES. *Then* X' *is a configuration of* $\mathcal{E}_r(\mathsf{P})$ *iff* X *is a configuration of* P, *where* $X' = \{(e, \mathbf{f}) \mid e \in X\}$.

Proof. Let $\mathsf{P} = (E, U, <, \#, \prec, \rhd)$. Consider $X \in \mathsf{Conf}_{r\mathrm{PES}}(\mathsf{P})$. As P is a cause-respecting and causal rPES we have that X is forward reachable, hence X is a configuration of the pPES $(E, <, \#)$, which we denote with P, and then $X' = \{(e, \mathbf{f}) \mid e \in X\}$ is a configuration also of the occurrence net associated to this event structure as, by Proposition 1, we have that $\mathsf{Conf}_{p\mathrm{PES}}(P) = \mathsf{Conf}_{\mathrm{PES}}(\mathsf{hc}(P))$. For the converse it is enough to observe that, up to renaming of events, $\mathcal{C}_r(\mathcal{E}_r(\mathsf{P}))$ is indeed P.

Clearly, if we start from a reversible occurrence net, we get an rPES from which a reversible occurrence net can be obtained having the same states (up to renaming of events).

Corollary 2. *Let* R *be a* RON. *Then* $\mathsf{St}(\mathcal{E}_r(\mathcal{C}_r(R))) = \mathsf{St}(R)$.

Example 11. Consider the rPES with four events $\{e_1, e_2, e_3, e_4\}$ such that $e_1 < e_3$ and $e_2 < e_4$, e_1 is in conflict with e_2 and this conflict is inherited along $<$. Furthermore, let e_1 and e_3 be reversible, and $e_3 \rhd \underline{e_1}$. The construction in Definition 18 gives the net below.

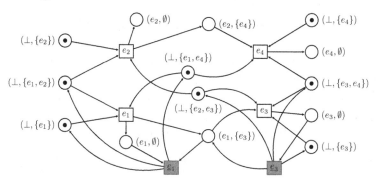

5   Conclusions and Future Work

The constructions we have proposed to associate a reversible occurrence net to a causal reversible prime event structure, and vice versa, are certainly driven by the classical ones (see [29]) for relating occurrence nets and prime event structures. The consequence of this approach is that the causality relation, either the one given in an rPES or the one induced by the flow relation in the occurrence net obtained ignoring the reversing events, is the one driving the construction. One of the other two relations of an rPES is substantially ignored (and we obtain from a RON a causal rPES where the reverse causality relation just says that an event can be reversed only after it has occurred) whereas the second (prevention) is tightly related to the causality relation: b is caused by a precisely when b prevents undoing of a. The notion of reversible occurrence net we have proposed suggests this construction, so the problem of finding which kind of net would correspond to, for example, a cause-respecting or even an arbitrary rPES remains open and certainly deserves to be investigated. It is however interesting to observe that the construction in Definition 18 gives a reversible occurrence net even when the rPES one started with is not a causal rPES. Consider the rPES with two events $\{e_1, e_2\}$ such that $e_1 < e_2$ and where the conflict and the prevention relations are empty. The only reversible event is e_1 and $e_1 \prec \underline{e}_1$. The set $\{e_2\}$ is a reachable configuration: we can remove e_1 from a reachable configuration $\{e_1, e_2\}$ by performing the event $\underline{e}_1$. This is an example of out-of-causal order computation. Given this rPES, our construction produces the following RON, which does not have $\{e_2\}$ among its configurations.

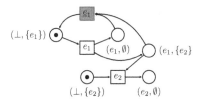

The constructions we have proposed are somehow the more adherent to what is usually done, based on the interpretation that *causality* implies that the event causing some other event somehow produces something that is used by the latter. This is not the only interpretation of what causality could mean. In fact, causality is often confused with the observation that two causally related events appear ordered in the same way in each possible execution, and when we talk about ordered execution, it should be stressed that this can be achieved in several ways, for instance using *inhibitor* arcs. Consider the net C:

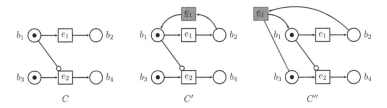

Here the event e_2 can be executed only after the event e_1 has been executed. However, e_1 does not produce a token (resource) that must be used by e_2. If we simply make the event e_1 reversible but do nothing to prevent reversing of e_1 before e_2 is reversed, then we would obtain the net C'. We could do better in C'' where we model prevention using so-called *read arcs* [20]. Hence, using inhibitor or read arcs seem feasible ways forward to capture more precisely the new relations of rPESes, including prevention. A similar approach has been already pursued in [8] to model so-called *modifiers* that are able to change the causality pattern of an event. This suggests that, for arbitrary rPESes, we need to find relations different from the flow relation to capture faithfully (forward and reverse) causal and prevention dependencies. This will be the subject of future research.

Acknowledgments. The authors would like to thank the reviewers for useful comments and suggestions.

References

1. Arbach, Y., Karcher, D.S., Peters, K., Nestmann, U.: Dynamic Causality in Event Structures. Logical Methods Comput. Sci. **14**(1) (2018)
2. Baldan, P., Busi, N., Corradini, A., Pinna, G.M.: Domain and event structure semantics for Petri nets with read and inhibitor arcs. Theoret. Comput. Sci. **323**(1–3), 129–189 (2004)
3. Baldan, P., Corradini, A., Montanari, U.: Contextual petri nets, asymmetric event structures and processes. Inf. Comput. **171**(1), 1–49 (2001)
4. Bartoletti, M., Cimoli, T., Pinna, G.M.: Lending petri nets. Sci. Comput. Program. **112**, 75–101 (2015)
5. Barylska, K., Koutny, M., Mikulski, L., Piątkowski, M.: Reversible computation vs. reversibility in petri nets. Sci. Comput. Program. **151**, 48–60 (2018)
6. Boudol, G.: Flow event structures and flow nets. In: Guessarian, I. (ed.) LITP 1990. LNCS, vol. 469, pp. 62–95. Springer, Heidelberg (1990). https://doi.org/10.1007/3-540-53479-2_4
7. Casu, G., Pinna, G.M.: Flow unfolding of multi-clock nets. In: Ciardo, G., Kindler, E. (eds.) PETRI NETS 2014. LNCS, vol. 8489, pp. 170–189. Springer, Cham (2014). https://doi.org/10.1007/978-3-319-07734-5_10
8. Casu, G., Pinna, G.M.: Petri nets and dynamic causality for service-oriented computations. In: Proceedings of SAC 2017, pp. 1326–1333. ACM (2017)
9. Danos, V., Krivine, J.: Reversible communicating systems. In: Gardner, P., Yoshida, N. (eds.) CONCUR 2004. LNCS, vol. 3170, pp. 292–307. Springer, Heidelberg (2004). https://doi.org/10.1007/978-3-540-28644-8_19
10. Danos, V., Krivine, J.: Transactions in RCCS. In: Abadi, M., de Alfaro, L. (eds.) CONCUR 2005. LNCS, vol. 3653, pp. 398–412. Springer, Heidelberg (2005). https://doi.org/10.1007/11539452_31
11. de Frutos Escrig, D., Koutny, M., Mikulski, Ł.: Reversing steps in petri nets. In: Donatelli, S., Haar, S. (eds.) PETRI NETS 2019. LNCS, vol. 11522, pp. 171–191. Springer, Cham (2019). https://doi.org/10.1007/978-3-030-21571-2_11
12. Giachino, E., Lanese, I., Mezzina, C.A.: Causal-consistent reversible debugging. In: Gnesi, S., Rensink, A. (eds.) FASE 2014. LNCS, vol. 8411, pp. 370–384. Springer, Heidelberg (2014). https://doi.org/10.1007/978-3-642-54804-8_26
13. Kuhn, S., Ulidowski, I.: A calculus for local reversibility. In: Devitt, S., Lanese, I. (eds.) RC 2016. LNCS, vol. 9720, pp. 20–35. Springer, Cham (2016). https://doi.org/10.1007/978-3-319-40578-0_2

14. Lanese, I., Lienhardt, M., Mezzina, C.A., Schmitt, A., Stefani, J.-B.: Concurrent flexible reversibility. In: Felleisen, M., Gardner, P. (eds.) ESOP 2013. LNCS, vol. 7792, pp. 370–390. Springer, Heidelberg (2013). https://doi.org/10.1007/978-3-642-37036-6_21

15. Lanese, I., Mezzina, C.A., Stefani, J.-B.: Reversibility in the higher-order π-calculus. Theoret. Comput. Sci. **625**, 25–84 (2016)

16. Lanese, I., Mezzina, C.A., Tiezzi, F.: Causal-consistent reversibility. Bull. EATCS **114** (2014)

17. Lanese, I., Palacios, A., Vidal, G.: Causal-consistent replay debugging for message passing programs. In: Pérez, J.A., Yoshida, N. (eds.) FORTE 2019. LNCS, vol. 11535, pp. 167–184. Springer, Cham (2019). https://doi.org/10.1007/978-3-030-21759-4_10

18. Langerak, R.: Bundle event structures: a non-interleaving semantics for LOTOS. FORTE 1992, vol. C-10, pp. 331–346 (1993). IFIP Transactions

19. Melgratti, H., Mezzina, C.A., Ulidowski, I.: Reversing P/T Nets. In: Riis Nielson, H., Tuosto, E. (eds.) COORDINATION 2019. LNCS, vol. 11533, pp. 19–36. Springer, Cham (2019). https://doi.org/10.1007/978-3-030-22397-7_2

20. Montanari, U., Rossi, F.: Contextual nets. Acta Informatica **32**(6) (1995)

21. Nielsen, M., Plotkin, G., Winskel, G.: Petri nets, event structures and domains, Part 1. Theoret. Comput. Sci. **13**, 85–108 (1981)

22. Philippou, A., Psara, K.: Reversible computation in petri nets. In: Kari, J., Ulidowski, I. (eds.) RC 2018. LNCS, vol. 11106, pp. 84–101. Springer, Cham (2018). https://doi.org/10.1007/978-3-319-99498-7_6

23. Phillips, I., Ulidowski, I.: Reversing algebraic process calculi. J. Logic Algebraic Program. **73**(1–2), 70–96 (2007)

24. Phillips, I., Ulidowski, I.: Reversibility and asymmetric conflict in event structures. J. Logic Algebraic Methods Program. **84**(6), 781–805 (2015)

25. Phillips, I., Ulidowski, I., Yuen, S.: A reversible process calculus and the modelling of the ERK signalling pathway. In: Glück, R., Yokoyama, T. (eds.) RC 2012. LNCS, vol. 7581, pp. 218–232. Springer, Heidelberg (2013). https://doi.org/10.1007/978-3-642-36315-3_18

26. Ulidowski, I., Phillips, I., Yuen, S.: Reversing event structures. New Generation Comput. **36**(3), 281–306 (2018)

27. van Glabbeek, R.J., Plotkin, G.D.: Configuration structures, event structures and petri nets. Theoret. Comput. Sci. **410**(41), 4111–4159 (2009)

28. Vassor, M., Stefani, J.-B.: Checkpoint/Rollback vs causally-consistent reversibility. In: Kari, J., Ulidowski, I. (eds.) RC 2018. LNCS, vol. 11106, pp. 286–303. Springer, Cham (2018). https://doi.org/10.1007/978-3-319-99498-7_20

29. Winskel, G.: Event structures. In: Brauer, W., Reisig, W., Rozenberg, G. (eds.) ACPN 1986. LNCS, vol. 255, pp. 325–392. Springer, Heidelberg (1987). https://doi.org/10.1007/3-540-17906-2_31

Involutory Turing Machines

Keisuke Nakano$^{(\boxtimes)}$

Research Institute of Electrical Communication, Tohoku University, Sendai, Japan
`k.nakano@acm.org`

Abstract. An involutory function, also called involution, is a function f that is its own inverse, i.e., $f(f(x)) = x$ holds whenever $f(x)$ is defined. This paper presents a computational model of involution as a variant of Turing machines, called an *involutory Turing machine*. The computational model is shown to be complete in the sense that not only does an involutory Turing machine always compute an involution but also every involutory computable function can be computed by an involutory Turing machine. As any involution is injective (hence reversible), any involutory Turing machine forms a standard reversible Turing machine that is backward deterministic. Furthermore, the existence of a universal involutory Turing machine is shown under an appropriate redefinition of universality given by Axelsen and Glück for reversible Turing machines. This work is motivated by characterizing bidirectional transformation languages.

Keywords: Involution · Reversible Turing machine · Universal Turing machine · Bidirectional transformation language · Time-symmetric machine

1 Introduction

An involutory function, also called involution, is a function that is its own inverse, i.e., $f(f(x)) = x$ holds whenever $f(x)$ is defined. In mathematics, because of their symmetric behavior, involutions have been used for solving functional equations and proving theorems, e.g., Zagier's one-sentence proof for Fermat's theorem on sums of two squares [12]. Even in computer science, involutions appear in cryptographic systems such as one-time pad and RC4.

This paper presents a computational model for involution as a variant of Turing machines with *function semantics*, where input and output words are specified by tapes of initial and final configurations, respectively. The idea to have such a model for involution is to impose a restriction on a standard Turing machine so that the reversed run of every valid run is valid. The restriction can be simply described by associating one transition rule with another according to a certain involution over states. We call it an *involutory Turing machine*. It is easy to find that an involutory Turing machine always computes an involution under the restriction.

© Springer Nature Switzerland AG 2020
I. Lanese and M. Rawski (Eds.): RC 2020, LNCS 12227, pp. 54–70, 2020.
https://doi.org/10.1007/978-3-030-52482-1_3

The present paper takes a further step. The involutory Turing machine is shown to be a 'complete' computational model for involution: any involutory computable function can be defined by an involutory Turing machine. That is, for a given non-involutory Turing machine that computes an involution, there exists an equivalent involutory Turing machine.

This work is inspired by Axelsen and Glück's work [1,2] where the expressiveness of *reversible Turing machines* is discussed. A reversible Turing machine is defined as a backward-deterministic Turing machine and hence computes only an injective function. They have shown that any injective computable function can be defined by a reversible Turing machine as we will show for involutory Turing machines. As an involutory function is a special kind of injective function, an involutory Turing machine can be regarded as a special reversible Turing machine.

Furthermore, this paper addresses the universality of involutory Turing machines as done by Axelsen and Glück [2] for reversible Turing machines. A standard Turing machine is said to be universal if it can simulate any Turing machine on arbitrary input, and it is known that there is a universal Turing machine. As for involutory Turing machines, there is no universal machine under the same definition of universality because the simulating function is not involutory. Therefore, we adopt an alternative definition of universality which has been introduced by Axelsen and Glück for reversible Turing machines. In their definition, the universal machine is allowed to preserve a given machine description as part of the output. We will show the existence of a universal involutory Turing machine under this redefinition.

In summary, the main contributions of this paper are as follows.

- An involutory Turing machine is proposed as a multi-tape Turing machine with restrictive transition rules and tape permutation. An involutory Turing machine always computes an involution.
- An involutory Turing machine is shown to be complete, i.e., every computable involution is defined by an involutory Turing machine.
- It is shown that for every k-tape involutory Turing machine, there exists a 2-tape involutory Turing machine that computes an isomorphic function.
- It is shown that there exists a universal involutory Turing machine in terms of an appropriate definition of universality.

In addition to the above, our design choice, limitations, and applications of involutory Turing machines will be discussed in Sect. 6. In particular, an application to bidirectional transformation will shed a light on a practical aspect of our computational model for involution.

The restriction imposed on Turing machines to be involutory coincides with *time symmetry* introduced by Gajardo et al. [5] for cellular automata to describe a corresponding physical notion. One might call our model a *time-symmetric Turing machine* in this sense. More detail is discussed as one of the related work in Sect. 7.

2 Preliminaries

The set of non-negative integers is denoted by $\mathbb{N}$. For $n \in \mathbb{N}$, the set $\{1, \ldots, n\}$ is denoted by $[n]$, in particular, $[0] = \emptyset$. The set of all words over an alphabet (that is a finite set of symbols) Σ is denoted by Σ^*. For convenience, we assume that a nested tuple of words can be regarded as a flattened one, e.g., $((w_1, w_2), w_3)$ and $(w_1, (w_2, w_3))$ may be identified with (w_1, w_2, w_3) for $w_1, w_2, w_3 \in \Sigma^*$.

For a (binary) relation $R \subseteq A \times B$, $a \mathrel{R} b$ stands for $(a, b) \in R$. The identity relation $Id_A \subseteq A \times A$ is $\{(a, a) \mid a \in A\}$. The composition of two relations $R \subseteq A \times B$ and $S \subseteq B \times C$, denoted by $S \circ R$, is given as $\{(a, c) \mid \exists b \in B, a \mathrel{R} b \wedge b \mathrel{S} c\}$. For a relation $R \subseteq A \times B$ over two sets A and B, the *inverse relation* $R^{-1} \subseteq B \times A$ is defined by $\{(b, a) \mid a \mathrel{R} b\}$. A relation $R \subseteq A \times A$ is said to be *symmetric* if $R^{-1} = R$. A relation $R \subseteq A \times B$ is said to be *functional* if $a \mathrel{R} b_1$ and $a \mathrel{R} b_2$ imply $b_1 = b_2$ for any $a \in A$ and $b_1, b_2 \in B$. A functional relation $R \subseteq A \times B$, written by $R : A \to B$, is simply called a (partial) *function* and $R(a)$ with $a \in A$ stands for $b \in B$ such that $a \mathrel{R} b$ if exists. A function $R : A \to B$ is said to be *total* if $R(a) \in B$ is defined for any $a \in A$. A function $R : A \to B$ is said to be *injective* if R^{-1} is functional. For any injective function $R : A \to B$ it is easy to see that $R^{-1} \circ R \subseteq Id_A$ and $R \circ R^{-1} \subseteq Id_B$ hold. A function $R : A \to B$ is said to be *bijective* if both R and R^{-1} are total and injective. A function $R : A \to A$ is called an *involutory* if R is symmetric. An involutory function is also called *involution*.

A *permutation* on $[k]$ is a bijective function over $[k]$ for a fixed integer $k \in \mathbb{N}$. A permutation can be expressed as the product of disjoint cycles, e.g., $(1\ 5\ 4)(3\ 7)$ denotes a permutation π such that $\pi(1) = 5$, $\pi(5) = 4$, $\pi(4) = 1$, $\pi(3) = 7$, $\pi(7) = 3$, and $\pi(i) = i$ for any other i. The inversion of a permutation is obtained by reversing every cycle, e.g., $((1\ 5\ 4)(3\ 7))^{-1} = (4\ 5\ 1)(7\ 3)$.

3 The Turing Machine and Its Known Variants

The Turing machine is one of the best-known computational models which can implement any computable function. A Turing machine manipulates symbols on a doubly-infinite tape of cells according to an internal state and a fixed transition relation. We use a triplet format [2] to represent the transition relation without loss of generality. Although it is well known that they are equivalent to single-tape Turing machines in power [10], we consider multi-tape Turing machines to make it easy to investigate various properties of involutory Turing machines. Moreover, our model of multi-tape Turing machines has a single instruction for permuting the order of tapes. This feature does not change the expressive power of Turing machines. As its byproduct, we can limit any other instruction only to the first tape. To apply an instruction to the other tape, we permute tapes so as for the tape to be the first before the instruction (and permute them back if needed).

Definition 3.1 (k-tape Turing machine). A *k-tape Turing machine* T is a tuple $(Q, \Sigma, q_{\text{ini}}, q_{\text{fin}}, \Delta)$ where Q is a finite set of *states*, Σ is a *tape alphabet* not containing the special blank symbol $\sqcup$, $q_{\text{ini}} \in Q$ is the *initial state*, $q_{\text{fin}} \in Q$ is the *final state*, and $\Delta = \Delta^{\text{rw}} \uplus \Delta^{\leftrightarrow} \uplus \Delta^{\updownarrow}$ is a ternary relation defining a set of *transition rules* where:

$$\Delta^{\text{rw}} \subseteq (Q \setminus \{q_{\text{fin}}\}) \times (\Sigma_{\sqcup} \times \Sigma_{\sqcup}) \times (Q \setminus \{q_{\text{ini}}\}) \quad (\text{SYMBOL RULES})$$
$$\Delta^{\leftrightarrow} \subseteq (Q \setminus \{q_{\text{fin}}\}) \times \{\leftarrow, \diamond, \rightarrow\} \times (Q \setminus \{q_{\text{ini}}\}) \quad (\text{MOVE RULES})$$
$$\Delta^{\updownarrow} \subseteq (Q \setminus \{q_{\text{fin}}\}) \times \Pi_k \times (Q \setminus \{q_{\text{ini}}\}) \quad (\text{PERMUTATION RULES})$$

where $\Sigma_{\sqcup}$ stands for $\Sigma \uplus \{\sqcup\}$ and Π_k is the set of all permutations over $[k]$. For $q, q' \in Q$, a *symbol rule* in Δ^{rw} has the form $(q, s{\Rightarrow}s', q')$ with $s, s' \in \Sigma_{\sqcup}$; a *move rule* in $\Delta^{\leftrightarrow}$ has the form (q, d, q') with $d \in \{\leftarrow, \diamond, \rightarrow\}$; a *permutation rule* in $\Delta^{\updownarrow}$ has the form $(q, \updownarrow\pi, q')$ with permutation $\pi \in \Pi_k$. A permutation rule is said to be *involutory* if π is involutory.

As presented in [2], symbol rules and move rules are independently given for the convenience of further discussion. Although these two kinds of actions are caused by a single rule in standard Turing machines [10], the separation of rules does not change the expressiveness of functions. It is easy to simulate a transition rule in a standard Turing machine by two transition rules and extra states in the present model. Moreover, the present model introduces permutation rules $(q, \updownarrow\pi, q')$, which permute k tapes without moving their heads in the order given by a permutation π. Again, they do not change the expressiveness because the operation can be simulated by a standard Turing machine with maintaining the left and right ends at the used cells for every tape to copy them to each other.

The configuration of a k-tape Turing machine is specified by the current internal state and k tapes with their tape head. The status of a tape with its head is represented by $\langle l, s, r \rangle \in \Sigma_{\sqcup}^{\omega} \times \Sigma_{\sqcup} \times \Sigma_{\sqcup}^{\omega}$ where s is the symbol at its head position and l and r are the left and right tapes of the head. Note that $\Sigma_{\sqcup}^{\omega}$ is the set of infinite words going infinitely to the right. Accordingly, l is 'mirrored' where its first symbol is the immediate left one of the head.

Definition 3.2 (Configuration). The *configuration* of a k-tape Turing machine $T = (Q, \Sigma, q_{\text{ini}}, q_{\text{fin}}, \Delta)$ is a tuple $(q, (\langle l_1, s_1, r_1 \rangle, \ldots, \langle l_k, s_k, r_k \rangle))$ where $q \in Q$ is an *internal state*, $l_i, r_i \in \Sigma_{\sqcup}^{\omega}$ for each $i \in [k]$ are the left and right of the i-th tape head and include only finite non-blank symbols, and $s_i \in \Sigma_{\sqcup}$ for each $i \in [k]$ is the symbol at the i-th tape head. The set of all configurations of T is written by $\mathcal{C}_T$.

Definition 3.3 (Computation step). Let $T = (Q, \Sigma, q_{\text{ini}}, q_{\text{fin}}, \Delta)$ be a k-tape Turing machine. Then a single *computation step* is defined as a relation $\vdash_T$ over

$\mathcal{C}_T$ such that

$$
\begin{aligned}
(q, (\langle l, s, r\rangle, \dots)) &\vdash_T (q', (\langle l, s', r\rangle, \dots)) & \text{when } (q, s{\Rightarrow}s', q') \in \Delta \\
(q, (\langle s'l, s, r\rangle, \dots)) &\vdash_T (q', (\langle l, s', sr\rangle, \dots)) & \text{when } (q, \leftarrow, q') \in \Delta \\
(q, (\langle l, s, r\rangle, \dots)) &\vdash_T (q', (\langle l, s, r\rangle, \dots)) & \text{when } (q, \diamond, q') \in \Delta \\
(q, (\langle l, s, s'r\rangle, \dots)) &\vdash_T (q', (\langle sl, s', r\rangle, \dots)) & \text{when } (q, \rightarrow, q') \in \Delta \\
(q, (t_1, \dots, t_k)) &\vdash_T (q', (t_{\pi(1)}, \dots, t_{\pi(k)})) & \text{when } (q, \updownarrow\pi, q') \in \Delta.
\end{aligned}
$$

The reflexive transitive closure of $\vdash_T$ is denoted by $\vdash_T^*$.

The semantics of a k-tape Turing machine T is given by a relation over k words based on $\vdash_T^*$ as below. We follow the style of Axelsen and Glück called a *function semantics* where an input and an output word are in the tape at the initial and the final configuration of a run, respectively, rather than the usual style with input and output tapes. This view makes it easier to capture the functional behavior of Turing machines. In the rest of the paper, a finite word $w \in \Sigma^*$ is used to represent an infinite word $w\sqcup^\omega \in \Sigma_\sqcup^\omega$; thereby ε denotes $\sqcup^\omega$.

Definition 3.4 (Function semantics of Turing machines). Let $T = (Q, \Sigma, q_{\mathsf{ini}}, q_{\mathsf{fin}}, \Delta)$ be a k-tape Turing machine. The *semantics* of T, denoted by $[\![T]\!]$, is given by the relation

$$
\begin{aligned}
[\![T]\!] = \{((w_1, \dots, w_k), (w_1', \dots, w_k')) \in (\Sigma^*)^k \times (\Sigma^*)^k \\
\mid (q_{\mathsf{ini}}, (\langle \varepsilon, \sqcup, w_1\rangle, \dots, \langle \varepsilon, \sqcup, w_k\rangle)) \vdash_T^* (q_{\mathsf{fin}}, (\langle \varepsilon, \sqcup, w_1'\rangle, \dots, \langle \varepsilon, \sqcup, w_k'\rangle))\}.
\end{aligned}
$$

Recall that we may write $[\![T]\!](w_1, \dots, w_k) = (w_1', \dots, w_k')$ if $[\![T]\!]$ is functional.

In the rest of the paper, for every Turing machine T it is assumed that for any sequence $(q_{\mathsf{ini}}, (\langle l_1, s_1, r_1\rangle, \dots, \langle l_k, s_k, r_k\rangle)) \vdash_T^* (q_{\mathsf{fin}}, (\langle l_1', s_1', r_1'\rangle, \dots, \langle l_k', s_k', r_k'\rangle))$ of computation steps, we have $(l_1, s_1) = \cdots = (l_k, s_k) = (\varepsilon, \sqcup)$ if and only if $(l_1', s_1') = \cdots = (l_k', s_k') = (\varepsilon, \sqcup)$. We call it the *tidiness* assumption.

Here are two examples of Turing machines. It is easy to see that they naturally conform to the tidiness assumption. Moreover, both examples are reversible as seen later.

Example 3.5. Let π be a permutation on $[k]$. The k-tape Turing machine $Perm(\pi) = (\{q_{\mathsf{ini}}, q_{\mathsf{fin}}\}, \Sigma, q_{\mathsf{ini}}, q_{\mathsf{fin}}, \{(q_{\mathsf{ini}}, \updownarrow\pi, q_{\mathsf{fin}})\})$ computes a function which permutes its arguments in accordance with π.

Example 3.6. The 1-tape Turing machine $T_{bnot} = (\{q_{\mathsf{ini}}, q_{\mathsf{bnot}}, q_{\mathsf{done}}, q_{\mathsf{back}}, q_{\mathsf{fin}}\}, \{0, 1\}, q_{\mathsf{ini}}, q_{\mathsf{fin}}, \Delta)$ with

$$
\begin{aligned}
\Delta = \{&(q_{\mathsf{ini}}, \sqcup{\Rightarrow}\sqcup, q_{\mathsf{next}}), \\
&(q_{\mathsf{next}}, \rightarrow, q_{\mathsf{bnot}}), (q_{\mathsf{bnot}}, 0{\Rightarrow}1, q_{\mathsf{next}}), (q_{\mathsf{bnot}}, 1{\Rightarrow}0, q_{\mathsf{next}}), (q_{\mathsf{bnot}}, \sqcup{\Rightarrow}\sqcup, q_{\mathsf{back}}), \\
&(q_{\mathsf{back}}, \leftarrow, q_{\mathsf{done}}), (q_{\mathsf{done}}, 0{\Rightarrow}0, q_{\mathsf{back}}), (q_{\mathsf{done}}, 1{\Rightarrow}1, q_{\mathsf{back}}), (q_{\mathsf{done}}, \sqcup{\Rightarrow}\sqcup, q_{\mathsf{fin}})\}
\end{aligned}
$$

computes a bitwise negation.

Definition 3.4 implies that the semantics of a Turing machine returns a tuple that consists of the same number of words as a given input. However, when the function either accepts (returns) only empty word for some specific arguments, we may regard it as a function whose input (output) tuple consists of fewer words. The next example $Dup(1)$ illustrates the case where a 2-tape Turing machine computes a function that takes a single word and returns a pair of words.

Example 3.7. A 2-tape Turing machine $Dup(1) = (Q, \Sigma, q_{ini}, q_{fin}, \Delta)$ with

$$Q = \{q_{ini}, q_{skip}, q_{check}, q_{back}, q_{get}, q_{put}, q_{done}, q_{fin}\} \cup \bigcup_{a \in \Sigma} \{q_{g\langle a\rangle}, q_{p\langle a\rangle}\}$$

$$\Delta = \{(q_{ini}, \sqcup{\Rightarrow}\sqcup, q_{skip}), (q_{skip}, \rightarrow, q_{check}), (q_{check}, \sqcup{\Rightarrow}\sqcup, q_{back}),$$
$$(q_{back}, \leftarrow, q_{get}), (q_{put}, \leftarrow, q_{done}), (q_{done}, \updownarrow(1\ 2), q_{back}), (q_{get}, \sqcup{\Rightarrow}\sqcup, q_{fin}), \} \cup$$
$$\bigcup_{a \in \Sigma} \{(q_{check}, a{\Rightarrow}a, q_{skip}), (q_{get}, a{\Rightarrow}a, q_{g\langle a\rangle}),$$
$$(q_{g\langle a\rangle}, \updownarrow(1\ 2), q_{p\langle a\rangle}), (q_{p\langle a\rangle}, \sqcup{\Rightarrow}a, q_{put})\}$$

computes a duplicate function, i.e., $[\![Dup(1)]\!](w) = (w, w)$ for any $w \in \Sigma^*$. Similarly, we can define a $2k$-tape Turing machine such that $[\![Dup(k)]\!](w_1, \ldots, w_k) = (w_1, \ldots, w_k, w_1, \ldots, w_k)$ for any $w_1, \ldots, w_k \in \Sigma^*$.

Definition 3.8 (Forward/backward determinism). Let $T = (Q, \Sigma, q_{ini}, q_{fin}, \Delta)$ be a k-tape Turing machine. Then T is *forward deterministic* if, for any distinct pair $(q, a_1, q_1), (q, a_2, q_2) \in \Delta$ of transition rules, we have $a_1 = s_1{\Rightarrow}s_1'$ and $a_2 = s_2{\Rightarrow}s_2'$ with some $s_1, s_1', s_2, s_2' \in \Sigma_\sqcup$ and $s_1 \neq s_2$. The Turing machine T is *backward deterministic* if, for any distinct pair $(q_1, a_1, q), (q_2, a_2, q) \in \Delta$ of transition rules, we have $a_1 = s_1{\Rightarrow}s_1'$ and $a_2 = s_2{\Rightarrow}s_2'$ with some $s_1, s_1', s_2, s_2' \in \Sigma_\sqcup$ and $s_1' \neq s_2'$.

The forward (backward) deterministic Turing machine has no pair of move rules which have the same source (target) state. With regard to a configuration step $C_1 \vdash_T C_2$, C_1 uniquely determines C_2 if T is forward deterministic while C_2 uniquely determines C_1 if T is backward deterministic. The definition of forward and backward determinism is exactly the same as *local* forward and backward determinism in [2].

Definition 3.9 (Reversible Turing machine). A k-tape Turing machine T is *reversible* if T is forward and backward deterministic.

Given an involutory function φ over a set Q of states such $\varphi(q_{ini}) = q_{fin}$ (hence, $\varphi(q_{fin}) = q_{ini}$), let us define a function $\widetilde{\varphi}$ which 'flips' transition rules in terms of φ. This function plays important roles to recognize properties of reversible and involutory Turing machines. The function $\widetilde{\varphi}$ is defined as a bijective function over transition rules by

$$\widetilde{\varphi}((q, (a_1, a_2, \ldots, a_k), q')) = (\varphi(q'), (a_1^{-1}, a_2^{-1}, \ldots, a_k^{-1}), \varphi(q))$$

where $(s \Rightarrow s')^{-1} = s' \Rightarrow s$, $(\leftarrow)^{-1} = \rightarrow$, $(\diamond)^{-1} = \diamond$, $(\rightarrow)^{-1} = \leftarrow$, and $(\updownarrow \pi)^{-1} = \updownarrow(\pi^{-1})$. The function $\widetilde{\varphi}$ is naturally extended for a set of transition rules and a Turing machine. For a set Δ of transition rules, $\widetilde{\varphi}(\Delta)$ represents $\{\widetilde{\varphi}(r) \mid r \in \Delta\}$. For a k-tape Turing machine $T = (Q, \Sigma, q_{ini}, q_{fin}, \Delta)$, $\widetilde{\varphi}(T)$ represents $(Q, \Sigma, q_{fin}, q_{ini}, \widetilde{\varphi}(\Delta))$. For a k-tape Turing machine T, $\widetilde{\varphi}(T)$ is forward (backward) deterministic if T is backward (forward) deterministic. It is easy to see that the function $\widetilde{\varphi}$ is involutory for any involutory function φ, that is, $\widetilde{\varphi}(\widetilde{\varphi}(x)) = x$ for any transition rule, any set of transition rules, and any Turing machine x as long as $\widetilde{\varphi}(x)$ is defined.

Let the function $\widetilde{\varphi}$ be extended for a configuration of a Turing machine as well so that $\widetilde{\varphi}((q, (t_1, \ldots, t_k))) = (\varphi(q), (t_1, \ldots, t_k))$. Then the following proposition holds straightforwardly.

Proposition 3.10. Let T be a k-tape Turing machine and φ be an involution over a set of states in T. Then, for any a computation step $C_1 \vdash_T C_2$, we have $\widetilde{\varphi}(C_2) \vdash_{\widetilde{\varphi}(T)} \widetilde{\varphi}(C_1)$.

The simplest function ι as such φ is given as $\iota(q_{ini}) = q_{fin}$, $\iota(q_{fin}) = q_{ini}$, and $\iota(q) = q$ for $q \in Q \setminus \{q_{ini}, q_{fin}\}$. Let us write T^{-1} for $\widetilde{\iota}(T)$. Then, for a given reversible Turing machine T, T^{-1} gives an inversion of T as shown by Bennett [3] and reformulated by Axelsen and Glück [2].

Theorem 3.11 (Semantics of reversible Turing machines). Given a k-tape reversible Turing machine T, $[\![T^{-1}]\!] = [\![T]\!]^{-1}$ holds.

Proof. For simplicity of the proof, only the case of $k = 1$ is shown. The proof can be easily generalized to the other cases. Let $T = (Q, \Sigma, q_{ini}, q_{fin}, \Delta)$ be a 1-tape reversible Turing machine. The equation $[\![T^{-1}]\!](w) = v$ holds if and only if $(q_{fin}, \langle \varepsilon, \sqcup, w \rangle) \vdash^*_{T^{-1}} (q_{ini}, \langle \varepsilon, \sqcup, v \rangle)$ by definition. From Proposition 3.10, $(q_{ini}, \langle \varepsilon, \sqcup, v \rangle) \vdash^*_T (q_{fin}, \langle \varepsilon, \sqcup, w \rangle)$ holds, which implies $[\![T]\!](v) = w$, i.e., $[\![T]\!]^{-1}(w) = v$. $\square$

A reversible Turing machine is a complete model in the sense that every injective computable function can be defined by a reversible Turing machine, which has been proved by Axelsen and Glück. Even though our computational model slightly differs from their one in that it has tape permutation rules, their proof of the statement works in our setting because our k-tape Turing machine can simulate theirs with k tapes and vice versa.

Theorem 3.12 (Expressiveness of reversible Turing machines [2]). The reversible Turing machines can compute exactly all injective computable functions. That is, given a k-tape Turing machine T such that $[\![T]\!]$ is injective, there is a k-tape reversible Turing machine T' such that $[\![T']\!] = [\![T]\!]$.

The Turing machines $Perm(\pi)$ given in Example 3.5, T_{bnot} given in Example 3.6, and $Dup(k)$ given in Example 3.7 are all reversible. In particular, the inverse $Dup(k)^{-1}$ computes a partial function that checks equivalence between the first k words and the last k words and returns the k words if the check succeeds.

Definition 3.13 (Concatenation of Turing machines). Let $T_1 = (Q_1, \Sigma, q_{\text{ini},1}, q_{\text{fin},1}, \Delta_1)$ and $T_2 = (Q_2, \Sigma, q_{\text{ini},2}, q_{\text{fin},2}, \Delta_2)$ be k-tape Turing machines where $Q_1 \cap Q_2 = \emptyset$ without loss of generality. The *concatenation* of T_1 and T_2, denoted by $T_2 \circ T_1$, is a k-tape Turing machine $(Q_1 \uplus Q_2, \Sigma, q_{\text{ini},1}, q_{\text{fin},2}, \Delta_1 \uplus \Delta_2 \uplus \{(q_{\text{fin},1}, \diamond, q_{\text{ini},2})\})$.

In the case where Q_1 and Q_2 are not disjoint, every state in either should be renamed before the concatenation. The reversibility of Turing machines is closed under concatenation as stated below. The proof is straightforward.

Proposition 3.14 (Concatenation of reversible Turing machines). If T_1 and T_2 are reversible Turing machines, so is $T_2 \circ T_1$.

The semantics of concatenation of two reversible Turing machines is equivalent to the function composition of their semantics as shown in the following theorem. Note that Turing machines to be concatenated are assumed tidy. The Turing machine obtained by the concatenation is also tidy.

Theorem 3.15 (Semantics of concatenation of reversible Turing machines). For two k-tape reversible Turing machines T_1 and T_2, we have $[\![T_2 \circ T_1]\!] = [\![T_2]\!] \circ [\![T_1]\!]$.

Proof. For simplicity of the proof, only the case of $k = 1$ is shown. The proof can be easily generalized to the other cases. Let $T_1 = (Q_1, \Sigma, q_{\text{ini},1}, q_{\text{fin},1}, \Delta_1)$ and $T_2 = (Q_2, \Sigma, q_{\text{ini},2}, q_{\text{fin},2}, \Delta_2)$ be k-tape Turing machines. When $[\![T]\!](w_1) = w_2$, we show that there exists w such that $[\![T_1]\!](w_1) = w$ and $[\![T_2]\!](w) = w_2$. By the construction of $T = T_2 \circ T_1$, there exists a sequence of computation steps $(q_{\text{ini},1}, \langle \varepsilon, \sqcup, w \rangle) \vdash^*_T (q_{\text{fin},2}, \langle \varepsilon, \sqcup, v \rangle)$. Because of the construction of transition rules of T, the sequence contains exactly one computation step induced by the rule $(q_{\text{fin},1}, \diamond, q_{\text{ini},2})$ which bridges Q_1 and Q_2. Hence, the sequence has the form $(q_{\text{ini},1}, \langle \varepsilon, \sqcup, w \rangle) \vdash^*_T (q_{\text{fin},1}, \langle l, s, w' \rangle) \vdash_T (q_{\text{ini},2}, \langle l, s, w' \rangle) \vdash^*_T (q_{\text{fin},2}, \langle \varepsilon, \sqcup, v \rangle)$. The tidiness assumption and determinism (coming from reversibility) of T_1 and T_2 result in $l = \varepsilon$, $s = \sqcup$, $[\![T_1]\!](w_1) = w'$, and $[\![T_2]\!](w') = w_2$. $\square$

The k-tape Turing machine T can be seen as the m-tape Turing machine when $k \leq m$ by leaving all $(k+1)$-th through m-th tapes and their heads unchanged. We write $Ext_{k \to m}(T)$ for the extended Turing machine.

Proposition 3.16 (Extended Turing machines). Let T be a k-tape Turing machine with $k \leq m$. Then we have $[\![Ext_{k \to m}(T)]\!](w_1, \ldots, w_k, w_{k+1}, \ldots, w_m) = ([\![T]\!](w_1, \ldots, w_k), w_{k+1}, \ldots, w_m)$ for any words $w_1, \ldots, w_k, w_{k+1}, \ldots, w_m$ whenever the right-hand side is defined. If T is reversible, so is $Ext_{k \to m}(T)$. Furthermore, $(Ext_{k \to m}(T))^{-1} = Ext_{k \to m}(T^{-1})$ holds.

4   Involutory Turing Machine

Involutory Turing machines are introduced and investigated in this section. As reversible Turing machines exactly characterize all injective computable functions, involutory Turing machines exactly characterize all involutory computable functions. As every involutory function is injective, an involutory Turing machine is defined as a special kind of reversible Turing machine. The tape reduction on the involutory Turing machines is also addressed in this section.

Definition 4.1 (Involutory Turing machine). Let $T = (Q, \Sigma, q_{ini}, q_{fin}, \Delta)$ be a k-tape Turing machine and φ be an involutory function over Q such that $\varphi(q_{ini}) = q_{fin}$ (hence $\varphi(q_{fin}) = q_{ini}$). Then T is *involutory* if T is reversible, $\widetilde{\varphi}(T) = T$ holds, and every permutation rule is involutory. The function φ is called a *state involution* of T.

Theorem 4.2 (Semantics of involutory Turing machine). If T is an involutory Turing machine T, then $[\![T]\!]$ is involutory.

Proof. Let $T = (Q, \Sigma, q_{ini}, q_{fin}, \Delta)$ be an involutory Turing machine with state involution φ. We show that $[\![T]\!](w) = v$ implies $[\![T]\!](v) = w$. Assume $[\![T]\!](w) = v$. By definition, we have $(q_{ini}, \langle \varepsilon, \sqcup, w \rangle) \vdash_T^* (q_{fin}, \langle \varepsilon, \sqcup, v \rangle)$. Since T is involutory, that is, $\widetilde{\varphi}(T) = T$, we have $(q_{ini}, \langle \varepsilon, \sqcup, v \rangle) \vdash_T^* (q_{fin}, \langle \varepsilon, \sqcup, w \rangle)$ by Proposition 3.10. $\square$

Example 4.3. The Turing machine $Perm(\pi)$ in Example 3.5 is involutory whenever π is involutory.

The Turing machine T_{bnot} in Example 3.6 is *not* involutory, although its semantics is involutory. We will see later that there exists an involutory Turing machine equivalent to a given Turing machine whenever its semantics is involutory.

The class of involutory Turing machines have one of the typical and trivial properties of involution, that is closed under conjugation, i.e., for any injective function g, $g^{-1} \circ f \circ g$ is involutory whenever so is f. In terms of Turing machines, the property is described by the following statement.

Lemma 4.4 (Closed under conjugation). Let T be a k-tape involutory Turing machine. For any k-tape reversible Turing machine T_r, the k-tape reversible Turing machine $T_r^{-1} \circ T \circ T_r$ is involutory.

Proof. Let $T = (Q, \Sigma, q_{ini}, q_{fin}, \Delta)$ be a k-tape involutory Turing machine with state involution φ, and $T_r = (Q_r, \Sigma_r, q_{ini,r}, q_{fin,r}, \Delta_r)$ be a k-tape reversible Turing machine. We assume that every state q_r of T_r^{-1} is renamed to $\bar{q}_r$ and let $\bar{Q}_r = \{ \bar{q}_r \mid q_r \in Q_r \}$. Since the k-tape Turing machine $T_c = T_r^{-1} \circ T \circ T_r$ is reversible from Proposition 3.14, it suffices to show the existence of a state involution of T_c. The state involution $\varphi_c : Q_c \to Q_c$ with $Q_c = \bar{Q}_r \uplus Q \uplus Q_r$ can be defined by $\varphi_c(\bar{q}_r) = q_r$ for $\bar{q}_r \in \bar{Q}_r$, $\varphi_c(q) = \varphi(q)$ for $q \in Q$, and $\varphi_c(q_r) = \bar{q}_r$ for $q_r \in Q_r$. $\square$

For an injective function f, a function $g(x, y) = (f(y), f^{-1}(x))$ is involutory because $g(g(x, y)) = (f(f^{-1}(x)), f^{-1}(f(y))) = (x, y)$ holds as long as $g(x, y)$ is defined. Similarly, a 2-tape involutory Turing machine can be constructed from a 1-tape reversible Turing machine. The following lemma shows a more general statement.

Lemma 4.5. (k-tape reversible to $2k$-tape involutory Turing machine). Given a k-tape reversible Turing machine T, there exists a $2k$-tape involutory Turing machine T' such that $[\![T']\!](w_1, \ldots, w_k, v_1, \ldots, v_k) = ([\![T]\!]^{-1}(v_1, \ldots, v_k), [\![T]\!](w_1, \ldots, w_k))$ for any input words $w_1, \ldots, w_k, v_1, \ldots, v_k$ of T.

Proof. Let $T = (Q, \Sigma, q_{\text{ini}}, q_{\text{fin}}, \Delta)$ be a k-tape reversible Turing machine. The corresponding $2k$-tape Turing machine T' is constructed as

$$Ext_{k \to 2k}(T)^{-1} \circ Perm(\pi) \circ Ext_{k \to 2k}(T)$$

where π is an involutory permutation on $[2k]$ such that $\pi(i) = k + i$ and $\pi(k + i) = i$ hold for any $i \in [k]$. The Turing machine T' is involutory by Lemma 4.4 since $Perm(\pi)$ in the middle is involutory.

As for the semantics of T', we can check the present statement by

$$
\begin{aligned}
&[\![T']\!](w_1, \ldots, w_k, v_1, \ldots, v_k) \\
&= [\![Ext_{k \to 2k}(T)^{-1} \circ Perm(\pi) \circ Ext_{k \to 2k}(T)]\!](w_1, \ldots, w_k, v_1, \ldots, v_k) \\
&= [\![Ext_{k \to 2k}(T)^{-1}]\!]([\![Perm(\pi)]\!]([\![Ext_{k \to 2k}(T)]\!](w_1, \ldots, w_k, v_1, \ldots, v_k))) \\
&= [\![Ext_{k \to 2k}(T)^{-1}]\!]([\![Perm(\pi)]\!]([\![T]\!](w_1, \ldots, w_k), v_1, \ldots, v_k)) \\
&= [\![Ext_{k \to 2k}(T)^{-1}]\!](v_1, \ldots, v_k, [\![T]\!](w_1, \ldots, w_k)) \\
&= ([\![T]\!]^{-1}(v_1, \ldots, v_k), [\![T]\!](w_1, \ldots, w_k)).
\end{aligned}
$$

$\square$

Now we show one of the main theorems which states any involutory computable function can be implemented by an involutory Turing machine. For any non-involutory Turing machine, an equivalent involutory Turing machine can be constructed whenever its semantics is involutory. Recall that in our function semantics of Turing machines a function some of whose arguments and results are always empty words is regarded as that with fewer arguments and results as mentioned in the previous section. In the following statement, for a given k-tape non-involutory Turing machine, a $2k$-tape involutory Turing machine is constructed whose semantics function has k arguments and k outputs that are always empty.

Theorem 4.6 (Expressiveness of involutory Turing machines). The involutory Turing machines can compute any involutory computable function. More specifically, given a k-tape Turing machine T such that $[\![T]\!]$ is involutory, there is a $2k$-tape involutory Turing machine T' such that $[\![T']\!] = [\![T]\!]$.

Proof. Let T be a k-tape Turing machine which computes an involution. Since an involution is injective, there exists a k-tape reversible Turing machine T_r such that $[\![T_r]\!] = [\![T]\!]$ by Theorem 3.12. Thus we have a $2k$-tape involutory Turing machine T_i such that $[\![T_i]\!](w_1, \ldots, w_k, v_1, \ldots, v_k) = ([\![T_r]\!]^{-1}(w_1, \ldots, w_k),$

$[\![T_r]\!](v_1, \ldots, v_k))$ by Lemma 4.5. Consider a $2k$-tape Turing machine given by $T' = Dup(k)^{-1} \circ T_i \circ Dup(k)$ which is involutory by Lemma 4.4. Then,

$$
\begin{aligned}
&[\![T']\!](w_1, \ldots, w_k) \\
&= [\![Dup(k)]\!]^{-1}([\![T_i]\!]([\![Dup(k)]\!](w_1, \ldots, w_k))) \\
&= [\![Dup(k)]\!]^{-1}([\![T_i]\!](w_1, \ldots, w_k, w_1, \ldots, w_k)) \\
&= [\![Dup(k)]\!]^{-1}([\![T_r]\!]^{-1}(w_1, \ldots, w_k), [\![T_r]\!](w_1, \ldots, w_k))
\end{aligned}
$$

holds where Theorem 3.11 and Theorem 3.15 are used. Since $[\![T_r]\!] = [\![T]\!]$ is involutory, two k-tuples of the argument of $[\![Dup(k)]\!]^{-1}$ are equal. By the definition of $[\![Dup(k)]\!]^{-1}$, we have $[\![T']\!](w_1, \ldots, w_k) = [\![T]\!](w_1, \ldots, w_k)$. $\qquad \square$

How expressive are multi-tape involutory Turing machines compared to those equipped with fewer tapes? It is well known that a multi-tape Turing machine can be simulated by a single-tape Turing machine with an injective encoding from a tuple of words to a single word. The simulation is called a *tape reduction*, which is also possible for reversible Turing machines [1, 2]. Concerning involutory Turing machines, any multi-tape involutory Turing machine can be simulated by a 2-tape involutory Turing machine whose semantics is a function over words that encode a tuple of words (where one of the tapes is always the empty word in the initial and final configuration).

Theorem 4.7 (k-tape to 2-tape involutory Turing machine). Given a k-tape involutory Turing machine $T = (Q, \Sigma, q_{\mathsf{ini}}, q_{\mathsf{fin}}, \Delta)$, there exists a 2-tape involutory Turing machine T' such that

$$
[\![T]\!](v_1, \ldots, v_k) = (w_1, \ldots, w_k) \quad \text{iff} \quad [\![T']\!](enc(v_1, \ldots, v_k)) = enc(w_1, \ldots, w_k)
$$

for any $v_1, \ldots, v_k, w_1, \ldots, w_k \in \Sigma^*$ where $enc : (\Sigma^*)^k \to (\Sigma \uplus \{\#\})^*$ is a simple encoding function for tuples with a separator $\# \notin \Sigma$ defined by $enc(x_1, \ldots, x_k) = x_1 \# \ldots \# x_k$.

Proof. Consider a function $f : (\Sigma \uplus \{\#\})^* \rightharpoonup (\Sigma \uplus \{\#\})^*$ such that $f(enc(v_1, \ldots, v_k)) = enc(w_1, \ldots, w_k)$ if and only if $[\![T]\!](v_1, \ldots, v_k) = (w_1, \ldots, w_k)$ for any $v_1, \ldots, v_k, w_1, \ldots, w_k \in \Sigma^*$. The function f is obviously computable. Since f is injective, there exists a 1-tape reversible Turing machine T_r whose semantics is equivalent to f. Furthermore, since $[\![T]\!]$ is involutory from Theorem 4.2, f is also involutory. By Theorem 4.6, there exists a 2-tape involutory Turing machine which concludes the statement of this theorem. $\qquad \square$

A tape reduction to a single-tape involutory Turing machine will be discussed in Sect. 6.

5   Universality of Involutory Turing Machine

A standard Turing machine is said to be universal if it simulates an arbitrary Turing machine. More exactly, a universal Turing machine takes a pair of words:

one is a Gödel number $\ulcorner T \urcorner$ (as a word) representing a Turing machine T and another is an input word of T. It returns the output word $[\![T]\!](x)$. The Gödel numbering $\ulcorner - \urcorner$ is an injective computable function that generates a word representation for a Turing machine. The notion of universality is called classical universality here to distinguish with another universality introduced later. For simplicity, only 1-tape Turing machines are considered which are to be simulated by a universal Turing machine. The results can be easily generalized to multi-tape Turing machines.

Definition 5.1 (Classical universality). A Turing machine U is said to be *classically universal* if $[\![U]\!](\ulcorner T \urcorner, x) = [\![T]\!](x)$ holds for any Turing machine T and its input word x of T.

No involutory Turing machine is classically universal since the function $[\![U]\!]$ in the definition above is obviously not involutory. Because the function is not even injective, no universal reversible Turing machine exists. Axelsen and Glück relaxed the definition of universality in a natural way; they showed that there exists a universal reversible Turing machine under the definition. We follow their definition for the universality of involutory Turing machines.

Definition 5.2 (Universality). An involutory Turing machine U is said to be *ITM-universal* if $[\![U]\!](\ulcorner T \urcorner, x) = (\ulcorner T \urcorner, [\![T]\!](x))$ holds for any involutory Turing machine T and its input word x of T.

The existence of an ITM-universal involutory Turing machine is easily obtained by the completeness of involutory Turing machines shown in Theorem 4.6.

Theorem 5.3. There exists an ITM-universal involutory Turing machine.

Proof. Let f be a function equivalent to the semantics of an involutory Turing machine to be ITM-universal given in Definition 5.2, i.e., $f(\ulcorner T \urcorner, x) = (\ulcorner T \urcorner, [\![T]\!](x))$ for any involutory Turing machine T and its input words of T. What we must show is that there exists an involutory Turing machine whose semantics is equivalent to f. Note that f is computable. By Theorem 4.6, it suffices to show that f is involutory. This is verified by $f(f(\ulcorner T \urcorner, x)) = f(\ulcorner T \urcorner, [\![T]\!](x)) = (\ulcorner T \urcorner, [\![T]\!]([\![T]\!](x))) = (\ulcorner T \urcorner, x)$ where the last equality comes from Theorem 4.2. □

Theorem 5.3 only shows the existence of an ITM-universal involutory Turing machine. The proof of the theorem relies on Theorem 3.12 (via Theorem 4.6) which requires an impractical generate-and-test inversion method [2, Lemma 3]. This kind of problem has already been recognized in proving the existence of universal reversible Turing machines by Axelsen and Glück [2]. They gave a solution to that by constructing a universal reversible Turing machine from a classically universal Turing machine. We employ their idea for the direct construction of an ITM-universal involutory Turing machine. Since their construction gives a non-involutory Turing machine, we shall show a different construction using Landauer embedding and Bennett's trick for a classically universal Turing machine.

Proposition 5.4 (Landauer embedding [2,8]**).** Let $T = (Q, \Sigma, q_{\mathrm{ini}}, q_{\mathrm{fin}}, \Delta)$ be a k-tape Turing machine. Then, there exists a $(k+1)$-tape reversible Turing machine $Lan(T)$ such that $[\![Lan(T)]\!](w_1, \ldots, w_k, \varepsilon) = ([\![T]\!](w_1, \ldots, w_k), \mathsf{trace}(T, w_1, \ldots, w_k))$ where trace is a function encoding a history of applied rules on the corresponding run into Σ^*.

As mentioned in [2], Bennett's trick gives an input-preserving reversible Turing machine for an arbitrary Turing machine.

Proposition 5.5 (Bennett's trick [3]**).** Let T be a k-tape Turing machine. Then, there exists a $(2k + 1)$-tape reversible Turing machine $Ben(T)$ such that $[\![Ben(T)]\!](w_1, \ldots, w_k) = (w_1, \ldots, w_k, [\![T]\!](w_1, \ldots, w_k))$.

For the proposition above, a similar proof to that of [2, Lemma 6] does work by $Ben(T) = Perm(\pi^{-1}) \circ Ext_{k+1 \to 2k+1}(Lan(T)^{-1}) \circ Perm(\pi) \circ Ext_{2k \to 2k+1}(Dup(k)) \circ Perm(\pi^{-1}) \circ Ext_{k+1 \to 2k+1}(Lan(T))$ with permutation $\pi = (k + 1 \ldots 2k + 1)$.

Theorem 5.6 (Universal Turing machine to ITM-universal involutory Turing machine). Let U be a classically universal Turing machine, i.e., $[\![U]\!](\ulcorner T \urcorner, x) = [\![T]\!](x)$ for any Turing machine T. Then, an involutory Turing machine U' defined by $U' = Ben(U)^{-1} \circ Perm((2\ 3)) \circ Ben(U)$ is ITM-universal.

Proof By Proposition 5.4 and Proposition 5.5, we obtain $[\![Ben(U)]\!](\ulcorner T \urcorner, x) = (\ulcorner T \urcorner, x, [\![T]\!](x))$ for any Turing machine $\ulcorner T \urcorner$ and its input x. Let T be a involutory Turing machine, i.e., $[\![T]\!]([\![T]\!](x)) = x$ by Theorem 4.2. Thus we have

$$
\begin{aligned}
[\![U']\!](\ulcorner T \urcorner, x) &= [\![Ben(U)]\!]^{-1}([\![Perm((2\ 3))]\!]([\![Ben(U)]\!](\ulcorner T \urcorner, x))) \\
&= [\![Ben(U)]\!]^{-1}([\![Perm((2\ 3))]\!](\ulcorner T \urcorner, x, [\![T]\!](x))) \\
&= [\![Ben(U)]\!]^{-1}(\ulcorner T \urcorner, [\![T]\!](x), x) \\
&= [\![Ben(U)]\!]^{-1}(\ulcorner T \urcorner, [\![T]\!](x), [\![T]\!]([\![T]\!](x))) \\
&= (\ulcorner T \urcorner, [\![T]\!](x))
\end{aligned}
$$

which indicates the ITM-universality of U'. □

6   Discussion

This section describes the design choice of permutation rules and the limitation of tape reduction for our involutory Turing machines. The applications of our computational model will also be discussed.

Design Choice. One may feel it unusual for the definition of a multi-tape Turing machine to have tape permutation rules. A k-tape Turing machine is typically defined by specifying a set of transition rules as

$$\Delta \subseteq (Q \setminus \{q_{\mathsf{fin}}\}) \times ((\Sigma_\sqcup \times \Sigma_\sqcup) \cup \{\leftarrow, \diamond, \rightarrow\})^k \times (Q \setminus \{q_{\mathsf{ini}}\}).$$

The typical definition forces one to rewrite or move at all tapes simultaneously[1]. An involutory Turing machine could be defined on this model with the same restriction $\widetilde{\varphi}(\Delta) = \Delta$ as ours. It is easy to see that the model always computes an involution by a similar proof to that of Theorem 4.2. However, it is not easy to show the expressiveness like Theorem 4.6 for the model without permutation rules. Although the author believes but cannot prove that the expressiveness does not hold without permutation rules, the readers may surmise it intuitively by trying to define a 2-tape Turing machine $Perm((1\ 2))$ that swaps an input pair. The simplest way to do this is first to swap each from left to right and then return the head back to the left end. Note that it does not conform to the restriction above to be involutory. The reversed run is no longer valid for any renaming states. There might exist a tricky way to implement the swap function without permutation rules. The author speculates that it is impossible, though.

Limitation of Tape Reduction. Theorem 4.7 states that any k-tape involutory Turing machine can be simulated by a 2-tape involutory Turing machine. A natural question is whether it is possible by a 1-tape involutory Turing machine. Again, the author believes it is impossible. Consider a 1-tape Turing machine T_{bnot} in Example 3.6, which is not involutory but whose semantics is involutory. By Theorem 4.6, there exists a 2-tape involutory Turing machine equivalent to T_{bnot}. It is found hard to define a 1-tape involutory Turing machine for a similar reason to the observation above on defining the swap function without permutation rules. The author speculates the reduction to a single tape is impossible in general but leaves the proof for future work as well.

Application to Bidirectional Transformation. This work is originally motivated by characterizing programming languages for bidirectional transformation, which enables us to synchronize multiple data and maintain their consistency. A typical bidirectional transformation is specified by a pair of forward ($get : S \rightarrow V$) and backward ($put : S \times V \rightarrow S$) transformations over sources S and views V where two functions are required to be consistent in some sense. More specifically, the following three laws are to be satisfied for the consistency (called *very-well-behavedness* in [4]):

$$put(s, get(s)) = s \qquad get(put(s, v)) = v \qquad put(put(s, v), v') = put(s, v')$$

for any $s \in S$ and $v, v' \in V$. Some bidirectional programming languages impose a syntactic restriction to programmers so that it conforms to the consistency. However, due to the restriction, it is hard to characterize how powerful each programming language is. As expressiveness of general programming languages can be characterized by Turing machines, we need a computational

---

[1] The union symbol $\cup$ may be replaced with $\times$ so that a read/write and a move action may happen at the same time. However, this makes it hard to give the inverse of a pair of actions, which is often required in the present work.

model to characterize all pairs of computable functions *get* and *put* that satisfy consistency.

An involutory Turing machine gives a partial solution to this problem because of its expressiveness. Consistency implies that a function $f : S \times V \to S \times V$ defined by $f(s, v) = (put(s, v), get(s))$ is involutory, that is, $f(f(s, v)) = (s, v)$ holds. Thereby any correct bidirectional program can be computed by a 2-tape involutory Turing machine under some encoding. Conversely, a 2-tape involutory Turing machine does not always specify a correct bidirectional program. The author believes that there exists a computational model given by an appropriately-restricted involutory Turing machine, which exactly covers all consistent bidirectional transformations. The present work will be a good starting point to characterize bidirectional programming languages.

Program Inversion. A program inverter *pinv* is a function that takes the Gödel number of a Turing machine T and returns that of a Turing machine whose semantics is the inverse of $[\![T]\!]$. i.e., $pinv(\ulcorner T \urcorner) = \ulcorner T \urcorner^{-1}$ holds. Axelsen and Glück have shown that there exists a 2-tape reversible Turing machine that computes *pinv*. They employ the result as a lemma to construct a universal reversible Turing machine from a classically universal Turing machine. Although we do not need such a lemma for the construction of a universal involutory Turing machine, the same statement also holds for the involutory Turing machine.

Theorem 6.1 (Program inverter as an involutory Turing machine). There exists a 2-tape involutory Turing machine T which computes a program inverter for reversible Turing machines, that is, $[\![T]\!](\ulcorner R \urcorner) = \ulcorner R^{-1} \urcorner$ holds for any reversible Turing machine R.

Proof. There exists a 1-tape reversible Turing machine T_r such that $[\![T_r]\!](\ulcorner R \urcorner) = \ulcorner R^{-1} \urcorner$ by [2, Lemma 15]. Since $[\![T_r]\!]$ is involutory, there exists a 2-tape involutory Turing machine whose semantics is equivalent to $[\![T_r]\!]$ by Theorem 4.6.   □

7   Related Work

This work is strongly inspired by Axelsen and Glück's [2]. They showed that (1) any injective computable function can be implemented by a reversible Turing machine, (2) the number of tapes of a reversible Turing machine can be reduced with preserving its semantics, (3) there exists a universal reversible Turing machine, and (4) a universal reversible Turing machine can be constructed from a universal Turing machine. In the present paper, we have addressed these properties for involutory Turing machines instead of reversible Turing machines. Regarding (1), (3), and (4), similar results have been obtained. Interestingly, their proofs are rather different from those of the corresponding theorems for reversible Turing machines. Regarding (2), we failed to find an equivalent single-tape involutory Turing machine for an arbitrary multi-tape involutory Turing machine. This might be an inherent limitation of involutory Turing machines as we have discussed in Sect. 6.

An involutory Turing machine may remind some readers of a symmetric Turing machine introduced by Lewis and Papadimitriou [9], where its computation step is symmetric. A symmetric Turing machine can be considered as a variant of an involutory Turing machine whose state involution is the identity function by ignoring the requirement of $\varphi(q_{\mathsf{ini}}) = q_{\mathsf{fin}}$ and $\varphi(q_{\mathsf{fin}}) = q_{\mathsf{ini}}$[2]. However, symmetric Turing machines give a computational model completely different from involutory Turing machines. A symmetric Turing machine defines an undirected graph specified by its configurations and computation steps; its run is a path from the initial one to the final one. This model has been introduced to specify the computational complexity of the undirected st-connectivity (USTCON) problem and is known to be at least as powerful as a deterministic Turing machine.

Gajardo, Kari, and Moreira [5] introduced *time symmetry* for cellular automata to import a notion in physical theories where forward and backward time directions cannot be distinguished. The time symmetry is specified by an involution which connects the corresponding states and transitions as involutory Turing machines do. Kutrib and Worsch [7] later ported the notion of time symmetry into finite automata and pushdown automata. Involutory Turing machines may be called *time-symmetric Turing machines* along this line. Nevertheless, our computational model should be called an involutory Turing machine in the present paper owing to our purpose to characterize all computable involutions unlike the previous time-symmetric machines: Gajardo et al.'s time-symmetric cellular automata compute a composition of two involutions but not a single involution. Although it would be worthwhile to investigate the time symmetry and other related properties of involutory Turing machines, they are left for future work.

8 Conclusion

A computational model for involution has been presented. The model is a variant of a multi-tape Turing machine, called an involutory Turing machine, which imposes a restriction on state transition rules so that the reversed run of every valid run should be valid. The model has been shown to be expressive enough in the sense that not only does an involutory Turing machine always compute an involution but also any involution can be computed by an involutory Turing machine. It has also been shown that there exists a universal involutory Turing machine that can simulate an arbitrary involutory Turing machine.

This work naturally introduces a notion of i-Turing completeness, i.e., a programming language L is said to be *i-Turing complete* if every program in L defines an involution and every involutory Turing machine can be simulated by a program in L. A similar notion called r-Turing completeness [1,2] has been employed for characterizing reversible programming languages [6,11]. As dis-

---

[2] Although the definition of a symmetric Turing machine in [9] differs from ours in another point that it allows transition rules to view the next cell of the head, this cannot change its expressiveness as mentioned in the paper.

cussed in Sect. 6, i-Turing completeness or its variant will be used to characterize bidirectional programming languages in the future.

Acknowledgment. I am grateful to Robert Glück who has kindly lectured to me about reversible Turing machines and their expressiveness. I also thank Kanae Tsushima for her observation on the involutoriness of bidirectional transformation and Mirai Ikebuchi for carefully proofreading the manuscript. Furthermore, I want to appreciate anonymous reviewers' fruitful comments on a close connection with time-symmetric machines. This work was partially supported by JSPS KAKENHI Grant Numbers JP17K00007, JP18H03204, and JP18H04093.

References

1. Axelsen, H.B., Glück, R.: What do reversible programs compute? In: Hofmann, M. (ed.) FoSSaCS 2011. LNCS, vol. 6604, pp. 42–56. Springer, Heidelberg (2011). https://doi.org/10.1007/978-3-642-19805-2_4
2. Axelsen, H.B., Glück, R.: On reversible turing machines and their function universality. Acta Inf. **53**(5), 509–543 (2016). https://doi.org/10.1007/s00236-015-0253-y
3. Bennett, C.H.: Logical reversibility of computation. IBM J. Res. Dev. **17**(6), 525–532 (1973)
4. Foster, N., Matsuda, K., Voigtländer, J.: Three complementary approaches to bidirectional programming. In: Gibbons, J. (ed.) Generic and Indexed Programming. LNCS, vol. 7470, pp. 1–46. Springer, Heidelberg (2012). https://doi.org/10.1007/978-3-642-32202-0_1
5. Gajardo, A., Kari, J., Moreira, A.: On time-symmetry in cellular automata. J. Comput. Syst. Sci. **78**(4), 1115–1126 (2012). https://doi.org/10.1016/j.jcss.2012.01.006
6. Glück, R., Yokoyama, T.: A linear-time self-interpreter of a reversible imperative language. Comput. Softw. **33**(3), 3_108–3_128 (2016)
7. Kutrib, M., Worsch, T.: Time-symmetric machines. In: Dueck, G.W., Miller, D.M. (eds.) RC 2013. LNCS, vol. 7948, pp. 168–181. Springer, Heidelberg (2013). https://doi.org/10.1007/978-3-642-38986-3_14
8. Landauer, R.: Irreversibility and heat generation in the computing process. IBM J. Res. Dev. **5**(3), 183–191 (1961). https://doi.org/10.1147/rd.53.0183
9. Lewis, H.R., Papadimitriou, C.H.: Symmetric space-bounded computation. Theor. Comput. Sci. **19**, 161–187 (1982)
10. Sipser, M.: Introduction to the theory of computation. PWS Publishing Company, Boston (1997)
11. Yokoyama, T., Axelsen, H.B., Glück, R.: Principles of a reversible programming language. In: Proceedings of the 5th Conference on Computing Frontiers, Ischia, Italy, 5–7 May 2008. pp. 43–54 (2008)
12. Zagier, D.: A one-sentence proof that every prime $p \equiv 1 \ (mod \ 4)$ is a sum of two squares. Am. Math. Monthly **97**(2), 144 (1990)

Event Structures for the Reversible Early Internal π-Calculus

Eva Graversen, Iain Phillips$^{(\boxtimes)}$ ⓘ, and Nobuko Yoshida ⓘ

Imperial College London, London, UK
i.phillips@imperial.ac.uk

Abstract. The π-calculus is a widely used process calculus, which models communications between processes and allows the passing of communication links. Various operational semantics of the π-calculus have been proposed, which can be classified according to whether transitions are unlabelled (so-called reductions) or labelled. With labelled transitions, we can distinguish early and late semantics. The early version allows a process to receive names it already knows from the environment, while the late semantics and reduction semantics do not. All existing reversible versions of the π-calculus use reduction or late semantics, despite the early semantics of the (forward-only) π-calculus being more widely used than the late. We define πIH, the first reversible early π-calculus, and give it a denotational semantics in terms of reversible bundle event structures. The new calculus is a reversible form of the internal π-calculus, which is a subset of the π-calculus where every link sent by an output is private, yielding greater symmetry between inputs and outputs.

1   Introduction

The π-calculus [18] is a widely used process calculus, which models communications between processes using input and output actions, and allows the passing of communication links. Various operational semantics of the π-calculus have been proposed, which can be classified according to whether transitions are unlabelled or labelled. Unlabelled transitions (so-called reductions) represent completed interactions. As observed in [25] they give us the internal behaviour of complete systems, whereas to reason compositionally about the behaviour of a system in terms of its components we need labelled transitions. With labelled transitions, we can distinguish early and late semantics [19], with the difference being that early semantics allows a process to receive (free) names it already knows from the environment, while the late does not. This creates additional causation in the early case between those inputs and previous output actions making bound names free. All existing reversible versions of the π-calculus use reduction semantics [14,26] or late semantics [7,17]. However the early semantics of the (forward-only) π-calculus is more widely used than the late, partly because it has a sound correspondence with contextual congruences [13,20].

We define πIH, the first reversible early π-calculus, and give it a denotational semantics in terms of reversible event structures. The new calculus is a reversible

ⓒ Springer Nature Switzerland AG 2020
I. Lanese and M. Rawski (Eds.): RC 2020, LNCS 12227, pp. 71–90, 2020.
https://doi.org/10.1007/978-3-030-52482-1_4

form of the internal π-calculus, or πI-calculus [24], which is a subset of the π-calculus where every link sent by an output is bound (private), yielding greater symmetry between inputs and outputs. It has been shown that the asynchronous π-calculus can be encoded in the asynchronous form of the πI-calculus [2].

The π-calculus has two forms of causation. *Structural* causation, as one would find in CCS, comes directly from the structure of the process, e.g. in $a(b).c(d)$ the action $a(b)$ must happen before $c(d)$. *Link* causation, on the other hand, comes from one action making a name available for others to use, e.g. in the process $a(x)|\overline{b}(c)$, the event $a(c)$ will be caused by $\overline{b}(c)$ making c a free name. Note that link causation as in this example is present in the early form of the πI-calculus though not the late, since it is created by the process receiving one of its free names. Restricting ourselves to the πI-calculus, rather than the full π-calculus lets us focus on the link causation created by early semantics, since it removes the other forms of link causation present in the π-calculus.

We base πIH on the work of Hildebrandt *et al.* [12], which used extrusion histories and locations to define a stable non-interleaving early operational semantics for the π-calculus. We extend the extrusion histories so that they contain enough information to reverse the πI-calculus, storing not only extrusions but also communications. Allowing processes to evolve, while moving past actions to a history separate from the process, is called dynamic reversibility [9]. By contrast, static reversibility, as in CCSK [21], lets processes keep their structure during the computation, and annotations are used to keep track of the current state and how actions may be reversed.

Event structures are a model of concurrency which describe causation, conflict and concurrency between events. They are 'truly concurrent' in that they do not reduce concurrency of events to the different possible interleavings. They have been used to model forward-only process calculi [3,6,27], including the πI-calculus [5]. Describing reversible processes as event structures is useful because it gives us a simple representation of the causal relationships between actions and gives us equivalences between processes which generate isomorphic event structures. True concurrency in semantics is particularly important in reversible process calculi, as the order actions can reverse in depends on their causal relations [22].

Event structure semantics of dynamically reversible process calculi have the added complexity of the histories and the actions in the process being separated, obscuring the structural causation. This was an issue for Cristescu *et al.* [8], who used rigid families [4], related to event structures, to describe the semantics of $R\pi$ [7]. Their semantics require a process to first reverse all actions to find the original process, map this process to a rigid family, and then apply each of the reversed memories in order to reach the current state of the process. Aubert and Cristescu [1] used a similar approach to describe the semantics of a subset of RCCS processes as configuration structures. We use a different tactic of first mapping to a statically reversible calculus, πIK, and then obtaining the event structure. This means that while we do have to reconstruct the original structure of the process, we avoid redoing the actions in the event structure.

Our πIK is inspired by CCSK and the statically reversible π-calculus of [17], which use communication keys to denote past actions. To keep track of link causation, keys are used in a number of different ways in [17]. In our case we can handle link causation by using keys purely to annotate the action which was performed using the key, and any names which were substituted during that action.

Although our two reversible variants of the πI-calculus have very different syntax and originate from different ideas, we show an operational correspondence between them in Theorem 4.6. We do this despite the extrusion histories containing more information than the keys, since they remember what bound names were before being substituted. The mapping from πIH to πIK bears some resemblance to the one presented from RCCS to CCSK in [16], though with some important differences. πIH uses centralised extrusion histories more similar to rhoπ [15] while RCCS uses distributed memories. Additionally, unlike CCS, πI has substitution as part of its transitions and memories are handled differently by πIK and πIH, and our mapping has to take this into account.

We describe denotational structural event structure semantics of πIK, partly inspired by [5,6], using reversible bundle event structures [10]. Reversible event structures [23] allow their events to reverse and include relations describing when events can reverse. Bundle event structures are more expressive than prime event structures, since they allow an event to have multiple possible conflicting causes. This allows us to model parallel composition without having a single action correspond to multiple events. While it would be possible to model πIK using reversible prime event structures, using bundle event structures not only gives us fewer events, it also lays the foundation for adding rollback to πIK and πIH, similarly to [10], which cannot be done using reversible prime event structures.

The structure of the paper is as follows: Sect. 2 describes πIH; Sect. 3 describes πIK; Sect. 4 describes the mapping from πIH to πIK; Sect. 5 recalls labelled reversible bundle event structures; and Sect. 6 gives event structure semantics of πIK. Proofs of the results presented in this paper can be found in the technical report [11].

2 πI-Calculus Reversible Semantics with Extrusion Histories

Stable non-interleaving, early operational semantics of the π-calculus were defined by Hildebrandt *et al.* in [12], using locations and extrusion histories to keep track of link causation. We will in this section use a similar approach to define a reversible variant of the πI-calculus, πIH, using the locations and histories to keep track of not just causation, but also past actions. The πI-calculus is a restricted variant of the π-calculus wherein output on a channel a, $\overline{a}(b)$, binds the name being sent, b, corresponding to the π-calculus process $(\nu b)\overline{a}\langle b\rangle.P$. This creates greater symmetry with the input $a(x)$, where the variable x is also bound. The syntax of πIH processes is:

$$P::= \sum_{i\in I}\alpha_i.P_i \mid P_0|P_1 \mid (\nu x)P \quad \alpha::= \overline{a}(b) \mid a(b)$$

The forward semantics of πIH can be seen in Table 1 and the reverse semantics can be seen in Table 2. We associate each transition with an action $\mu :: = \alpha \mid \tau$ and a location u (Definition 2.1), describing where the action came from and what changes are made to the process as a result of the action. We store these location and action pairs in extrusion and communication histories associated with processes, so $(\overline{H}, \underline{H}, H) \vdash P$ means that if (μ, u) is an action and location pair in the output history $\overline{H}$ then μ is an output action, which P previously performed at location u. Similarly $\underline{H}$ contains pairs of input actions and locations and H contains triples of two communicating actions and the location associated with their communication. We use $\mathbf{H}$ as shorthand for $(\overline{H}, \underline{H}, H)$.

Definition 2.1 (Location [12]). *A location u of an action μ is one of the following:*

1. *$l[P][P']$ if μ is an input or output, where $l \in \{0,1\}^*$ describes the path taken through parallel compositions to get to μ's origin, P is the subprocess reached by following the path before μ has been performed, and P' is the result of performing μ in P.*
2. *$l \langle 0l_0[P_0][P_0'], 1l_1[P_1][P_1'] \rangle$ if $\mu = \tau$, where $l0l_0[P_0][P_0']$ and $l1l_1[P_1][P_1']$ are the locations of the two actions communicating.*

The path l can be empty if the action did not go through any parallel compositions.

We also use the operations on extrusion histories from Definition 2.2. These (1) add a branch to the path in every location, (2) isolate the extrusions whose locations begin with a specific branch, (3) isolate the extrusions whose locations begin with a specific branch and then remove the first branch from the locations, and (4) add a pair to the history it belongs in.

Definition 2.2 (Operations on extrusion histories [12]). *Given an extrusion history $(\overline{H}, \underline{H}, H)$, for $H^* \in \{\overline{H}, \underline{H}, H\}$ we have the following operations for $i \in \{0,1\}$:*

1. *$iH^* = \{(\mu, iu) \mid (\mu, u) \in H^*\}$*
2. *$[i]H^* = \{(\mu, iu) \mid (\mu, iu) \in H^*\}$*
3. *$[\check{i}]H^* = \{(\mu, u) \mid (\mu, iu) \in H^*\}$*
4. *$\mathbf{H} + (\mu, u) = \begin{cases} (\overline{H} \cup \{L\}, \underline{H}, H) & \text{if } (\mu, u) = (\overline{a}(n), u) \\ (\overline{H}, \underline{H} \cup \{L\}, H) & \text{if } (\mu, u) = (a(x), u) \\ (\overline{H}, \underline{H}, H \cup \{L\}) & \text{if } (\mu, u) = (a(x), \overline{a}(n), l\langle u_0, u_1 \rangle) \end{cases}$*

The forwards semantics of πIH have six rules. In [OUT] the action is an output, the location is the process before and after doing the output, and they are added to the output history. The equivalent reverse rule, [OUT^{-1}], similarly removes the pair from the history and transforms the process from the second part of the location back to the first. The input rule [IN] works similarly, but performs a substitution on the received name and adds the pair to the input history instead. In [PAR$_i$] we isolate the parts of the histories whose locations start with i and use those to perform an action in P_i, getting $\mathbf{H}'_i \vdash P'_i$. It then

Table 1. Semantics of πIH (forwards rules)

$$\frac{u = [\sum_{i \in I} \alpha_i.P_i][P_j] \quad \alpha_j = \overline{a}(n) \quad j \in I}{\mathbf{H} \vdash \sum_{i \in I} \alpha_i.P_i \xrightarrow[u]{\alpha_j} (\overline{H} \cup \{(\overline{a}(n), u)\}, \underline{H}, H) \vdash P_j} \; [\text{OUT}]$$

$$\frac{u = [\sum_{i \in I} \alpha_i.P_i][P_j] \quad P_j' = P_j[x := n] \quad \alpha_j = a(x) \quad j \in I}{\mathbf{H} \vdash \sum_{i \in I} \alpha_i.P_i \xrightarrow[u]{a(n)} (\overline{H}, \underline{H} \cup \{(a(n), u)\}, H) \vdash P_j'} \; [\text{IN}]$$

$$\frac{([i]\overline{H}, [i]\underline{H}, [i]H) \vdash P_i \xrightarrow[u]{\mu} \mathbf{H}_i' \vdash P_i' \quad P_{1-i}' = P_{1-i} \quad \text{if } \mu = \overline{a}(n) \text{ then } n \notin \mathsf{fn}(P_{1-i})}{\mathbf{H} \vdash P_0 | P_1 \xrightarrow[iu]{\mu} ((\overline{H} \setminus [i]\overline{H}) \cup i\overline{H_i'}, (\underline{H} \setminus [i]\underline{H}) \cup i\underline{H_i'}, (H \setminus [i]H) \cup iH_i') \vdash P_0'|P_1'} \; [\text{PAR}_i]$$

$$([i]\overline{H}, [i]\underline{H}, [i]H) \vdash P_i \xrightarrow[v_i]{\alpha_i} \mathbf{H}_i' \vdash P_i' \quad \alpha_i = \overline{a}(n) \quad \alpha_j = a(n)$$
$$([j]\overline{H}, [j]\underline{H}, [j]H) \vdash P_j \xrightarrow[v_j]{\alpha_i} \mathbf{H}_j' \vdash P_j' \quad j = 1 - i \quad n \notin \mathsf{fn}(P_j)$$
$$\frac{}{\mathbf{H} \vdash P_0 | P_1 \xrightarrow[(0v_0, 1v_1)]{\tau} (\overline{H}, \underline{H}, H \cup \{((\alpha_0, \alpha_1, \langle 0v_0, 1v_1 \rangle))\}) \vdash (\nu n)(P_0'|P_1')} \; [\text{COM}_i]$$

$$\frac{\mathbf{H} \vdash P \xrightarrow[u]{\mu} \mathbf{H}' \vdash P' \quad x \notin n(\mu)}{\mathbf{H} \vdash (\nu x)P \xrightarrow[u]{\mu} \mathbf{H}' \vdash (\nu x)P'} \; [\text{SCOPE}] \qquad \frac{P \equiv P' \quad \mathbf{H} \vdash P' \xrightarrow[u]{\mu} \mathbf{H}' \vdash Q' \quad Q' \equiv Q}{\mathbf{H} \vdash P \xrightarrow[u]{\mu} \mathbf{H}' \vdash Q} \; [\text{STR}]$$

replaces the part of the histories parts of the histories whose locations start with i with $\mathbf{H}_i'$ when propagating the action through the parallel. A communication in [COM$_i$] adds memory of the communication to the history. The rules [SCOPE] and [STR] are standard and self-explanatory.

The reverse rules use the extrusion histories to find a location $l[P][P']$ such that the current state of the subprocess at l is P', and change it to P.

In these semantics structural congruence, consisting only of α-conversion together with $!P \equiv !P|P$ and $(\nu\, a)(\nu b)P \equiv (\nu\, b)(\nu\, a)P$, is primarily used to create and remove extra copies of a replicated process when reversing the action that happened before the replication. Since we use locations in our extrusion histories, we try to avoid using structural congruence any more than necessary. However, not using it for parallel composition would mean that we would need some other way of preventing traces such as $\mathbf{H} \vdash !P \xrightarrow[u]{\mu} \overset{\mu}{\underset{u}{\rightsquigarrow}} \mathbf{H} \vdash !P|P$, which allows a process to reach a state it could not reach via a parabolic trace. Using structural congruence for replication does not cause any problems for the locations, as we can tell past actions originating in each copy of P apart by the path in their location, with actions from the ith copy having a path of i 0s followed by a 1.

Table 2. Semantics of reversible πIH (reverse rules)

$$\frac{u = [\sum_{i \in I} \alpha_i.P_i][P_j] \quad \alpha_j = \overline{a}(n) \quad j \in I \quad (\overline{a}(n), u) \in \overline{H}}{\mathbf{H} \vdash P_j \overset{\alpha_j}{\underset{u}{\rightsquigarrow}} (\overline{H} \setminus \{(\overline{a}(n), u)\}, \underline{H}, H) \vdash \sum_{i \in I} \alpha_i.P_i} \; [\mathrm{OUT}^{-1}]$$

$$\frac{u = [\sum_{i \in I} \alpha_i.P_i][P_j] \quad P_j' = P_j[x := n] \quad \alpha_j = a(x) \quad j \in I \quad (a(n), u) \in \underline{H}}{\mathbf{H} \vdash P_j' \overset{a(n)}{\underset{u}{\rightsquigarrow}} (\overline{H}, \underline{H} \setminus \{(a(n), u)\}, H) \vdash \sum_{i \in I} \alpha_i.P_i} \; [\mathrm{IN}^{-1}]$$

$$\frac{([i]\overline{H}, [i]\underline{H}, [i]H) \vdash P_i \overset{\alpha}{\underset{u}{\rightsquigarrow}} \mathbf{H}_i' \vdash P_i' \quad P_{1-i}' = P_{1-i} \text{ if } \alpha = \overline{a}(n) \text{ then } n \notin \mathrm{fn}(P_{1-i})}{\mathbf{H} \vdash P_0 | P_1 \overset{\alpha}{\underset{iu}{\rightsquigarrow}} ((\overline{H} \setminus [i]\overline{H}) \cup i\overline{H_i'}, (\underline{H} \setminus [i]\underline{H}) \cup i\underline{H_i'}, (H \setminus [i]H) \cup iH_i') \vdash P_0' | P_1'} \; [\mathrm{PAR}_i^{-1}]$$

$$\frac{([i]\overline{H} \cup \{(\overline{a}(n), v_i)\}, [i]\underline{H}, [i]H) \vdash P_i \overset{\overline{a}(n)}{\underset{v_i}{\rightsquigarrow}} \mathbf{H}_i' \vdash P_i' \quad \alpha_i = \overline{a}(n) \quad \alpha_j = a(n)}{([j]\overline{H}, [j]\underline{H} \cup \{(a(n), v_j)\}, [j]H) \vdash P_j \overset{a(n)}{\underset{v_j}{\rightsquigarrow}} \mathbf{H}_j' \vdash P_j' \quad j = 1 - i \quad n \notin \mathrm{fn}(P_j)}{\mathbf{H} \vdash (\nu n)(P_0 | P_1) \overset{\tau}{\underset{(0v_0, 1v_1)}{\rightsquigarrow}} (\overline{H}, \underline{H}, H \setminus \{((\alpha_0, \alpha_1, \langle 0v_0, 1v_1 \rangle))\} \vdash P_0' | P_1'} \; [\mathrm{COM}_i^{-1}]$$

$$\frac{\mathbf{H} \vdash P \overset{\mu}{\underset{u}{\rightsquigarrow}} \mathbf{H}' \vdash P' \quad x \notin n(\alpha)}{\mathbf{H} \vdash (\nu x)P \overset{\mu}{\underset{u}{\rightsquigarrow}} \mathbf{H}' \vdash (\nu x)P'} \; [\mathrm{SCOPE}^{-1}] \qquad \frac{P \equiv P' \quad \mathbf{H} \vdash P' \overset{\alpha}{\underset{u}{\rightsquigarrow}} \mathbf{H}' \vdash Q' \quad Q' \equiv Q}{\mathbf{H} \vdash P \overset{\alpha}{\underset{u}{\rightsquigarrow}} \mathbf{H}' \vdash Q} \; [\mathrm{STR}^{-1}]$$

Example 2.3. Consider the process $(a(x).\overline{x}(d)|\overline{a}(c))|b(y)$. If we start with empty histories, each transition adds actions and locations:

$(\emptyset, \emptyset, \emptyset) \vdash (a(x).\overline{x}(d)|\overline{a}(c))|b(y)$

$\qquad\qquad\qquad\qquad\qquad\qquad \xrightarrow{\quad\tau\quad}_{0\langle 0[a(x).\overline{x}(d)][\overline{c}(d)], 1[\overline{a}(c)][0]\rangle}$

$(\emptyset, \emptyset, \{(a(c), \overline{a}(c), 0\langle 0[a(x).\overline{x}(d)][\overline{c}(d)], 1[\overline{a}(c)][0]\rangle\}) \vdash (\nu c)(\overline{c}(d)|0)|b(y)$

$\qquad\qquad\qquad\qquad\qquad\qquad \xrightarrow{\quad\overline{c}(d)\quad}_{00[\overline{c}(d)][0]}$

$(\{(\overline{c}(d), 00[\overline{c}(d)][0])\}, \emptyset, \{(a(c), \overline{a}(c), 0\langle 0[a(x).\overline{x}(d)][\overline{c}(d)], 1[\overline{a}(c)][0]\rangle\}) \vdash (\nu c)(0|0)|b(y)$

$\qquad\qquad\qquad\qquad\qquad\qquad \xrightarrow{\quad b(d)\quad}_{1[b(y)][0]}$

$(\{(\overline{c}(b), 00[\overline{c}(b)][0])\}, \{(b(d), 1[b(y)][0])\}, \{(a(c), \overline{a}(c), 0\langle 0[a(x).\overline{x}(d)][\overline{c}(d)], 1[\overline{a}(c)][0]\rangle\}) \vdash (0|0)|0$

We show that our forwards and reverse transitions correspond.

Proposition 2.4 (Loop).

1. *Given a πIH process P and an extrusion history $\mathbf{H}$, if $\mathbf{H} \vdash P \xrightarrow{\alpha}_{u} \mathbf{H}' \vdash Q$, then*

   $\mathbf{H}' \vdash Q \overset{\alpha}{\underset{u}{\rightsquigarrow}} \mathbf{H} \vdash P.$

2. *Given a forwards-reachable πIH process P and an extrusion history $\mathbf{H}$, if $\mathbf{H} \vdash P \overset{\alpha}{\underset{u}{\rightsquigarrow}} \mathbf{H}' \vdash Q$, then $\mathbf{H}' \vdash Q \xrightarrow{\alpha}_{u} \mathbf{H} \vdash P.$*

3 πI-Calculus Reversible Semantics with Annotations

In order to define event structure semantics of πIH, we first map from πIH to a statically reversible variant of πI-calculus, called πIK. πIK is based on previous statically reversible calculi πK [17] and CCSK [21]. Both of these use *communication keys* to denote past actions and which other actions they have interacted with, so $a(x)|\overline{a}(b) \xrightarrow{\tau[n]} a(b)[n]|\overline{a}(b)[n]$ means a communication with the key n has taken place between the two actions. We apply this idea to define early semantics of πIK, which has the following syntax:

$$P:: = \alpha.P \mid \alpha[n].P \mid P_0 + P_1 \mid P_0|P_1 \mid (\nu x)P \quad \alpha:: = \overline{a}(b) \mid a(b)$$

The primary difference between applying communication keys to CCS and the πI-calculus is the need to deal with substitution. We need to keep track of not only which actions have communicated with each other, but also which names were substituted when. We do this by giving the substituted names a key, $a_{[n]}$, but otherwise treating them the same as those without the key, except when undoing the input associated with n.

Table 3. πIK forward semantics

$$\frac{\mathsf{std}(P) \quad P' = P[x := b_{[n]}]}{a(x).P \xrightarrow{a(b)[n]} a(b)[n].P'} \qquad \frac{\mathsf{std}(P)}{\overline{a}(b).P \xrightarrow{\overline{a}(b)[n]} \overline{a}(b)[n].P}$$

$$\frac{P \xrightarrow{\mu[m]} P' \quad m \neq n \quad \text{if } \mu = \overline{a}(x) \text{ then } x \notin n(\alpha)}{\alpha[n].P \xrightarrow{\mu[m]} \alpha[n].P'} \qquad \frac{P_0 \xrightarrow{\mu[n]} P_0' \quad \mathsf{std}(P_1)}{P_0 + P_1 \xrightarrow{\mu[n]} P_0' + P_1}$$

$$\frac{P_0 \xrightarrow{\mu[n]} P_0' \quad \mathsf{fsh}[n](P_1) \quad \text{if } \mu = \overline{a}(b) \text{ then } b \notin \mathsf{fn}(P_1)}{P_0|P_1 \xrightarrow{\mu[n]} P_0'|P_1} \qquad \frac{P_0 \xrightarrow{a(b)[n]} P_0' \quad P_1 \xrightarrow{\overline{a}(b)[n]} P_1'}{P_0|P_1 \xrightarrow{\tau[n]} (\nu b)(P_0'|P_1')}$$

$$\frac{P \xrightarrow{\mu[m]} P' \quad a \notin n(\mu)}{(\nu a)P \xrightarrow{\mu[m]} (\nu a)P'} \qquad \frac{P \equiv Q \xrightarrow{\mu[n]} Q' \equiv P'}{P \xrightarrow{\mu[n]} P'}$$

Table 4. πIK reverse semantics

$$\frac{\mathsf{std}(P) \quad x \notin n(P) \quad P' = P[b_{[m]} := x]}{a(b)[m].P \rightsquigarrow^{a(b)[m]} a(x).P'} \qquad \frac{\mathsf{std}(P)}{\overline{a}(b)[n].P \rightsquigarrow^{\overline{a}(b)[n]} \overline{a}(b).P}$$

$$\frac{P \rightsquigarrow^{\mu[m]} P' \quad m \neq n}{\alpha[n].P \rightsquigarrow^{\mu[m]} \alpha[n].P'} \qquad \frac{P_0 \rightsquigarrow^{\mu[n]} P_0' \quad \mathsf{std}(P_1)}{P_0 + P_1 \rightsquigarrow^{\mu[n]} P_0' + P_1}$$

$$\frac{P_0 \rightsquigarrow^{\mu[n]} P_0' \quad \mathsf{fsh}[n](P_1) \quad \text{if } \mu = \overline{a}(b) \text{ then } b \notin \mathsf{fn}(P_1)}{P_0|P_1 \rightsquigarrow^{\mu[n]} P_0'|P_1} \qquad \frac{P_0 \rightsquigarrow^{a(b)[n]} P_0' \quad P_1 \rightsquigarrow^{\overline{a}(b)[n]} P_1'}{(\nu b)(P_0|P_1) \rightsquigarrow^{\tau[n]} P_0'|P_1'}$$

$$\frac{P \rightsquigarrow^{\mu[m]} P' \quad a \notin n(\mu)}{(\nu a)P \rightsquigarrow^{\mu[m]} (\nu a)P'} \qquad \frac{P \equiv Q \rightsquigarrow^{\mu[n]} Q' \equiv P'}{P \rightsquigarrow^{\mu[n]} P'}$$

Table 3 shows the forward semantics of πIK. The reverse semantics can be seen in Table 4. We use α to range over input and output actions and μ over input, output, and τ. We use $\mathsf{std}(P)$ denote that P is a *standard process*, meaning it does not contain any past actions (actions annotated with a key), and $\mathsf{fsh}[n](P)$ to denote that a key n is fresh for P. Names in past actions are always free. Our semantics very much resemble those of CCSK, with the exceptions of substitution and ensuring that any name being output does not appear elsewhere in the process. The semantics use structural congruence as defined in Table 5.

Table 5. Structural congruence

$P \vert 0 \equiv P$	$P_0 \vert P_1 \equiv P_1 \vert P_0$	$P_0 \vert (P_1 \vert P_2) \equiv (P_0 \vert P_1) \vert P_2$
$P + 0 \equiv P$	$P_0 + P_1 \equiv P_1 + P_0$	$P_0 + (P_1 + P_2) \equiv (P_0 + P_1) + P_2$
$!P \equiv !P \vert P$	$(\nu x)(\nu y)P \equiv (\nu y)(\nu x)P$	$(\nu a)(P_0 \vert P_1) \equiv ((\nu a)P_0 \vert P_1)$ if $a \notin n(P_1)$

We again show a correspondence between forward and reverse transitions.

Proposition 3.1 (Loop).

1. *Given a process P, if $P \xrightarrow{\mu[n]} Q$ then $Q \overset{\mu[n]}{\rightsquigarrow} P$.*
2. *Given a forwards reachable process P, if $P \overset{\mu[n]}{\rightsquigarrow} Q$ then $Q \xrightarrow{\mu[n]} P$.*

4   Mapping from πIH to πIK

We will now define a mapping from πIH to πIK and show that we have an operational correspondence in Theorem 4.6. The extrusion histories store more information than the keys, as they keep track of which names were substituted, as illustrated by Example 4.1. This means we lose some information in our mapping, but not information we need.

Example 4.1. Consider the processes $(\emptyset, \{(a(b), [a(x)][0])\}, \emptyset) \vdash 0$ and $a(b)[n]$. These are the result of $a(x)$ receiving b in the two different semantics. We can see that the extrusion history remembers that the input name was x before b was received, but the keys do not remember, and when reversing the action could use any name as the input name. This does not make a great deal of difference, as after reversing $a(b)$, the process with the extrusion history can also α-convert x to any name.

Since we intend to define a mapping from processes with extrusion histories to processes with keys, we first describe how to add keys to substituted names in a process in Definition 4.2. We have a function, S, which takes a process, P_1, in which we wish to add the key $[n]$ to all those names which were x in a previous state of the process, P_2, before being substituted for some other name in an input action with the key $[n]$.

Definition 4.2 (Substituting in πIK-process to correspond with processes with extrusion histories). *Given a πIK process P_1, a πI-calculus process without keys, P_2, a key n, and a name x, we can add the key n to any names which x has been substituted with, by applying $S(P_1, P_2, [n], x)$, defined as:*

1. $S(0, 0, [n], x) = 0$

2. $S\left(\sum_{i \in I} P_{i1}, \sum_{i \in I} P_{i2}, [n], x\right) = \sum_{i \in I} S(P_{i1}, P_{i2}, [n], x)$

3. $S(P_1 | Q_1, P_2 | Q_2, [n], x) = S(P_1, P_2, [n], x) | S(Q_1, Q_2, [n], x)$

4. $S((\nu a)P_1, (\nu b)P_2, [n], x) = P_1'$ *where:*
   if $x = b$ then $P_1' = P_1$ and otherwise $P_1' = (\nu a)S(P_1, P_2, [n], x)$.

5. $S(\alpha_1.P_1, \alpha_2.P_2, [n], x) = \alpha_1'.P_1'$ *where:*
   if $\alpha_2 \in \{x(c), \overline{x}(c)\}$ then $\alpha_1' = \alpha_{1_{[n]}}$ and otherwise $\alpha_1' = \alpha_1$;
   if $\alpha_2 \in \{c(x), \overline{c}(x)\}$ then $P_1' = P_1$ and otherwise $P_1' = S(P_1, P_2, [n], x)$.

6. $S(\alpha_1[m].P_1, \alpha_2.P_2, [n], x) = \alpha_1'[m].P_1'$ *where:*
   if $\alpha_2 \in \{x(c), \overline{x}(c)\}$ then $\alpha_1' = \alpha_{1_{[n]}}$ and otherwise $\alpha_1' = \alpha_1$;
   if $\alpha_2 \in \{c(x), \overline{c}(x)\}$ then $P_1' = P_1$ and otherwise $P_1' = S(P_1, P_2, [n], x)$.

7. $S(!P_1, !P_2, [n], x) = !S(P_1, P_2, [n], x)$

8. $S(P_1 | P_1', !P_2, [n], x) = S(P_1, !P_2, [n], x) | S(P_1', P_2, [n], x)$

9. $S(!P_1, P_2 | P_2', [n], x) = S(!P_1, P_2, [n], x) | S(P_1, P_2', [n], x)$

where $a(b)_{[n]} = a_{[n]}(b)$ and $\overline{a}(b)_{[n]} = \overline{a}_{[n]}(b)$

Being able to annotate our names with keys, we can define a mapping, E, from extrusion histories to keys in Definition 4.4. E iterates over the extrusions, having one process which builds πIK-process, and another that keeps track of which state of the original πIH process has been reached. When turning an extrusion into a keyed action, we use the locations as key and also give each extrusion an extra copy of its location to use for determining where the action came from. This way we can use one copy to iteratively go through the process, removing splits from the path as we go through them, while still having another intact copy of the location to use as the final key. In $E(\mathbf{H} \vdash P, P')$, $\mathbf{H}$ is a history of extrusions which need to be turned into keyed actions, P is the process these keyed actions should be added to, and P' is the state the process would have reached, had the added extrusions been reversed instead of turned into keyed actions.

If E encounters a parallel composition in P (case 2), it splits its extrusion histories in three. One part, $\mathbf{H}_{\mathsf{shared}}$ contains the locations which have an empty path, and therefore belong to actions from before the processes split. Another part contains the locations beginning with 0, and goes to the first part of the process. And finally the third part contains the locations beginning with 1, and goes to the second part of the process.

E can add an action – and the choices not picked when that action was performed – to P (cases 3, 4) when the associated location has an empty path and has P' as its result process. When turning an input memory from the history into a past input action in the process (case 4), we use S (Definition 4.2) to add keys to the substituted names. When E encounters a restriction (case 5), it moves a memory that can be used inside the restriction inside. It does this iteratively until there are no such memories left in the extrusion histories. We apply E to a process in Example 4.5.

Definition 4.3. *The function* lcopy *gives each member of an extrusion history an extra copy of its location:*

$$\text{lcopy}(H^*) = \{(\mu, u, u) \mid (\mu, u) \in H^*\}$$
$$\text{lcopy}(\overline{H}, \underline{H}, H) = (\text{lcopy}(\overline{H}), \text{lcopy}(\underline{H}), \text{lcopy}(H))$$

Definition 4.4. *Given a* πIH *process,* $\mathbf{H} \vdash P$, *we can create an equivalent* πIK *process,* $E(\text{lcopy}(\mathbf{H}) \vdash P, P) = P'$ *defined as*

1. $E((\emptyset, \emptyset, \emptyset) \vdash P, P') = P$
2. $E(\mathbf{H} \vdash P_0 | P_1, P_0' | P_1') = E(\mathbf{H}_{\text{shared}} \vdash P_0'' | P_1'', P_0''' | P_1''')$ where:

   $\mathbf{H}_{\text{shared}} = (\{(\alpha, u, u') \mid (\alpha, u, u') \in \overline{H} \text{ and } u \neq iu''\}, \{(\alpha, u, u') \mid (\alpha, u, u') \in \underline{H} \text{and } u \neq iu''\}, \emptyset)$

   $P_0'' = E((\overline{H_0}, \underline{H_0}, H_0) \vdash P_0, P_0')$ where:

   $\overline{H_0} = \{(\overline{a}(b), u_0, u_0') \mid (\overline{a}(b), 0u_0, u_0') \in \overline{H} \text{ or } (\overline{a}(b), \alpha_1, \langle 0u_0, 1u_1 \rangle, u_0') \in H\}$

   $\underline{H_0} = \{(a(b), u_0, u_0') \mid (a(b), 0u_0, u_0') \in \underline{H} \text{ or } (a(b), \alpha_1, \langle 0u_0, 1u_1 \rangle, u_0') \in H\}$

   $H_0 = \{(\alpha, \alpha', u, u') \mid (\alpha, \alpha', 0u, u') \in H\}$

   $P_1'' = E((\overline{H_1}, \underline{H_1}, H_1) \vdash P_1, P_1'))$ where:

   $\overline{H_1} = \{(\overline{a}(b), u_1, u_1') \mid (\overline{a}(b), 1u_1, u_1') \in \overline{H} \text{ or } (\alpha_0, \overline{a}(b), \langle 0u_0, 1u_1 \rangle, u_1') \in H\}$

   $\underline{H_1} = \{(a(b), u_1, u_1') \mid (a(b), 1u_1, u_1') \in \underline{H} \text{ or } (\alpha_0, a(b), \langle 0u_0, 1u_1 \rangle, u_1') \in H\}$

   $H_1 = \{(\alpha, \alpha', u, u') \mid (\alpha, \alpha', 1u, u') \in H\}$

   $\mathbf{H_i} \vdash P_i' \xrightarrow[u_{i,0}]{\alpha_{i,0}} \cdots \xrightarrow[u_{i,n}]{\alpha_{i,n}} (\emptyset, \emptyset, \emptyset) \vdash P_i'''$ for $i \in \{0, 1\}$

3. $E((\overline{H} \cup \{(\overline{a}(b), [Q][P'], u)\}, \underline{H}, H) \vdash P, P') = E(\mathbf{H} \vdash \overline{a}(b)[u].P + \sum_{i \in I \setminus \{j\}} \alpha_i.P_i, Q)$

   $if Q = \sum_{i \in I} \alpha_i.P_i, \overline{a}(b) = \alpha_j$, and $P' = P_j$
4. $E((\overline{H}, \underline{H} \cup \{(a(b), [Q][P'], u)\}, H) \vdash P, P') =$
   $$E(\mathbf{H} \vdash a(b)[u].S(P, P_j, [u], x) + \sum_{i \in I \setminus \{j\}} \alpha_i.P_i, Q)$$

   $if Q = \sum_{i \in I} \alpha_i.P_i, a(x) = \alpha_j$, and $P' = P_j[x := b]$
5. $E(\mathbf{H} \vdash (\nu x)P, (\nu x)P') = E(\mathbf{H} - (\alpha, u, u') \vdash P'', (\nu x)Q')$
   $where P'' = (\nu x)E((\emptyset, \emptyset, \emptyset) + (\alpha, u, u') \vdash P, P')$

   $if (\alpha, u, u') \in \overline{H} \cup \underline{H} \text{ and } (\emptyset, \emptyset, \emptyset) + (\alpha, u, u) \vdash P \xrightarrow[u]{\alpha} (\emptyset, \emptyset, \emptyset) \vdash Q'$
6. $E(\mathbf{H} \vdash P, !P') = E(\mathbf{H} \vdash P | P, !P' | P')$ if there exists $(\alpha, u, u') \in \overline{H} \cup \underline{H} \cup H$ such that $u \neq [Q][Q']$.

Example 4.5. We will now apply E to the process

$$(\{(\overline{b}(c), u_2)\}, \emptyset, \{(b(a), \overline{b}(a), \langle 0u_0, 1u_1 \rangle)\}) \vdash a(x) \mid 0$$

with locations $u_0 = [b(y).y(x)][a(x)]$, $u_1 = [\overline{b}(a)][0]$, and $u_2 = [\overline{b}(c).(b(y).y(x) \mid \overline{b}(a)][b(y).y(x) \mid \overline{b}(a)]$. We perform

$$E(\mathsf{lcopy}((\{(\overline{b}(c), u_2)\}, \emptyset, \{(b(a), \overline{b}(a), \langle 0u_0, 1u_1 \rangle)\})) \vdash a(x) \mid 0, a(x) \mid 0)$$

Since we are at a parallel, we use Case 2 of Definition 4.4 to split the extrusion histories into three to get $E((\{(\overline{b}(c), u_2, u_2)\}, \emptyset, \emptyset) \vdash P_0 \mid P_1, b(y).y(x) \mid \overline{b}(a))$ where $P_0 = E((\emptyset, \{(b(a), u_0, \langle 0u_0, 1u_1 \rangle)\}, \emptyset) \vdash a(x), a(x))$ and $P_1 = E((\{(\overline{b}(a), u_1, \langle 0u_0, 1u_1 \rangle)\}, \emptyset, \emptyset) \vdash 0, 0)$.
To find P_0, we look at u_0, and find that it has $a(x)$ as its result, meaning we can apply Case 4 to obtain $E((\emptyset, \emptyset, \emptyset) \vdash b(a)[\langle 0u_0, 1u_1 \rangle].S(a(x), y(x), [\langle 0u_0, 1u_1 \rangle], y), b(y).y(x))$. And by applying Case 5 of Definition 4.2, $S(a(x), y(x), [\langle 0u_0, 1u_1 \rangle], y) = a_{[\langle 0u_0, 1u_1 \rangle]}(x)$. Since we have no more extrusions to add, we apply Case 1 to get our process $P_0 = b(a)[\langle 0u_0, 1u_1 \rangle].a_{[\langle 0u_0, 1u_1 \rangle]}(x)$.
To find P_1, we similarly look at u_1 and find that we can apply Case 3. This gives us $P_1 = \overline{b}(a)[\langle 0u_0, 1u_1 \rangle].0$.
We can then apply Case 3 to $E((\{(\overline{b}(c), u_2, u_2)\}, \emptyset, \emptyset) \vdash P_0 \mid P_1, b(y).y(x) \mid \overline{b}(a))$. This gives us our final process,

$$\overline{b}(c)[k'].b(a)[k].a_{[k]}(x) \mid \overline{b}(a)[k].0$$

where $k = \langle 0u_0, 1u_1 \rangle$ and $k' = u_2$

We can then show, in Theorem 4.6, that we have an operational correspondence between our two calculi and E preserves transitions. Item 1 states that every transition in πIH corresponds to one in πIK process generated by E, and Item 2 vice versa.

Theorem 4.6. *Given a reachable πIH process, $\mathbf{H} \vdash P$, and an action, μ,*

1. *if there exists a location u such that $\mathbf{H} \vdash P \xrightarrow{\mu}_u \mathbf{H}' \vdash P'$ then there exists a*

   key, m, such that $E(\mathsf{lcopy}(\mathbf{H}) \vdash P, P) \xrightarrow{\mu[m]} E(\mathsf{lcopy}(\mathbf{H}') \vdash P', P')$;

2. *if there exists a key, m, such that $E(\mathsf{lcopy}(\mathbf{H}) \vdash P, P) \xrightarrow{\mu[m]} P''$, then there*

   exists a location, u, and a πIH process, $\mathbf{H}' \vdash P'$, such that $\mathbf{H} \vdash P \xrightarrow{\mu}_u \mathbf{H}' \vdash P'$ and $P'' \equiv E(\mathsf{lcopy}(\mathbf{H}') \vdash P', P')$.

5   Bundle Event Structures

In this section we will recall the definition of *labelled reversible bundle event structures* (LRBESs), which we intend to use later to define the event structure semantics of πIK and through that πIH. We also describe some operations on

LRBESs, which our semantics will make use of. This section is primarily a review of definitions from [10]. We use bundle event structures, rather than the more common prime event structures, because LRBESs yield more compact event structures with fewer events and simplifies parallel composition.

An LRBES consists of a set of events, E, a subset of which, F, are reversible, and three relations on them. The bundle relation, $\mapsto$, says that if $X \mapsto e$ then one of the events of X must have happened before e can and all events in X are in conflict with each other. The conflict relation, $\sharp$, says that if $e \sharp e'$ then e and e' cannot occur in the same configuration. The prevention relation, $\rhd$, says that if $e \rhd \underline{e'}$ then e' cannot reverse after e has happened. Since the event structure is labelled, we also have a set of labels Act, and a labelling function λ from events to labels. We use $\underline{e}$ to denote e being reversed, and e^* to denote either e or $\underline{e}$.

Definition 5.1 (Labelled Reversible Bundle Event Structure [10]). *A labelled reversible bundle event structure is a 7-tuple $\mathcal{E} = (E, F, \mapsto, \sharp, \rhd, \lambda, \mathsf{Act})$ where:*

1. *E is the set of events;*
2. *$F \subseteq E$ is the set of reversible events;*
3. *the bundle set, $\mapsto \subseteq 2^E \times (E \cup \underline{F})$, satisfies $X \mapsto e^* \Rightarrow \forall e_1, e_2 \in X.e_1 \neq e_2 \Rightarrow e_1 \sharp e_2$ and for all $e \in F$, $\{e\} \mapsto \underline{e}$;*
4. *the conflict relation, $\sharp \subseteq E \times E$, is symmetric and irreflexive;*
5. *$\rhd \subseteq E \times \underline{F}$ is the prevention relation.*
6. *$\lambda : E \to \mathsf{Act}$ is a labelling function.*

An event in an LRBES can have multiple possible causes as defined in Definition 5.2. A possible cause X of an event e is a conflict-free set of events which contains a member of each bundle associated with e and contains possible causes of all events in X.

Definition 5.2 (Possible Cause). *Given an LRBES, $\mathcal{E} = (E, F, \mapsto, \sharp, \rhd, \lambda, \mathsf{Act})$ and an event $e \in E$, $X \subseteq E$ is a possible cause of e if*

- *$e \notin X$, X is finite, whenever $X' \mapsto e$ we have $X' \cap X \neq \emptyset$;*
- *for any $e', e'' \in \{e\} \cup X$, we have $e' \not\sharp e''$ ($X \cup \{e\}$ is conflict-free);*
- *for all $e' \in X$, there exists $X'' \subseteq X$, such that X'' is a possible cause of e';*
- *there does not exist any $X''' \subset X$, such that X''' is a possible cause of e.*

Since we want to compare the event structures generated by a process to the operational semantics, we need a notion of transitions on event structures. For this purpose we use configuration systems (CSs), which event structures can be translated into.

Definition 5.3 (Configuration system [23]). *A configuration system (CS) is a quadruple $\mathcal{C} = (E, F, \mathsf{C}, \to)$ where E is a set of events, $F \subseteq E$ is a set of reversible events, $\mathsf{C} \subseteq 2^E$ is the set of configurations, and $\to \subseteq \mathsf{C} \times 2^{E \cup \underline{F}} \times \mathsf{C}$ is a labelled transition relation such that if $X \xrightarrow{A \cup \underline{B}} Y$ then:*

- *$X, Y \in \mathsf{C}$, $A \cap X = \emptyset$; $B \subseteq X \cap F$; and $Y = (X \setminus B) \cup A$;*

– for all $A' \subseteq A$ and $B' \subseteq B$, we have $X \xrightarrow{A' \cup B'} Z \xrightarrow{(A \setminus A') \cup (B \setminus B')} Y$, meaning $Z = (X \setminus B') \cup A' \in \mathsf{C}$.

Definition 5.4 (From LRBES to CS [10]). *We define a mapping C_{br} from LRBESs to CSs as: $C_{br}((E, F, \mapsto, \sharp, \rhd, \lambda, \mathsf{Act})) = (E, F, \mathsf{C}, \rightarrow)$ where:*

1. $X \in \mathsf{C}$ *if X is conflict-free;*
2. *For $X, Y \in \mathsf{C}$, $A \subseteq E$, and $B \subseteq F$, there exists a transition $X \xrightarrow{A \cup B} Y$ if:*
   (a) $Y = (X \setminus B) \cup A$; $X \cap A = \emptyset$; $B \subseteq X$; *and $X \cup A$ conflict-free;*
   (b) *for all $e \in B$, if $e' \rhd \underline{e}$ then $e' \notin X \cup A$;*
   (c) *for all $e \in A$ and $X' \subseteq E$, if $X' \mapsto e$ then $X' \cap (X \setminus B) \neq \emptyset$;*
   (d) *for all $e \in B$ and $X' \subseteq E$, if $X' \mapsto \underline{e}$ then $X' \cap (X \setminus (B \setminus \{e\})) \neq \emptyset$.*

For our semantics we need to define a prefix, restriction, parallel composition, and choice. Causal prefixing takes a label, μ, an event, e, and an LRBES, $\mathcal{E}$, and adds e to $\mathcal{E}$ with the label μ and associating every other event in $\mathcal{E}$ with a bundle containing only e. Restriction removes a set of events from an LRBES.

Definition 5.5 (Causal Prefixes [10]). *Given an LRBES $\mathcal{E}$, a label μ, and an event e, $(\mu)(e).\mathcal{E} = (E', F', \mapsto', \sharp', \rhd', \lambda', \mathsf{Act}')$ where:*

1. $E' = E \cup e$
2. $F' = F \cup e$
3. $\mapsto' = \mapsto \cup (\{\{e\}\} \times (E \cup \{\underline{e}\}))$
4. $\sharp' = \sharp$
5. $\rhd' = \rhd \cup (E \times \{\underline{e}\})$
6. $\lambda' = \lambda[e \mapsto \mu]$
7. $\mathsf{Act}' = \mathsf{Act} \cup \{\mu\}$

Removing a set of labels L from an LRBES removes not just events with labels in A but also events dependent on events with labels in L.

Definition 5.6 (Removing labels and their dependants). *Given an event structure $\mathcal{E} = (E, F, \mapsto, \sharp, \rhd, \lambda, \mathsf{Act})$ and a set of labels $L \subseteq \mathsf{Act}$, we define $\rho_{\mathcal{E}}(L) = X$ as the maximum subset of E such that*

1. *if $e \in X$ then $\lambda(e) \notin L$;*
2. *if $e \in X$ then there exists a possible cause of e, x, such that $x \subseteq X$.*

A choice between LRBESs puts all the events of one event structure in conflict with the events of the others.

Definition 5.7 (Choice [10]). *Given LRBESs $\mathcal{E}_0, \mathcal{E}_1, \ldots, \mathcal{E}_n$, the choice between them is $\sum_{0 \leq i \leq n} \mathcal{E}_i = (E, F, \mapsto, \sharp, \rhd, \lambda, \mathsf{Act})$ where:*

1. $E = \bigcup_{0 \leq i \leq n} \{i\} \times E_i$
2. $F = \bigcup_{0 \leq i \leq n} \{i\} \times F_i$
3. $X \mapsto e^*$ *if $e = (i, e_i)$, $X_i \mapsto_i e_i^*$, and $X = \{i\} \times X_i$*
4. $(i, e) \sharp (j, e')$ *if $i \neq j$ or $e \sharp_i e'$*
5. $(i, e) \rhd (j, e')$ *if $i \neq j$ or $e \sharp_i e'$*
6. $\lambda(j, e) = \lambda_j(e)$
7. $\mathsf{Act} = \bigcup_{0 \leq i \leq n} \mathsf{Act}_i$

Definition 5.8 (Restriction [10]). *Given an LRBES, $\mathcal{E} = (E, F, \mapsto, \sharp, \rhd, \lambda, \mathsf{Act})$, restricting $\mathcal{E}$ to $E' \subseteq E$ creates $\mathcal{E} \restriction E' = (E', F', \mapsto', \sharp', \rhd', \lambda', \mathsf{Act}')$ where:*

1. $F' = F \cap E'$;
2. $\mapsto' = \mapsto \cap (\mathcal{P}(E') \times (E' \cup \underline{F'}))$;
3. $\sharp' = \sharp \cap (E' \times E')$;

4. $\rhd' = \rhd \cap (E' \times \underline{F'})$;
5. $\lambda' = \lambda \restriction_{E'}$;
6. $\mathsf{Act} = \mathsf{ran}(\lambda')$.

For parallel composition we construct a product of event structures, which consists of events corresponding to synchronisations between the two event structures. The possible causes of an event (e_0, e_1) contain a possible cause of e_0 and a possible cause of e_1.

Definition 5.9 (Parallel [10]). *Given two LRBESs $\mathcal{E}_0 = (E_0, F_0, \mapsto_0, \sharp_0, \rhd_0, \lambda_0, \mathsf{Act}_0)$ and $\mathcal{E}_1 = (E_1, F_1, \mapsto_1, \sharp_1, \rhd_1, \lambda_1, \mathsf{Act}_1)$, their parallel composition $\mathcal{E}_0 \times \mathcal{E}_1 = (E, F, \mapsto, \sharp, \rhd, \lambda, \mathsf{Act})$ with projections π_0 and π_1 where:*

1. *$E = E_0 \times_* E_1 = \{(e, *) \mid e \in E_0\} \cup \{(*, e) \mid e \in E_1\} \cup \{(e, e') \mid e \in E_0 \text{ and } e' \in E_1\}$;*
2. *$F = F_0 \times_* F_1 = \{(e, *) \mid e \in F_0\} \cup \{(*, e) \mid e \in F_1\} \cup \{(e, e') \mid e \in F_0 \text{ and } e' \in F_1\}$;*
3. *for $i \in \{0, 1\}$ we have $(e_0, e_1) \in E$, $\pi_i((e_0, e_1)) = e_i$;*
4. *for any $e^* \in E \cup \underline{F}$, $X \subseteq E$, $X \mapsto e^*$ iff there exists $i \in \{0, 1\}$ and $X_i \subseteq E_i$ such that $X_i \mapsto \pi_i(e)^*$ and $X = \{e' \in E \mid \pi_i(e') \in X_i\}$;*
5. *for any $e, e' \in E$, $e \sharp e'$ iff there exists $i \in \{0, 1\}$ such that $\pi_i(e) \sharp_i \pi_i(e')$, or $\pi_i(e) = \pi_i(e') \neq \bot$ and $\pi_{1-i}(e) \neq \pi_{1-i}(e')$;*
6. *for any $e \in E$, $e' \in F$, $e \rhd \underline{e'}$ iff there exists $i \in \{0, 1\}$ such that $\pi_i(e) \rhd_i \pi_i(e')$.*

7. $\lambda(e) = \begin{cases} \lambda_0(e_0) & \text{if } e = (e_0, *) \\ \lambda_1(e_1) & \text{if } e = (*, e_1) \\ \tau & \text{if } e = (e_0, e_1) \text{ and either } \lambda_0(e_0) = a(x) \text{ and } \lambda_1(e_1) = \bar{a}(x) \\ & \text{or } \lambda_0(e_0) = \bar{a}(x) \text{ and } \lambda_1(e_1) = a(x) \\ 0 & \text{otherwise} \end{cases}$

8. $\mathsf{Act} = \{\tau\} \cup \mathsf{Act}_0 \cup \mathsf{Act}_1$

6   Event Structure Semantics of πIK

In this section we define event structure semantics of πIK using the LRBESs and operations defined in Sect. 5. Theorems 6.3 and 6.4 give us an operational correspondence between a πIK process and the generated event structure. Together with Theorem 4.6, this gives us a correspondence between a πIH process and the event structure it generates by going via a πIK process.

As we want to ensure that all free and bound names in our process are distinct, we modify our syntax for replication, assigning each replication an infinite set, $\mathbf{x}$, of names to substitute into the place of bound names in each created copy of the process, so that

$$!_{\mathbf{x}} P \equiv {!}_{\mathbf{x} \setminus \{x_0, \ldots, x_k\}} P | P\{^{x_0, \ldots, x_k}/_{a_0, \ldots, a_k}\} \text{ if } \{x_0, \ldots, x_k\} \subseteq \mathbf{x}$$

$$\text{and } \mathsf{bn}(P) = \{a_0, \ldots, a_k\}$$

Before proceeding to the semantics we also define the standard bound names of a process P, $\mathsf{sbn}(P)$, meaning the names that would be bound in P if every action was reversed, in Definition 6.1.

Definition 6.1. *The standard bound names of a process* P, $\mathsf{sbn}(P)$, *are defined as:*

$$\mathsf{sbn}(a(x).P') = \{x\} \cup \mathsf{sbn}(P') \qquad \mathsf{sbn}(a(x)[m].P') = \{x\} \cup \mathsf{sbn}(P')$$
$$\mathsf{sbn}(\overline{a}(x).P') = \{x\} \cup \mathsf{sbn}(P') \qquad \mathsf{sbn}(\overline{a}(x)[m].P') = \{x\} \cup \mathsf{sbn}(P')$$
$$\mathsf{sbn}(P_0|P_1) = \mathsf{sbn}(P_0) \cup \mathsf{sbn}(P_1) \qquad \mathsf{sbn}(P_0 + P_1) = \mathsf{sbn}(P_0) \cup \mathsf{sbn}(P_1)$$
$$\mathsf{sbn}(\nu x)P' = \{x\} \cup \mathsf{sbn}(P') \qquad \mathsf{sbn}(!_{\mathsf{x}}P) = \mathbf{x}$$

We can now define the event structure semantics in Table 6. We do this using rules of the form $\{\!| P |\!\}_{(\mathcal{N},l)} = \langle \mathcal{E}, \mathsf{Init}, k \rangle$ where l is the level of unfolding of replication, $\mathcal{E}$ is an LRBES, Init is the initial configuration, $\mathcal{N} \supseteq n(P)$ is a set of names, which any input in the process could receive, and $k : \mathsf{Init} \to \mathcal{K}$ is a function assigning communication keys to the past actions, which we use in parallel composition to determine which synchronisations of past actions to put in Init. We define $\{\!| P |\!\}_{\mathcal{N}} = \sup_{l \in \mathbb{N}} \{\!| P |\!\}_{(\mathcal{N},l)}$.

The denotational semantics in Table 6 make use of the LRBES operators defined in Sect. 5. The choice and output cases are straightforward uses of the choice and causal prefix operators. The input creates a case for prefixing an input of each name in $\mathcal{N}$ and a choice between the cases. We have two cases for restriction, one for restriction originating from a past communication and another for restriction originating from the original process. If the restriction does not originate from the original process, then we ignore it, otherwise we remove events which would use the restricted channel and their causes. The parallel composition uses the parallel operator, but additionally needs to consider link causation caused by the early semantics. Each event labelled with an input of a name in standard bound names gets a bundle consisting of the event labelled with the output on that name. And each output event is prevented from reversing by the input names receiving that name. This way, inputs on extruded names are caused by the output that made the name free. Replication substitutes the names and counts down the level of replication.

Note that the only difference between a future and a past action is that the event corresponding to a past action is put in the initial state and given a communication key.

Example 6.2. Consider the process $a(b)[n] \mid \overline{a}(b)[n]$. Our event structure semantics generate an LRBES $\{\!| a(x)[n] \mid \overline{a}(b[n]) |\!\}_{\{a,b,x\}} = \langle (E, F, \mapsto, \sharp, \rhd, \lambda, \mathsf{Act}), \mathsf{Init}, k \rangle$ where:

$$E = F = \{a(b), a(a), a(x), \overline{a}(b), \tau\} \qquad \lambda(e) = e$$
$$\{\overline{a}(b)\} \mapsto a(b) \qquad\qquad\qquad \mathsf{Act} = \{a(b), a(a), a(x), \overline{a}(b), \tau\}$$
$$a(b) \sharp a(a), \ a(b) \sharp a(x), \ a(a) \sharp a(x), \qquad \mathsf{Init} = \{\tau\}$$
$$a(b) \sharp \tau, \ a(a) \sharp \tau, \ a(x) \sharp \tau, \ \overline{a}(b) \sharp \tau \qquad k(\tau) = n$$
$$a(b) \rhd \overline{a}(b)$$

From this we see that (1) receiving b is causally dependent on sending b, (2) all the possible inputs on a are in conflict with one another, (3) the synchronisation between the input and the output is in conflict with either happening on their own, and (4) since the two past actions have the same key, the initial state contains their synchronisation.

Table 6. Denotational event structure semantics of πIK

$\{\![0]\!\}_{(\mathcal{N},l)} = \quad \langle(\emptyset,\emptyset,\emptyset,\emptyset,\emptyset,\emptyset,\emptyset),\emptyset,\emptyset\rangle$

$\{\![P_0 + P_1]\!\}_{(\mathcal{N},l)} = \quad \langle\mathcal{E}_0 + \mathcal{E}_1, \{0\}\times\mathsf{Init}_0 \cup \{1\}\times\mathsf{Init}_1, k((i,e)) = k_i(e)\rangle$ where
$\quad\quad \{\![P_i]\!\} = \langle\mathcal{E}_i,\mathsf{Init}_i,k_i\rangle$ for $i\in\{0,1\}$

$\{\![\overline{a}(n).P]\!\}_{(\mathcal{N},l)} = \quad \langle\overline{a}(n)(e).\mathcal{E}_P,\mathsf{Init}_P,k_P\rangle$ for some fresh $e\notin E$ where
$\quad\quad \{\![P]\!\}_{(\mathcal{N},l)} = \langle\mathcal{E}_P,\mathsf{Init}_P,k_P\rangle$

$\{\![a(x).P]\!\}_{(\mathcal{N},l)} = \quad \Big\langle\sum_{n\in(\mathcal{N}\backslash\mathsf{sbn}(P))} a(n)(e).\mathcal{E}_{P_n}, \bigcup_{n\in(\mathcal{N}\backslash\mathsf{sbn}(P))}\{n\}\times\mathsf{Init}_{P_n}, (n,e)\mapsto k_{P_n}(e)\Big\rangle$
$\quad\quad$ for some fresh $e_n\notin E_n$ where
$\quad\quad \{\![P[x:=n]]\!\}_{(\mathcal{N},l)} = \langle\mathcal{E}_{P_n},\mathsf{Init}_{P_n},k_{P_n}\rangle$

$\{\![\overline{a}(n)[m].P]\!\}_{(\mathcal{N},l)} = \quad \langle\overline{a}(n)(e).\mathcal{E}_P,\mathsf{Init}_P\cup\{e\},k_P[e\mapsto m]\rangle$ for some fresh $e\notin E$ where
$\quad\quad \{\![P]\!\}_{(\mathcal{N},l)} = \langle\mathcal{E}_P,\mathsf{Init}_P,k_P\rangle$

$\{\![a(b)[m].P]\!\}_{(\mathcal{N},l)} = \quad \Big\langle\sum_{n\in(\mathcal{N}\backslash\mathsf{sbn}(P))} a(n)(e_n).\mathcal{E}_{P_n}, \big(\bigcup_{n\in(\mathcal{N}\backslash\mathsf{sbn}(P))}\{n\}\times\mathsf{Init}_{P_n}\big)\cup\{(b,e_b)\}, k\Big\rangle$
$\quad\quad$ for some fresh $e_n\notin E_n$ where
$\quad\quad \{\![P[b_{[m]}:=n]]\!\}_{(\mathcal{N},l)} = \langle\mathcal{E}_{P_n},\mathsf{Init}_{P_n},k_{P_n}\rangle$
$\quad\quad k((n,e)) = \begin{cases} m & \text{if } e=e_b \text{ and } n=b \\ k_{P_n}(e) & \text{otherwise} \end{cases}$

$\{\![(\nu a)P]\!\}_{(\mathcal{N},l)} = \quad \langle\mathcal{E}\restriction E_\alpha,\mathsf{Init}\cap E_\alpha,k\restriction E_\alpha\rangle$ where:
$\quad\quad \{\![P]\!\}_{(\mathcal{N},l)} = \langle\mathcal{E},\mathsf{Init},k\rangle$
$\quad\quad E_\alpha = \rho(\{\alpha\mid a\in n(\alpha)\})$
$\quad\quad$ if whenever there exist past actions $b(a)[m]$ and $\overline{b}(a)[m]$ in P then
$\quad\quad$ they are guarded by a restriction (νa) in P

$\{\![(\nu a)P]\!\}_{(\mathcal{N},l)} = \quad \langle\mathcal{E},\mathsf{Init},k\rangle$ where:
$\quad\quad \{\![P]\!\}_{(\mathcal{N},l)} = \langle\mathcal{E},\mathsf{Init},k\rangle$
$\quad\quad$ if there exist past actions $b(a)[m]$ and $\overline{b}(a)[m]$ in P which
$\quad\quad$ are not guarded by a restriction (νa) in P

$\{\![P_0|P_1]\!\}_{(\mathcal{N},l)} = \quad \langle(E,F,\mapsto,\sharp,\rhd,\lambda,\mathsf{Act})\restriction\{e\mid\lambda(e)\neq 0\},\mathsf{Init},k\rangle$ where
$\quad\quad$ for $i\in\{0,1\}$, $\{\![P_i]\!\}_l = \langle\mathcal{E}_i,\mathsf{Init}_i,k_i\rangle$
$\quad\quad (E_0,F_0,\mapsto_0,\sharp_0,\rhd_0)\times(E_0,F_0,\mapsto_0,\sharp_0,\rhd_0) = (E,F,\mapsto',\sharp,\rhd')$
$\quad\quad \mathsf{Init} = \{(e_0,*)\mid e_0\in\mathsf{Init}_0 \text{ and } \nexists e_1\in\mathsf{Init}_1.k_1(e_1)=k_0(e_0)\}\cup$
$\quad\quad \{(*,e_1)\mid e_1\in\mathsf{Init}_1 \text{ and } \nexists e_0\in\mathsf{Init}_0.k_1(e_1)=k_0(e_0)\}\cup$
$\quad\quad \{(e_0,e_1)\mid e_0\in\mathsf{Init}_0 \text{ and } e_1\in\mathsf{Init}_1 \text{ and } k_1(e_1)=k_0(e_0)\}$
$\quad\quad X\mapsto e$ if $X\mapsto' e$ or there exists $x\in\mathsf{no}(\lambda(e))$ such that
$\quad\quad X = \{e'\mid\exists a.\lambda(e')=\overline{a}(x)\}$ and $x\in\mathsf{sbn}(P)$
$\quad\quad e\rhd\underline{e'}$ if either $e\rhd'\underline{e'}$ or there exists $x\in\mathsf{no}(\lambda(e))$ and a such that $\lambda(e')=\overline{a}(x)$
$\quad\quad k(e) = \begin{cases} k_0(e_0) & \text{if } e=(e_0,*) \\ k_1(e_1) & \text{if } e=(*,e_1) \\ k_0(e_0) & \text{if } e=(e_0,e_1) \end{cases}$

$\{\![!_{\mathbf{x}}P]\!\}_{(\mathcal{N},0)} = \quad \langle(\emptyset,\emptyset,\emptyset,\emptyset,\emptyset,\emptyset,\emptyset),\emptyset,\emptyset\rangle$

$\{\![!_{\mathbf{x}}P]\!\}_{(\mathcal{N},l)} = \quad \{\![!_{\mathbf{x}\backslash\{x_0,\dots,x_k\}}P\mid P\{^{x_0,\dots,x_k}/_{a_0,\dots,a_k}\}]\!\}_{(\mathcal{N},l-1)}$ if $\{x_0,\dots,x_k\}\subseteq\mathbf{x}$
$\quad\quad$ and $\mathsf{bn}(P) = \{a_0,\dots,a_k\}$

We show in Theorems 6.3 and 6.4 that given a process P with a conflict-free initial state, including any reachable process, performing a transition $P\xrightarrow{\mu[m]}P'$ does not affect the event structure, as $\{\![P]\!\}_\mathcal{N}$ and $\{\![P']\!\}_\mathcal{N}$ are isomorphic. It also means we have an event e labelled μ such that e is available in P's initial state, and P''s initial state is P's initial state with e added. A similar event can be removed to correspond to a reverse action.

Theorem 6.3. *Let P be a forwards reachable process wherein all bound and free names are different and let $\mathcal{N} \supseteq n(P)$ be a set of names. If (1) $\{\!\lfloor P \rfloor\!\}_{\mathcal{N}} = \langle \mathcal{E}, \mathsf{Init}, k \rangle$ where $\mathcal{E} = (E, F, \mapsto, \sharp, \rhd, \lambda, \mathsf{Act})$, and Init is conflict-free, and (2) there exists a transition $P \xrightarrow{\mu[m]} P'$ such that $\{\!\lfloor P' \rfloor\!\}_{\mathcal{N}} = \langle \mathcal{E}', \mathsf{Init}', k' \rangle$, then there exists an isomorphism $f : \mathcal{E} \to \mathcal{E}'$ and a transition in $C_{br}(\mathcal{E})$, $\mathsf{Init} \xrightarrow{\{e\}} X$, such that $\lambda(e) = \mu$, $f \circ k' = k[e \mapsto m]$, and $f(X) = \mathsf{Init}'$.*

Theorem 6.4. *Let P be a forwards reachable process wherein all bound and free names are different and let $\mathcal{N} \supseteq n(P)$ be a set of names. If (1) $\{\!\lfloor P \rfloor\!\}_{\mathcal{N}} = \langle \mathcal{E}, \mathsf{Init}, k \rangle$ where $\mathcal{E} = (E, F, \mapsto, \sharp, \rhd, \lambda, \mathsf{Act})$, and (2) there exists a transition $\mathsf{Init} \xrightarrow{\{e\}} X$ in $C_{br}(\mathcal{E})$, then there exists a transition $P \xrightarrow{\mu[m]} P'$ such that $\{\!\lfloor P' \rfloor\!\}_{\mathcal{N}} = \langle \mathcal{E}', \mathsf{Init}', k' \rangle$ and an isomorphism $f : \mathcal{E} \to \mathcal{E}'$ such that $\lambda(e) = \mu$, $f \circ k' = k[e \mapsto m]$, and $f(X) = \mathsf{Init}'$.*

By Theorems 4.6, 6.3, and 6.4 we can combine the event structure semantics of πIK and mapping E (Definition 4.4) and get an operational correspondence between $\mathbf{H} \vdash P$ and the event structure $\{\!\lfloor E(\mathsf{lcopy}(\mathbf{H}) \vdash P, P) \rfloor\!\}_{n(E(\mathsf{lcopy}(\mathbf{H}) \vdash P, P))}$.

7   Conclusion and Future Work

All existing reversible versions of the π-calculus use reduction semantics [14,26] or late semantics [7,17], despite the early semantics being used more widely than the late in the forward-only setting. We have introduced πIH, the first reversible early π-calculus. It is a reversible form of the *internal* π-calculus, where names being sent in output actions are always bound. As well as structural causation, as in CCS, the early form of the internal π-calculus also has a form of link causation created by the semantics being early, which is not present in other reversible π-calculi. In πIH past actions are tracked by using extrusion histories adapted from [12], which move past actions and their locations into separate histories for dynamic reversibility. We mediate the event structure semantics of πIH via a statically reversible version of the internal π-calculus, πIK, which keeps the structure of the process intact but annotates past actions with keys, similarly to πK [17] and CCSK [21]. We showed that a process πIH with extrusion histories can be mapped to a πIK process with keys, creating an operational correspondence (Theorem 4.6).

The event structure semantics of πIK, and by extension πIH, are defined inductively on the syntax of the process. We use labelled reversible bundle event structures [10], rather than prime event structures, to get a more compact representation where each action in the calculus has only one corresponding event. While causation in the internal π-calculus is simpler that in the full π-calculus, our early semantics means that we still have to handle link causation, in the form of an input receiving a free name being caused by a previous output of that free name. We show an operational correspondence between πIK processes and their event structure representations in Theorems 6.3 and 6.4. Cristescu *et al.* [8] have used rigid families [4], related to event structures, to describe the semantics of Rπ [7]. However, unlike our denotational event structure semantics, their semantics require one to reverse every action in the process before applying the mapping to a rigid family, and then redo every reversed action in the rigid family. Our approach of using a static calculus as an intermediate step means we get the current state of the event structure immediately, and do not need to redo the past steps.

Future Work: We could expand the event structure semantics of πIK to πK. This would entail significantly more link causation, but would give us event structure semantics of a full π-calculus. Another possibility is to expand πIH to get a full reversible early π-calculus.

Acknowledgements. We thank Thomas Hildebrandt and Håkon Normann for discussions on how to translate their work on π-calculus with extrusion histories to a reversible setting. We thank the anonymous reviewers of RC 2020 for their helpful comments.

This work was partially supported by an EPSRC DTP award; also by the following EPSRC projects: EP/K034413/1, EP/K011715/1, EP/L00058X/1, EP/N027833/1, EP/T006544/1, EP/N028201/1 and EP/T014709/1; and by EU COST Action IC1405 on Reversible Computation.

References

1. Aubert, C., Cristescu, I.: Contextual equivalences in configuration structures and reversibility. JLAMP **86**(1), 77–106 (2017). https://doi.org/10.1016/j.jlamp.2016.08.004
2. Boreale, M.: On the expressiveness of internal mobility in name-passing calculi. Theoret. Comput. Sci. **195**(2), 205–226 (1998). https://doi.org/10.1016/S0304-3975(97)00220-X
3. Boudol, G., Castellani, I.: Permutation of transitions: an event structure semantics for CCS and SCCS. In: de Bakker, J.W., de Roever, W.-P., Rozenberg, G. (eds.) REX 1988. LNCS, vol. 354, pp. 411–427. Springer, Heidelberg (1989). https://doi.org/10.1007/BFb0013028
4. Castellan, S., Hayman, J., Lasson, M., Winskel, G.: Strategies as concurrent processes. Electron. Notes Theor. Comput. Sci. **308**, 87–107 (2014). https://doi.org/10.1016/j.entcs.2014.10.006
5. Crafa, S., Varacca, D., Yoshida, N.: Compositional event structure semantics for the internal π-calculus. In: Caires, L., Vasconcelos, V.T. (eds.) CONCUR 2007. LNCS, vol. 4703, pp. 317–332. Springer, Heidelberg (2007). https://doi.org/10.1007/978-3-540-74407-8_22
6. Crafa, S., Varacca, D., Yoshida, N.: Event structure semantics of parallel extrusion in the Pi-calculus. In: Birkedal, L. (ed.) FoSSaCS 2012. LNCS, vol. 7213, pp. 225–239. Springer, Heidelberg (2012). https://doi.org/10.1007/978-3-642-28729-9_15
7. Cristescu, I., Krivine, J., Varacca, D.: A compositional semantics for the reversible pi-calculus. LICS, pp. 388–397. IEEE Computer Society, Washington, DC (2013). https://doi.org/10.1109/LICS.2013.45

8. Cristescu, I., Krivine, J., Varacca, D.: Rigid families for the reversible π-calculus. In: Devitt, S., Lanese, I. (eds.) RC 2016. LNCS, vol. 9720, pp. 3–19. Springer, Cham (2016). https://doi.org/10.1007/978-3-319-40578-0_1

9. Danos, V., Krivine, J.: Reversible communicating systems. In: Gardner, P., Yoshida, N. (eds.) CONCUR 2004. LNCS, vol. 3170, pp. 292–307. Springer, Heidelberg (2004). https://doi.org/10.1007/978-3-540-28644-8_19

10. Graversen, E., Phillips, I., Yoshida, N.: Event structure semantics of (controlled) reversible CCS. In: Kari, J., Ulidowski, I. (eds.) RC 2018. LNCS, vol. 11106, pp. 102–122. Springer, Cham (2018). https://doi.org/10.1007/978-3-319-99498-7_7

11. Graversen, E., Phillips, I., Yoshida, N.: Event structures for the reversible early internal pi-calculus. arXiv:2004.01211 [cs.FL] (2020). https://arxiv.org/abs/2004.01211

12. Hildebrandt, T.T., Johansen, C., Normann, H.: A stable non-interleaving early operational semantics for the Pi-calculus. In: Drewes, F., Martín-Vide, C., Truthe, B. (eds.) LATA 2017. LNCS, vol. 10168, pp. 51–63. Springer, Cham (2017). https://doi.org/10.1007/978-3-319-53733-7_3

13. Honda, K., Yoshida, N.: On reduction-based process semantics. TCS **151**(2), 437–486 (1995). https://doi.org/10.1016/0304-3975(95)00074-7

14. Lanese, I., Mezzina, C.A., Stefani, J.-B.: Reversing higher-order Pi. In: Gastin, P., Laroussinie, F. (eds.) CONCUR 2010. LNCS, vol. 6269, pp. 478–493. Springer, Heidelberg (2010). https://doi.org/10.1007/978-3-642-15375-4_33

15. Lanese, I., Mezzina, C.A., Stefani, J.B.: Reversibility in the higher-order π-calculus. Theoret. Comput. Sci. **625**, 25–84 (2016). https://doi.org/10.1016/j.tcs.2016.02.019

16. Medić, D., Mezzina, C.A.: Static VS dynamic reversibility in CCS. In: Devitt, S., Lanese, I. (eds.) RC 2016. LNCS, vol. 9720, pp. 36–51. Springer, Cham (2016). https://doi.org/10.1007/978-3-319-40578-0_3

17. Medic, D., Mezzina, C.A., Phillips, I., Yoshida, N.: A parametric framework for reversible pi-calculi. In: EXPRESS/SOS, pp. 87–103 (2018). https://doi.org/10.4204/EPTCS.276.8

18. Milner, R., Parrow, J., Walker, D.: A calculus of mobile processes, I and II. Inf. Comput. **100**(1), 1–77 (1992). https://doi.org/10.1016/0890-5401(92)90008-4

19. Milner, R., Parrow, J., Walker, D.: Modal logics for mobile processes. Theoret. Comput. Sci. **114**(1), 149–171 (1993). https://doi.org/10.1016/0304-3975(93)90156-N

20. Milner, R., Sangiorgi, D.: Barbed bisimulation. In: Kuich, W. (ed.) ICALP 1992. LNCS, vol. 623, pp. 685–695. Springer, Heidelberg (1992). https://doi.org/10.1007/3-540-55719-9_114

21. Phillips, I., Ulidowski, I.: Reversing algebraic process calculi. JLAMP **73**(1–2), 70–96 (2007). https://doi.org/10.1016/j.jlap.2006.11.002

22. Phillips, I., Ulidowski, I.: Reversibility and models for concurrency. Electron. Notes Theor. Comput. Sci. **192**(1), 93–108 (2007). https://doi.org/10.1016/j.entcs.2007.08.018

23. Phillips, I., Ulidowski, I.: Reversibility and asymmetric conflict in event structures. JLAMP **84**(6), 781–805 (2015). https://doi.org/10.1016/j.jlamp.2015.07.004

24. Sangiorgi, D.: π-calculus, internal mobility, and agent-passing calculi. Theoret. Comput. Sci. **167**(1), 235–274 (1996). https://doi.org/10.1016/0304-3975(96)00075-8

25. Sewell, P., Wojciechowski, P.T., Unyapoth, A.: Nomadic pict: programming languages, communication infrastructure overlays, and semantics for mobile computation. ACM Trans. Program. Lang. Syst. **32**(4), 121–1263 (2010). https://doi.org/10.1145/1734206.1734209
26. Tiezzi, F., Yoshida, N.: Reversible session-based pi-calculus. JLAMP **84**(5), 684–707 (2015). https://doi.org/10.1016/j.jlamp.2015.03.004
27. Winskel, G.: Event structure semantics for CCS and related languages. In: Nielsen, M., Schmidt, E.M. (eds.) ICALP 1982. LNCS, vol. 140, pp. 561–576. Springer, Heidelberg (1982). https://doi.org/10.1007/BFb0012800

Programming Languages

Hermes: A Language for Light-Weight Encryption

Torben Ægidius Mogensen[✉]

DIKU, University of Copenhagen, Universitetsparken 5, 2100 Copenhagen, Denmark
torbenm@di.ku.dk

Abstract. Hermes is a domain-specific language for writing light-weight encryption algorithms: It is reversible, so it is not necessary to write separate encryption and decryption procedures, and it avoids several types of side-channel attacks, both by ensuring no secret values are left in memory and by ensuring that operations on secret data spend time independent of the value of this data, thus preventing timing-based attacks. We show a complete formal specification of Hermes, argue absence of timing-based attacks (under reasonable assumptions), and compare implementations of well-known light-weight encryption algorithms in Hermes and C.

1 Introduction

Recent work [12] have investigated using the reversible language Janus [5,19] for writing encryption algorithms. Janus is a structured imperative language where all statements are reversible. A requirement for reversibility is that no information is ever discarded: No variable is destructively overwritten in such a way that the original value is lost. Instead, it must be updated in a reversible manner or swapped with another variable. Since encryption is by nature reversible, it seems natural to write these in a reversible programming language. Additionally, reversible languages requires that all intermediate variables are cleared to 0 before they are discarded, which ensures that no information that could potentially be used for side-channel attacks is left in memory. But non-cleared variables is not the only side-channel attack used against encryption: If the time used to encrypt data can depend on the values of the data and the encryption key, attackers can gain (some) information about the data or the key simply by measuring the time used for encryption. Janus has control structures the timing of which depend on the values of variables, so it does not protect against timing-based attacks.

So we propose a new reversible language, Hermes, specifically designed to address these concerns. Although somewhat inspired by Janus, Hermes has some significant differences, as we shall see below. An early version of the Hermes language was presented in [7]. Experiments using this language have indicated a need for a type system that separates secret and public data. In the early version, the (informally specified) type system distinguishes constants, loop variables, and all else, with constants and loop variables being considered non-secret and

© Springer Nature Switzerland AG 2020
I. Lanese and M. Rawski (Eds.): RC 2020, LNCS 12227, pp. 93–110, 2020.
https://doi.org/10.1007/978-3-030-52482-1_5

all else being secret. This early language is, however, too restrictive in many cases and too permissive in other cases:

- Loop bounds and array sizes were constants, so algorithms with variable-size keys or data would have to have a procedure for each size.
- Loop counters could in the early version of Hermes only be updated by constant values, which may also be too restrictive.
- Procedure parameters are not distinguished by secrecy, so loop counters could not be passed as parameters. By classifying parameters as public or secret, loop counters can now be passed as public parameters.
- Any value was allowed as index to an array, but since timing can depend on the index value (due to caching), this is a potential side channel. By limiting array indices to public values, this can be avoided.

So we propose a new version of Hermes that uses public and secret types, with strong restrictions on operations on secret values. Constants and loop counters are public, all other variables are by default secret, but can be declared public. The type system not only tracks flow of information similar to binding-time analysis [3], trust analysis [8], and information flow analysis [11] but also imposes restrictions to ensure reversibility and (under reasonable assumptions) avoid timing-based side-channel attacks.

$$
\begin{aligned}
Program \quad &\rightarrow Procedure^{+} \\
\\
Procedure &\rightarrow \textbf{id} \ (\ Args \ ) \ Stat \\
\\
Args \quad &\rightarrow Type \ \textbf{id} \quad | \quad Type \ \textbf{id[]} \quad | \quad Args \ , \ Args \\
\\
Type \quad &\rightarrow \texttt{secret IntType} \quad | \quad \texttt{public IntType} \\
\\
Stat \quad &\rightarrow \ ; \\
& \ | \ Lval \ \textbf{update} \ Exp \ ; \\
& \ | \ Lval \ \texttt{<->} Lval \quad | \quad \textbf{if} \ (\ Exp \ ) \ Lval \ \texttt{<->} Lval \\
& \ | \ \textbf{for} \ (\ \textbf{id} = Exp \ ; \ Exp \ ) \ Stat \\
& \ | \ \texttt{call id} \ (\ Lvals); \quad | \quad \texttt{uncall id} \ (\ Lvals); \\
& \ | \ \{ \ Decls1 \ Stat^* \} \\
\\
Exp \quad &\rightarrow Lval \quad | \quad \textbf{numConst} \quad | \quad \texttt{size id} \\
& \ | \ Exp \ \textbf{binOp} \ Exp \quad | \quad \textbf{unOp} \ Exp \\
\\
Lval \quad &\rightarrow \textbf{id} \quad | \quad \textbf{id} \ [\ Exp \ ] \\
\\
Lvals \quad &\rightarrow Lval \quad | \quad Lval \ , \ Lvals \\
\\
VarSpec \quad &\rightarrow \textbf{id} \quad | \quad \textbf{id} \ [\ Exp \ ] \\
\\
Decls \quad &\rightarrow \\
& \ | \ Type \ VarSpec \ ; \ Decls \\
& \ | \ \texttt{const id} = \textbf{numConst} \ ; \ Decls
\end{aligned}
$$

Fig. 1. Core syntax of Hermes

2   Hermes Syntax

The core syntax of Hermes is shown in Fig. 1. The grammar uses tokens specified in boldface. These are described below.

id denotes identifiers. An identifier starts with a letter and can contain letters, digits, and underscores.

numConst denotes decimal or hexadecimal integers using C-style notation.

IntType denotes names of integer types. These can be u8, u16, u32, and u64, representing unsigned integers of 8, 16, 32 or 64 bits.

unOp denotes an unary operator on numbers. This can be bitwise negation (~).

binOp denotes an unary operator on numbers. This can be one of +, -, *, /, %, &, |, ^, ==, !=, <, >, <=, >=, <<, and >>. All arithmetic is modulo 2^{64}. Comparison operators return $2^{64}-1$ (all ones) when the comparison is true and 0 when the comparison is false. Note that this is different from their behaviour in C, where they return 1 and 0, respectively. &, |, and ^ are bitwise logical operators.

update denotes an update operator. This can be one of +=, -=, ^=, <<=, and >>=. The first three operators have the same meaning as in C. <<= is a left rotate. The rotation amount is modulo the size of the L-value being rotated, so if, for example, x is an 8-bit variable, x <<= 13; will rotate x left by 5 bits. >>= is a right rotate using similar rules. Note that the meaning of <<= and >>= differ from their meaning in C, where they represent shift-updates.

3   The Type System of Hermes

Values in Hermes are all 64 bit unsigned integers, and they can be secret or public. Scalar and array variables additionally impose a number size (8, 16, 32 or 64 bits). A constant just has the type constant, which is implicitly a 64-bit number. So we have:

$$
\begin{aligned}
ValType &\rightarrow \textsf{secret} \mid \textsf{public} \\
VarType &\rightarrow \textsf{constant} \mid ValType^{Size} \mid ValType^{Size}\,\textsf{[]} \\
Size &\rightarrow 8 \mid 16 \mid 32 \mid 64
\end{aligned}
$$

We use t with optional subscript to denote a value type, τ with optional subscript to denote a variable type, and z with optional subscript to denote a size. So t^z denotes the special case of variable types where the variable is a scalar non-constant. We define a partial order $\sqsubseteq$ as the reflexive extension of public $\sqsubseteq$ secret and a least upper bound operator $\sqcup$ induced by this partial order. We use this to make the result secret when secret and public values are mixed.

3.1   L-Values and Expressions

Variable environments, denoted by ρ with optional subscript, bind identifiers (denoted by x with optional subscript) to variable types. Environments are functions, so $\rho(x)$ is the variable type that x is bound to in ρ. We update environments using the notation $\rho[x \mapsto \tau]$, which creates a new environment that is identical to ρ, except that x is bound to τ.

Sequents for typing expressions, denoted by e with optional subscript, are of the form $\rho \vdash_E e : ValType$, and sequents for typing L-values (denoted by l with optional subscript) are of the form $\rho \vdash_L l : VarType$. In order to make updates, swaps, and parameter passing reversible, we must impose restrictions to avoid aliasing and similar clashes. To do this, we introduce functions that find variables in expressions or parts of expressions. $V()$ finds the variables in an expression or L-value, $R()$ finds the root variable of an L-value, and $V()_I$ finds the variables in index expressions in an L-value.

$$
\begin{aligned}
V(n) &= \emptyset & V(x) &= \{x\} \\
V(x[e]) &= \{x\} \cup V(e) & V(\neg e) &= V(e) \\
V(e_1 \odot e_2) &= V(e_1) \cup V(e_2) & V(\text{size } x) &= \emptyset \\
\\
R(x) &= x & V_I(x) &= \emptyset \\
R(x[e]) &= x & V_I(x[e]) &= V(e)
\end{aligned}
$$

Note that $V()$ does not include variables in size-expressions, as these are harmless in terms of aliasing.

We specify rules for L-values and expressions in Fig. 2.

For L-values, the rule for variables says that a variable has the type specified by the environment. The rule for array access says that the array variable must have an array type and the index expression must be public. This ensures that timing of memory accesses (which can depend on the address, but not the accessed value) does not leak secret information. The rules for constants state that a constant is public. n denotes an integer constant. The rule for non-constant L-values say that the L-value must be a scalar and that the expression type is the value type part of the type of the L-value. The rule for an unary operator $\neg$ just say that the result has the same type as its argument. The rules for a binary operator $\odot$ is more complex. If any of the arguments are secret, the result is also secret. Additionally, some potentially time-variant operations are not allowed on secret values. We assume a set TV of time-variant operators is given. This will typically contain division and modulo operators, but can also contain multiplication if the target architecture does not have a constant-time multiplication instruction. The last rule states that the size of an array is a public value.

3.2   Statements and Local Declarations

A seqent for a statement s is of the form $\Gamma, \rho \vdash_S s$ and states that given a procedure environment Γ and variable environment ρ, the statement s is well typed. A procedure environment binds procedure names to lists of variable types. The type rules for statements are shown in Fig. 3.

The first rule says that the empty statement is well typed. To ensure reversibility, the rule for updates (where $\oplus=$ denotes an update operator) says

$$\frac{}{\rho \vdash_L x : \rho(x)}\text{(Variable)}$$

$$\frac{\rho(x) = t^z\,[]\quad \rho \vdash_E e : \texttt{public}}{\rho \vdash_L x[e] : t^z}\text{(ArrayAccess)}$$

$$\frac{}{\rho \vdash_E n : \texttt{public}}\text{(Constant1)}$$

$$\frac{\rho \vdash_L l : \texttt{constant}}{\rho \vdash_E l : \texttt{public}}\text{(Constant2)}$$

$$\frac{\rho \vdash_L l : t^z}{\rho \vdash_E l : t}\text{(L-val)}$$

$$\frac{\rho \vdash_E e : t}{\rho \vdash_E \neg e : t}\text{(UnOp)}$$

$$\frac{\rho \vdash_E e_1 : t_1 \quad \rho \vdash_E e_2 : t_2 \quad t_1 \sqcup t_2 = \texttt{public}}{\rho \vdash_E e_1 \odot e_2 : \texttt{public}}\text{(BinOp1)}$$

$$\frac{\rho \vdash_E e_1 : t_1 \quad \rho \vdash_E e_2 : t_2 \quad t_1 \sqcup t_2 = \texttt{secret} \quad \odot \notin TV}{\rho \vdash_E e_1 \odot e_2 : \texttt{secret}}\text{(BinOp2)}$$

$$\frac{\rho(x) = t^z\,[]}{\rho \vdash_E \texttt{size}\,x : \texttt{public}}\text{(Size)}$$

Fig. 2. Type rules for L-values and expressions

that the root variable of the L-val must not occur in the expression. Furthermore, if the expression is secret, the L-Val must also be secret. The rule for a swap states that the two L-values must have exactly the same type, and that the root variable of one side can not occur in index expressions on the other side. The rule for conditional swap additionally requires that the root variables of the L-values do not occur in the condition and that the condition is no more secret than the L-values. The rule for loops state that the loop bounds must be public, and that the loop variable is implicitly declared to be a public 64-bit variable local to the loop body. The rules for procedure calls state that the types of the argument L-values must match those found in the procedure environment. Furthermore, to avoid aliasing and ensure reversibility, the root variable of one argument can not occur in another argument. The rule for blocks states that all statements in the block must be well typed in the environment that is extended by the local declarations. Static scoping is used. The bottom of Fig. 3 show the rules for extending environments.

Sequents for declarations are of the form $\rho \vdash_D d \rightsquigarrow \rho_1$, and state that the declaration d extends the environment ρ to ρ_1. The first rule state that an empty declaration does not change the environment. The rule for constant declarations extends the environment with the constant name bound to $\texttt{constant}$. The rules for variable declarations are straightforward. The rules for array declarations require that the expression that determines the size of an array must be public, and that the array variable can not shadow any variable used in this expression.

3.3 Procedures and Programs

The rules for declarations of procedures and programs are shown in Fig. 4. A sequent of the form $\vdash pgm$ states that pgm is a valid program. $\vdash_P p \rightsquigarrow \Gamma$ states

$$\frac{}{\Gamma, \rho \vdash_S \ ;} \text{(Empty)}$$

$$\frac{\rho \vdash_L l : t_0^z \quad \rho \vdash_E e : t_1 \quad R(l) \notin V(e) \quad t_1 \sqsubseteq t_0}{\Gamma, \rho \vdash_S l \oplus= e} \text{(Update)}$$

$$\frac{\rho \vdash_L l_1 : t^z \quad \rho \vdash_L l_2 : t^z \quad R(l_1) \notin V_I(l_2) \quad R(l_2) \notin V_I(l_1)}{\Gamma, \rho \vdash_S l_1 \mathrel{<->} l_2} \text{(Swap)}$$

$$\frac{\begin{array}{c}\rho \vdash_L l_1 : t_0^z \quad \rho \vdash_L l_2 : t_0^z \quad \rho \vdash_E e : t_1 \quad t_1 \sqsubseteq t_0 \\ R(l_1) \notin V_I(l_2) \cup V(e) \quad R(l_2) \notin V_I(l_1) \cup V(e)\end{array}}{\Gamma, \rho \vdash_S \text{if } (e)\, l_1 \mathrel{<->} l_2} \text{(SwapC)}$$

$$\frac{\rho \vdash_E e_1 : \texttt{public} \quad \rho \vdash_E e_2 : \texttt{public} \quad \Gamma, \rho[x \mapsto \texttt{public}^{64}] \vdash_S s}{\Gamma, \rho \vdash_S \text{for } (x = e_1 ; e_2)\, s} \text{(ForLoop)}$$

$$\frac{\begin{array}{c}\Gamma(f) = (\tau_1, \ldots, \tau_n) \quad \forall i \in [1, n] : \rho \vdash_L l_i : \tau_i \\ \forall i, j \in [1, n] : i \neq j \Rightarrow R(l_i) \notin V(l_j)\end{array}}{\Gamma, \rho \vdash_S \texttt{call } f(l_1, \ldots, l_n) ;} \text{(Call)}$$

$$\frac{\Gamma, \rho \vdash_S \texttt{call } f(l_1, \ldots, l_n) ;}{\Gamma, \rho \vdash_S \texttt{uncall } f(l_1, \ldots, l_n) ;} \text{(Uncall)}$$

$$\frac{\rho \vdash_D d \rightsquigarrow \rho_1 \quad \forall i \in [1, n] : \Gamma, \rho_1 \vdash_S s_i}{\Gamma, \rho \vdash_S \{d\; s_1 \ldots s_n\}} \text{(Block)}$$

$$\frac{}{\rho \vdash_D \;\rightsquigarrow \rho} \text{(EmptyDecl)} \qquad \frac{\rho[x \mapsto t^z] \vdash_D d \rightsquigarrow \rho_1}{\rho \vdash_D t \texttt{ uz } x;\; d \rightsquigarrow \rho_1} \text{(VarDecl)}$$

$$\frac{\rho[x \mapsto \texttt{constant}] \vdash_D d \rightsquigarrow \rho_1}{\rho \vdash_D \texttt{const } x = n;\; d \rightsquigarrow \rho_1} \text{(ConstDecl)}$$

$$\frac{\rho \vdash_E e : \texttt{public} \quad x \notin V(e) \quad \rho[x \mapsto t^z[\,]] \vdash_D d \rightsquigarrow \rho_1}{\rho \vdash_D t \texttt{ uz } x[e];\; d \rightsquigarrow \rho_1} \text{(ArrayDecl)}$$

Fig. 3. Type rules for statements and declarations

that a procedure p generates a procedure environment Γ, $\Gamma \vdash^P p$ states that, given the procedure environment Γ, the procedure p is valid, and $\vdash_A a \rightsquigarrow V/\overline{\tau}$ states that the argument list a generates the variable list V and the type list $\overline{\tau}$. We use $\uplus$ to append two (variable or type) lists and $\cap$ to represent the set of elements common to two lists.

The rule for programs first builds a procedure environment, ensuring that no procedure is declared twice, and then checks that all procedures are well typed in this procedure environment. Procedures can all call each other. The *Procedure1* rule builds a procedure environment for a single procedure, and *Procedure2* checks that a single procedure is well typed. Both use rules for building a list of argument names and types, ensuring no name occurs twice.

$$\frac{\forall i \in [1,n] : \vdash_P p_i \rightsquigarrow [f_i \mapsto (\overline{\tau_i})] \quad \forall i,j \in [1,n] : i \neq j \Rightarrow f_i \neq f_j}{\forall i \in [1,n] : [f_1 \mapsto (\overline{\tau_1}), \ldots, f_n \mapsto (\overline{\tau_n})] \vdash^P p_i}$$
$$\overline{\vdash p_1 \ldots p_n} \text{(Program)}$$

$$\frac{\vdash_A a \rightsquigarrow V/\overline{\tau}}{\vdash_P f(a) \; s \rightsquigarrow [f \mapsto \overline{\tau}]} \text{(Procedure1)}$$

$$\frac{\vdash_A a \rightsquigarrow [x_1, \ldots, x_n]/[\tau_1, \ldots, \tau_n] \quad \Gamma, [x_1 \mapsto \tau_1, \ldots, x_n \mapsto \tau_n] \vdash_S s}{\Gamma \vdash^P f(a) \; s} \text{(Procedure2)}$$

$$\frac{\vdash_A a_1 \rightsquigarrow V_1/\overline{\tau_1} \quad \vdash_A a_2 \rightsquigarrow V_2/\overline{\tau_2} \quad V_1 \cap V_2 = \emptyset}{\vdash_A a_1 , a_2 \rightsquigarrow V_1 \uplus V_2/\overline{\tau_1} \uplus \overline{\tau_2}} \text{(ArgList)}$$

$$\frac{}{\vdash_A t \; uz \, x \rightsquigarrow [x]/[t^z]} \text{(Scalar)} \qquad \frac{}{\vdash_A t \; uz \, x[] \rightsquigarrow [x]/[t^z []]} \text{(Array)}$$

Fig. 4. Type rules for procedures and programs

4   Run-Time Semantics of Hermes

The run-time semantics of Hermes does not distinguish secret and public values – type checking ensures that no secrets leak into public variables – so values in Hermes are just sized numbers. Expressions all evaluate to 64 bit numbers, which are only truncated when used to update variables or array elements, which can be 8, 16, 32, or 64 bits in size. An array has an element size, a vector size, and a vector of elements of the vector size. The sizes of scalar variables and the element sizes of array are known at compile time, but for specification convenience they are part of the run-time environments. A compiler can check sizes at compile time, so the run-time environments bind names (or offsets) to locations only. Similarly, named constants can be eliminated at compile time, so they do not need to be part of the run-time environments.

Environments (η) bind constants to their value and variables to their integer sizes (8, 16, 32, or 64) and locations.

Stores (σ) bind locations to values. The value of a scalar variable is an 8, 16, 32, or 64 bit integer, and the value of an array is a record (struct) of its vector size and its vector. The elements of the vector are locations holding 8, 16, 32, or 64 bit integers, according to the integer size of the array.

We use the same notation for environments as in the type semantics, but we also use the update notation as a pattern: If η_1 is known, we use the notation $\eta_2[x \mapsto v] = \eta_1$ to say that η_2 is equal to η_1 with the *latest* binding of x removed. This means that earlier bindings of x are retained in the environment and can be retrieved. The environments are stack-like: Bindings are removed in the opposite order in which they are created. Stores, on the other hand, do not need to retain older bindings of locations, so when a new value is bound to a location, the old value can be forgotten. We use the notation $\sigma[\lambda := v]$ when updating stores. While this is not immediately evident from the semantic rules, there is only be one store in use at any given time, and locations are disposed of in the opposite order of their creation, so the store acts like and can be implemented as a global stack, allocating new zero-initialised locations on the top of the stack and removing them in the opposite order of their allocation.

We use a family of functions $newlocation_z$ where z an integer size (8, 16, 32, or 64) that takes a store σ returns a new store σ_1 and location λ of size z such that λ is bound to zero in σ_1, and the dual function $disposelocation_z$ that takes a storeσ_1 and a location λ and returns a store σ obtained by removing (unstacking) λ from σ_1, after checking that the contents of λ in σ_1 is 0. If not, the result is undefined. If $(\sigma_1, \lambda) = newlocation_z(\sigma)$, then $\sigma = disposelocation_z(\sigma_1\lambda)$.

We also use a family of functions $newarray_z$ that each take a store σ and a vector size vs and returns a new store σ_1 and a location λ that in the new store is bound to two fields: $\sigma_1(\lambda) = (vs, ve)$, where vs is the vector size at this location, and ve is a vector of new locations for the elements of the vector, all of which are bound to zero in the new store. We use array notation to access elements of a vector. $newarray_z$ also have duals, $disposearray_z$, that each take a store σ_1, a vector size vs, and a location λ and returns a new store σ where the array at λ has been removed (unstacked). It checks that the vector size at the location matches vs, and that all vector elements are locations with zero as content. If either of these is not true, the result is undefined. If $(\sigma_1, \lambda) = newarray_z(\sigma, vs)$, then $\sigma = disposearray_z(\sigma_1, vs, \lambda)$.

$$\frac{}{\sigma, \eta \models_L x @ \eta(x)} \text{(Variable/Constant)}$$

$$\frac{\eta(x) = (z, \lambda) \quad \sigma(\lambda) = (vs, ve) \quad \sigma, \eta \models_E e \to i \quad i < vs}{\sigma, \eta \models_L x[e] @ (z, ve[i])} \text{(ArrayElement)}$$

$$\frac{}{\sigma, \eta \models_E n \to n} \text{(Constant1)} \qquad \frac{\eta(x) = (n, \text{null})}{\sigma, \eta \models_E x \to n} \text{(Constant2)}$$

$$\frac{\sigma, \eta \models_L l @ (z, \lambda)}{\sigma, \eta \models_E l \to \sigma(\lambda) \uparrow_z} \text{(L-val)} \qquad \frac{\sigma, \eta \models_E e \to v}{\sigma, \eta \models_E \neg e \to I(\neg)(v)} \text{(UnOp)}$$

$$\frac{\sigma, \eta \models_E e_1 \to v_1 \quad \sigma, \eta \models_E e_2 \to v_2}{\sigma, \eta \models_E e_1 \odot e_2 \to I(\odot)(v_1, v_2)} \text{(BinOp)} \qquad \frac{\eta(x) = (z, \lambda) \quad \sigma(\lambda) = (vs, ve)}{\sigma, \eta \models_E \textbf{size } x \to vs} \text{(Size)}$$

Fig. 5. Semantic rules for L-values and expressions

4.1   L-Values and Expressions

Figure 5 shows the evaluation rules for L-values and expressions. L-values evaluate to locations, and expressions to 64-bit integers. Sequents for L-values are of the form $\sigma, \eta \models_L l @ (z, \lambda)$ and state that the L-value l is stored at location λ which is of size z. We use a special case for constants: When $\lambda = \text{null}$, l is a constant equal to z. null is a null location where no values are stored.

$$
\begin{aligned}
I(;) &= \; ; & I(l \; \hat{} = e;) &= \; l \; \hat{} = e; \\
I(l \; += e;) &= \; l \; -= e; & I(l \; -= e;) &= \; l \; += e; \\
I(l \; <<= e;) &= \; l \; >>= e; & I(l \; >>= e;) &= \; l \; <<= e; \\
& I(l_1 <\text{->} l_2;) = \; l_1 <\text{->} l_2; \\
& I(\text{if } (c) \; l_1 <\text{->} l_2;) = \; \text{if } (c) \; l_1 <\text{->} l_2; \\
& I(\text{for } (x = e_1; e_2) \; s) = \; \text{for } (x = e_2; e_1) \; I(s) \\
I(\text{call } f(as);) &= \; \text{uncall } f(as); & I(\text{uncall } f(as);) &= \; \text{call } f(as); \\
& I(\{d \; s_1 \dots s_n\}) = \; \{d \; I(s_n) \dots I(s_1)\}
\end{aligned}
$$

Fig. 6. Inverting statements

Sequents of the form $\sigma, \eta \models_E e \rightarrow v$, state that e evaluates to v.

We use a function I that binds operator symbols to the functions they represent. So $I(+)$ is a function that takes a pair of integers and returns their sum (modulo 2^{64}) and $I(\hat{})$ is a function that takes a single 64-bit integer and returns its bitwise negation. I takes a pair of an update operator and an integer size and returns a function that takes two integers of this size and returns a third integer of this size. Note that the actual updating is not done by this function. For example, $I(<<=,8)$ is a function that takes two 8-bit integers and returns the first rotated left by the second modulo 8. So $I(<<=,8)(129,18) = I(<<=,8)(129,2) = 6$. I is defined outside the semantic rules. Recall that comparison operators return 0 when the relation is false and $2^{64}-1$ when the relation is true.

The rule for variables and constants says that the size and location of a scalar variable or constant is found in the environment. The rule for array elements states that the location of the variable is bound in the store to a pair of vector size and vector elements, that the index expression must evaluate to a value less than the vector size, and that the location of the array element is found in the vector of elements. The type system guarantees that the location is not null and that it is bound to a pair, but it does not ensure that the index is within bounds, so this is checked at runtime. If the index it out of bounds, the effect is undefined.

The two first rules for expressions handle constants. The first handles simple number constants, which evaluate to themselves, and the second handles named constants that are bound to pairs of values and null locations. The rule for L-values finds the location of the L-value and gets its contents from the store, and then extends the value to 64 bits. For this, we use a postfix operator $\uparrow_z$ that extends a z-bit value to 64 bits. The rules for unary and binary operators evaluate the operand(s) and then applies the semantic operator to the value(s) of the operand(s). Finally, the rule for **size** finds the size of the array in the store. The type system ensures that the location is not null and that it is bound to a pair.

4.2 Statements

To handle **uncall** in the semantics for statements, we need to "run" statements backwards. To this end, we use the function I in Fig. 6 to invert statements:

In a type-correct program, the effect of first executing s and then $I(s)$ is, if s terminates without error, a null effect: The store is in the same state as before s was executed. Proving this is tedious, but relatively uncomplicated. The main complications are declarations and that some statements are only reversible if the aliasing constraint in th etype system hold. We do, however, not at the time have a complete proof written down.

Statements transform stores into stores, while keeping the environment unchanged. Sequents for running statements are of the form $\Delta, \eta \models_S s : \sigma_0 \rightleftharpoons \sigma_1$ and state that, given a procedure environment Δ and a variable environment η, a statement s reversibly transforms a store σ_0 to a store σ_1.

The rules for statements are shown in Fig. 7. The rule for the empty statement states that it does not change the store. The rule for updates finds the value v of the L-value and the value w of the expression. It then truncates w to s bits (using the $\downarrow_s$ operator), performs the operation (restricted to s bits) between the two values, and stores the result in the location of the L-value.

The rule for swap finds the values of the two L-values in the store and updates the store with these swapped. There are two rules for conditional swap: The first rule states that if the condition evaluates to 0 (false), there is no change in the store. The other rule states that if the condition evaluates to a non-zero (true) value, the effect on the store is like an unconditional swap. Note that this does not imply that the condition is evaluated twice if it is non-zero, nor that the timing differs. It is up to the implementation to ensure invariant timing.

The rule for loops first evaluate the loop bounds, allocates a new location in the store, and stores the first bound at the location, applies helper rules $\models_F$ using an environment where the loop counter is bound to the location, and then disposes of the location in the resulting store. There are two helper rules: One for when the loop counter is equal to the second bound, and one where it does not. Both use the location and the value of the second bound.

The rule for `call` finds the sized locations of the arguments, looks the procedure up in the procedure environment to get the list of parameter names and the body of the procedure. It then creates a new environment that binds the parameter names to the argument locations and executes the body in this environment. This implements call-by-reference parameter passing. The rule for `uncall` is similar, but it is the inverse of the body that is executed. The type system guarantees that the sizes of the given parameters are the same as the sizes of the declared parameters.

The rule for blocks uses the declarations to extend the environment and store, executes the body, and uses the declarations to restrict the store.

4.3 Declarations

The rules for declarations is shown in Fig. 8. There are two kinds of sequents for declarations: $\eta_0, \sigma_0 \models_D d \rightsquigarrow \eta_1, \sigma_1$ says that the declaration d extends η_0 and σ_0 to η_1 and σ_1. Conversely, $\eta_0, \sigma_0 \models_D^{inv} d \rightsquigarrow \eta_1, \sigma_1$ says that "undoing" the declaration d restricts η_0 to η_1 and σ_0 to σ_1.

$$\frac{}{\Delta, \eta \models_S \; ; \; : \sigma \rightleftharpoons \sigma}(\text{Empty})$$

$$\frac{\sigma, \eta \models_L l @ (z, \lambda) \quad \sigma(\lambda) = v_1 \quad \sigma, \eta \models_E e \rightarrow v_2}{\Delta, \eta \models_S l \oplus= e; \; : \sigma \rightleftharpoons \sigma[\lambda := I(\oplus=, z)(v_1, v_2 \downarrow_z)]}(\text{Update})$$

$$\frac{\sigma, \eta \models_L l_1 @ (z, \lambda_1) \quad \sigma, \eta \models_L l_2 @ (z, \lambda_2) \quad \sigma(\lambda_1) = v_1 \quad \sigma(\lambda_1) = v_1}{\Delta, \eta \models_S l_1 \texttt{<->} l_2; \; : \sigma \rightleftharpoons \sigma[\lambda_1 := v_2, \lambda_2 := v_1]}(\text{Swap})$$

$$\frac{\sigma, \eta \models_E e \rightarrow v \quad v = 0}{\Delta, \eta \models_S \texttt{if} \; (e) \; l_1 \texttt{<->} l_2; \; : \sigma \rightleftharpoons \sigma}(\text{CondSwap1})$$

$$\frac{\sigma, \eta \models_E e \rightarrow v \quad v \neq 0}{\sigma, \eta \models_L l_1 @ (z, \lambda_1) \quad \sigma, \eta \models_L l_2 @ (z, \lambda_2) \quad \sigma(\lambda_1) = v_1 \quad \sigma(\lambda_2) = v_2}{\Delta, \eta \models_S \texttt{if} \; (e) \; l_1 \texttt{<->} l_2; \; : \sigma \rightleftharpoons \sigma[\lambda_1 := v_2, \lambda_2 := v_1]}(\text{CondSwap2})$$

$$\frac{\sigma, \eta \models_E e_1 \rightarrow v_1 \quad \sigma, \eta \models_E e_2 \rightarrow v_2}{(\sigma_1, \lambda) = newlocation_{64}(\sigma) \quad \sigma_2 = \sigma_1[\lambda := v_1]}{\Delta, \eta[x \mapsto (64, \lambda)], \lambda, v_2 \models_F s : \sigma_2 \rightleftharpoons \sigma_3 \quad \sigma_4 = disposelocation_{64}(\sigma_3, \lambda)}{\Delta, \eta \models_S \texttt{for} \; (x=e_1; e_2) \; s : \sigma \rightleftharpoons \sigma_4}(\text{ForLoop})$$

$$\frac{\sigma(\lambda) = v}{\Delta, \eta, \lambda, v \models_F s : \sigma \rightleftharpoons \sigma}(\text{Loop1})$$

$$\frac{\sigma(\lambda) \neq v \quad \Delta, \eta \models_S s : \sigma \rightleftharpoons \sigma_1 \quad \eta, \lambda, v \models_F s : \sigma_1 \rightleftharpoons \sigma_2}{\Delta, \eta, \lambda, v \models_F s : \sigma \rightleftharpoons \sigma_2}(\text{Loop2})$$

$$\frac{\forall i \in [1, n] : \sigma, \eta \models_L l_i @ (z_i, \lambda_i) \quad \Delta f = ([(x_1, z_1), \ldots, (x_n, z_n)], s)}{\Delta, [x_1 \mapsto (z_1, \lambda_1), \ldots, x_n \mapsto (z_n, \lambda_n)] \models_S s : \sigma \rightleftharpoons \sigma_1}{\Delta, \eta \models_S \texttt{call} \; f(l_1, \ldots, l_n); \; : \sigma \rightleftharpoons \sigma_1}(\text{Call})$$

$$\frac{\forall i \in [1, n] : \sigma, \eta \models_L l_i @ (z_i, \lambda_i) \quad \Delta f = ([(x_1, z_1), \ldots, (x_n, z_n)], s)}{\Delta, [x_1 \mapsto (z_1, \lambda_1), \ldots, x_n \mapsto (z_n, \lambda_n)] \models_S I(s) : \sigma \rightleftharpoons \sigma_1}{\Delta, \eta \models_S \texttt{call} \; f(l_1, \ldots, l_n); \; : \sigma \rightleftharpoons \sigma_1}(\text{Uncall})$$

$$\frac{\eta, \sigma \models_D d \rightsquigarrow \eta_0, \sigma_0}{\forall i \in [1, n] : \Delta, \eta_0 \models_S s_i : \sigma_{i-1} \rightleftharpoons \sigma_i}{\eta_0, \sigma_n \models_D^{inv} d \rightsquigarrow \eta, \sigma_{n+1}}{\Delta, \eta \models_S \{d \; s_1 \ldots s_n\} : \sigma_0 \rightsquigarrow \sigma_{n+1}}(\text{Block})$$

Fig. 7. Semantic rules for statements

The first two rules say that the empty declaration has no effect. The next two rules state that a constant declaration extends the environment but leaves the store unchanged. Recall that constants are stored in the environment by using a null location. The rules for variable and array declarations do not distinguish secret and public values. In the forwards direction, a new location (bound to zero) is created for the variable and the variable is bound to the location. In the backwards direction, $disposelocation_z$ verifies that the location is bound to zero before it is removed from the store. In the forwards direction, a new

$$\overline{\eta,\sigma \models_D \leadsto \eta,\sigma}\,(\text{EmptyDecl}) \qquad \overline{\eta,\sigma \models_D^{inv} \leadsto \eta,\sigma}\,(\text{EmptyDeclInv})$$

$$\frac{\eta[x \mapsto (n,\text{null})],\sigma \models_D d \leadsto \eta_1,\sigma_1}{\eta,\sigma \models_D \textbf{const}\ x = n;d \leadsto \eta_1,\sigma_1}\,(\text{ConstDecl})$$

$$\frac{\eta,\sigma \models_D^{inv} d \leadsto \eta_1,\sigma_1 \quad \eta_2[x \mapsto (n,\text{null})] = \eta_1}{\eta,\sigma \models_D^{inv} \textbf{const}\ x = n;d \leadsto \eta_2,\sigma_1}\,(\text{ConstDeclInv})$$

$$\frac{(\sigma_1,\lambda) = newlocation_z(\sigma) \quad \eta[x \mapsto (z,\lambda)],\sigma_1 \models_D d \leadsto \eta_2,\sigma_2}{\eta,\sigma \models_D t\ \textbf{uz}\ x;d \leadsto \eta_2,\sigma_2}\,(\text{VarDecl})$$

$$\frac{\begin{array}{c}\eta,\sigma \models_D^{inv} d \leadsto \eta_1,\sigma_1\\ \eta_2[x \mapsto (z,\lambda)] = \eta_1 \quad \sigma_2 = disposelocation_z(\sigma_1,\lambda)\end{array}}{\eta,\sigma \models_D^{inv} t\ \textbf{uz}\ x;d \leadsto \eta_2,\sigma_2}\,(\text{VarDeclInv})$$

$$\frac{\begin{array}{c}\sigma,\eta \models_E e \rightarrow n \quad (\sigma_1,\lambda) = newarray_z(\sigma,n)\\ \eta[x \mapsto (z,\lambda)],\sigma_1 \models_D d \leadsto \eta_2,\sigma_2\end{array}}{\eta,\sigma \models_D t\ \textbf{uz}\ x[e];d \leadsto \eta_2,\sigma_2}\,(\text{ArrayDecl})$$

$$\frac{\begin{array}{c}\eta,\sigma \models_D^{inv} d \leadsto \eta_1,\sigma_1\\ \sigma_1,\eta \models_E e \rightarrow n \quad \eta_2[x \mapsto (z,\lambda)] = \eta_1 \quad \sigma_1(\lambda) = (n,ve)\\ \sigma_2 = disposearray_z(\sigma_1,z,\lambda)\end{array}}{\eta,\sigma \models_D^{inv} t\ \textbf{uz}\ x[e];\text{d} \leadsto \eta_2,\sigma_2}\,(\text{ArrayDeclInv})$$

Fig. 8. Semantic rules for declarations

zeroed array is created in the store and the variable is bound to its location in the environment. In the backwards direction is it verified that the expression evaluates to the array size, and $disposearray_z$ checks that the elements of the array are all bound to 0 in the store and removes the array from the store. Note that the rules for undeclaring things treat the declarations in reverse order.

4.4 Procedures and Programs

The rules for procedures and programs are shown in Fig. 9. There is no `main` function and no input/output in Hermes, so it is assumed that procedures are called from outside Hermes. Therefore, the semantics of a program is just creating a procedure environment Δ. The external program can call (or uncall) a procedure in this environment by providing a store and a list of locations for the procedure parameters. The rule for procedures creates a procedure environment for a single procedure. This binds the procedure name to a list of (name, integer size) pairs and the body of the procedure. The environments are combined using $\uplus$ in the rule for programs. Additional rules describe external calls to Hermes. These are very like the rules for calls in statements, except that the locations are given directly instead of being derived from a list of L-values.

$$\frac{\forall i \in [1,n] : \models_P p_i \gg \Delta_i}{\models p_1 \dots p_n \gg \Delta_1 \uplus \dots \uplus \Delta_n}(\text{Program}) \qquad \frac{\models_A a \hookrightarrow xs}{\models_P f(a)\ s \gg [f \mapsto (xs, s)]}(\text{Procedure})$$

$$\frac{\models_A a_1 \hookrightarrow xs_1 \quad \models_A a_2 \hookrightarrow xs_2}{\models_A a_1, a_2 \hookrightarrow xs_1 \uplus xs_2}(\text{ArgList})$$

$$\frac{}{\models_A t\ \text{uz}\ x \hookrightarrow [(x,z)]}(\text{Scalar}) \qquad \frac{}{\models_A t\ \text{uz}\ x[] \hookrightarrow [(x,z)]}(\text{Array})$$

$$\frac{\Delta f = ([(x_1, z_1), \dots, (x_n, z_n)], s)}{\Delta, [x_1 \mapsto (z_1, \lambda_1), \dots, x_n \mapsto (z_n, \lambda_n)] \models_S s : \sigma \rightleftharpoons \sigma_1}{\Delta, \sigma, [\lambda_1, \dots, \lambda_n] \models_X \text{call } f \Rightarrow \sigma_1}(\text{Xcall})$$

$$\frac{\Delta f = ([(x_1, z_1), \dots, (x_n, z_n)], s)}{\Delta, [x_1 \mapsto (z_1, \lambda_1), \dots, x_n \mapsto (z_n, \lambda_n)] \models_S R(s) : \sigma \rightleftharpoons \sigma_1}{\Delta, \sigma, [\lambda_1, \dots, \lambda_n] \models_X \text{uncall } f \Rightarrow \sigma_1}(\text{Xuncall})$$

Fig. 9. Semantic rules for procedures and programs

5   Code Examples

In the examples, we use some syntactic sugar that the Hermes compiler expands into the core syntax during parsing. The statements $Lval$++;, $Lval$--;, and if (Exp) $Lval$ update Exp; are expanded to $Lval$ += 1;, $Lval$ -= 1;, and $Lval$ update $(Exp\ != 0)$ & (Exp);, respectively. The latter works because 0 is a neutral element for all the update operators used in Hermes. A declaration that specifies a number of variables and arrays of the same type is expanded to a sequence of individual declarations, and if secret or public is omitted from a declaration, secret is assumed. For example, the declarations public u32 x, a[n]; u64 z; is just a shorter way to write the equivalent public u32 x; public u32 a[n]; secret u64 z;. Operator precedences can be overridden by parentheses.

Figure 10 (top) shows Hermes code for the TEA encryption algorithm [14], a simple cypher used mainly for teaching. Only the encryption function is shown – decryption is done by uncalling the encryption function. The sizes of v and k are 2 and 4, respectively. Compare to the equivalent program in C [17] at the bottom of Fig. 10. Apart from using updates and swaps, the main difference is that the C version requires an explicit decryption function, which is not needed in Hermes. Also, the local variables are in Hermes cleared to 0 by "uncomputation", where the C version leaves these uncleared.

Figure 11 shows Hermes and C code for the central part of RC5 [9], another simple algorithm. The Hermes program shows size s being used as a loop bound, which makes the procedure independent of the size of the expanded key. Since C does not have a rotate operator, the C version [15] uses a macro for this. And since C does not have a swap operator, the central loop is unrolled so one iteration in the C version correspond to two iterations in the Hermes version. Again, C needs an explicit decryption function (not shown), which is not required in Hermes. Key expansion in RC5 (not shown) is not reversible, so to

```
encrypt (u32 v[], u32 k[])
{
    u32 v0, v1, k0, k1, k2, k3;
    public u32 sum;
    const delta = 0x9E3779B9;              /* key schedule constant */
    v0 <-> v[0]; v1 <-> v[1];                        /* set up */
    k0 += k[0]; k1 += k[1]; k2 += k[2]; k3 += k[3];  /* cache key */
    for (i=0; 32) {                         /* basic cycle start */
        sum += delta;
        v0 += ((v1<<4) + k0) ^ (v1 + sum) ^ ((v1>>5) + k1);
        v1 += ((v0<<4) + k2) ^ (v0 + sum) ^ ((v0>>5) + k3);
        i++;
    }                       /* end cycle, now clear local variables */
    k0 -= k[0]; k1 -= k[1]; k2 -= k[2]; k3 -= k[3]; sum -= 0xC6EF3720;
    v[0] <-> v0; v[1] <-> v1;               /* return coded values */
}
```

```
void encrypt (uint32_t v[2], uint32_t k[4]) {
    uint32_t v0=v[0], v1=v[1], sum=0, i;  /* set up */
    uint32_t delta=0x9E3779B9;              /* key schedule constant */
    uint32_t k0=k[0], k1=k[1], k2=k[2], k3=k[3];  /* cache key */
    for (i=0; i<32; i++) {                  /* basic cycle start */
        sum += delta;
        v0 += ((v1<<4) + k0) ^ (v1 + sum) ^ ((v1>>5) + k1);
        v1 += ((v0<<4) + k2) ^ (v0 + sum) ^ ((v0>>5) + k3);
    }                                       /* end cycle */
    v[0]=v0; v[1]=v1;
}

void decrypt (uint32_t v[2], uint32_t k[4]) {
    uint32_t v0=v[0], v1=v[1], sum=0xC6EF3720, i;  /* sum=32*delta */
    uint32_t delta=0x9E3779B9;              /* key schedule constant */
    uint32_t k0=k[0], k1=k[1], k2=k[2], k3=k[3];  /* cache key */
    for (i=0; i<32; i++) {                  /* basic cycle start */
        v1 -= ((v0<<4) + k2) ^ (v0 + sum) ^ ((v0>>5) + k3);
        v0 -= ((v1<<4) + k0) ^ (v1 + sum) ^ ((v1>>5) + k1);
        sum -= delta;
    }                                       /* end cycle */
    v[0]=v0; v[1]=v1;
}
```

Fig. 10. TEA in Hermes (top) and C (bottom)

implement this in Hermes requires storing additional values i "garbage" array. Th garbage array is reset to zeroes when the expanded key (after calling the central procedure) is uncomputed by **uncalling** the key expansion procedure.

Figure 12 shows Hermes code for speck128 [1,18] (a cypher used by NSA). Again, only encoding is shown. The main thing to note is that the R procedure are found in two copies, one (Rs) where the k parameter is secret, and one (Rp) where it is public. This is because two of the calls pass a public loop counter to k, while the other two calls pass part of a secret key to k. An extension to the type system that avoids this codeduplication is being investigated. Some

```
rc5(u32 ct[], u32 S[])
{
  u32 A, B;
  A <-> ct[0];  B <-> ct[1];
  A += S[0];  B += S[1];
  for(i=2; size S) {
    A ^= B; A <<= B; A += S[i];
    B <-> A;
    i++;
  }
  ct[0] <-> A;  ct[1] <-> B;
}
```

```
#define ROL(x,r)  ((x<<r)|(x>>(64-r)))

void RC5_ENCRYPT(WORD *pt, WORD *ct)
{
  WORD i, A=pt[0]+S[0], B=pt[1]+S[1];
  for(i = 1; i <= 12; i++)
  {
    A = ROL(A ^ B, B) + S[2*i];
    B = ROL(B ^ A, A) + S[2*i + 1];
  }
  ct[0] = A;  ct[1] = B;
}
```

Fig. 11. RC5 core in Hermes (left) and C (right)

```
speck128(u64 ct[], u64 K[])
{
  u64 y, x, b, a;
  y <-> ct[0];  x <-> ct[1];  b += K[0];  a += K[1];

  call Rs(x, y, b);
  for (i=0; 32) {
    call Rp(a, b, i);  i++;
    call Rs(x, y, b);
  }
  for (i=32; 0) {   /* restore a and b */
    i--; uncall Rp(a, b, i);
  }
  y <-> ct[0];  x <-> ct[1];  b -= K[0];  a -= K[1];
}

Rs(u64 x, u64 y, secret u64 k)
{ x >>= 8; x += y; x ^= k; y <<= 3; y ^= x; }

Rp(u64 x, u64 y, public u64 k)
{ x >>= 8; x += y; x ^= k; y <<= 3; y ^= x; }
```

Fig. 12. Speck128 in Hermes

uncomputation is needed to restore a and b to 0. This is not found in the standard C implementation, where these are left uncleared.

We have implemented several other encryption algorithms in Hermes, including Red Pike [16] (a cypher used by GCHQ) and Blowfish [10] (designed as a replacement for DES). With the exception of key expansion, this was relatively straight forward.

6   Conclusion and Future Work

We have presented a language Hermes for writing light-weight encryption functions. Hermes ensures reversibility, so decryption can be done by executing encryption procedures backwards, and can (given a suitable implementation) protect against certain forms of side-channel attacks, such as timing based attacks and leaks to memory. Hermes has a formal semantics for both the type system and runtime behavior. These semantics can be used to prove both that secret information does not leak into publica variables and that type-correct programs are, indeed, reversible, but we do not have complete proofs for this at the moment, mainly because we expect Hermes to evolve over time, so we have postponed proofs until Hermes settles to a more stable form. The semantic rules do not specify what happens if a condition in a rule fails, for example when an array bound is exceeded. For the type rules, the obvious behaviour is an error message. For the run-time semantics, it is less clear. Run-time error messages can be helpful in locating errors, but they can potentially leak information about secret values. So it might be better to continue execution with some default behaviour.

We have in Standard ML made a reference interpreter for Hermes which closely follows the semantic rules. The interpreter does not guarantee time-invariant operations, and it reports errors when run-time errors are detected. We also have an implementation of Hermes in WebAssembly [2]. We are working on extending this to target CT-Wasm [13], a variant of WebAssembly that has a public/secret type system similar to the one used here. Targeting CT-Wasm should preserve the safety features of Hermes. Note that the aliasing restrictions in Hermes make call-by-reference indistinguishable from call-by-value-return, so this can be used as an optimisation when WebAssembly, as planned, supports multiple return values.

We are currently working on implementing the Advanced Encryption Standared (AES) in Hermes. An issue with AES is that it uses secret information as array indexes, which the current Hermes does not allow, so to implement it may require a relaxation of this restriction, for example by ensuring the array is fully cached, so access time is independent of the index. We are also considering other extensions to Hermes, including sized boolean types (with values 0 and $2^z - 1$) and read-only parameters to procedures. The latter will avoid the need of duplicating the R procedure in Fig. 12. We are also considering additional control structures, but will only add them by need. A more precise alias analysis could relax some of the restrictions on parameter passing, but we have not found any examples where this matters. At the moment, index checks and checks that variables and arrays are zeroed before being disposed are done at run time. Static verification of these would be beneficial, for efficiency and safety both.

Some side-channel attacks (such as Spectre [4]) target speculative execution. By partially evaluating [3,6] Hermes programs with all public values (typically key and block lengths) considered static will leave a straight-line unconditional sequence of operations only involving secret values and constants, thus avoiding speculative execution. This has the added benefit that it is easier to eliminate index checks and checks for variables being zero at the end of blocks.

Public-key cyphers are not trivially reversible – that would defeat the purpose – so implementing these in Hermes it not obvious. A possibility is to let the encryption function return not only the cypher text, but also additional "garbage" information that must be discarded before transmitting the cypher text. Similarly, decryption also produces garbage in addition to the original text. As such, the reversibility of Hermes is not exploited, but is rather a hindrance. The safety features still apply, though.

We thank our colleagues Ken Friis Larsen and Michael Kirkedal for co-supervising some student projects about Hermes and for fruitful discussions, and we thank the students who worked on these projects.

References

1. Beaulieu, R., Shors, D., Smith, J., Treatman-Clark, S., Weeks, B., Wingers, L.: The SIMON and SPECK families of lightweight block ciphers. Cryptology ePrint Archive, Report 2013/404 (2013). https://eprint.iacr.org/2013/404
2. Haas, A., et al.: Bringing the web up to speed with Webassembly. SIGPLAN Not. **52**(6), 185–200 (2017)
3. Hatcliff, J., Mogensen, T.Æ., Thiemann, P. (eds.): DIKU 1998. LNCS, vol. 1706. Springer, Heidelberg (1999). https://doi.org/10.1007/3-540-47018-2
4. Kocher, P., et al.: Exploiting speculative execution. Spectre attacks (2018). meltdownattack.com
5. Lutz, C.: Janus: a time-reversible language. A letter to Landauer (1986). http://www.tetsuo.jp/ref/janus.pdf
6. Mogensen, T.Æ: Partial evaluation of the reversible language Janus. In: Khoo, S.-C., Siek, J.G. (eds.) PEPM 2011, pp. 23–32. ACM (2011)
7. Mogensen, T.Æ.: Hermes: a reversible language for writing encryption algorithms (work in progress). In: Bjørner, N., Virbitskaite, I., Voronkov, A. (eds.) PSI 2019. LNCS, vol. 11964, pp. 243–251. Springer, Cham (2019). https://doi.org/10.1007/978-3-030-37487-7_21
8. Palsberg, J., Ørbæk, P.: Trust in the λ-calculus. In: Mycroft, A. (ed.) SAS 1995. LNCS, vol. 983, pp. 314–329. Springer, Heidelberg (1995). https://doi.org/10.1007/3-540-60360-3_47
9. Rivest, R.L.: The RC5 encryption algorithm. Dr. Dobb's J. **20**(1), 146–148 (1995)
10. Schneier, B.: Description of a new variable-length key, 64-bit block cipher (Blowfish). In: Anderson, R. (ed.) FSE 1993. LNCS, vol. 809, pp. 191–204. Springer, Heidelberg (1994). https://doi.org/10.1007/3-540-58108-1_24
11. Smith, G.: Principles of secure information flow analysis. In: Christodorescu, M., Jha, S., Maughan, D., Song, D., Wang, C. (eds.) Malware Detection, pp. 291–307. Springer, Boston (2007). https://doi.org/10.1007/978-0-387-44599-1_13
12. Táborský, D., Larsen, K.F., Thomsen, M.K.: Encryption and reversible computations. In: Kari, J., Ulidowski, I. (eds.) RC 2018. LNCS, vol. 11106, pp. 331–338. Springer, Cham (2018). https://doi.org/10.1007/978-3-319-99498-7_23
13. Watt, C., Renner, J., Popescu, N., Cauligi, S., Stefan, D.: CT-Wasm: type-driven secure cryptography for the web ecosystem. CoRR, abs/1808.01348 (2018)
14. Wheeler, D.J., Needham, R.M.: TEA, a tiny encryption algorithm. In: Preneel, B. (ed.) FSE 1994. LNCS, vol. 1008, pp. 363–366. Springer, Heidelberg (1995). https://doi.org/10.1007/3-540-60590-8_29
15. Wikipedia: RC5. https://en.wikipedia.org/wiki/RC5. Accessed Feb 2019
16. Wikipedia: Red pike (cipher). https://en.wikipedia.org/wiki/Red_Pike_(cipher). Accessed Feb 2019

17. Wikipedia: Tiny encryption algorithm. https://en.wikipedia.org/wiki/Tiny_Encryption_Algorithm. Accessed Jan 2019
18. Wikipedia: Speck (cipher). https://en.wikipedia.org/wiki/Speck_(cipher). Accessed Feb 2019
19. Yokoyama, T., Axelsen, H.B., Glück, R.: Principles of a reversible programming language. In: Proceedings of the 5th Conference on Computing frontiers, CF 2008, pp. 43–54. ACM, New York (2008)

Reversible Programming Languages Capturing Complexity Classes

Lars Kristiansen[1,2(✉)]

[1] Department of Informatics, University of Oslo, Oslo, Norway
[2] Department of Mathematics, University of Oslo, Oslo, Norway
larsk@math.uio.no

Abstract. We argue that there is a link between implicit computational complexity theory and the theory of reversible computation. We show that the complexity classes ETIME and P can be captured by inherently reversible programming languages.

1 Introduction

The title above is inspired by the title of a paper I co-authored with Paul Voda more than 15 years ago: *Programming languages capturing complexity classes* [10]. In that paper we related the computational power of fragments of programming languages to complexity classes defined by imposing time and space constraints on Turing machines. Around that time, I authored and co-authored a number of related papers, e.g. [8,9,11], all of which were clearly inspired by work in *implicit computational complexity theory* from the 1990s, e.g., Bellatoni and Cook [2], Leivant [12,13] and, particularly, Jones [5,6].

Complexity classes like P, FP, NP, LOGSPACE, EXPTIME, and so on, are defined by imposing explicit resource bounds on a particular machine model, namely the Turing machine. E.g., FP is defined as the class of functions computable in polynomial time on a deterministic Turing machine. The definition puts constraints on the resources available to the Turing machines, but no constraints on the algorithms available to them. A Turing machine may compute a function in the class by any imaginable algorithm as long as it works in polynomial time. Implicit computational complexity theory studies classes of functions (problems, languages) that are defined without imposing explicit resource bounds on machine models, but rather by imposing linguistic constraints on the way algorithms can be formulated. When we explicitly restrict our language for formulating algorithms, that is, our programming language, then we may implicitly restrict the computational resources needed to execute algorithms. If we manage to find a restricted programming language that captures a complexity class, then we will have a so-called implicit characterization. A seminal example is Bellatoni and Cook's [2] characterization of FP. They give a functional programming language (which they call a function algebra). This language consists of a few initial functions and two definition schemes (safe composition and safe primitive recursion) which allow us to define new functions. These schemes put

© Springer Nature Switzerland AG 2020
I. Lanese and M. Rawski (Eds.): RC 2020, LNCS 12227, pp. 111–127, 2020.
https://doi.org/10.1007/978-3-030-52482-1_6

rather severe syntactical restrictions on how we can define functions, but they do not refer to polynomially bounded Turing machines or any other kind of resource bounded computing machinery. It is not easy to write programs when we have to stick to these schemes, even experienced programmers might find it hard to multiply two numbers but, be that as it may, this is a programming language that yields an implicit characterization of a complexity class. It turns out that a function can be computed by a program written in Bellantoni & Cook's language if and only if it belongs to the complexity class FP.

There is an obvious link between implicit computational complexity and reversible computing. A programming language based on natural reversible operations will impose restrictions on the way algorithms can be formulated, and thus, also restrictions on the computational resources needed to execute algorithms. Hence, the following question knocks at the door: Will it be possible find reversible programming languages that capture some of the standard complexity classes? The answer turns out to be YES. We will present a reversible language that captures, or if you like, gives an implicit characterization of, the (maybe not very well-known) complexity class ETIME. A few small modifications of this language yield a reversible language that captures the very well-known complexity class P.

Our languages are based on a couple of naturally reversible operations. To increase, or decrease, a natural number by 1 modulo a base b is such an operation: $\ldots 0, 1, 2, \ldots, b - 2, b - 1, 0, 1, 2 \ldots$. The successor of $b - 1$ becomes 0, and then $b - 1$ becomes the predecessor of 0. Thus, "increase" and "decrease" are the reverse of each other. To move an element from the top of one stack to the top of another stack is another such operation as we can simply move the element back to the stack it came from.

This paper addresses students and researchers interested in programming languages, reversible computations and computer science in general, they will not necessarily be experts in computability or complexity theory. We will give priority to readability over technical accuracy, but still this is a fairly technical paper, and we will assume that the reader is faintly acquainted with Turing machines and basic complexity theory (standard textbooks are Arora and Barac [1], Jones [7] and Sipser [16]).

Implicit computational complexity theory is definitely a broader and richer research area than our short discussion above may indicate. More on the subject can be found in Dal Lago [3].

2 Reversible Bottomless Stack (RBS) Programs

An infinite sequence of natural numbers $s_1, s_2, s_3, \ldots$ is a *bottomless stack* if there exists k such that $s_i = 0$ for all $i > k$. We use $\langle x_1, \ldots, x_n, 0^*]$ to denote the bottomless stack $s_1, s_2, s_3, \ldots$ where $s_i = x_i$ when $i \leq n$, and $s_i = 0$ when $i > n$. We say that x_1 is the *top element* of $\langle x_1, \ldots, x_n, 0^*]$. Observe that 0 is the top element of the stack $\langle 0^*]$. Furthermore, observe that $\langle 0, 0^*]$ is the same stack as $\langle 0^*]$ (since $\langle 0, 0^*]$ and $\langle 0^*]$ denote the same sequence of natural numbers). We will refer to $\langle 0^*]$ as the *zero stack*.

THE SYNTAX OF RBS

$$X \in \textbf{Variable} \quad ::= \quad \text{X}_1 \mid \text{X}_2 \mid \text{X}_3 \mid \ldots$$
$$com \in \textbf{Command} \quad ::= \quad X^+ \mid X^- \mid (X \text{ to } X) \mid com; com$$
$$\mid \quad \texttt{loop } X \; \{ \, com \, \}$$

Fig. 1. The syntax of the language RBS. The variable X in the loop command is not allowed to occur in the loop's body.

The syntax of the imperative programming language RBS is given in Fig. 1. Any element in the syntactic category **Command** will be called a *program*, and we will use the word *command* and the word *program* interchangeably throughout the paper. We will now explain the semantics of RBS.

An RBS program manipulates bottomless stacks, and each program variable holds such a stack. The input to a program is a single natural number m. When the execution of the program starts, the input m will be stored at the top of the stack hold by X_1, that is, we have $\text{X}_1 = \langle m, 0^*]$. All other variables occurring in the program hold the zero stack when the execution starts. A program is executed in a *base* b which is determined by the input: we have $b = \max(m + 1, 2)$ if $\text{X}_1 = \langle m, 0^*]$ when the execution starts. The execution base b is kept fixed during the entire execution.

Let X and Y be program variables. We will now explain how the primitive commands work. The command (X to Y) pops off the top element of the stack held by X and pushes it onto the stack held by Y, that is

$$\{\text{X} = \langle x_1, \ldots, x_n, 0^*] \wedge \text{Y} = \langle y_1, \ldots, y_m, 0^*]\} \, (\text{X to Y})$$
$$\{\text{X} = \langle x_2 \ldots, x_n, 0^*] \wedge \text{Y} = \langle x_1, y_1, \ldots, y_m, 0^*]\}.$$

The command X^+ increases the the top element of the stack held by X by $1 \pmod{b}$, that is

$$\{\text{X} = \langle x_1, \ldots, x_n, 0^*]\} \, \text{X}^+ \, \{\text{X} = \langle x_1 + 1 \pmod{b}, x_2 \ldots, x_n, 0^*]\}.$$

The command X^- decreases the the top element of the stack held by X by $1 \pmod{b}$, that is

$$\{\text{X} = \langle x_1, \ldots, x_n, 0^*]\} \, \text{X}^- \, \{\text{X} = \langle x_1 - 1 \pmod{b}, x_2 \ldots, x_n, 0^*]\}.$$

Observe that we have

$$\{\text{X} = \langle b - 1, x_2 \ldots, x_n, 0^*]\} \, \text{X}^+ \, \{\text{X} = \langle 0, x_2 \ldots, x_n, 0^*]\}$$

and

$$\{\text{X} = \langle 0, x_2 \ldots, x_n, 0^*]\} \, \text{X}^- \, \{\text{X} = \langle b - 1, x_2 \ldots, x_n, 0^*]\}$$

when b is the base of the execution.

The semantics of the command $C_1 ; C_2$ is as expected. This is the standard composition of the commands C_1 and C_2, that is, first C_1 is executed, then C_2 is executed. The command loop X $\{C\}$ executes the command C repeatedly k times in a row where k is the top element of the stack held by X. Note that the variable X is not allowed to occur in C and, moreover, the command loop X $\{C\}$ will not modify the stack held by X.

Example 1. Let C_1 be the program loop X_1 $\{ X_2^+ \}$; $(X_2 \text{ to } X_1)$. We have

$$\{X_1 = \langle 17, 0^*] \wedge X_2 = \langle 0^*]\} \, C_1 \, \{X_1 = \langle 17, 17, 0^*] \wedge X_2 = \langle 0^*]\}.$$

Let C_2 be the program loop X_1 $\{ X_2^+ \}$; X_2^+; $(X_2 \text{ to } X_1)$. We have

$$\{X_1 = \langle 17, 0^*] \wedge X_2 = \langle 0^*]\} \, C_2 \, \{X_1 = \langle 0, 17, 0^*] \wedge X_2 = \langle 0^*]\}$$

since the execution base is 18. All numbers stored on stacks during an execution will be strictly less than the execution base, and thus, less than or equal to $\max(m, 1)$ where m is the input. □

Intuitively, it should be clear that RBS programs are reversible in a very strong sense. RBS is an *inherently reversible* programming language in the terminology of Matos [14]. If we like, we can of course state this insight more formally. The next definition and the following theorem will be a step in that direction.

Definition 2. We define *reverse command* of C, written C^R, inductively over the structure C:

- $(X_i^+)^R = X_i^-$
- $(X_i^-)^R = X_i^+$
- $(X_i \text{ to } X_j)^R = (X_j \text{ to } X_i)$
- $(C_1 ; C_2)^R = C_2^R ; C_1^R$
- $(\text{loop } X_i \, \{ C \})^R = \text{loop } X_i \, \{ C^R \}.$

□

Theorem 3. *Let C be a program, and let $X_1, \ldots, X_n$ be the variables occurring in C. Furthermore, let m be any natural number. We have*

$$\{X_1 = \langle m, 0^*] \wedge \bigwedge_{i=2}^{n} X_i = \langle 0^*]\} \, C; C^R \, \{X_1 = \langle m, 0^*] \wedge \bigwedge_{i=2}^{n} X_i = \langle 0^*]\}.$$

It is a nice, and maybe even challenging, exercise to write up a decent proof Theorem 3, even if it should be pretty clear that the theorems holds. We will offer a proof in the next section. The reader not interested in the details of the proof, may skip that section.

We will now define the set of problems that can be decided by an RBS programs. To that end, we need to determine how an RBS program should accept, and how an RBS program should reject, its input. Any reasonable convention will do, and we will just pick a simple and convenient one.

EXAMPLE

Program:	Comments:
	(* $X_1 = \langle m, 0^*]$ *)
X_1 to X_9;	(* the top elements of X_9 is m *)
X_2^+;	(* $X_1 = \langle 0^*]$ and $X_2 = \langle 1, 0^*]$ *)
loop X_9 {	(* repeat m times *)
X_1 to X_3;	
X_2 to X_1;	(* swap the top elements of X_1 and X_2 *)
X_3 to X_2 }	

Fig. 2. The program accepts every even number and rejects every odd number.

Definition 4. An RBS program C accepts the natural number m if C executed with input m terminates with 0 at the top of the stack hold by X_1, otherwise, C rejects m.

A problem is a set of natural numbers.[1] An RBS program C *decides the problem A* if C accepts all m that belong to A and rejects all m that do not belong to A. Let $\mathcal{S}$ denote class of problems decidable by an RBS program. □

Let A be the set of even numbers. Then A is a problem. Figure 2 shows an RBS program that decides A.

Now, any RBS program decides a problem, and $\mathcal{S}$ is obviously a well-defined class of computable (decidable) problems. We have defined $\mathcal{S}$ by a reversible programming language. We have not defined $\mathcal{S}$ by imposing resource bounds on Turing machines or any other machine models. What can we say about the computational complexity of the problems we find in $\mathcal{S}$? May it be the case that $\mathcal{S}$ equals a complexity class?

3   The Proof of Theorem 3

This section is dedicated to a detailed proof of Theorem 3 (readers not interested may jump ahead to Sect. 4). First, we need some terminology and notation: We will say that a (bottomless) stack is a *b-stack* if every number stored on the stack is strictly smaller than b. Furthermore, we will use $\mathcal{V}(C)$ to denote the set of program variables occurring in the command C, and for any positive integer m and any command C, we define the command C^m by $C^1 \equiv C$ and $C^{m+1} \equiv C^m$; C.

Now, assume that C is an RBS command with $\mathcal{V}(C) \subseteq \{X_1, \ldots, X_n\}$. Furthermore, assume that C is executed in base b and that $\alpha_1, \ldots, \alpha_n, \beta_1, \ldots, \beta_n$ are b-stacks. With these assumptions in mind, we make the following claim:

---

[1] It is pretty standard in computability and complexity theory to define a problem as a set of natural numbers.

$$\text{If } \{\bigwedge_{\ell=1}^{n} X_\ell = \alpha_\ell\} \, C \, \{\bigwedge_{\ell=1}^{n} X_\ell = \beta_\ell\}, \text{ then } \{\bigwedge_{\ell=1}^{n} X_\ell = \beta_\ell\} \, C^R \, \{\bigwedge_{\ell=1}^{n} X_\ell = \alpha_\ell\}.$$

(claim)

Theorem 3 follows straightforwardly from this claim. So all we need to do is to prove the claim.

We will of course carry out induction on the structure of the command C, and our proof will split into the tree base cases (i) $C \equiv X_i^+$, (ii) $C \equiv X_i^-$ and (iii) $C \equiv (X_j \, \text{to} \, X_i)$ and the two inductive cases (iv) $C \equiv C_1 \,; C_2$ and $C \equiv \text{loop} \, X_i \, \{C_0\}$ (see Fig. 1).

Case (i). Assume

$$\{\bigwedge_{\ell=1}^{n} X_\ell = \alpha_\ell\} \, X_i^+ \, \{\bigwedge_{\ell=1}^{n} X_\ell = \beta_\ell\}.$$

Then we also have $\{X_i = \alpha_i\} \, X_i^+ \, \{X_i = \beta_i\}$ where

$$\alpha_i = \langle m_1, m_2, \ldots, m_k, 0^*] \quad \text{and} \quad \beta_i = \langle m_1 + 1 \, (\text{mod } b), m_2, \ldots, m_k, 0^*]$$

for some $m_1, \ldots, m_k < b$. We have $(m_1 + 1 \, (\text{mod } b)) - 1 \, (\text{mod } b) = m_1$ when $m_1 < b$. Thus we have $\{X_i = \beta_i\} \, X_i^- \, \{X_i = \alpha_i\}$. By Definition 2, we have $\{X_i = \beta_i\} \, (X_i^+)^R \, \{X_i = \alpha_i\}$. Now, since neither X_i^+ nor $(X_i^+)^R$ will modify any stack held by a variable X_j where $j \neq i$, we also have

$$\{\bigwedge_{\ell=1}^{n} X_\ell = \beta_\ell\} \, (X_i^+)^R \, \{\bigwedge_{\ell=1}^{n} X_\ell = \alpha_\ell\}.$$

This concludes the proof of case (i). The proofs of the cases (ii) and (iii) are very similar to the proof of case (i). We leave the details to the reader and proceed with the inductive cases.

Case (iv). Assume

$$\{\bigwedge_{\ell=1}^{n} X_\ell = \alpha_\ell\} \, C_1 \,; C_2 \, \{\bigwedge_{\ell=1}^{n} X_\ell = \beta_\ell\}.$$

Then there exist b-stacks $\gamma_1, \ldots, \gamma_n$ such that

$$\{\bigwedge_{\ell=1}^{n} X_\ell = \alpha_\ell\} \, C_1 \, \{\bigwedge_{\ell=1}^{n} X_\ell = \gamma_\ell\} \quad \text{and} \quad \{\bigwedge_{\ell=1}^{n} X_\ell = \gamma_\ell\} \, C_2 \, \{\bigwedge_{\ell=1}^{n} X_\ell = \beta_\ell\}.$$

We apply our induction hypothesis both to C_1 and to C_2 and conclude

$$\{\bigwedge_{\ell=1}^{n} X_\ell = \gamma_\ell\} \, C_1^R \, \{\bigwedge_{\ell=1}^{n} X_\ell = \alpha_\ell\} \quad \text{and} \quad \{\bigwedge_{\ell=1}^{n} X_\ell = \beta_\ell\} \, C_2^R \, \{\bigwedge_{\ell=1}^{n} X_\ell = \gamma_\ell\}.$$

It follows that

$$\{\bigwedge_{\ell=1}^{n} X_\ell = \beta_\ell\} \; C_2^R \, ; \, C_1^R \; \{\bigwedge_{\ell=1}^{n} X_\ell = \alpha_\ell\}.$$

Finally, as Definition 2 states that $(C_1 \, ; \, C_2)^R = C_2^R \, ; \, C_1^R$, we have

$$\{\bigwedge_{\ell=1}^{n} X_\ell = \beta_\ell\} \; (C_1 \, ; \, C_2)^R \; \{\bigwedge_{\ell=1}^{n} X_\ell = \alpha_\ell\}.$$

This completes the proof of case (iv).

Case (v). Assume

$$\{\bigwedge_{\ell=1}^{n} X_\ell = \alpha_\ell\} \; \texttt{loop } X_i \; \{\, C_0 \,\} \; \{\bigwedge_{\ell=1}^{n} X_\ell = \beta_\ell\} \qquad (*)$$

and let m be the top element of the stack α_i.

If $m = 0$, we have

$$\{\bigwedge_{\ell=1}^{n} X_\ell = \alpha_\ell\} \; \texttt{loop } X_i \; \{\, C_0 \,\} \; \{\bigwedge_{\ell=1}^{n} X_\ell = \alpha_\ell\}.$$

as the command C_0 will not be executed at all. Thus, we also have

$$\{\bigwedge_{\ell=1}^{n} X_\ell = \alpha_\ell\} \; \texttt{loop } X_i \; \{\, C_0^R \,\} \; \{\bigwedge_{\ell=1}^{n} X_\ell = \alpha_\ell\}.$$

and by Definition 2, we have

$$\{\bigwedge_{\ell=1}^{n} X_\ell = \alpha_\ell\} \; (\texttt{loop } X_i \; \{\, C_0 \,\})^R \; \{\bigwedge_{\ell=1}^{n} X_\ell = \alpha_\ell\}.$$

This proves that the claim holds when $m = 0$. We are left to prove that the claim holds when $m > 0$. Thus, in the remainder of this proof we assume that $m > 0$.

First we prove

$$\text{If } \{\bigwedge_{\ell=1}^{n} X_\ell = \alpha_\ell\} \; C_0^m \; \{\bigwedge_{\ell=1}^{n} X_\ell = \beta_\ell\}, \text{ then } \{\bigwedge_{\ell=1}^{n} X_\ell = \beta_\ell\} \; (C_0^R)^m \; \{\bigwedge_{\ell=1}^{n} X_\ell = \alpha_\ell\}.$$
$$(\dagger)$$

by a secondary induction on m.

Let $m = 1$. Then we have $C_0^m \equiv C_0$, and an application of our main induction hypothesis to C_0 yields $(\dagger)$. Let $m > 1$. Then we have

$$C_0^m \equiv C_0^{m-1} \, ; \, C_0 \quad \text{and} \quad (C_0^R)^m \equiv C_0^R \, ; \, (C_0^R)^{m-1}$$

and (†) holds by our induction hypothesis on m and case (iv) above. This concludes the proof of (†).

We are now ready to complete our proof the claim. By (*), we have

$$\{ \bigwedge_{\ell=1}^{n} X_\ell = \alpha_\ell \} \ C_0^m \ \{ \bigwedge_{\ell=1}^{n} X_\ell = \beta_\ell \}.$$

By (†), we have

$$\{ \bigwedge_{\ell=1}^{n} X_\ell = \beta_\ell \} \ (C_0^R)^m \ \{ \bigwedge_{\ell=1}^{n} X_\ell = \alpha_\ell \}.$$

Since $X_i \notin \mathcal{V}(C_0)$, we have $\beta_i = \alpha_i$, and thus, the top element of β_i is the same as the top element of α_i, namely m. It follows that

$$\{ \bigwedge_{\ell=1}^{n} X_\ell = \beta_\ell \} \ \texttt{loop } X_i \ \{ C_0^R \} \ \{ \bigwedge_{\ell=1}^{n} X_\ell = \alpha_\ell \}.$$

Finally, as Definition 2 states that $\texttt{loop } X_i \ \{ C_0^R \} = (\texttt{loop } X_i \ \{ C_0 \})^R$, we have

$$\{ \bigwedge_{\ell=1}^{n} X_\ell = \beta_\ell \} \ (\texttt{loop } X_i \ \{ C_0 \} \ )^R \ \{ \bigwedge_{\ell=1}^{n} X_\ell = \alpha_\ell \}.$$

This completes the proof of case (v).

4   Simulation of Turing Machines

4.1   A General Strategy

Let us first see how we can simulate a Turing machine in a standard way in a standard high-level language. Thereafter we will discuss how we can simulate a Turing machine in our rudimentary reversible language. In the standard language we will of course be able to simulate any Turing machine, no matter how much time and space resources the machine requires. In the reversible language we will only be able to simulate those Turing machines that run in time $O(2^{kn})$ (where k is a constant and n is the length of the input).

We assume some familiarity with Turing machines. The reader is expected to know that a Turing machine computes by writing symbols from a finite alphabet $a_1, \ldots, a_A$ on an infinite tape which is divided into cells; know that one of the cells is scanned by the machine's head; know a there is a finite number of states $q_1, \ldots, q_Q$; and so on.

The input w will be available on the tape when a Turing machine M starts, and the actions taken by M will be governed by a finite transition table. Each entry of the table is a 5-tuple

$$a_i, q_k, a_j, D, q_\ell \tag{*}$$

where a_i, a_j are alphabet symbols; q_k, q_ℓ are states; and D is ether "left" or "right". Such a tuple is called a transition and tells M what to do when it scans the symbol a_j in state q_k: in that case M should write the symbol a_j, move its head one position in the direction given by D, and then proceed in state q_ℓ. We restrict our attention to deterministic Turing machines, and for each alphabet symbol a_i and each non-halting state q_k, there will be one, and only one, transition that starts with a_i, q_k. So a Turing machine knows exactly what to do until it reaches one its halting states, and then it simply halts (if it halts in a dedicated state q_{accept}, it accepts its input; if it halts in a dedicated state q_{reject}, it rejects its input). This entails that we can simulate a Turing machine by a sequence of if-then statements embedded into a while-loop. We need one if-then statement for each transition:

⟨initiate the tape with the input w⟩
while ⟨M is not in a halting state⟩ **do**
if ⟨a_1 is scanned in state q_1⟩ **then** ⟨do what should be done⟩;
if ⟨a_2 is scanned in state q_1⟩ **then** ⟨do what should be done ⟩;
$\vdots$ $\vdots$
if ⟨a_A is scanned in state q_Q⟩ **then** ⟨do what should be done ⟩
end-while.

Minimum one transition will be executed each time the loop's body is executed, and the running time of M (on input w) will more or less be the number of times the body is executed. (It might happen that more than one transition is executed when the loop's body is executed once, but that will not cause any trouble.) In order to simulate the actions taken by the transitions, we need a representation of the computing machinery. We need to keep track of the current state, we need to keep track of the symbols on the tape, and we need to identify the scanned cell. The current state can simply be stored in a register STATE, but how should we deal with the tape? The tape is divided into an infinite sequence of cells

$$C_1, C_2, C_2, \ldots, C_{s-1}, C_s, C_{s+1}, \ldots$$

where one of the cells C_s is scanned by the head. Only finitely many of these cells will contain anything else than the blank symbol. Let us say that C_i contains blank when $i > B_0$. In order to simulate the machine it will obviously be sufficient to store the symbols in the cells $C_1, C_2, \ldots, C_B$ where $B = \max(B_0, s) + 1$. In addition we need to keep track of the scanned cell C_s. A convenient way to deal with the situation will be to use a stack STACK_L, a register SCAN, another stack STACK_R, and store the tape content in the following way:

C_{s-1}		C_{s+1}
$\vdots$		$\vdots$
C_1	C_s	C_B
STACK_L	SCAN	STACK_R

Now we can mimic the movements of the head by pushing and popping alphabet symbols in the obvious way, and the transition (*) can be implemented by a program of the form

> if SCAN = a_i and STATE = q_k then
> { SCAN := a_j; ... push and pop ... ; STATE := q_ℓ }.

4.2   Can RBS Programs Simulate Turing Machines?

The input to an RBS program is a natural number, and we will thus discuss to what extent an RBS program can simulate a Turing machine that takes a single natural number as input.

We have seen that a program with only one while-loop can simulate a Turing machine (and we will for sure need at least one while-loop in order to simulate an arbitrary Turing machine). Now, while-loops are not available in RBS, and the best we can do in order to simulate a Turing machine is to use a fixed number of nested for-loops:

> loop Y_1 { loop Y_2 { ... loop Y_k { ⟨sequence of if-then statements⟩ } ... }}.

Since an RBS program cannot increase the numerical value of its input, the body of each of these loops will be executed maximum $\max(m, 1)$ times where m is the input to the RBS program (and to the Turing machine the program simulates). Thus it is pretty clear that we cannot simulate a Turing machine if its running time is not bounded by m^k for some constant k. This corresponds to a bound $2^{k|m|}$ where k is a constant and $|m|$ is the length of the input m, that is, $|m|$ equals the number of symbols needed to represent the natural number m in binary notation. In the following we will see that any Turing machine that uses such an amount of computation time can be simulated by an RBS program.

It turns out that an RBS program can simulate the transitions of a Turing machine M in essentially the same way as the high-level program sketched above, given that the input to M is sufficiently large (on small inputs the simulation might fail). Stacks are directly available in RBS, and thus an RBS program can easily represent the tape and mimic the movements of the head. On the other hand, assignment statements and if-then statements are not directly available. This makes things a bit tricky. Let us first see how RBS programs to a certain extent can simulate programs written in a non-reversible programming language called LOOP⁻.

4.3   LOOP⁻ Programs

The syntax of LOOP⁻ is given in Fig. 3. Any element in the syntactic category **Command** will be called a program. A LOOP⁻ program manipulates natural numbers, and each program variable holds a single natural number. The command X := k assigns the fixed number k to the variable X. The command X := Y assigns the number hold by the variable Y to the variable X. The command

THE SYNTAX OF LOOP⁻

$$X \in \textbf{Variable} \quad ::= \quad \mathtt{X}_1 \mid \mathtt{X}_2 \mid \mathtt{X}_3 \mid \ldots$$
$$k \in \textbf{Constant} \quad ::= \quad 0 \mid 1 \mid 2 \mid 3 \mid \ldots$$
$$com \in \textbf{Command} \quad ::= \quad X := k \mid X := X \mid \mathtt{pred}(X) \mid com\,;\,com$$
$$\mid \quad \mathtt{loop}\ X\ \{\,com\,\}$$

Fig. 3. The syntax of the language LOOP⁻. The variable X in the loop command is not allowed to occur in the loop's body.

$\mathtt{pred}(\mathtt{X})$ decreases the value hold by the variable $\mathtt{X}$ by 1 if the value is strictly greater than 0; and leave the value hold by $\mathtt{X}$ unchanged if the value is 0. Furthermore, the command $\mathtt{C}_1\,;\,\mathtt{C}_2$ is the standard composition of the commands $\mathtt{C}_1$ and $\mathtt{C}_2$, and the command $\mathtt{loop}\ \mathtt{X}\ \{\mathtt{C}\}$ executes the command $\mathtt{C}$ repeatedly k times in a row where k in the number hold by $\mathtt{X}$. Note that the variable $\mathtt{X}$ is not allowed to occur in $\mathtt{C}$ and that the command $\mathtt{loop}\ \mathtt{X}\ \{\mathtt{C}\}$ does not modify the value held by $\mathtt{X}$.

An RBS program can represent a LOOP⁻ variable $\mathtt{X}$ holding natural number k by a variable $\mathtt{X}$ (we use the same variable name) holding the stack $\langle k, 0^* \rangle$. The command $\mathtt{X} := k$ can then be simulated by the program

$$(\mathtt{X\,to\,Z});\ \underbrace{\mathtt{X}^+;\mathtt{X}^+;\ \ldots\mathtt{X}^+}_{\text{increase } k \text{ times}}$$

where $\mathtt{Z}$ is an auxiliary variable ($\mathtt{Z}$ works as a trash bin). Now, observe that this will only work if the base of execution is strictly greater than k, but that will good enough to us. The command $\mathtt{X} := \mathtt{Y}$ can be simulated by the program

$$(\mathtt{X\,to\,Z});\ \mathtt{loop}\ \mathtt{Y}\ \{\,\mathtt{X}^+\,\}$$

where $\mathtt{Z}$ is an auxiliary variable ($\mathtt{Z}$ works as a trash bin). Furthermore, the command $\mathtt{pred}(\mathtt{X})$ can be simulated by a program that uses auxiliary variables $\mathtt{Y}$ and $\mathtt{Z}$ (which represent natural numbers) and the simulations of the assignment statements given above:

$$\mathtt{Z} := 0;\ \mathtt{Y} := \mathtt{X};\ \mathtt{loop}\ \mathtt{Y}\ \{\,\mathtt{X} := \mathtt{Z};\ \mathtt{Z}^+\,\}.$$

This shows how RBS programs can simulate all the primitive LOOP⁻ commands. It is easy to see that

- the RBS command $\mathtt{C}_1'\,;\,\mathtt{C}_2'$ simulates the LOOP⁻ command $\mathtt{C}_1\,;\,\mathtt{C}_2$ if $\mathtt{C}_1'$ simulates $\mathtt{C}_1$ and $\mathtt{C}_2'$ simulates $\mathtt{C}_2$
- the RBS command $\mathtt{loop}\ \mathtt{X}\ \{\,\mathtt{C}'\,\}$ simulates the LOOP⁻ command $\mathtt{loop}\ \mathtt{X}\ \{\,\mathtt{C}\,\}$ if $\mathtt{C}'$ simulates $\mathtt{C}$.

Hence, any LOOP⁻ program can be simulated by an RBS program given that the input is sufficiently large. On small inputs simulations might fail since the simulation of the assignment $X := k$ only works if the execution base is strictly greater than k.

The LOOP$^-$ language turns out to be more expressive than one might expect at a first glance, and all sorts of conditional statements and if-then constructions are available in the language. As an example, let us see how we can implement the construction

$$\text{if } X = Y \text{ then } C_1 \text{ else } C_2.$$

We will need some axillary variables X', Y', Z, U which do not occur in any of the commands C_1 and C_2. First we execute the program

$$X' := X; \, Y' := Y; \, \text{loop } X \, \{ \, \text{pred}(Y') \, \}; \, \text{loop } Y \, \{ \, \text{pred}(X') \, \}.$$

This program sets both X' and Y' to 0 if X and Y hold the same number. If X and Y hold different numbers, one of the two variables X', Y' will be set to a number strictly greater than 0. Then we execute the program

$$\begin{aligned} &Z := 1; \, U := 1; \\ &\text{loop } X' \, \{ \, Z := 0 \, \}; \, \text{loop } Y' \, \{ \, Z := 0 \, \}; \\ &\text{loop } Z \, \{ \, C_1; \, U := 0 \, \}; \, \text{loop } U \, \{ \, C_2 \, \}. \end{aligned}$$

The composition of these two programs executes the program C_1 exactly once (and C_2 will not be executed at all) if X and Y hold the same number. If X and Y hold different numbers, C_2 will be executed exactly once (and C_1 will not be executed at all). The reader should note that this implementation of if-then-else construction does not contain any assignments of the form $X := k$ where $k > 1$.

It is proved in Kristiansen [8] that LOOP$^-$ captures the complexity class LINSPACE, that is, the set of problems decidable in space $O(n)$ on a deterministic Turing machine (n is the length of the input). Hence, the considerations above indicate that LINSPACE $\subseteq \mathcal{S}$. However, we are on our way to proving a stronger result, namely that LINSPACE $\subseteq \mathcal{S} =$ ETIME. The equality LINSPACE $\overset{?}{=}$ ETIME is one of the many notorious open problems of complexity theory. The general opinion is that the equality does not hold.

4.4 RBS Programs that Simulates Time-Bounded Turing Machines

We have seen that RBS programs (nearly) can simulate LOOP$^-$ programs. LOOP$^-$ can assign constants to registers and perform if-then-else constructions. This helps us to see how to an RBS program can simulate an arbitrary $2^{k|m|}$ time Turing machine M. Such a program may be of the form

$$\begin{aligned} &\langle \text{initiate the tape with the input } m \rangle; \\ &Y_1 := \langle \text{the input } m \rangle; \, Y_2 := \langle \text{the input m} \rangle; \, \ldots; \, Y_k := \langle \text{the input m} \rangle; \\ &\text{loop } Y_1 \, \{ \, \text{loop } Y_2 \, \{ \, \ldots \text{loop } Y_k \, \{ \, T_1; \, T_2; \, \ldots; \, T_r \, \} \ldots \} \}. \end{aligned}$$

We represent the symbols in M's alphabet $a_1, \ldots a_A$ by the numbers $1, \ldots, A$ and M's states $q_1, \ldots q_Q$ by the numbers $1, \ldots, Q$. We use two stacks to hold the content of the tape, and we use registers STATE and SCAN to hold respectively the current state and the scanned cell. Each T_s will take care of a transition a_i, q_k, a_j, D, q_ℓ and be of the form

```
if SCAN = i and STATE = k then { SCAN := j; ... push and pop ... ; STATE := ℓ }.
```

We are left with a minor problem: This will not work for small inputs. This will only work if the base of execution $b = \max(m + 1, 2)$ is strictly greater than $\max(A, Q)$. Only then will the simulating program be able to perform the necessary assignments of constants to variables. In some sense we cannot deal with this problem. An RBS program will not be able to simulate (in any reasonable sense of the word) an arbitrary $2^{k|m|}$ time Turing machine M on small inputs, but still there will be an RBS program that decides the same problem as M.

We have seen that it suffices to assign the constants 0 and 1 to variables in order to implement the if-then-else construction in LOOP⁻. This entails that the if-then-else construction will work on small inputs as the base of execution always will be strictly greater than 1. Hence, if the problem A is decided by a $2^{k|m|}$ time Turing machine M, there will also be an RBS program that decides A. This program will be of the form

```
X := ⟨the input m⟩ ;
if X = 0 then ⟨give correct output for m = 0⟩
else { pred(X);
if X = 0 then ⟨give correct output for m = 1⟩
else { pred(X);
if X = 0 then ⟨give correct output for m = 2⟩
   ⋮
else {⟨the input is big enough, ...
   ... simulate M, accept if M accepts, reject if M rejects ⟩} ... } }.
```

5   Main Results

5.1   A Characterization of ETIME

Definition 5. Let $|m|$ denote the number of digits required to write the natural number m in binary notation. For any natural number k, let $ETIME_k$ be the class of problems decidable in time $O(2^{k|m|})$ on a deterministic Turing machine. Let $ETIME = \bigcup_{i \in \mathbb{N}} ETIME_i$. □

Theorem 6. $\mathcal{S} = ETIME$.

Proof. The proof of the inclusion $\mathcal{S} \subseteq$ ETIME should be straightforward to anyone experienced with Turing machines. Assume $A \in \mathcal{S}$ (we will argue that $A \in$ ETIME). Then there is an RBS program C that decides A. Let m be the input to C. Each loop in C will be executed maximum $m + 1$ times since the base of execution will be $\max(m+1, 2)$. Thus, there exist constants k_0, k_1 (not depending on m) such that $k_0(m+1)^{k_1}$ bounds the number of primitive commands executed by C on input m. A Turing machine can simulate the execution of C on input m with polynomial overhead. Thus there exist constants k_2, k_3 such that $k_2(m+1)^{k_3}$ bounds the number of steps a Turing machine needs to decide if m is in A. There exists k such that $k_2(m+1)^{k_3} < 2^{k|m|}$. Hence, $A \in \text{ETIME}$. This proves the inclusion $\mathcal{S} \subseteq \text{ETIME}$.

We turn to proof of the inclusion $\text{ETIME} \subseteq \mathcal{S}$. Assume $A \in \text{ETIME}$ (we will argue that $A \in \mathcal{S}$). Then there is a $O(2^{k|m|})$ time Turing machine M that decides A. Now, M will run in time $2^{k_0|m|}$ when k_0 is sufficiently large. In the previous section we saw that there will be an RBS program that decides the same problem as M. Hence, $A \in \mathcal{S}$. This proves the inclusion $\text{ETIME} \subseteq \mathcal{S}$.   □

5.2   A Characterization of P

Would it not be nice if we could find a reversible language that captures a complexity class that is a bit more attractive than ETIME? Now, P is for a number of reasons, which the reader might be aware of, one of most popular and important complexity classes. Luckily, it turns out that a few modifications of RBS yield a characterization of P.

First we modify the way RBS programs receive input. The input will now be a string over some alphabet. Any alphabet that contains at least two symbols will do and, for convenience, we will stick to the alphabet $\{a, b\}$. The base of execution will at program start be set to the length of the input. Otherwise, nearly everything is kept as before: Every variable will still hold a bottomless stack storing natural numbers. All commands available in the original version of RBS will be available in the new version. A program will still accept its input by terminating with 0 at the top of the stack held by X_1, otherwise, the program rejects its input. Moreover, all variables including X_1, the variable that used to import the input, hold the zero stack when the execution of a program starts.

Next we extend RBS by two commands with the syntax

$$\texttt{case   inp[}X\texttt{]=a:} \; \{ com \} \quad \text{and} \quad \texttt{case   inp[}X\texttt{]=b:} \; \{ com \}$$

where X is a variable and com is a command which does not contain X. These commands make it possible for a program to access its input. The input is a string $\alpha_0\alpha_1, \dots, \alpha_{b-1}$ where b is the execution base and $\alpha_i \in \{a, b\}$. Assume that X_j holds a stack where top element is k. The command

$$\texttt{case   inp[}X_j\texttt{]=a:} \; \{ \, \texttt{C} \, \}$$

executes the command C if $\alpha_k = a$, otherwise, the command does nothing. The command

$$\texttt{case   inp[}X_j\texttt{]=b:} \; \{ \, \texttt{C} \, \}$$

executes the command C if $\alpha_k = b$, otherwise, the command does nothing.

EXAMPLE

Program:	Comments:
	(* all stacks hold the zero stack *)
X_2^-	(* the top element of X_2 is $b - 1$ *)
loop X_2 {	(* repeat $b - 1$ times *)
case inp[X_3]=b:	(* X_3 is a pointer into the input *)
{ X_1 to X_9;	(* X_1 holds the zero stack *)
X_1^+	(* top element of X_1 is 1 *)
};	
X_3^+	(* move pointer to the right *)
};	(* end of loop *)
case inp[X_3]=a:	(* top element of X_3 is $b - 1$ *)
{ X_1 to X_9; X_1^+ }	

Fig. 4. The program accepts any string that starts with a nonempty sequence of a's and ends with a single b (the input to a program should at least contain two symbols). The program rejects any string that is not of this form. The program accepts by terminating with $X_1 = \langle 0^*]$ and rejects by terminating with $X_1 = \langle 1, 0^*]$.

We still have a reversible language. The two new commands are reversible. The variable X_j is not allowed to occur in C and will consequently not be modified by C. Thus, for $x \in \{a, b\}$, we may extend Definition 2 by

$$\left(\text{case} \quad \text{inp}[X_j]\text{=x: } \{ C \} \right)^R = \text{case} \quad \text{inp}[X_j]\text{=x: } \{ C^R \}.$$

and Theorem 3 will still hold.

To avoid confusion we will use RBS' to denote our new version of RBS. We require that the input to an RBS' program is of length at least 2 (so we exclude the empty string and the one-symbol strings a and b). This is of course a bit artificial, but it seems to be the most convenient way to deal with a few annoying problems of technical nature. Accordingly, we also require that every string in a language (see the definition below) is of length at least 2.

Definition 7. A language L is a set of strings over the alphabet $\{a, b\}$, moreover, every string in L is of length at least 2.

An RBS' program C decides the language L if C accepts every string that belongs to L and rejects every string that does not belong to L. Let S' be class of languages decidable by an RBS' program.

Let $|w|$ denote the length of the string w. For any natural number k, let P_k be the class of languages decidable in time $O(|w|^k)$ on a deterministic Turing machine. Let $P = \bigcup_{i \in \mathbb{N}} P_i$.   □

Figure 4 shows an RBS' program which decides the language given by the regular expression $a^* ab$.

The proof of the next theorem is very similar to the proof of Theorem 6, and the reader should be able to provide the details. Just recall that the execution base of an RBS′ program is set to the length of the input. Hence, the number of primitive instructions executed by an RBS′ program will be bounded by $|w|^k$ where $|w|$ is the length of the input w and k is a sufficiently large constant, and moreover, an RBS′ program of the form

$$\texttt{loop}\, Y_1 \, \{\, \texttt{loop}\, Y_2 \, \{\, \ldots \texttt{loop}\, Y_k \, \{\, \langle \ldots \text{ a list of transitions } \ldots \rangle \,\} \ldots \}\}.$$

will execute $\langle \ldots$ a list of transitions $\ldots \rangle$ exactly $|w|^k$ times if each and one of the variables $Y_1, \ldots Y_k$ holds a stack where the top element is $|w|$.

Theorem 8. $\mathcal{S}' = P$.

6   Some Final Remarks

We have argued that there is a link between implicit computational complexity theory and the theory of reversible computation, and we have showed that both ETIME and P can be captured by inherently reversible programming languages. In general, implicit characterizations are meant to shed light on the nature of complexity classes and the many notoriously hard open problems involving such classes. Implicit characterizations by reversible formalisms might yield some new insights in this respect. It is beyond the scope of this paper to discuss or interpret the theorems proved above any further, but one might start to wonder how different aspects of reversibility relate to time complexity, space complexity and nondeterminism.

The author is not aware of any work in reversible computing that is closely related to the work presented above, but some work of Matos [14] is at least faintly related. Matos characterizes the primitive recursive functions by an inherently reversible loop-language.[2] Paolini et al. [15] do also characterize the primitive recursive functions by a reversible formalism. Their work is of a recursion-theoretic nature and has a different flavor than ours, but it is possible that such studies might lead to interesting characterizations of complexity classes.

We finish off this paper by suggesting a small research project. It should be possible to extend RBS to an inherently reversible higher-order language. First-order programs will be like the ones defined and explained above. Second-order programs will manipulate stacks of stacks, third-order programs will manipulate stacks of stacks of stacks, and so on. This will induce a hierarchy: the class of problems decidable by a first-order RBS program, the class of problems decidable by a second-order RBS program, ... by a third-order RBS program, and so on. By the same token, RBS′ will induce a hierarchy: the class of languages decidable by a first-order RBS′ program, the class of languages decidable by a second-order RBS′ program, and so on. These two hierarchies should be compared to the alternating time-space hierarchies studied in Goerdt [4], Jones [6], Kristiansen and Voda [10] and many other papers.

---

[2] The result is not stated very clearly in the paper. See the footnote at page 2066.

References

1. Arora, S., Barak, B.: Computational Complexity: A Modern Approach. Cambridge University Press, Cambridge (2009)
2. Bellantoni, S.J., Cook, S.: A new recursion-theoretic characterizations of the polytime functions. Comput. Complex. **2**, 97–110 (1992)
3. Dal Lago, U.: A short introduction to implicit computational complexity. In: Bezhanishvili, N., Goranko, V. (eds.) ESSLLI 2010-2011. LNCS, vol. 7388, pp. 89–109. Springer, Heidelberg (2012). https://doi.org/10.1007/978-3-642-31485-8_3
4. Goerdt, A.: Characterizing complexity classes by higher type primitive recursive definitions. Theoret. Comput. Sci. **100**, 45–66 (1992)
5. Jones, N.D.: LOGSPACE and PTIME characterized by programming languages. Theoret. Comput. Sci. **228**, 151–174 (1999)
6. Jones, N.D.: The expressive power of higher-order types or, life without CONS. J. Funct. Program. **11**, 55–94 (2001)
7. Jones, N.D.: Computability and Complexity from a Programming Perspective. The MIT Press, Cambridge (1997)
8. Kristiansen, L.: Neat function algebraic characterizations of LOGSPACE and LINSPACE. Comput. Complex. **14**, 72–88 (2005)
9. Kristiansen, L., Niggl, K.-H.: On the computational complexity of imperative programming languages. Theoret. Comput. Sci. **318**, 139–161 (2004)
10. Kristiansen, L., Voda, P.J.: Programming languages capturing complexity classes. Nord. J. Comput. **12**, 89–115 (2005)
11. Kristiansen, L., Voda, P.J.: Complexity classes and fragments of C. Inf. Process. Lett. **88**, 213–218 (2003)
12. Leivant, D.: A foundational delineation of computational feasibility. In: Proceedings Sixth Annual IEEE Symposium on Logic in Computer Science, pp. 39–47. IEEE (1991)
13. Leivant, D.: Stratified functional programs and computational complexity. In: POPL 1993: Proceedings of the 20th ACM SIGPLAN-SIGACT Symposium on Principles of Programming Languages, pp. 325–333. ACM, New York (1993)
14. Matos, A.B.: Linear programs in a simple reversible language. Theoret. Comput. Sci. **290**, 2063–2074 (2003)
15. Paolini, L., Piccolo, M., Roversi, L.: On a class of reversible primitive recursive functions and its Turing-complete extensions. New Gener. Comput. **36**, 233–256 (2018)
16. Sipser, M.: Introduction to the Theory of Computation. PWS Publishing Company, Boston (1997)

On the Expressivity of Total Reversible Programming Languages

Armando B. Matos[1], Luca Paolini[2(✉)] [iD], and Luca Roversi[2] [iD]

[1] Departamento de Ciência de Computadores, Universidade do Porto,
Porto, Portugal
armandobcm@yahoo.com
[2] Dipartimento di Informatica, Università degli Studi di Torino, Turin, Italy
{luca.paolini,luca.roversi}@unito.it

Abstract. SRL is a reversible programming language conceived as a restriction of imperative programming languages. Each SRL program that mentions n registers defines a bijection on n-tuples of integers. Despite its simplicity, SRL is strong enough to grasp a wide class of computable bijections and to rise non-trivial programming issues. We advance in the study of its expressivity. We show how to choose among alternative program-branches by checking if a given value is positive or negative. So, we answer some longstanding questions that the literature poses. In particular, we prove that SRL is primitive recursive complete and that its program equivalence is undecidable.

Keywords: Reversible programming languages · Imperative programming languages · Primitive recursive functions · Decidability

1 Introduction

Reversible computing is an unconventional form of computing that identifies an interesting restriction of the classical digital computing model which, perhaps surprisingly, still is Turing-complete [3]. Classical computation is deterministic in a forward manner, i.e. each state is followed by a unique state. The reversible computation is a classic computation which is also required to be backward-deterministic: every state has a unique predecessor state.

The research interest for reversible computing is emerged in a plethora of situations (see [25] for a survey). Inside the classical computing, often we come across this subject inadvertently and accidentally. Think about lossless compression, cryptographic procedures, view-update problem, and so on. However, the interest for the reversible paradigm in the classical computing is far broader than that, because it is linked to the ubiquitous backtracking mechanism. Albeit specific researches on these classic arguments have been developed, the quest for an overall theory of reversible computing has been initially motivated from a different search: the interest for thermodynamic issues of the computation. This

© Springer Nature Switzerland AG 2020
I. Lanese and M. Rawski (Eds.): RC 2020, LNCS 12227, pp. 128–143, 2020.
https://doi.org/10.1007/978-3-030-52482-1_7

research goal can potentially contribute to decrease energy consumption, systems overheat and, battery stockpiling in portable systems. Furthermore, we like to remind that the reversible computation is intimately linked to emerging computing models, like, for example, the quantum computing paradigm.

The literature proposes several reversible languages (see [25] for a survey). We focus our attention on SRL and its variants, namely a family of total reversible programming languages introduced in [10]. These languages have been conceived as a restriction of the LOOP language defined in [14,15]. The LOOP language identifies a sub-class of programs that exist inside WHILE programming languages and which correspond the class of primitive recursive functions, crucial in recursion theory. The distinguishing difference between SRL languages and LOOP, or WHILE ones, is that their registers store both positive and negative integers (like standard programming languages) and not only natural numbers. The three instructions common to every variant of SRL are the increment (viz. inc R), the decrement (viz. dec R) and the iteration (viz. for R(P), where P is a subprogram that cannot modify the content of register R). Registers contain values in $\mathbb{Z}$ and a program that mentions n registers defines a bijection $\mathbb{Z}^n \to \mathbb{Z}^n$.

For each program P of SRL, we can build the program P^{-1} that reverses the behavior of P in an effective way. I.e., executing P^{-1} just after P is equivalent to the identity. Patently, increment and decrement are mutual inverses. On the other hand, for R(P) iterates n times the execution of P, whenever $n \geq 0$, and iterates n times the execution of the inverse of P whenever $n \leq 0$; so, it can be used to invert itself.

Despite the instruction set of SRL is quite limited, its operational semantics is unexpectedly complex. The literature [10,12,13,18,21] leaves many questions open, mainly concerning the relation between SRL and the class of computable bijections[1], which form a core of computable functions [10,19,20,22–24].

We aim at answering some of those questions.

1. Is the program equivalence of SRL decidable?
2. Is it decidable if a program of SRL behaves as the identity?
3. Is it possible to decide whether a given program is an inverse of a second one?
4. Is SRL primitive-recursive complete?
5. Is SRL sufficiently expressive to represent RPP [21] or RPRF [18,20]?

Patently, these questions are correlated in many ways. Quite trivially 1, 2 and 3 are equivalent. Also 4 and 5 are because RPP and RPRF are primitive-recursive correct and complete. A positive answer to 4 would imply a positive answer to 5 and a negative one to 1 because the equivalence between primitive-recursive functions is undecidable [26, Ch. 3].

In this work we answer to all of them by solving the open problem in [21]: "It is an open problem if the conditional instruction of RPP can be implemented in SRL." Encoding a conditional behavior as a program of SRL allows to compile programs of RPP and RPRF in SRL, so answering question 5. Since RPP is

---

[1] We remark that, traditionally, computable bijections are studied on natural numbers, while in this setting, studies extend them, w.l.o.g., to the whole set of integers.

primitive-recursive complete [21], then SRL is, answering question 4. So, the program equivalence for SRL is undecidable because that one of primitive recursive functions is [26, Ch.3]. This answers questions 1, 2 and 3.

Contents. Section 2 introduces SRL and some useful notations. Section 3 introduces the representation of truth values. Section 4 shows how to test numbers and zero. Section 5 shows how RPP can be represented in SRL. Conclusions are in Sect. 6.

2   The Language SRL

SRL is a reversible programming language [10,11,25] that Armando Matos distills from a variant of Meyer and Ritchie's LOOP language [14,15]. Specifically, SRL restricts a FOR language that, in its turn, is a total restriction of any WHILE programming language (a.k.a. IMP) [5,9,26]. A FOR language is in [17] which revisits results in [14,15] about the relation between programming and primitive recursive functions.

The choice of letting SRL-languages to operate on all integers eases the design of a reversible language because $\mathbb{Z}$, endowed with sum, is a group while $\mathbb{N}$ is not. Therefore, the registers that a program of SRL uses store values of $\mathbb{Z}$. Each program P defines a bijection $\mathbb{Z}^n \to \mathbb{Z}^n$, where $n \geq 1$ is an upper bound to the number of registers that occur in P. As a terminology, we take "mentioned" and "used" as synonymous of "occur" in a sentence like "registers that occur in P". The inverse of P is P^{-1}, i.e. the inverse bijection that P represents. We shall explain how to get P^{-1} from P in a few.

The minimal dialect of SRL languages we focus on is as follows:

Definition 1. *Let* R *be a meta-variable denoting register names that we range over by lowercase letters, possibly with subscripts and superscripts. Valid SRL-programs are the programs generated by the following grammar:*

$$P ::= \text{inc } R \mid \text{dec } R \mid \text{for } R(P) \mid P; P \tag{1}$$

that, additionally, satisfy the following linear constraint*: for* $r(P)$ *is part of a valid program iff* r *is not used in* P *as argument of* inc *or* dec*.*

The operational semantics of SRL says that (i) inc x increments the content of the register x by 1; (ii) dec x decrements the content of the register x by 1; (iii) $P_0; P_1$ is the sequential composition of 2 programs that we execute from left to right; and, (iv) if $n \in \mathbb{Z}$ is the initial content of the register r then, for $r(P)$ executes, either $\underbrace{P; \ldots; P}_{n}$ whenever $n \geq 0$, or $\underbrace{P^{-1}; \ldots; P^{-1}}_{|n|}$ whenever $n \leq 0$, where $|n|$ is the absolute value of n. We notice that executing for $r(P)$ cannot alter the value in r because of the linear constraint on the syntax.

The inverse of an SRL-program is obtained by transforming inc x, dec x, $P_0; P_1$ and for $r(P)$ in dec x, inc x, $P_1^{-1}; P_0^{-1}$ and for $r(P^{-1})$, respectively. More on SRL, its extensions, as well as results about it, is in [10,11,21,25].

For the sake of simplicity, the following notation concisely and formally allows to see SRL programs as bijective functions.

Notation 1 (Register names). *Without loss of generality, we shall only consider* SRL-*programs whose registers' names are a single letter, typically r, indexed by means of different natural numbers. Also, we assume that, if a program mentions $n \in \mathbb{N}$ registers, then $r_0, \ldots, r_{n-1}$ are their names.*

We use vectors of integers to denote the contents of all registers as a whole, both for input and output. If a vector contains n integers then, we say that n is its size and we index such integers from 0 to $n - 1$. The idea is that the content of the register r_i is in position i of the vector. As for quantum computing [16], we represent such vectors as column arrays written downwards.

Notation 2. *Let P be a* SRL *program that respects Notation 1. Let $n \in \mathbb{N}$ be an upper bound of the indexes of the registers that P uses. Let $|v_{in}\rangle$ and $|v_{out}\rangle$ denote (column) vectors of size n. Then, $|v_{in}\rangle P |v_{out}\rangle$ denotes that P sets the content of its register with the values in $|v_{out}\rangle$, starting from registers set to the values in $|v_{in}\rangle$. Slightly abusing our notation:*

$$|v_1\rangle P_1 |v_2\rangle \cdots |v_k\rangle P_k |v_{k+1}\rangle$$

is the computation of $P_1; \ldots; P_n$ applied to $|v_1\rangle$ with the value of the registers' intermediate contents made explicitly.

We conclude with simple examples of SRL programs that use ancillary registers. Specifically, a register is said to be a "*zero-ancilla*" whenever we assume that its initial value is 0; when its initial value is different, we are just not interested in the behaviour of the program.

Lemma 1 (Integer-Negation). *If r_1 is used as a zero-ancilla then:*

$$\text{for } r_0(\text{dec } r_1); \text{for } r_1(\text{inc } r_0); \text{for } r_1(\text{inc } r_0); \text{for } r_0(\text{dec } r_1); \tag{2}$$

inverts the sign of the value in r_0.

Proof. Let $a \in \mathbb{Z}$. It is easy to see that:

$$\left|\begin{matrix}a\\0\end{matrix}\right| \text{ for } r_0(\text{dec } r_1); \left|\begin{matrix}a\\-a\end{matrix}\right| \text{ for } r_1(\text{inc } r_0); \left|\begin{matrix}0\\-a\end{matrix}\right| \text{ for } r_1(\text{inc } r_0); \left|\begin{matrix}-a\\-a\end{matrix}\right| \text{ for } r_0(\text{dec } r_1); \left|\begin{matrix}-a\\0\end{matrix}\right|.$$

$\square$

We remark that (2) resets the zero-ancilla to zero, so that it can be reused for as many applications of (2) as we need. So, we can use the macro neg r_i as a name of (2), hiding an additional zero-initialized ancillary register.

Lemma 2 (Swap). *If r_2 is used as a zero-ancilla then:*

$$\text{for } r_0(\text{inc } r_2); \text{for } r_2(\text{dec } r_0); \text{for } r_1(\text{inc } r_0);$$
$$\text{for } r_0(\text{dec } r_1); \text{for } r_2(\text{inc } r_1); \text{for } r_1(\text{dec } r_2); \tag{3}$$

swaps the content of r_0 and r_1, and leaves the zero-ancilla clean.

Proof. Let $a, b \in \mathbb{Z}$. It is easy to see that:

$$\begin{vmatrix} a \\ b \\ 0 \end{vmatrix} \text{ for } r_0(\mathsf{inc}\, r_2); \begin{vmatrix} a \\ b \\ a \end{vmatrix} \text{ for } r_2(\mathsf{dec}\, r_0); \begin{vmatrix} 0 \\ b \\ a \end{vmatrix} \text{ for } r_1(\mathsf{inc}\, r_0); \begin{vmatrix} b \\ b \\ a \end{vmatrix}$$

$$\text{ for } r_0(\mathsf{dec}\, r_1); \begin{vmatrix} b \\ 0 \\ a \end{vmatrix} \text{ for } r_2(\mathsf{inc}\, r_1); \begin{vmatrix} b \\ a \\ a \end{vmatrix} \text{ for } r_1(\mathsf{dec}\, r_2); \begin{vmatrix} b \\ a \\ 0 \end{vmatrix}.$$

$\square$

We shall use the macro:

$$\mathsf{swap}(r_i, r_j) \tag{4}$$

as a name of (3) which mentions two distinct registers r_i and r_j and which hides an additional zero-initialized ancillary register. Remarkably, that unique silent zero-ancilla can be used by all swaps and negations that possibly occur in a program. For completeness, we recall that swap and negation, analogous to the ones here above, are taken as primitive operations in variants of SRL [10, 11].

3   Representing Truth Values

In order to represent truth values in SRL, we conventionally use a pair of registers.

Definition 2 (Truth values). *A pair of registers is called* truth-pair *whenever one register contains 0 and the other contains 1. If 1 is in the first register, then the truth-pair encodes **true**. Otherwise, 1 is in the second register and the truth-pair encodes **false**.*

Definition 2 recalls the representation of qbits in quantum computing [16] and, indeed, it has been inspired by the quantum programming languages designed in [22, 23]. Definition 2 relies on some observations:

1. "for", natively included in SRL, works as a basic conditional operator. If r contains 1, then for $r(P)$ executes P once. Furthermore, the program:

$$\mathsf{for}\, r_0(P); \mathsf{for}\, r_1(Q)$$

   simulates an "if-then-else" whenever r_0, r_1 is a truth-pair which drives the mutually exclusive selection between P and Q.
2. It is easy to negate a truth-value by means of $\mathsf{swap}(r_i, r_j)$, as defined in (3), which, we recall, uses a silent additional ancilla.

A first application of truth-pairs is to check the parity of a register's content.

Lemma 3 (isEven). *Given the truth-pair r_1, r_2 set to true, for $r_0(\mathsf{swap}(r_1, r_2))$ decides the parity of the number in r_0. It leaves r_1, r_2 set true iff the content of r_0 is even.*

Proof. Let $n \in \mathbb{Z}$. Then:

$$\begin{vmatrix} n \\ 1 \\ 0 \end{vmatrix} \text{ for } r_0(\text{swap}(r_1, r_2)); \begin{vmatrix} n \\ b_{even} \\ b_{odd} \end{vmatrix}, \tag{5}$$

where both b_{even} is 1 (b_{odd} is zero) if and only if n is even and b_{odd} is 1 (b_{even} is zero) if and only if n is odd. $\square$

We observe that a truth-pair can drive for $r_1(P)$; for $r_2(Q)$ to simulate an "if-then-else" that chooses between P and Q. Once chosen, we can set the truth-pair back to its initial content by applying the inverse of (5), i.e. Bennet's trick [1–3], in accordance with programming strategy widely used in [21]. In principle, Bennet's trick allows to reuse the truth-pair for a further parity test.

Lemma 3 justifies the use of the macro isEven(r_i, r_j, r_k) as a name for (5), provided that r_i, r_j, r_k are distinct registers and that r_j, r_k form a truth-pair. If the content of r_i is even the truth-value contained in r_j, r_k is not changed, otherwise it is logically negated. We also note that the inverse of (5) is for $r_i(\text{swap}(r_j, r_k))$, because the swap is commutative on its arguments.

An Euclidean division by 2 on positive numbers, relying on Lemma 3, divides the dividend, an integer, by the divisor, yielding a quotient and a remainder smaller than the divisor.

Lemma 4 (Halve). *Let r_1, r_2 be a truth-pair initialized to true. Let r_3 be a zero-ancilla. Then:*

$$\text{for } r_0(\text{swap}(r_1, r_2)); \text{for } r_1(\text{inc } r_3)) \tag{6}$$

halves the content of r_0, leaves the quotient of the integer division by 2, which is decremented by one in the case r_0 contains a negative odd number, in r_3 and, finally, lives the remainder in r_2.

Proof. Let $n \geq 0$. Then:

$$\begin{vmatrix} n \\ 1 \\ 0 \\ 0 \end{vmatrix} \text{ for } r_0(\text{swap}(r_1, r_2)); \text{for } r_1(\text{inc } r_3)); \begin{vmatrix} n \\ b_{even} \\ b_{odd} \\ n/2 \end{vmatrix}$$

where b_{even} and b_{odd} flag the parity of the value in r_0 in accordance with Lemma 3. In particular, r_1, r_2 contain 1, 0, respectively, iff the remainder of the division is zero. Otherwise, r_1, r_2 contain 0, 1, respectively. If $n < 0$, then:

$$\begin{vmatrix} n \\ 1 \\ 0 \\ 0 \end{vmatrix} \text{ for } r_0(\text{swap}(r_1, r_2)); \text{for } r_1(\text{inc } r_3)); \begin{vmatrix} n \\ b_{even} \\ b_{odd} \\ n/2 - b_{odd} \end{vmatrix}$$

where b_{even} and b_{odd} flag the parity of the value in r_0 in accordance with Lemma 3. $\square$

Lemma 4 justifies the use of the macro halve$(r_i)(r_j)(r_k)(r_h)$ as a name for (6) in order to halve the value in r_i, whenever r_i, r_j, r_k and r_h are pairwise distinct. Clearly, halve silently assumes the use of an additional zero-ancilla.

4   Testing SRL-Registers

We here discuss how to check if an integer number is smaller than -1 in order to leave the answer in a truth-pair. The test is crucial to answer longstanding questions about the expressivity of SRL, firstly posed in [10] and reiterated in other papers [12, 13, 18, 20, 21].

The *Fundamental Theorem of Arithmetic* is the starting point [4, p. 23]:

"... Any integer not zero can be expressed as a unit (± 1) times a product of positive primes. This expression is unique except for the order on which the primes factors occur. ..."

Technically, every integer $n \neq 0$ has *prime-decomposition* $(\pm 1)2^k p_1 p_2 \cdots p_m$, unique up to the order of its factors. For every $k, m \geq 0$ and $1 \leq i \leq m$, the factor p_i is a prime, positive and odd number not smaller than 3. The *odd-core* of n, decomposed as $(\pm 1)2^k p_1 p_2 \cdots p_m$, is $(\pm 1)p_1 p_2 \cdots p_m$. For instance, 21 is prime-decomposed as either $(1) \cdot 2^0 \cdot 3 \cdot 7$ or $(1) \cdot 2^0 \cdot 7 \cdot 3$ with odd-core 21, and -90 is prime-decomposed in $(-1) \cdot 2^1 \cdot 3 \cdot 3 \cdot 5$ with odd-core -45.

Proposition 1. *Let $n \neq 0$ be an integer and let $(\pm 1)2^k p_1 p_2 \cdots p_m$ be the prime-decomposition of n, for some $k, m \geq 0$.*

1. *$k \leq |n|$, where $|n|$ is the absolute value of n.*
2. *For each $h \leq k$, the division of n by 2^h returns $(\pm 1)2^{k-h} p_1 p_2 \cdots p_m$ as quotient and 0 as remainder.*
3. *The division of n by 2^k returns an odd number. So, dividing n by 2^{k+1} has 1 as its remainder.*

Proof. Trivial.   □

Crucially, for each $j \in \mathbb{N}$, if we divide 0 by 2^j, then 0 is both remainder and quotient. Therefore, given an integer N and an integer M greater than N, we can show that a program of SRL exists which iteratively divides N by 2 for M times. If N is 0, the only reminder we can obtain is 0. Otherwise, a remainder equal to 1 necessarily shows up.

Theorem 3 here below defines the program. It assumes the existence of two occurrences of N. One is the dividend, the other drives the iteration. We remark that producing a copy of a given N costs just a single zero-ancilla more.

Theorem 3 (isLessThanOne). *Let r_2, r_3 and r_5, r_6 be truth-pairs initialized to true and let r_4 be a zero-ancilla. Let both r_0 and r_1 contain the value N. Then:*

$$
\text{for } r_0 \left(
\begin{array}{ll}
\text{for } r_5(\text{for } r_1(\text{ swap}(r_2, r_3); \text{ for } r_2(\text{inc } r_4)\,)); & \text{/* SP0 */} \\
\text{for } r_3(\text{swap}(r_5, r_6)); & \text{/* SP1 */} \\
\text{for } r_5(\text{ for } r_4(\text{dec } r_1); \text{ for } r_1(\text{dec } r_4)\,); & \text{/* SP2 */} \\
\text{for } r_6 \left(
\begin{array}{l}
\text{for } r_1(\text{ for } r_2(\text{dec } r_4); \text{ swap}(r_2, r_3)\,)); \\
\text{for } r_1(\text{inc } r_4); \text{ for } r_4(\text{inc } r_1)
\end{array}
\right) & \text{/* SP3 */}
\end{array}
\right) \quad (7)
$$

leaves true in the truth-pair r_5, r_6 if and only if N is strictly lower than 1.

Proof. Both r_0, r_1 contain N because r_0 iterates as many times as required, and r_1 is the dividend. Some remarks are worth doing.

- The comments /* SP0 */... name the part of program to their left that begins with "for".
- We can think of r_1, r_2, r_3, r_4 as the arguments of halve, i.e. we could rewrite SP0 as for r_5(halve(r_1, r_2, r_3, r_4)). So, Lemma 4, implies that SP0 halves r_1, leaving the quotient in r_4 and the remainder in r_3.
- Only swap-operations modify truth pairs.
- It would be sufficient to initialize r_0 with any number greater than the exponent of 2 in the prime-decomposition of N.
- Making explicit the statement requirements,

REGISTER-NAME	r_0 r_1 r_2 r_3 r_4 r_5 r_6
CONTENT	N N 1 0 0 1 0

sums up the input for SRL program (7).

The behaviour of the SRL program (7) can described by considering three cases: $N = 0$, $N > 0$ and $N < 0$.

- Let $N = 0$. Then (7) does nothing and result is immediate. We remark that the result does not change if we arbitrarily modify the value in r_0.
- Let $N \geq 1$. The outermost "for r_0" iterates its body as many times as N and the computation proceeds as discussed in the following.
  1. Let us consider SP0. If the truth-pair r_5, r_6 contains true, the program (7) executes halve(r_1, r_2, r_3, r_4) once. Lemma 4 implies that the value of r_1 does not change, that the remainder is stored in the truth-pair r_2, r_3 and that the result of dividing r_1 by 2 is in r_4. Otherwise, the truth-pair r_5, r_6 contains false and nothing is done.
  2. Let us consider SP1. We observe that only SP1 can modify r_5, r_6. If the truth-pair r_2, r_3 contains true, i.e. r_1 has even value in it, then nothing is done. Otherwise, the truth-pair r_2, r_3 contains false, i.e. r_1 contains an odd number. Then, SP1 yields the global result by setting the truth-pair r_5, r_6 to false.
  3. Let us consider SP2 which, we remark, is crucial that the program (7) executes at most once. Let the truth-pair r_5, r_6 contain true. We both subtract from r_1 half of its value, which is in r_4 after we execute SP0, and we reset r_4 to zero. This sets r_1, r_2, r_3 and r_4 for the next halve-iteration. If the truth-pair r_5, r_6 contains false, then nothing is done.
  4. Let us consider SP3. If the truth-pair r_5, r_6 contains true, then nothing is done. Globally, this means that the body of SP3 cannot run until r_1 is possibly set with an odd value. If the truth-pair r_5, r_6 contains false, then we must consider two cases in order to ensure that SP3 leaves the value false in the truth-pair r_2, r_3.
     - Let r_1 contain an odd value n after executing SP1, which sets r_5, r_6 to false, and which is followed by SP2 that, doing nothing, leaves register's contents unchanged. Since for r_1(for r_2(dec r_4); swap(r_2, r_3)) is the inverse of halve(r_1, r_2, r_3, r_4), then:

$$\begin{vmatrix} N \\ n \\ 0 \\ 1 \\ n/2 \\ 0 \\ 1 \end{vmatrix} \overset{\text{for } r_1(\text{for } r_2(\text{dec } r_4); \text{swap}(r_2,r_3));}{\underbrace{}_{\text{halve}(r_1,r_2,r_3,r_4)^{-1}}} \begin{vmatrix} N \\ n \\ 1 \\ 0 \\ 0 \\ 0 \\ 1 \end{vmatrix} \text{for } r_1(\text{inc } r_4); \begin{vmatrix} N \\ n \\ 1 \\ 0 \\ n \\ 0 \\ 1 \end{vmatrix} \text{for } r_4(\text{inc } r_1) \begin{vmatrix} N \\ 2n \\ 1 \\ 0 \\ n \\ 0 \\ 1 \end{vmatrix}.$$

To sum up, (i) the truth-pair r_2, r_3 is restored to true, (ii) the contents of r_1 and r_4 are now both even. Specifically, r_1 contains an even value and r_4 doubles that value.

- Let r_1 contain an even value n. This sub-case can only occur when the preceding sub-case, with r_1 initially set to an odd value n, has already occurred once. Moreover, both SP0, SP1 and SP2 cannot not change the content of the registers anymore, because r_5, r_6 contain the false and r_1 is doubled by every iteration in order to permanently maintain true in the pair r_2, r_3. Then:

$$\begin{vmatrix} N \\ n \\ 1 \\ 0 \\ n/2 \\ 0 \\ 1 \end{vmatrix} \overset{\text{for } r_1(\text{for } r_2(\text{dec } r_4); \text{swap}(r_2,r_3));}{\underbrace{}_{\text{halve}(r_1,r_2,r_3,r_4)^{-1}}} \begin{vmatrix} N \\ n \\ 1 \\ 0 \\ 0 \\ 0 \\ 1 \end{vmatrix} \text{for } r_1(\text{inc } r_4); \begin{vmatrix} N \\ n \\ 1 \\ 0 \\ n \\ 0 \\ 1 \end{vmatrix} \text{for } r_4(\text{inc } r_1) \begin{vmatrix} N \\ 2n \\ 1 \\ 0 \\ n \\ 0 \\ 1 \end{vmatrix}.$$

To sum up, (i) the truth-pair r_2, r_3 remains true, (ii) the contents of r_1 and r_4 are both even. Specifically, r_1 contains an even value and r_4 doubles that value.

- Let $N \leq -1$. By definition, for $r_0(P)$ executes P^{-1} as many times as n_0 if n_0 is the value of r_0. We have to check that (7) doubles the content of r_1 before checking its parity. Hence, r_1 can never be read off with an odd number in it. Thus, (7) simply checks the parity of r_1 and doubles r_1, at every of its iterations, according to the following details:

  - Let us consider SP3. The body of the outermost "for" of SP3 never executes, for the truth-pair r_5, r_6 contains true all along the execution.
  - Let us call B_{SP2} the body for $r_4(\text{dec } r_1)$; for $r_1(\text{dec } r_4)$ of SP2. Then, every iteration of (7) executes B_{SP2}. Since N is negative and r_5 contains 1, we have to consider B_{SP2}^{-1}, i.e. for $r_1(\text{inc } r_4)$; for $r_4(\text{inc } r_1)$. Moreover, since r_1 contains a negative number, we remark that the outermost occurrence of "for" in B_{SP2}^{-1} further inverts its body. Since $N \leq -1$, we consider a generic negative number n. Thus:

$$\begin{vmatrix} N \\ n < 0 \\ 1 \\ 0 \\ 0 \\ 1 \\ 0 \end{vmatrix} \text{for } r_1(\text{dec } r_4); \begin{vmatrix} N \\ n \\ 1 \\ 0 \\ -n \\ 1 \\ 0 \end{vmatrix} \text{for } r_4(\text{dec } r_1) \begin{vmatrix} N \\ n + n \\ 1 \\ 0 \\ -n \\ 1 \\ 0 \end{vmatrix},$$

where both n and $n + n$ are negative, so $-n$ is positive.

  - Let us consider SP1. Since the truth-pair r_2, r_3 is never changed from its initial value true, the body of the outermost occurrence of "for" in SP1 is always skipped.

- Let us consider SP0 and let name for r_5(for r_1(swap(r_2, r_3); for r_2(inc r_4))), i.e. the body of SP0, as B_{SP0}. Every iteration of (7) executes B_{SP0} because the initial true value in the truth-pair r_5, r_6 never changes. Since N is negative, we consider B_{SP0}^{-1}, i.e. for r_5(for r_1(for r_2(dec r_4); swap(r_2, r_3);)). Nevertheless, also r_1 contains a negative number, thus the body of for (r_1) is subject to a further inversion that annihilates the first one. Since $N \leq -1$, we consider a generic negative number n. Thus:

$$\begin{vmatrix} N \\ 2n \\ 1 \\ 0 \\ -n \\ 1 \\ 0 \end{vmatrix} \text{ for } r_5(\text{for } r_1(\text{ swap}(r_2, r_3); \text{ for } r_2(\text{inc } r_4))) \begin{vmatrix} N \\ 2n \\ 1 \\ 0 \\ 0 \\ 1 \\ 0 \end{vmatrix}.$$

Summing up, in the case $N \leq -1$ each iteration executes two steps: (i) SP2 copies the content of r_1 in r_4 and doubles r_1; (ii) SP0 resets r_4 to zero and leaves all other registers unchanged.   □

Concluding observations and remarks on (7) follow.

We can drop the constraint that both r_0 and r_1 contain the same value by letting r_1 be a zero-ancilla and starting (7) with for r_0(inc r_1), to recover the current assumptions of Theorem 3. Therefore:

$$\text{isLessThanOne}(r_{j_0}, r_{j_1}, r_{j_2}, r_{j_3}, r_{j_4}, r_{j_5}, r_{j_6}) \tag{8}$$

can be a name for the program (7) that we assume to apply to distinct registers such that: (i) r_{j_2}, r_{j_3} and r_{j_5}, r_{j_6} are truth-pairs with initial value set true, and (ii) r_{j_1}, r_{j_4} are variables with initial value set 0. Under these assumptions, after executing isLessThanOne($r_{j_0}, r_{j_1}, r_{j_2}, r_{j_3}, r_{j_4}, r_{j_5}, r_{j_6}$), the truth-pair r_{j_5}, r_{j_6} still contains true if and only if r_{j_0} was containing either zero or a negative integer.

Using one more additional zero-ancilla would allow to further simplify (7) in the minimal version of SRL that we program with in this work: all the explicit uses of the swap-macros would disappear. In accordance with Theorem 3, isLessThanOne always returns the content of r_{j_0} unchanged. Yet, in accordance with Theorem 3, isLessThanOne always returns the truth-pair r_{j_2}, r_{j_3} clean. Therefore, w.l.o.g., it is possible to use it silently. On the other hand, the truth-pair r_{j_5}, r_{j_6} is used for the result and so it cannot be used silently. Worst, the registers r_{j_1}, r_{j_4} are left "dirty", i.e. containing useless values for our goal. It is an open question if a program, equivalent to (7), exists that stops with all ancillary variables, but the truth-pair r_5, r_6 that contains the result, clean, i.e. with their starting values in them.

The program (7) of Theorem 3 and its sub-procedures, have been checked by using the Haskell meta-interpreter in [11, page 86]. The main drawback of isLessThanOne is that the value of r_1 grows exponentially. More precisely, let N be an integer different from zero and $(\pm1)2^k p_1 p_2 \cdots p_m$ its prime-decomposition with odd-core $d = p_1 p_2 \cdots p_m$. If N is positive, then the above program leaves the value $d * 2^{N-k}$ in r_1. If N is negative, then value is $N * 2^N$. We leave the problem of eliminating the exponential blow up as open.

5 Expressivity

We here prove that SRL can represent all Primitive Recursive functions (PR). We begin by recalling what Reversible Primitive Permutations (RPP) are. Second, we show that SRL can represent every element of RPP. Since RPP can express all PR [21], then SRL enjoys the same property.

By analogy with PR, we build RPP by means of composition schemes that we apply to base functions. RPP contains total reversible endofunctions on tuples of integers, i.e. elements of $\mathbb{Z}^n$ for some $n \in \mathbb{N}$.

Definition 3 (Reversible Primitive Permutations [21]). *Reversible Primitive Permutations (RPP) is a sub-class of endofunctions on $\mathbb{Z}^n$ for some $n \in \mathbb{N}$. In order to identify the endofunctions of RPP specifically defined on $\mathbb{Z}^k$, for some given k, we write RPP^k with the following meaning:*

- *RPP^1 includes the identity function I, the successor function S that increments an integer, the predecessor function P that decrements an integer, the negation function N that inverts the sign of an integer;*
- *RPP^2 includes the transposition χ that exchanges two integers;*
- *If $f, g \in \mathsf{RPP}^k$ then, their series-composition $(f \, \mathring{,} \, g)$ belongs to RPP^k. It is the function that sequentially applies f and g to the k-tuple of integers provided as input (i.e., it is the programming composition that applies functions from left to right);*
- *If $f \in \mathsf{RPP}^j$ and $g \in \mathsf{RPP}^k$, for some $j, k \in \mathbb{N}$, then the parallel composition $(f \parallel g)$ belongs to RPP^{j+k}. It is the function that applies f on the first j arguments and, in parallel, applies g on the other ones;*
- *If $f \in \mathsf{RPP}^k$, then the finite iteration $\mathsf{It}\,[f]$ belongs to RPP^{k+1} and it is the function defined as:*

$$\mathsf{It}\,[f]\,(x_1, \ldots, x_k, z) := ((\overbrace{f \, \mathring{,} \ldots \mathring{,} \, f}^{|z|}) \parallel \mathsf{I})\,(x_1, \ldots, x_k, z);$$

- *Let $f, g, h \in \mathsf{RPP}^k$. The selection $\mathsf{If}\,[f, g, h]$ belongs to RPP^{k+1} and it is the function defined as:*

$$\mathsf{If}\,[f, g, h]\,(\langle x_1, \ldots, x_k, z \rangle) := \begin{cases} (f \parallel \mathsf{I})\,(\langle x_1, \ldots, x_k, z \rangle) & \text{if } z > 0 \text{ ,} \\ (g \parallel \mathsf{I})\,(\langle x_1, \ldots, x_k, z \rangle) & \text{if } z = 0 \text{ ,} \\ (h \parallel \mathsf{I})\,(\langle x_1, \ldots, x_k, z \rangle) & \text{if } z < 0 \text{ .} \end{cases}$$

Summing up, RPP [21] is a quite simple language that simplifies the reversible language presented in [18]. We recall from [21] that no reversible programming language can represent all and only the total reversible functions and that an algorithm exists, which is linear both in time and space, able to generate the inverse of every element in RPP.

Many notions of definability exist. Good references are [17, 20, 21], for example. Typically, they deal with classes of functions that yield single value as result. However, SRL-programs and RPP functions return tuples. In order to relate SRL and RPP to classes of single-value return functions we introduce what definability means in our context:

Definition 4 (Definability). *Let f be an endofunction on $\mathbb{Z}^k$. The function f is* definable *whenever there is a program P that involves $k+h$ registers, for some $h \in \mathbb{N}$, such that: if the first k registers are initialized to $v_0, \ldots, v_{k-1}$ and the others are initialized to zero, then the application of P sets the first k registers to $f(v_0, \ldots, v_{k-1})$. Moreover, f is* r-definable *whenever P ends by also resetting the last h registers to zero.*

Clearly, a reversible programming language like SRL can r-define reversible functions only. Also, from the definition here above, it follows that the definition of SRL and RPP can be strengthened to explicitly construct the inverse of any of their elements. We mean that, if P is a program of SRL, for example, it is easy to see that P r-defines f iff P^{-1} r-defines f^{-1}.

Theorem 4 (RPP-definability). *If $f \in$ RPP, then there is an SRL-program P that r-defines it.*

Proof. By induction, if $f \in$ RPP^k, then we prove that there is a program P P^* that r-defines f and uses $k + h$ registers, for some $h \in \mathbb{N}$.

- If f is either an identity, a successor or a predecessor, then it can be easily r-defined with no additional register. If f is a negation, then it can be r-defined by using the procedure of Lemma 1, by using one additional register. If f is a transposition, then it can be r-defined by using the procedure of Lemma 2 with a one additional register.
- Let $f = f_1 \, \mathring{,} \, f_2 \in$ RPP^k. By induction, there is P_i that r-defines f_i by using the registers $r_0, \ldots, r_{k+h_i-1}$ $(1 \leq i \leq 2)$. Then $P_1; P_2$ r-defines f by using $h = \max\{h_1, h_2\}$ additional registers (reset to zero by both P_1 and P_2).
- Let $f = (f_1 \parallel f_2)$ such that $f_i \in$ RPP^{k_i} $(1 \leq i \leq 2)$ and $k_1 + k_2 = k$. By induction, there is P_i that r-defines f_i by using the registers $r_0, \ldots, r_{k_i+h_i-1}$. Let P_1^* be the program P_1 where $r_{k_1}, \ldots, r_{k_1+h_1-1}$ (viz. its h additional registers) are simultaneously renamed $r_k, \ldots, r_{k+h_1-1}$. Let P_2^* be the program P_2 where $r_0, \ldots, r_{k_2+h_2-1}$ are simultaneously renamed $r_{k_1}, \ldots, r_{k_1+k_2+h_2-1}$. Then f is r-defined by $P_1^*; P_2^*$ with $\max\{h_1, h_2\}$ additional registers.
- Let $f = $ It $[f']$ where $f' \in$ RPP$^{k'}$ $(k = k' + 1)$. By induction, there is P' using the registers $r_0, \ldots, r_{k'-1}, \ldots, r_{k'+h'-1}$ that r-defines f' with h' additional registers. The register r_k is expected to drive the execution of It $[f]$, thus we denote P^* the program P' where each register with index r_i $(i \geq k)$ are renamed r_{i+1}.
  We use isLessThanOne in (8) in order to check the content of r_k using $8+1$ registers, the distinguished one being a zero-ancilla that occurrences of swap in (4) relies on. In this work we do not focus on minimizing the number of additional variables. We are looking for a program that receives the input in the first k registers and it uses $h' + 8 + 1$ additional zero-ancillae. Thus $r_1, \ldots, r_{k'+h'}$ (except r_k) are used by P^*, while $r_k, r_{k+h'+1}, \ldots, r_{k+h'+7}$ are the eight registers that supply the input of isLessThanOne and $r_{k+h'+8}$ is sometimes used to reverse a procedure.

We r-define It $[f']$ by means of the following program (named $P_{\mathsf{lt}[f']}$):

$$\mathsf{inc}\, r_{k+h'+1}; \mathsf{inc}\, r_{k+h'+5}; \tag{9}$$

$$\mathsf{inc}\, r_k; \mathsf{isLessThanOne}(r_k, r_{k+h'+1}, \ldots, r_{k+h'+6}); \mathsf{dec}\, r_k; \tag{10}$$

$$\mathsf{for}\, r_{k+h'+6}(\mathsf{for}\, r_k(P^*)); \tag{11}$$

$$\mathsf{for}\, r_{k+h'+5}(\mathsf{dec}\, r_{k+h'+8}; \mathsf{for}\, r_{k+h'+8}(\mathsf{for}\, r_k(P^*)); \mathsf{inc}\, r_{k+h'+8}) \tag{12}$$

$$\mathsf{inc}\, r_k; \left(\mathsf{isLessThanOne}(r_k, r_{k+h'+1}, \ldots, r_{k+h'+6})\right)^{-1}; \mathsf{dec}\, r_k; \tag{13}$$

$$\mathsf{dec}\, r_{k+h'+5}; \mathsf{dec}\, r_{k+h'+1}; \tag{14}$$

Line (9) initializes the truth-pairs $r_{k+h'+2}, r_{k+h'+3}$ and $r_{k+h'+5}, r_{k+h'+6}$ to true. I.e., it prepares the execution of isLessThanOne in accordance with the requirements of Theorem 3. Line (10) increments the content of r_k before testing it. It results that the truth-pair $r_{k+h'+5}, r_{k+h'+6}$ is left to true if and only if the content of r_k is strictly less than zero. Finally, it restores r_k to its initial value. Let n be the content of r_k. Line (11), if n is positive, then $r_{k+h'+5}, r_{k+h'+6}$ is false and P^* is executed n times. Otherwise, $r_{k+h'+6}$ contains 0 and nothing is done. Line (12), if n is strictly negative, then $r_{k+h'+5}$ contains 1 and P^* is executed $|n|$ times because $r_{k+h'+8}$ is set to -1 so that for $r_{k+h'+8}$ ensures the inversion of the application of P^*, which, in its turn, was inverted by the negative value n. Lines (13) and (14) reset all additional registers to zero, implementing Bennet's trick locally to this procedure.

Albeit the execution of It $[f']$ amounts to a non predetermined number of sequential compositions of f', we emphasize that the number of ancillae that the translation $P_{\mathsf{lt}[f']}$ requires is bounded because (i) the number of ancillae that P' contain is, in its turn, bounded (by induction), and (ii) P' r-defines f', meaning that P' leaves its ancillae clean at the end of each iteration, whatever number of compositions are involved.

– Let $f = \mathsf{If}\, [f_1, f_0, f_2]$ such that $f_1, f_0, f_2 \in \mathsf{RPP}^k$. This case is simpler than the preceding one. We need to adapt the construction in Theorem 3's proof in order to write two programs that check if the given argument is bigger, or lesser, than one and that leave their answer in a truth-pair. We notice that two nested for are necessary to trigger the application of g, because we have to check that the value driving the selection is neither bigger, nor lesser than one. $\square$

Since all primitive recursive functions are definable in RPP by [21, Th. 5], Theorem 4 immediately implies that SRL can express every element of PR. Therefore, we answer the open questions that we recall in the introduction.

6 Conclusions

Many essential reversible programming languages appear in the literature. A survey is in [25], albeit we should add many recent proposals as, for instance, R-WHILE [6], R-CORE [7], RPRF [18], RPP [21], RFUN [8]. Some comparative discussion is useful to frame the relevance of the presented result.

SRL has been conceived by distilling the reversible core of the language LOOP [14,15]. For this reason SRL enjoys two main characterizing features, up to some details. First, it allows to program total procedures only. Second, it is also a (reversible) core of a standard imperative programming language.

Almost all reversible programming languages are conceived to be Turing-complete, so the first feature distinguishes SRL from them. We do not consider this feature, that it shares with RPRF and RPP, as a limitation. The relevance of studying classes of total functions only is unquestionable, since results about Primitive Recursive Functions (see [17] as instance) like Kleene Normalization Theorem, Grzegorczyk Hierarchies, and so on. Turing-complete languages are not immediately suitable for such kinds of investigations until the identification of a minimal total core of programs/functions in them. Thanks to its conciseness and expressive power, that we studied in this paper, we consider SRL as the best candidate for theoretical investigations in analogy with that done on primitive recursive functions.

Let us consider the second feature. Janus has been the first reversible programming language distilled from an imperative structured programming language. Many interesting extensions and paradigmatic languages stem from it, in particular the recent R-WHILE and R-CORE. Their primitives are based on iterators that may not terminate (roughly while-iterators) and which are somewhat stretched to behave reversibly, by incorporating some form of "assertion". Quite interestingly, the introduction of R-CORE relies on the observation that a possibly non terminating iterator of R-WHILE can encode the conditional. However, these languages neglect the very standard imperative total iterator for. It is worth to emphasize that modifying the semantics of "for" (in SRL) by not inverting its body when applied to negative numbers, in analogy with the iterator in RPP, we obtain a version of SRL straightforwardly included in the core of standard imperative programming languages. Furthermore, our expressivity results still hold for such a variant of SRL. On the other hand, we wonder if all the reversible while-iterators have to be extended with some exiting-test, that are not standard in classical languages. We leave this as a further open question.

References

1. Axelsen, H.B., Glück, R.: On reversible Turing machines and their function universality. Acta Informatica **53**(5), 509–543 (2016). https://doi.org/10.1007/s00236-015-0253-y
2. Axelsen, H.B., Glück, R.: On reversible turing machines and their functionuniversality. Acta Informatica **53**(5), 509–543 (2016). https://doi.org/10.1007/s00236-015-0253-y
3. Bennett, C.H.: Logical reversibility of computation. IBM J. Res. Dev. **17**(6), 525–532 (1973). https://doi.org/10.1147/rd.176.0525
4. Birkhoff, G., Mac Lane, S.: A Survey of Modern Algebra, 4th edn. Macmillan, New York (1977)
5. Calude, C.: Theories of Computational Complexity. Elsevier (1988), annals of Discrete Mathematics - Monograph 35

6. Glück, R., Yokoyama, T.: A linear-time self-interpreter of a reversible imperative language. Comput. Softw. **33**(3), 108–128 (2016). https://doi.org/10.11309/jssst.33.3_108
7. Glück, R., Kaarsgaard, R.: A categorical foundation for structured reversible flowchart languages: Soundness and adequacy. Log. Methods Comput. Sci. **14**(3) Sepember 2018. https://doi.org/10.23638/LMCS-14(3:16)2018, https://lmcs.episciences.org/4802
8. Jacobsen, P.A.H., Kaarsgaard, R., Thomsen, M.K.: CoreFun: A typed functional reversible core language. In: Kari, J., Ulidowski, I. (eds.) Reversible Computation. pp. 304–321. Springer (2018)
9. Kristiansen, L., Niggl, K.H.: On the computational complexity of imperative programming languages. Theoret. Comput. Sci. **318**(1–2), 139–161 (2004). https://doi.org/10.1016/j.tcs.2003.10.016
10. Matos, A.B.: Linear programs in a simple reversible language. Theoret. Comput. Sci. **290**(3), 2063–2074 (2003). https://doi.org/10.1016/S0304-3975(02)00486-3
11. Matos, A.B.: Register reversible languages (work in progress). Technical report, LIACC (2014). https://www.dcc.fc.up.pt/~acm/questionsv.pdf
12. Matos, A.B., Paolini, L., Roversi, L.: The fixed point problem for general and for linear SRL programs is undecidable. In: Aldini, A., Bernardo, M. (eds.) Proceedings of the 19th Italian Conference on Theoretical Computer Science, Urbino, Italy, 18–20 September 2018. CEUR Workshop Proceedings, vol. 2243, pp. 128–139. CEUR-WS.org (2018). http://ceur-ws.org/Vol-2243/paper12.pdf
13. Matos, A.B., Paolini, L., Roversi, L.: The Fixed Point Problem of aSimple Reversible Language. Theor. Comput. Sci. **813**, 143–154 (2020). https://doi.org/10.1016/j.tcs.2019.10.005. http://www.sciencedirect.com/science/article/pii/S0304397519306280
14. Meyer, A.R., Ritchie, D.M.: Computational complexity and program structure. Technical report. RC 1817, IBM (1967)
15. Meyer, A.R., Ritchie, D.M.: The complexity of loop programs. In: Proceedings of the 22nd National Conference of the ACM, pp. 465–469. ACM, New York (1967). https://doi.org/10.1145/800196.806014
16. Nielsen, M.A., Chuang, I.L.: Quantum Computation and Quantum Information: 10th Anniversary Edition, 10th edn. Cambridge University Press, New York (2011)
17. Odifreddi, P.: Classical Recursion Theory - The Theory of Functions and Sets of Natural Numbers, vol. I. Studies in Logic and the Foundations of Mathematics, Elsevier North Holland (1989)
18. Paolini, L., Piccolo, M., Roversi, L.: A class of reversible primitive recursive functions. Electron. Notes Theor. Comput. Sci. **322**(18605), 227–242 (2016). https://doi.org/10.1016/j.entcs.2016.03.016
19. Paolini, L., Piccolo, M., Roversi, L.: A Certified Study of a Reversible Programming Language. In: Uustalu, T. (ed.) 21st International Conference on Types for Proofs and Programs (TYPES 2015). Leibniz International Proceedings in Informatics (LIPIcs), vol. 69, pp. 7:1–7:21. Schloss Dagstuhl - Leibniz-Zentrum fuer Informatik, Germany (2018). https://doi.org/10.4230/LIPIcs.TYPES.2015.7
20. Paolini, L., Piccolo, M., Roversi, L.: On a class of reversible primitive recursive functions and its turing-complete extensions. New Gener. Comput. **36**(3), 233–256 (2018). https://doi.org/10.1007/s00354-018-0039-1
21. Paolini, L., Piccolo, M., Roversi, L.: A class of Recursive Permutations which is Primitive Recursive complete. Theor. Comput. Sci. **813**, 218–233 (2020).https://doi.org/10.1016/j.tcs.2019.11.029. Submitted to the journal in 2016

22. Paolini, L., Piccolo, M., Zorzi, M.: QPCF: higher-order languages and quantum circuits. J. Autom. Reasoning **63**(4), 941–966 (2019). https://doi.org/10.1007/s10817-019-09518-y
23. Paolini, L., Roversi, L., Zorzi, M.: Quantum programming made easy. In: Ehrhard, T., Fernández, M., Paiva, V.d., Tortora de Falco, L. (eds.) Proceedings Joint International Workshop on Linearity & Trends in Linear Logic and Applications. Electronic Proceedings in Theoretical Computer Science, Oxford, UK, 7–8 July 2018, vol. 292, pp. 133–147. Open Publishing Association (2019). https://doi.org/10.4204/EPTCS.292.8
24. Paolini, L., Zorzi, M.: qPCF: a language for quantum circuit computations. In: Gopal, T.V., Jäger, G., Steila, S. (eds.) TAMC 2017. LNCS, vol. 10185, pp. 455–469. Springer, Cham (2017). https://doi.org/10.1007/978-3-319-55911-7_33
25. Perumalla, K.: Introduction to Reversible Computing. CRC Press, Boca Raton (2014)
26. Schoning, U.: Gems of Theoretical Computer Science. Springer, Heidelberg (1998)

Toward a Curry-Howard Equivalence
for Linear, Reversible Computation

Work-in-Progress

Kostia Chardonnet[1,2,3(✉)], Alexis Saurin[2,3], and Benoît Valiron[1,2]

[1] Université Paris-Saclay, CNRS, CentraleSupélec,
Laboratoire de Recherche en Informatique, 91405 Orsay, France
{kostia,benoit.valiron}@lri.fr
[2] Université de Paris, IRIF, CNRS, 75013 Paris, France
alexis.saurin@irif.fr
[3] Équipe πr^2, Inria, Paris, France

Abstract. In this paper, we present a linear and reversible language with inductive and coinductive types, together with a Curry-Howard correspondence with the logic μMALL: linear logic extended with least and greatest fixed points allowing inductive and coinductive statements. Linear, reversible computation makes an important sub-class of quantum computation without measurement. In the latter, the notion of purely quantum recursive type is not yet well understood. Moreover, models for reasoning about quantum algorithms only provide complex types for classical datatypes: there are usually no types for purely quantum objects beside tensors of quantum bits. This work is a first step towards understanding purely quantum recursive types.

Keywords: Reversible computation · Linear logic · Curry-Howard

1 Introduction

Computation and logic are two faces of the same coin. For instance, consider a proof s of $A \to B$ and a proof t of A. With the logical rule *Modus-Ponens* one can construct a proof of B: Fig. 1 features a graphical presentation of the corresponding proof. Horizontal lines stand for deduction steps—they separate conclusions (below) and hypotheses (above). These deduction steps can be stacked vertically up to axioms in order to describe complete proofs. In Fig. 1 the proofs of A and $A \to B$ are symbolized with vertical ellipses. The ellipsis annotated with s indicates that s is a complete proof of $A \to B$ while t stands for a complete proof of A.

$$\frac{\begin{array}{cc} \overset{s}{\vdots} & \overset{t}{\vdots} \\ A \to B & A \end{array}}{B}$$

Fig. 1. Modus-Ponens

This connection is known as the *Curry-Howard correspondence* [4,8]. In this general framework, types correspond to formulas and programs to proofs, while

© Springer Nature Switzerland AG 2020
I. Lanese and M. Rawski (Eds.): RC 2020, LNCS 12227, pp. 144–152, 2020.
https://doi.org/10.1007/978-3-030-52482-1_8

program evaluation is mirrored with proof simplification (the so-called cut-elimination). The Curry-Howard correspondence formalizes the fact that the proof s of $A \rightarrow B$ can be regarded as a *function*—parametrized by an argument of type A—that produces a proof of B whenever it is fed with a proof of A. Therefore, the computational interpretation of Modus-Ponens corresponds to the *application* of an argument (i.e. t) of type A to a function (i.e. s) of type $A \rightarrow B$. When computing the corresponding program, one substitutes the parameter of the function with t and get a result of type B. On the logical side, this corresponds to substituting every axiom introducing A in the proof s with the full proof t of A. This yields a direct proof of B without any invocation of the "lemma" $A \rightarrow B$.

Paving the way toward the verification of critical softwares, the Curry-Howard correspondence provides a versatile framework. It has been used to mirror first and second-order logics with dependent-type systems [3,10], separation logics with memory-aware type systems [9,13], resource-sensitive logics with differential privacy [6], logics with monads with reasoning on side-effects [11,17], etc.

This paper is concerned with the case of reversible computation, a sub-class of *pure* quantum computation. In general quantum computation, one has access to a co-processor holding a "quantum" memory. This memory consists of "quantum" bits having a peculiar property: their state cannot be duplicated, and the operations one can perform on them are unitary, reversible operations. The co-processor comes with an interface to which one can send instructions to allocate, update or read quantum registers. Quantum memories can be used to solve classical problems faster than with purely conventional means. Quantum programming languages are nowadays pervasive [5] and several formal approaches based on logical systems have been proposed to relate to this model of computation [12,14,16]. However, all of these languages rely on a purely *classical* control-flow: quantum computation is reduced to describing a list of instructions—a quantum circuit—to be sent to the co-processor. In particular, in this model operations performed on the quantum memory only act on quantum bits and tensors thereof, while the classical computer enjoys the manipulation of any kind of data with the help of rich type systems.

This extended abstract aims at proposing a type system featuring inductive and coinductive types for a purely reversible language, first step towards a rich quantum type system. We base our study on the approach presented in [15]. In this model, reversible computation is restricted to two main types: the tensor, written $a \otimes b$ and the co-product, written $a \oplus b$. The former corresponds to the type of all pairs of elements of type a and elements of type b, while the latter represents the disjoint union of all elements of type a and elements of type b. For instance, a bit can be typed with $\mathbb{1} \oplus \mathbb{1}$, where $\mathbb{1}$ is a type with only one element. The language in [15] offers the possibility to code isos—reversible maps—with pattern matching. An iso is for instance the swap operation, typed with $a \otimes b \leftrightarrow b \otimes a$. The language also permits higher-order operations on isos, so that an iso can be parametrized by another iso, and is extended with lists

$$\frac{}{A \vdash A} \ id \qquad \frac{\Gamma_1, A \vdash \Delta_1 \quad \Gamma_2 \vdash \Delta_2, A}{\Gamma_1, \Gamma_2 \vdash \Delta_1, \Delta_2} \ cut \qquad \frac{\Delta \vdash A}{\Delta, \mathbb{1} \vdash A} \ \mathbb{1}_L$$

$$\frac{}{\vdash \mathbb{1}} \ \mathbb{1}_R \qquad \frac{\Delta, A, B \vdash C}{\Delta, A \otimes B \vdash C} \ \otimes_L \qquad \frac{\Delta \vdash A \quad \Gamma \vdash B}{\Delta, \Gamma \vdash A \otimes B} \ \otimes_R$$

$$\frac{\Delta, A \vdash C \quad \Delta, B \vdash C}{\Delta, A \oplus B \vdash C} \ \oplus_L \qquad \frac{\Delta \vdash A_i}{\Delta \vdash A_1 \oplus A_2} \ \oplus_R^i \ i \in \{1, 2\} \qquad \frac{A[X \leftarrow \mu X.A] \vdash B}{\mu X.A \vdash B} \ \mu_L$$

$$\frac{A \vdash B[X \leftarrow \mu X.B]}{A \vdash \mu X.B} \ \mu_R \qquad \frac{A[X \leftarrow \nu X.A] \vdash B}{\nu X.A \vdash B} \ \nu_L \qquad \frac{A \vdash B[X \leftarrow \nu X.B]}{A \vdash \nu X.B} \ \nu_R$$

Fig. 2. Rules for μMALL. .

(denoted with $[a]$). For instance, one can type a map operation acting on all the elements of a list with $(a \leftrightarrow b) \rightarrow ([a] \leftrightarrow [b])$. However, if [15] hints at an extension toward pure quantum computation, the type system is not formally connected to any logical system.

The main contribution of this work is a Curry-Howard correspondence for a purely reversible typed language in the style of [15]. We capitalize on the logic μMALL [1,2]: an extension of the additive and multiplicative fragment of linear logic with least and greatest fixed points allowing inductive and coinductive statements. This logic contains both a tensor and a co-product, and its strict linearity makes it a good fit for a reversible type system.

2 Background on μMALL

The logic μMALL [1,2] is an extension of the additive and multiplicative fragment of linear logic [7]. The syntax of linear logic is extended with the formulas $\mu X.A$ and its dual $\nu X.A$ (where X is a type variable occuring in A), which can be understood at the least and greatest fixed points of the operator $X \mapsto A$. These permit inductive and coinductive statements. We are only interested in a fragment of μMALL which contains the tensor, the plus, the unit and the μ and ν connectives. Note that our system only deals with closed formulas. Our syntax of formulas is $A, B ::= \mathbb{1} \mid X \mid A \otimes B \mid A \oplus B \mid \mu X.A \mid \nu X.A$. The derivation rules are shown in Fig. 2. They defined a binary relation $\Delta \vdash \Gamma$ on set of formulas defined inductively. For each rule the assumptions are above the line while the conclusion is under. In the rules, the comma stands for the disjoint union: observe that each formula has to be used exactly once and cannot be duplicated or erased. In μMALL one can for instance define the type of natural numbers as $\mu X.\mathbb{1} \oplus X$, of lists of type A as $\mu X.\mathbb{1} \oplus (A \otimes X)$ and of streams of type A as $\nu X.A \otimes X$.

We consider proofs to be potentially non-well-founded derivation trees: they are not necessarily finite as we can for instance consider the formula $\mu X.X$ and apply the rule μ_R an infinite number of times. Among non well-founded proof-objects we distinguish the regular derivation trees that we call circular

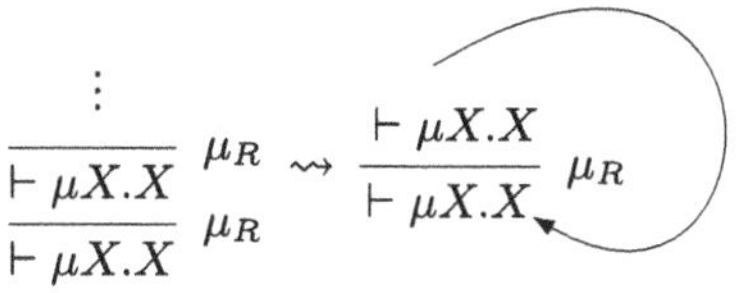

$$\cfrac{\cfrac{\vdots}{\vdash \mu X.X}\ \mu_R}{\cfrac{\vdash \mu X.X}{\vdash \mu X.X}\ \mu_R}\ \mu_R \quad\rightsquigarrow\quad \cfrac{\vdash \mu X.X}{\vdash \mu X.X}\ \mu_R$$

$$\cfrac{\cfrac{\vdots}{\vdash \mu X.X}\ \mu_R \qquad \cfrac{\vdots}{\mu X.X \vdash \mathsf{F}}\ \mu_L}{\vdash \mathsf{F}}\ \text{cut}$$

Fig. 3. Circular representation of proofs.

Fig. 4. Degenerated proof.

pre-proofs. These trees can then be represented in a compact manner, see Fig. 3. One problem with such a proof-system is to determine whether or not infinite derivations are indeed proofs. Indeed, if every infinite derivation is accepted as a proof, it would be possible to prove any formula F, as shown in Fig. 4.

To answer this problem, μ**MALL** comes with a validity criterion for derivations. It roughly says that a derivation is valid if, in every infinite branch of the derivation, there exists an infinite number of rules μ_L or an infinite number of rules ν_R. The intuition is that since $\mu X.A$ formulas represent least fixed points, their objects are finite. An infinite number of rule μ_R would mean producing an infinite object, which is not possible. On the other hand, we can explore an arbitrarily large object as input with the rule μ_L. For the other case, since $\nu X.A$ formulas represent greatest fixed points, their object are infinite. We therefore want to ensure that we can produce infinite objects: hence the infinite number of rules ν_R. This criterion can be understood in a more operational way as a requirement for productivity.

3 Our Language

Our language is based on the one presented in [15]. We build on the reversible part of the paper by extending the language to support both a more general rewriting system and inductive and coinductive types. The language is defined by layers. Terms and types are presented in Table 1, while typing derivations, based on μ**MALL** ,can be found in Tables 2 and 3. The language consists of the following pieces.

Basic Type. They are first-order and typed with base types. The constructors $\texttt{inj}_l$ and $\texttt{inj}_r$ represent the choice between either the left or right-hand side of a type of the form $A \oplus B$; the constructor $\langle,\rangle$ builds pairs of elements (with the corresponding type constructor $\otimes$); $\texttt{fold}$ and $\texttt{pack}$ respectively represent inductive and coinductive structure for the types $\mu X.A$ and $\nu X.A$. A value can serve both as a result and as a pattern in the clause of an iso. Generalized patterns are used as special patterns: $\texttt{v}_g : A$ can match any value of type A. Terms are expressions at "surface-level": applying an iso always gives a term, whereas it is an expression only when the argument is a generalized pattern.

Table 1. Terms and types

(Base types)	$A, B ::= \mathbb{1} \mid A \oplus B \mid A \otimes B \mid \mu X.A \mid \nu X.A$
(Isos, first-order)	$\alpha ::= A \leftrightarrow B$
(Isos, higher-order)	$T ::= \alpha_1 \rightarrow \cdots \rightarrow \alpha_n \rightarrow \alpha$
(Values)	$v ::= () \mid x \mid \text{inj}_l \, v \mid \text{inj}_r \, v \mid \langle v_1, v_2 \rangle \mid$
	$\quad \text{fold } v \mid \text{pack } v$
(Generalized pattern)	$v_g ::= () \mid x \mid \langle v_g, v_g \rangle \mid \omega \, v_g \mid \text{let } v_g = v_g \text{ in } v_g \mid$
	$\quad \text{fold } v_g \mid \text{pack } v_g$
(Expressions)	$e ::= v_g \mid \text{inj}_r \, e \mid \text{inj}_l \, e \mid \langle e, e \rangle \mid$
	$\quad \text{fold } e \mid \text{pack } e \mid \text{let } v_g = v_g \text{ in } e$
(Isos)	$\omega ::= \{e_1 \leftrightarrow e_1' \mid \dots \mid e_n \leftrightarrow e_n'\} \mid \lambda f.\omega \mid$
	$\quad \mu f.\omega \mid f \mid \omega_1 \, \omega_2 \mid \text{inv } \omega$
(Terms)	$t ::= () \mid x \mid \text{inj}_l \, t \mid \text{inj}_r \, t \mid \langle t_1, t_2 \rangle \mid$
	$\quad \text{fold } t \mid \text{pack } t \mid \omega \, t \mid \text{let } v_g = v_g \text{ in } t$

First-Order Isos. An iso of type α acts on terms of base types. An iso is a function of type $A \leftrightarrow B$, defined as a set of clauses of the form $\{e_1 \leftrightarrow e_1' \mid \dots \mid e_n \leftrightarrow e_n'\}$. The tokens e_i and e_i' in the clauses are expressions. Compared to the original language in [15], we allow general expressions both on the left and on the right of a clause. In order to apply an iso to a term, the iso must be of type $A \leftrightarrow B$ and the term of type A. In the typing rules of isos, the OD predicate (taken from [15] and not described in this paper) syntactically enforces the exhaustivity and non-overlapping conditions that the left-hand-side and right-hand-side of clauses should satisfy. Exhaustivity for an iso $\{e_1 \leftrightarrow e_1' \mid \dots \mid e_n \leftrightarrow e_n'\}$ of type $A \leftrightarrow B$ means that the expressions on the left (resp. on the right) of the clauses describe all possible values for the type A (resp. the type B). Non-overlapping means that two expressions cannot match the same value. For instance, the left and right injections $\text{inj}_l \, e$ and $\text{inj}_r \, e'$ are non-overlapping while a pattern v_g is always exhaustive.

Higher-Order Isos. An iso of type T manipulate other isos as basic blocks. Since isos represent closed computations, iso-variable are non-linear and can be duplicated at will while term-variable are linear. The constructions $\lambda f.\omega$ and $\omega_1 \, \omega_2$ represent respectively the abstraction of a function and the application of an iso to another. The construction $\mu g.\omega$ represents the creation of a recursive function, rewritten as $\omega[g := \mu g.\omega]$ by the operational semantics. The typing rule for $\mu g.\omega$ has a productivity criterion. Indeed, since isos can be non-terminating (because of coinduction), productivity is important to ensure that we work with total functions. These checks are crucial to make sure that our isos are indeed bijections in the mathematical sense. The construction $\text{inv } \omega$ corresponds to the inversion of the iso ω. If ω is of type $A \leftrightarrow B$ then $\text{inv } \omega$ is of type $B \leftrightarrow A$.

Finally, our language is equipped with a rewrite system ($\rightarrow$) on terms. The evaluation of an iso applied to an argument works with pattern-matching. The

Table 2. Typing of terms and expressions

$$\frac{}{\emptyset;\Psi \vdash_e () : \mathbb{1}} \quad \frac{}{x : A;\Psi \vdash_e x : A} \quad \frac{\Delta;\Psi \vdash_e t : A}{\Delta;\Psi \vdash_e \text{inj}_l\, t : A \oplus B} \quad \frac{\Delta;\Psi \vdash_e t : B}{\Delta;\Psi \vdash_e \text{inj}_r\, t : A \oplus B}$$

$$\frac{\Delta_1;\Psi \vdash_e t_1 : A \quad \Delta_2;\Psi \vdash_e t_2 : B}{\Delta_1,\Delta_2;\Psi \vdash_e \langle t_1,t_2 \rangle : A \otimes B} \quad \frac{\Delta;\Psi \vdash t : A[X \leftarrow \nu X.A]}{\Delta;\Psi \vdash \text{pack}\, t : \nu X.A}$$

$$\frac{\Psi \vdash_\omega \omega : A \leftrightarrow B \quad \Delta;\Psi \vdash_e t : A}{\Delta;\Psi \vdash_e \omega\, t : B} \quad \frac{\Delta;\Psi \vdash_e t : A[X \leftarrow \mu X.A]}{\Delta;\Psi \vdash_e \text{fold}\, t : \mu X.A}$$

$$\frac{\Gamma;\Psi \vdash_e v_{g_1} : A \quad \Delta_1;\Psi \vdash_e v_{g_2} : A \quad \Gamma,\Delta_2;\Psi \vdash_e t : B}{\Delta_1,\Delta_2;\Psi \vdash_e \text{let}\, v_{g_1} = v_{g_2} \text{ in } t : B}$$

Table 3. Typing of isos

$$\frac{\begin{array}{ccc} \Delta_1;\Psi \vdash_e e_1 : A & \dots & \Delta_n;\Psi \vdash_e e_n : A \quad \text{OD}_A\{e_1,\dots,e_n\} \\ \Delta_1;\Psi \vdash_e e_1' : B & \dots & \Delta_n;\Psi \vdash_e e_n' : B \quad \text{OD}_B\{e_1',\dots,e_n'\} \end{array}}{\Psi \vdash_\omega \{e_1 \leftrightarrow e_1' \mid \dots \mid e_n \leftrightarrow e_n'\} : A \leftrightarrow B.}$$

$$\frac{\Psi, f : \alpha \vdash_\omega \omega : T}{\Psi \vdash_\omega \lambda f.\omega : \alpha \to T} \quad \frac{}{\Psi, f : \alpha \vdash_\omega f : \alpha} \quad \frac{\Psi \vdash_\omega \omega_1 : \alpha \to T \quad \Psi \vdash_\omega \omega_2 : \alpha}{\Psi \vdash_\omega \omega_1\omega_2 : T}$$

$$\frac{\Psi \vdash_\omega \omega : T^\perp}{\Psi \vdash_\omega \text{inv}\, \omega : T} \quad \frac{\Psi, f : \alpha \vdash_\omega \omega : \alpha_1 \to \dots \to \alpha_n \to \alpha \quad \mu f.\omega \text{ is productive}}{\Psi \vdash_\omega \mu f.\omega : \alpha_1 \to \dots \to \alpha_n \to \alpha}$$

non-overlapping and exhaustivity conditions guarantee subject-reduction (see Proposition 3.1).

Example 3.1. Encoding of the isomorphism *map* in our language, where $[\,]$ is the empty list and :: is the list construction. The iso *map* is of type $(A \leftrightarrow B) \to ([A] \leftrightarrow [B])$ where $[A]$ is the type of lists of type A. This iso takes an iso of type $A \leftrightarrow B$ as argument and apply it to each element of the list given as argument:

$$\lambda f.\mu g.\left\{ \begin{array}{ll} [\,] & \leftrightarrow [\,] \\ h::t & \leftrightarrow (f\ h)::(g\ t) \end{array} \right\} : (A \leftrightarrow B) \to [A] \leftrightarrow [B]).$$

Example 3.2. We can define the iso of type : $A \oplus (B \oplus C) \leftrightarrow C \oplus (A \oplus B)$ as

$$\left\{ \begin{array}{l} \text{inj}_l\, a \leftrightarrow \text{inj}_r\, \text{inj}_l\, a \\ \text{inj}_r\, \text{inj}_l\, b \leftrightarrow \text{inj}_r\, \text{inj}_r\, b \\ \text{inj}_r\, \text{inj}_r\, c \leftrightarrow \text{inj}_l\, c \end{array} \right\}.$$

Remark 3.1. In our two examples, the left and right-hand side of the $\leftrightarrow$ on each function respect both the criteria of exhaustivity—every-value of each type is being covered by at least one expression—and non-overlapping—no two expressions cover the same value. Both isos are therefore bijections.

Property 3.1. *The language features subject reduction: If $\vdash t : A$ and $t \to t'$ then we have $\vdash t' : A$. Moreover, it enjoys confluence: Let $\to^*$ be the reflexive, transitive closure of $\to$. If $t \to^* t_1$ and $t \to^* t_2$ then there exists t_3 such that $t_1 \to^* t_3$ and $t_2 \to^* t_3$.*   □

We conjecture that well-typed isos are indeed isomorphisms:

Conjecture 3.1. *For all $\omega : A \leftrightarrow B$, $v : A$ and $u : B$ then $((\mathtt{inv}\,\omega) \circ \omega)\,v \to^* v$ and $(\omega \circ \mathtt{inv}\,\omega)\,u \to^* u$.*

4   Towards Curry-Howard

An iso $\vdash \omega : A \leftrightarrow B$ corresponds to both a computation sending a value of type A to a result of type B and a computation sending a value of type B to a result of type A. We can mechanically translate such an iso to a pair of derivations $\pi, \pi^\perp$ in μMALL , where π is a proof of $A \vdash B$ and $\pi^\perp$ is a proof of $B \vdash A$. This mechanical translation constructs circular pre-proofs, as discussed in Sect. 2. We however still need to show that the obtained derivations respect the validity criterion for circular proof.

Once proven, we would obtain a *static* correspondence between programs and proofs. We would however still need to show that this entails a *dynamic* correspondence between the evaluation procedure of our language and the cut-elimination procedure of μMALL. For that, we would need to make sure that the proofs we obtain are indeed isomorphisms, meaning that if we cut the aforementioned proofs π and $\pi^\perp$, performing the cut-elimination procedure would give either the identity on A or the identity on B.

Conjecture 4.1. *Validity of proofs. If $\vdash \omega : A \leftrightarrow B$ then the μMALL derivations $\pi : A \vdash B$ and $\pi^\perp : B \vdash A$ of ω are valid.*
Isomorphism of Proofs. Provided that the above holds, we moreover have

$$\cfrac{}{A \vdash A}\,id \quad\rightsquigarrow\quad \cfrac{\cfrac{\pi^\perp}{B \vdash A} \quad \cfrac{\pi}{A \vdash B}}{A \vdash A}\,cut \qquad\qquad \cfrac{\cfrac{\pi}{A \vdash B} \quad \cfrac{\pi^\perp}{B \vdash A}}{B \vdash B}\,cut \quad\rightsquigarrow\quad \cfrac{}{B \vdash B}\,id$$

Simulation of Evaluation. Provided that t is a value and v is a normal form, if $\omega\,t \to^* v$, if π is the proof corresponding to $\omega\,t$, and if π' is the proof corresponding to v, then $\pi \to^* \pi'$ with the cut-elimination procedure.

Example 4.1. Consider the iso that, given an iso f and a list $[x_1, x_2, \dots, x_n]$ returns the list $[f\,x_1, (\mathtt{inv}\,f)\,x_2, f\,x_3, (\mathtt{inv}\,f)\,x_4, \dots]$ written as:

$$\mu g.\lambda f. \begin{Bmatrix} [\,] & \leftrightarrow [\,] \\ h :: t & \leftrightarrow (f\,h) :: ((g\,(\mathtt{inv}\,f)\,)t) \end{Bmatrix} : (A \leftrightarrow A) \to ([A] \leftrightarrow [A]) \tag{1}$$

We define the two mutually recursive proofs π_1 and π_2 by $\pi_1 = \Pi(\psi_f, \pi_2)$ and $\pi_2 = \Pi(\psi_{f^\perp}, \pi_1)$ where ψ_f and $\psi_{f^\perp}$ correspond to the isos f and $\mathtt{inv}\,f$. The proof associated with the iso in Eq. (1) is π_1. The proof $\Pi(\phi_1, \phi_2)$ is shown in Fig. 5.

$$
\dfrac{\dfrac{\dfrac{\dfrac{\dfrac{\dfrac{}{\vdash \mathbb{1}}\,\mathbb{1}_R}{\vdash \mathbb{1} \oplus (A \otimes [A])}\,\oplus^1_R}{\vdash [A]}\,\mu_R}{\mathbb{1} \vdash [A]}\,\mathbb{1}_L \qquad \dfrac{\dfrac{\dfrac{\dfrac{\dfrac{\dfrac{\phi_1}{A \vdash A} \quad \dfrac{}{A \vdash A}\,\mathrm{id}}{A \vdash A}\,\mathtt{cut} \qquad \dfrac{\dfrac{\phi_2}{[A] \vdash [A]} \quad \dfrac{}{[A] \vdash [A]}\,\mathrm{id}}{[A] \vdash [A]}\,\mathtt{cut}}{A, [A] \vdash A \otimes [A]}\,\otimes_R}{A, [A] \vdash \mathbb{1} \oplus (A \otimes [A])}\,\oplus^2_R}{A, [A] \vdash [A]}\,\mu_R}{A \otimes [A] \vdash [A]}\,\otimes_L}{\mathbb{1} \oplus (A \otimes [A]) \vdash [A]}\,\oplus_L}{[A] \vdash [A]}\,\mu_L
$$

Fig. 5. Proof corresponding to Example 4.1.

5 Conclusion

We presented a higher-order, linear, reversible language with inductive and coinductive types together with an interpretation of programs into derivations in the logic μMALL. This work is still in progress: A number of proofs still need to be completed. After completing the proofs of our current conjectures, we want to extend our language to linear combinations of terms in order to study purely quantum recursive types and generalized quantum loops: in [15], lists are the only recursive type which is captured and recursion is terminating. The logic μMALL would help providing a finer understanding of termination and non-termination.

Acknowledgments. This work was supported in part by the French National Research Agency (ANR) under the research project SoftQPRO ANR-17-CE25-0009-02, and by the DGE of the French Ministry of Industry under the research project PIA-GDN/QuantEx P163746-484124.

References

1. Baelde, D., Doumane, A., Saurin, A.: Infinitary proof theory: the multiplicative additive case. In: Proceedings of CSL. LIPIcs, vol. 62, pp. 42:1–42:17 (2016)
2. Baelde, D., Miller, D.: Least and Greatest Fixed Points in Linear Logic. In: Dershowitz, N., Voronkov, A. (eds.) LPAR 2007. LNCS (LNAI), vol. 4790, pp. 92–106. Springer, Heidelberg (2007). https://doi.org/10.1007/978-3-540-75560-9_9
3. Bertot, Y., Castéran, P.: Interactive Theorem Proving and Program Development - Coq'Art. Springer, Heidelberg (2004). https://doi.org/10.1007/978-3-662-07964-5
4. Curry, H.B.: Functionality in combinatory logic. Proc. Nat. Acad. Sci. U.S.A. **20**(11), 584 (1934)
5. Fingerhuth, M., Babej, T., Wittek, P.: Open source software in quantum computing. PLoS ONE **13**(12), 1–28 (2018). https://doi.org/10.1371/journal.pone.0208561
6. Gaboardi, M., Haeberlen, et al.: Linear dependent types for differential privacy. In: Proceedings of POPL, pp. 357–370. ACM (2013). https://doi.org/10.1145/2429069.2429113

7. Girard, J.Y.: Linear logic. Theoret. Comput. Sci. **50**(1), 1–101 (1987)
8. Howard, W.A.: The formulae-as-types notion of construction. To HB Curry: Essays on Combinatory Logic, Lambda Calculus and Formalism **44**, 479–490 (1980)
9. Jung, R., Jourdan, et al.: RustBelt: securing the foundations of the Rust programming language. PACMPL 2(POPL), 66:1–66:34 (2018). https://doi.org/10.1145/3158154
10. Leroy, X.: Formal verification of a realistic compiler. Commun. ACM **52**(7), 107–115 (2009). https://doi.org/10.1145/1538788.1538814
11. Maillard, K., Hritcu, C., Rivas, E., Muylder, A.V.: The next 700 relational program logics. PACMPL 4(POPL), 4:1–4:33 (2020). https://doi.org/10.1145/3371072
12. Paykin, J., Rand, R., Zdancewic, S.: QWIRE: a core language for quantum circuits. In: Proceedings of POPL, pp. 846–858. ACM (2017). https://doi.org/10.1145/3009837.3009894
13. Reynolds, J.C.: Separation logic: a logic for shared mutable data structures. In: Proceedings of LICS, pp. 55–74. IEEE Computer Society (2002). https://doi.org/10.1109/LICS.2002.1029817
14. Rios, F., Selinger, P.: A categorical model for a quantum circuit description language. Proceedings of QPL. ENTCS **266**, 164–178 (2017). https://doi.org/10.4204/EPTCS.266.11
15. Sabry, A., Valiron, B., Vizzotto, J.K.: From Symmetric Pattern-Matching to Quantum Control. In: Baier, C., Dal Lago, U. (eds.) FoSSaCS 2018. LNCS, vol. 10803, pp. 348–364. Springer, Cham (2018). https://doi.org/10.1007/978-3-319-89366-2_19
16. Selinger, P., Valiron, B.: A lambda calculus for quantum computation with classical control. Math. Struct. Comput. Sci. **16**(3), 527–552 (2006)
17. Swamy, N., Hritcu, C., Keller, C., et al.: Dependent types and multi-monadic effects in F. In: Proceedings of POPL, pp. 256–270. ACM (2016). https://doi.org/10.1145/2837614.2837655

A Tutorial Introduction to Quantum Circuit Programming in Dependently Typed Proto-Quipper

Peng Fu[1($\boxtimes$)], Kohei Kishida[2], Neil J. Ross[1], and Peter Selinger[1]

[1] Dalhousie University, Halifax, NS, Canada
{frank-fu,neil.jr.ross,peter.selinger}@dal.ca
[2] University of Illinois, Urbana-Champaign, IL, USA
kkishida@illinois.edu

Abstract. We introduce dependently typed Proto-Quipper, or Proto-Quipper-D for short, an experimental quantum circuit programming language with linear dependent types. We give several examples to illustrate how linear dependent types can help in the construction of correct quantum circuits. Specifically, we show how dependent types enable programming families of circuits, and how dependent types solve the problem of type-safe uncomputation of garbage qubits. We also discuss other language features along the way.

Keywords: Quantum programming languages · Linear dependent types · Proto-Quipper-D

1 Introduction

Quantum computers can in principle outperform conventional computers at certain crucial tasks that underlie modern computing infrastructures. Experimental quantum computing is in its early stages and existing devices are not yet suitable for practical computing. However, several groups of researchers, in both academia and industry, are now building quantum computers (see, e.g., [2,11,17]). Quantum computing also raises many challenging questions for the programming language community [18]: How should we design programming languages for quantum computation? How should we compile and optimize quantum programs? How should we test and verify quantum programs? How should we understand the semantics of quantum programming languages?

In this paper, we focus on quantum circuit programming using the linear dependently typed functional language Proto-Quipper-D.

The no-cloning property of quantum mechanics states that one cannot in general copy the state of a qubit. Many existing quantum programming languages, such as Quipper [9,10], QISKit [22], Q# [27], Cirq [5], or ProjectQ [26], do not enforce this property. As a result, programmers have to ensure that references to qubits within a program are not duplicated or discarded. Linear types

© Springer Nature Switzerland AG 2020
I. Lanese and M. Rawski (Eds.): RC 2020, LNCS 12227, pp. 153–168, 2020.
https://doi.org/10.1007/978-3-030-52482-1_9

have been used for resource aware programming [7,28] and it is now well-known that they can be used to enforce no-cloning [25]. A variety of programming languages use linear types for quantum circuit programming, e.g., Proto-Quipper-S [24], Proto-Quipper-M [23], and QWire [20]. All well-typed programs in these languages satisfy the no-cloning property.

Dependent types [15] have been one of the main focuses in programming language and type system research in the past decades. Dependent types make it possible to express program invariants and constraints using types [1,3,6]. In the context of quantum circuit programming, dependent types are useful for expressing parameterized families of circuits. For example, one can define a function that inputs a size and outputs a circuit of the corresponding size. Because the type of the output circuit is indexed by the size argument, errors due to an attempt to compose mismatched circuits are detected at compile time. Another important application of dependent types is the type-safe management of garbage qubits, which we discuss in Sect. 4.

We introduce an experimental quantum circuit programming language called dependently typed Proto-Quipper, or Proto-Quipper-D for short. Following Quipper, Proto-Quipper-D is a functional language with quantum data types and aims to provide high-level abstractions for constructing quantum circuits. Like its predecessors Proto-Quipper-S and Proto-Quipper-M, the Proto-Quipper-D language relies on linear types to enforce no-cloning. Proto-Quipper-D additionally features the use of linear dependent types to facilitate the type-safe construction of circuit families [21]. This paper provides a practical introduction to programming in Proto-Quipper-D.

The paper is structured around several programming examples that showcase the use of linear dependent types in Proto-Quipper-D.

- We give an introduction to dependent types by showing how to use them to prove basic properties of addition in Sect. 2.
- We show how to program with families of quantum circuits in Sect. 3.
- We give a new application of existential dependent types and show how it simplifies the construction of certain reversible quantum circuits in Sect. 4.

An implementation of Proto-Quipper-D is available at: https://gitlab.com/frank-peng-fu/dpq-remake.

2   An Introduction to Dependent Types

Proto-Quipper-D supports programming by recursion and pattern matching. For example, the following is a program that defines the addition of Peano numbers.

```
data Nat = Z | S Nat

add : !(Nat -> Nat -> Nat)
add n m =
  case n of
    Z -> m
    S n' -> S (add n' m)
```

In the above program, we use the keyword **data** to define an algebraic data type in the style of Haskell 98 [13]. The type checker will analyze the data type declaration and determine that **Nat** is a *parameter type* (or *non-linear type*). In Proto-Quipper-D, parameter types are types that can be freely duplicated and discarded. The addition function has type !(Nat -> Nat -> Nat). The exclamation mark (pronounced "bang") in front of a function type makes that type a parameter type. This means that addition is a reusable function, i.e., it can be used multiple times. The type of a non-reusable function would be of the form a -> b and in particular would not be prefixed by a !. In contrast to a reusable function, a non-reusable function must be used exactly once. This guarantees that any quantum data embedded in the function does not get inadvertently duplicated or discarded. Proto-Quipper-D requires all top-level declarations to have parameter types, making them reusable.

With dependent types, we can even encode properties of programs in types. In Proto-Quipper-D, dependent function types are of the form (x : A) -> B, where the type B may optionally mention the variable x. We can think of this dependent function type as the universal quantification $\forall x : A . B$ of predicate logic. Dependent types therefore allow us to represent properties of programs as types. For example, the following programs correspond to proofs of basic properties of addition.

```
addS : ! (p : Nat -> Type) -> (n m : Nat) ->
            p (add n (S m)) -> p (add (S n) m)
addS p n m h =
  case n of
    Z -> h
    S n' -> addS (λ y -> p (S y)) n' m h

addZ : ! (p : Nat -> Type) -> (n : Nat) -> p (add n Z) -> p n
addZ p n h = case n of
                Z -> h
                S n' -> addZ (λ y -> p (S y)) n' h
```

The type of **addS** expresses the theorem that for all natural numbers n and m, we have $n + Sm = Sn + m$. However, rather than using an equality symbol, we use the so-called *Leibniz equality*. Leibniz defined two things to be equal if they have exactly the same properties. Therefore, the type of **addS** states that for any property p : Nat -> Type of natural numbers, and for all natural numbers n, m, if add n (S m) has the property p, then add (S n) m has the property p. Similarly, the type of **addZ** expresses the fact that $n + Z = n$.

Note how the types of dependent type theory play a dual role: on the one hand, they can be read as types specifying the inputs and outputs of functional programs; on the other hand, they can be read as logical statements. This is the so-called *propositions-as-types* paradigm [8]. For example, the last arrow "->" in the type of **addS** can be interpreted both as a function type and as the logical implication symbol. This works because a proof of an implication is actually a function that transforms evidence for the hypothesis into evidence for the conclusion.

Indeed, not only does the type of the function addS corresponds to a theorem, but the actual code of addS corresponds to its proof. For example, in the branch when n is Z, the variable h has type p (add Z (S m)), which equals p (S m) by the definition of add. This branch is expecting an expression of type p (add (S Z) m), which equals p (S m) by definition of add, so the type-checking of h succeeds.

In practice, we can sometimes use the above equality proofs to convert one type to another. We will give examples of this in Sect. 3.2. However, we emphasize that Proto-Quipper-D is designed for quantum circuit programming, not general theorem proving like languages such as Coq and Agda. The only kind of primitive propositions we can have are equalities, and the support of dependent data types is limited to *simple types*, as discussed in Sect. 3.1.

3   Programming Quantum Circuits

We use the keyword object to introduce simple linear objects such as bits and qubits, representing primitive wires in circuits. We use the keyword gate to introduce a primitive gate. As far as Proto-Quipper-D is concerned, gates are uninterpreted; they simply represent basic boxes that can be combined into circuits. Each primitive gate has a type specifying its inputs and outputs.

```
object Qubit
object Bit

gate H : Qubit -> Qubit
gate CNot : Qubit -> Qubit -> Qubit * Qubit
gate Meas : Qubit -> Bit
gate Discard : Bit -> Unit
gate Init0 : Unit -> Qubit
gate C_X : Qubit -> Bit -> Qubit * Bit
gate C_Z : Qubit -> Bit -> Qubit * Bit
```

The above code declares primitive types Qubit and Bit and a number of gates. For example, the gate H is a reusable linear function of type !(Qubit -> Qubit), which, by convention, represents the Hadamard gate. Note that the type checker automatically adds the ! to gate declarations, so it is not necessary to do so manually. The type expression Qubit * Qubit denotes the tensor product of two qubits, and thus, the controlled-not gate CNot has two inputs and two outputs (where, by convention, the first input is the target and the second is the control). By linearity, the arguments of the CNot can only be used once. Thus, an expression such as CNot x x will be rejected by the type checker because the argument x is used twice. The gate Meas corresponds to a measurement, turning a qubit into a classical bit. The type Unit represents the unit of the tensor product, i.e., a bundle of zero wires. Thus, the gate Discard can be used to discard a classical bit, and the gate Init0 can be used to initialize a qubit (by convention, in state $|0\rangle$). We also introduce two classically-controlled gates C_X and C_Z.

The following program produces a circuit that generates a Bell state:

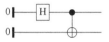

```
bell00 : !(Unit -> Qubit * Qubit)
bell00 u =
  let x = Init0 ()
      y = Init0 ()
      x' = H x
      (y, x') = CNot y x'
  in (y, x')
```

The initialization gate Init0 inputs a unit, denoted by (), and outputs a qubit. If we want to display the circuit generated by the function bell00, we can use Proto-Quipper's box function:

```
bell00Box : Circ(Unit, Qubit * Qubit)
bell00Box = box Unit bell00
```

The box function inputs a circuit-generating function such as bell00 and produces a completed circuit of type Circ(Unit, Qubit * Qubit). In the Proto-Quipper-D interactive shell, we can then type :d bell00Box to display the circuit.

The following program implements quantum teleportation.

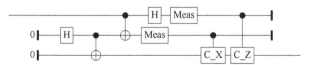

```
bellMeas : !(Qubit -> Qubit -> Bit * Bit)
bellMeas x y =
  let (x', y') = CNot x y
      y'' = H y'
  in (Meas x', Meas y'')

tele : !(Qubit -> Qubit)
tele phi =
  let (bob, alice) = bell00 ()
      (a', phi') = bellMeas alice phi
      (bob', a'') = C_X bob a'
      (r, phi'') = C_Z bob' phi'
      u = Discard phi''
      u = Discard a''
  in r
```

3.1 Simple Types

Following Quipper, Proto-Quipper-D makes a distinction between *parameters* and *states*. Parameters are values that are known at circuit generation time, while states are only known at circuit execution time. For example, the type Nat represents a parameter, while the type Qubit represents a state.

In Proto-Quipper-D, we use the concept of *simple types* to describe states. As discussed earlier, simple types can be introduced using the keyword object. In practice, it is more common to create simple types by composing existing ones. For example, Qubit * Qubit is also a simple type. For this reason, we call the tensor product a *simple type constructor*. In Proto-Quipper-D, the programmer can also define families of new simple types using the simple keyword. For example, the following defines a type family Vec, and Vec Qubit n is a simple type.

```
simple Vec a : Nat -> Type where
    Vec a Z = VNil
    Vec a (S n) = VCons a (Vec a n)
```

The expression Nat -> Type is a *kind expression*. It means that Vec a n is a type whenever n is a natural number. The two clauses after the simple keyword are the definition of the type Vec a n. The first clause says that an element of the type Vec a Z can be constructed by the constructor VNil. The second clause says that an element of the type Vec a (S n) can be constructed by applying the constructor VCons to a term of type a and a term of type Vec a n. Therefore, Vec a n represents a vector of n elements of type a.

The type Vec a n is an example of *dependent data type*, where the data type Vec a n depends on some term n of type Nat. In the interpreter, we can query the types of VNil and VCons (by typing :t VNil). They have the following types.

```
VNil : forall (a : Type) -> Vec a Z
VCons : forall (a : Type) -> forall (n : Nat) ->
              a -> Vec a n -> Vec a (S n)
```

In Proto-Quipper-D, all data constructors are reusable, so there is no need for them to have an explicit bang-type. The leading forall keyword means that programmers do not need to supply that argument when calling the function. We call such quantification *irrelevant quantification*. For example, when using VCons, we only need to give it two arguments, one of type a and one of type Vec a n.

The simple data type declaration is currently the only way to introduce dependent data types in Proto-Quipper-D. Semantically, simple types corresponds to states. Syntactically, a simple type can uniquely determine the size and the constructors of its data. The type checker will check whether a simple data type declaration is well-defined. Note that not all dependent data types are simple types. For example, the following declaration will not pass the type checker.

```
simple ColorVec a : Nat -> Type where
  ColorVec a Z = CNil
  ColorVec a (S n) = VConsBlue a (ColorVec a n)
  ColorVec a (S n) = VConsRed a (ColorVec a n)
```

The `ColorVec` data type is ambiguous when the parameter is `S n`, as the constructor in this case can be either `VConsBlue` or `VConsRed`.

In general, checking whether a simple type is well-defined is equivalent to deciding whether a general recursive function is well-defined and terminating, which is undecidable. Currently, Proto-Quipper-D checks whether a simple data type declaration is well-defined using the same criterion as checking primitive recursion [14].

3.2 Using Leibniz Equality

Suppose we want to define a function that reverses the order of the components in a vector. One way to do this is to use an accumulator: we traverse the vector while prepending each element to the accumulator. This can be expressed by the `reverse_aux` function defined below.

```
reverse_aux : ! (a : Type) -> (n m : Nat) ->
                    Vec a n -> Vec a m -> Vec a (add n m)
reverse_aux a n m v1 v2 =
  case n of
    Z -> let VNil = v1 in v2
    S n' ->
      let VCons q qs = v1 in
      let ih = reverse_aux a n' (S m) qs (VCons q v2) in
      addS (Vec a) n' m ih
```

Note that the type of `reverse_aux` indicates that the length of the output vector is the sum of the lengths of the input vectors. In the definition for `reverse_aux`, we use `v1` and `v2` exactly once in each branch, which respects linearity. In the second branch of `reverse_aux`, the type checker expects an expression of type `Vec a (add (S n') m)`, but the expression `ih`, obtained from the recursive call, has type `Vec a (add n' (S m))`. We therefore use the theorem `addS` from Sect. 2 to convert the type to `Vec a (add (S n') m)`. We can then use `reverse_aux` to define the `reverse_vec` function, which requires a similar type conversion.

```
reverse_vec : ! (a : Type) -> (n : Nat) -> Vec a n -> Vec a n
reverse_vec a n v = addZ (Vec a) n (reverse_aux a n Z v VNil)
```

3.3 Families of Quantum Circuits

We can use simple data types such as vectors to define functions that correspond to families of circuits. As an example, we consider the well-known quantum

Fourier transform [19]. The quantum Fourier transform is the map defined by

$$|a_1, \ldots, a_n\rangle \mapsto \frac{(|0\rangle + e^{2\pi i 0.a_1 a_2 \ldots a_n}|1\rangle) \ldots (|0\rangle + e^{2\pi i 0.a_{n-1} a_n}|1\rangle)(|0\rangle + e^{2\pi i 0.a_n}|1\rangle)}{2^{n/2}}.$$

where $0.a_1 \ldots a_n$ is the binary fraction $a_1/2 + a_2/4 + \ldots + a_n/2^n$. Circuits for the quantum Fourier transform can be constructed using the Hadamard gate H and the controlled rotation gates $R(k)$ defined by

$$R(k) = \begin{pmatrix} 1 & 0 & 0 & 0 \\ 0 & 1 & 0 & 0 \\ 0 & 0 & 1 & 0 \\ 0 & 0 & 0 & e^{2\pi i/2^k} \end{pmatrix}.$$

The family of gates $R(k)$ can be declared in Proto-Quipper-D as follows:

```
gate R Nat : Qubit -> Qubit -> Qubit * Qubit
```

Applying the Hadamard gate to the first qubit produces the following state

$$H_1|a_1, \ldots, a_n\rangle = \frac{1}{\sqrt{2}}(|0\rangle + e^{2\pi i 0.a_1}|1\rangle) \otimes |a_2, \ldots, a_n\rangle,$$

where the subscript on the gate indicates the qubit on which the gate acts. We then apply a sequence of controlled rotations using the the first qubit as the target. This yields

$$R(n)_{1,n} \ldots R(2)_{1,2} H_1|a_1, \ldots, a_n\rangle = \frac{1}{2^{1/2}}(|0\rangle + e^{2\pi i 0.a_1 a_2 \ldots a_n}|1\rangle) \otimes |a_2, \ldots, a_n\rangle,$$

where the subscripts i and j in $R(k)_{i,j}$ indicate the target and control qubit, respectively. When $n = 5$, the above sequence of gates corresponds to the following circuit.

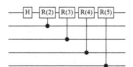

To construct such a circuit in Proto-Quipper-D, we first define the rotate function, which will produce a cascade of rotations with a single target. The rotations in the above circuit are then generated by oneRotation 4.

```
rotate : ! forall (y : Nat) -> Nat ->
              Qubit -> Vec Qubit y -> Qubit * Vec Qubit y
rotate k q v =
    case v of
      VNil -> (q, VNil)
      VCons x xs ->
        let (q', x') = R k q x
            (q'', xs') = rotate (S k) q' xs
        in (q'', VCons x' xs')
```

```
oneRotation : ! (n : Nat) ->
                  Circ(Qubit * Vec Qubit n, Qubit * Vec Qubit n)
oneRotation n =
  box (Qubit * Vec Qubit n)
    (λ x -> let (q, v) = x in rotate 2 (H q) v)
```

The `rotate` function uses the input vector v for controls and recursively applies
the rotation gate R to the target qubit q, updating the rotation angle at each
step. To program the full quantum Fourier transform, we apply the Hadamard
and controlled rotations recursively to the rest of input qubits.

```
qft : ! forall (n : Nat) -> Vec Qubit n -> Vec Qubit n
qft v =
  case v of
    VNil -> VNil
    VCons q qs ->
      let q' = H q
          (q'', qs') = rotate 2 q' qs
          qs'' = qft qs'
      in VCons q'' qs''
```

```
qftBox : ! (n : Nat) -> Circ(Vec Qubit n, Vec Qubit n)
qftBox n = box (Vec Qubit n) qft
```

For example, `qftBox 5` generates the following circuit.

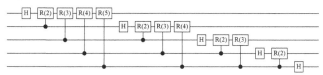

The input qubits of the circuit above use a big-endian ordering. We can
convert to little-endian ordering by reversing the input vector.

```
qftBoxLittle : ! (n : Nat) -> Circ(Vec Qubit n, Vec Qubit n)
qftBoxLittle n = box (Vec Qubit n) (λ v -> qft (reverse_vec Qubit n v))
```

Then `qftBoxLittle 5` generates the following circuit.

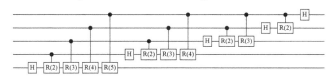

3.4   Type Classes for Simple Types and Parameter Types

Proto-Quipper-D is equipped with a type class mechanism that allows the user
to define type classes and instances [29]. In addition, Proto-Quipper-D has two
built-in type classes called `Simple` and `Parameter`, which are useful for programming with simple types and parameter types, respectively. The user cannot

directly define instances for these two classes. Instead, instances for `Simple` and `Parameter` are automatically generated from data type declarations.

When a simple data type is defined, the type checker automatically makes the type an instance of the `Simple` class and, if appropriate, of the `Parameter` class. Similarly, when algebraic data types such as `List` and `Nat` are defined, the type checker makes instances of the `Parameter` class when possible. For example, consider the following programs.

```
data List a = Nil | Cons a (List a)

kill : ! forall a -> (Parameter a) => a -> Unit
kill x = ()

test1 : !(List Nat -> Unit)
test1 x = kill x

test2 : !(List Qubit -> Unit)
test2 x = kill x
```

The argument of the function `kill` must be a parameter. The expression `test1` is well-typed, because `List Nat` is a member of the `Parameter` class. But `test2` fails to type-check because `List Qubit` is not a member of the `Parameter` class.

Simple types are useful for describing the types of certain operations that require a circuit, rather than a family of circuits. Examples are boxing, unboxing, and reversing a circuit:

```
box : (a : Type) -> forall (b : Type) ->
        (Simple a, Simple b) => !(a -> b) -> Circ(a, b)

unbox : forall (a b : Type) ->
        (Simple a, Simple b) => Circ(a, b) -> !(a -> b)

reverse : forall (a b : Type) ->
        (Simple a, Simple b) => Circ(a, b) -> Circ(b, a)
```

The type of `box` implies that only functions of simple type can be turned into boxed circuits. The following program will not type-check because `List Qubit` is not a simple type.

```
boxId : Circ(List Qubit , List Qubit)
boxId = box (List Qubit) (λ x -> x)
```

With the built-in function **reverse**, we can now compute the inverse of qftBox.

```
boxQftRev : ! (n : Nat) -> Circ(Vec Qubit n, Vec Qubit n)
boxQftRev n = reverse (qftBox n)
```

By definition, the family of circuits represented by `boxQftRev` is obtained by taking the inverse of every member of the family of circuits represented `qftBox`. For example, `boxQftRev 5` generates the following circuit.

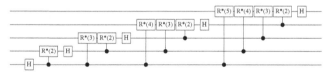

4   Type-Safe Management of Garbage Qubits

In quantum computing, it is often necessary to provide classical oracles to a quantum algorithm. These oracles are reversible implementations of classical boolean functions. Consider the example of the single bit full adder. If the inputs are `a`, `b` and `carryIn`, then the boolean expression `xor (xor a b) carryIn` calculates the sum of `a`, `b` and `carryIn` while the boolean expression `(a && b) || (a && carryIn) || (b && carryIn)` calculates the output carry.

We can implement the single bit adder as a reversible quantum circuit. Suppose that the boolean operations `xor`, `||`, and `&&` are given as reversible circuits of type `!(Qubit -> Qubit -> Qubit * Qubit)`. Here, the first qubit in the output of each function is the result of the operation, whereas the second qubit is a "garbage" qubit that cannot be discarded since this would violate linearity. As a result, the following naive implementation of the adder generates 7 garbage qubits and has a 9-tuple of qubits as its return type.

```
adder : ! (Qubit -> Qubit -> Qubit ->
              Qubit * Qubit * Qubit * Qubit * Qubit *
                Qubit * Qubit * Qubit * Qubit)
adder a b carryIn =
  let (a1, a2, a3) = copy3 a
      (b1, b2, b3) = copy3 b
      (carryIn1, carryIn2, carryIn3) = copy3 carryIn
      (g1, r) = xor a1 b1
      (g2, s) = xor carryIn1 r
      (g3, c1) = a2 && b2
      (g4, c2) = a3 && carryIn2
      (g5, c3) = b3 && carryIn3
      (g6, c4) = c1 || c2
      (g7, carryOut) = c4 || c3
  in (s, carryOut, g1, g2, g3, g4, g5, g6, g7)
```

Due to linearity, the copying of a classical qubit must be explicit. In the code above, `copy3` is a function that produces three copies of a qubit that is in a classical state, i.e., `copy3` corresponds to the following circuit.

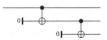

The above implementation of the adder is hard to read and awkward to compose with other circuits, because its type keeps track of all the garbage qubits produced throughout the computation. In Proto-Quipper-D, we solve this problem using monads [12], existential dependent types, and existential circuit boxing.

Instead of using the type `!(Qubit -> Qubit -> Qubit * Qubit)`, we give xor, `||`, and `&&` the type `!(Qubit -> Qubit -> WithGarbage Qubit)`, where `WithGarbage` is a monad that will take care of the garbage qubits. The idiomatic implementation of the full adder in Proto-Quipper-D is the following.

```
adder : !(Qubit -> Qubit -> Qubit -> WithGarbage (Qubit * Qubit))
adder a b carryIn = do
  let (a1, a2, a3) = copy3 a
      (b1, b2, b3) = copy3 b
      (carryIn1, carryIn2, carryIn3) = copy3 carryIn
  s <- [| xor (xor a1 b1) (pure carryIn1)|]
  carryOut <- [|[|(a2 && b2) || (a3 && carryIn2)|] || (b3 && carryIn3)|]
  return (s, carryOut)
```

Proto-Quipper-D implements idiom brackets [16] of the form `[| f a b c |]`. This expression will be translated to `join (ap (ap (ap (pure f) a) b) c)`, where `ap`, `pure` and `join` have the following types.

```
ap  : ! forall (a b : Type) -> forall (m : Type -> Type) ->
          (Monad m) => m (a -> b) -> m a -> m b

pure : ! forall (m : Type -> Type) ->
          (Monad m) => forall (a : Type) -> a -> m a

join : ! forall (a : Type) -> forall (m : Type -> Type) ->
          (Monad m) => m (m a) -> m a
```

We now briefly discuss the definition of the `WithGarbage` monad.

```
data WithGarbage a = WG ((n : Nat) * Vec Qubit n) a

instance Monad WithGarbage where
  return x = WG (Z, VNil) x
  bind wg f = let WG ng r = wg
                  (n, g) = ng
                  WG mg' r' = f r
                  (m, g') = mg'
              in WG (add n m, append g g') r'
```

The type `(x : A) * B` is an *existential dependent type*, corresponding to the existential quantification $\exists x : A . B$ of predicate logic. Just as for dependent function types, the type B may optionally mention the variable x. The elements of the type (n : Nat) * Vec Qubit n are pairs (n, v), where n : Nat and v : Vec Qubit n. Thus, WithGarbage a contains a vector of qubits of a unknown length and a value of type a. In the definition of the WithGarbage monad, the return function does not generate any garbage qubits. The bind function combines the garbage qubits from the two computations wg and f. Note that it uses the append function to concatenate two vectors.

The standard way to dispose of a qubit (and turn it into garbage) is via the following dispose method.

```
class Disposable a where
  dispose : a -> WithGarbage Unit

instance Disposable Qubit where
  dispose q = WG (1, VCons q VNil) ()
```

So for example, we can implement xor as follows. Note that the implemented circuit is not optimal, but it serves to illustrate the point.

```
xor : !(Qubit -> Qubit -> WithGarbage Qubit)
xor x y =
  do let z = Init0 ()
         (z', x') = CNot z x
         (z'', y') = CNot z' y
     dispose x'
     dispose y'
     return z''
```

Using the WithGarbage monad, we can program almost as if the extra garbage qubits do not exist. Next, we need a type-safe way to uncompute the garbage qubits. We achieve this with the function with_computed below, which takes a garbage-producing function and turns it into a function that produces no garbage. The implementation of with_computed relies on the following built-in function:

```
existsBox : (a : Type) -> forall (b : Type) ->
            (Simple a, Parameter b) => (p : b -> Type) ->
            !(a -> (n : b) * p n) ->
            (n : b) * ((Simple (p n)) => Circ(a, p n))
```

Intuitively, the existsBox construct is used to box an existential function. It takes a circuit generating function of type !(a -> (n : b) * p n) as input and turns it into an *existential circuit* of the type (n : b) * Circ(a, p n). Using existsBox, we can define with_computed:

```
with_computed : ! forall d ->  (a b c : Type) ->
                (Simple a, Simple b) =>
                !(a -> WithGarbage b) ->
                !(c * b -> d * b) -> (c * a -> d * a)
```

```
with_computed a b c f g input =
  let (y, x) = input
      (_,circ) = existsBox a (λx->Vec Qubit x*b) (λz->unGarbage (f z))
      h' = unbox circ
      (v, r) = h' x
      circ_rev = unbox (reverse circ)
      (d, r') = g (y, r)
      res = circ_rev (v, r')
  in (d, res)
```

The `with_computed` function inputs a function `f : a -> WithGarbage b` and a second function `g : c * b -> d * b`, and produces a garbage-free circuit `c * a -> d * a` corresponding to the following diagram. Of course each wire may correspond to multiple qubits, as specified in its type.

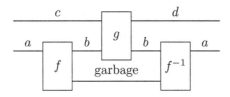

Note that this construction is type-safe, because it guarantees that there will be no uncollected garbage, regardless of how much garbage the function f actually produces. However, Proto-Quipper-D does not guarantee the *semantic* correctness of the resulting circuit; it could happen that a qubit that is supposed to be returned in state $|0\rangle$ is returned in some other state. Since semantic correctness is in general undecidable, Proto-Quipper-D makes no attempt to prove it. Consequently, a failure of semantic correctness is considered to be a programming error, rather than a type error. However, the *syntactic* correctness of the generated circuits is guaranteed by the type system.

Using the `with_computed` function and a few helper functions, we can obtain the following reversible version of `adder`.

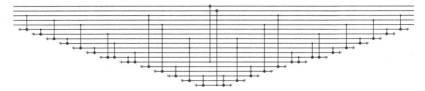

5   Case Studies

Beyond the simple examples that were considered in this tutorial, we have conducted two nontrivial programming case studies using Proto-Quipper-D. The first one is an implementation of the binary welded tree algorithm [4], which features the use of the dependent vector data type. The second is a boolean oracle for determining the winner of a completed game of Hex, which features the use the of `WithGarbage` and `State` monads. Both implementations are distributed with Proto-Quipper-D, in `test/BWT.dpq` and `test/Hex3.dpq`, respectively. The largest oracle contains 457,383 gates. For this oracle, type checking is nearly instantaneous (it takes less than 1 second), and circuit generation takes about 2.5 min on a 3.5 GHz CPU (4 cores), 16 GB memory desktop machine.

6   Conclusion

In this tutorial, we introduced the quantum programming language Proto-Quipper-D through a series of examples. Proto-Quipper-D is an experimental language and is currently under active development. Due to space constraints, we did not discuss all of the features of Proto-Quipper-D. Our goal was to highlight the use of linear and dependent types in quantum circuit programming. All the programs in the tutorial are available in `test/Tutorial.dpq` of the Proto-Quipper-D distribution.

Acknowledgements. This work was supported by the Air Force Office of Scientific Research under award number FA9550-15-1-0331. Any opinions, findings and conclusions or recommendations expressed in this material are those of the authors and do not necessarily reflect the views of the U.S. Department of Defense.

References

1. Agda Documentation. https://agda.readthedocs.io/en/v2.6.0.1/. Accessed 01 Feb 2020
2. Arute, F., et al.: Quantum supremacy using a programmable superconducting processor. Nature **574**, 505–510 (2019). (84 authors)
3. Bove, A., Dybjer, P.: Dependent types at work. In: Bove, A., Barbosa, L.S., Pardo, A., Pinto, J.S. (eds.) LerNet 2008. LNCS, vol. 5520, pp. 57–99. Springer, Heidelberg (2009). https://doi.org/10.1007/978-3-642-03153-3_2
4. Childs, A.M., Cleve, R., Deotto, E., Farhi, E., Gutmann, S., Spielman, D.A.: Exponential algorithmic speedup by a quantum walk. In: Proceedings of the 35th Annual ACM Symposium on Theory of Computing, pp. 59–68 (2003)
5. Circ. https://cirq.readthedocs.io/en/stable/. Accessed 01 Feb 2020
6. Coq Documentation. https://coq.inria.fr/documentation/. Accessed 01 Feb 2020
7. Girard, J.Y.: Linear Logic. Theor. Comput. Sci. **50**(1), 1–101 (1987)
8. Girard, J.Y., Lafont, Y., Taylor, P.: Proofs and Types. Cambridge University Press, Cambridge (1989)
9. Green, A.S., Lumsdaine, P.L.F., Ross, N.J., Selinger, P., Valiron, B.: An introduction to quantum programming in Quipper. In: Dueck, G.W., Miller, D.M. (eds.) RC 2013. LNCS, vol. 7948, pp. 110–124. Springer, Heidelberg (2013). https://doi.org/10.1007/978-3-642-38986-3_10
10. Green, A.S., Lumsdaine, P.L., Ross, N.J., Selinger, P., Valiron, B.: Quipper: a scalable quantum programming language. In: Proceedings of the 34th Annual ACM SIGPLAN Conference on Programming Language Design and Implementation, vol. 48(6), pp. 333–342. ACM (2013)
11. IBM Quantum Experience. https://quantum-computing.ibm.com. Accessed 01 Feb 2020

12. Jones, M.P.: Functional programming with overloading and higher-order polymorphism. In: Jeuring, J., Meijer, E. (eds.) AFP 1995. LNCS, vol. 925, pp. 97–136. Springer, Heidelberg (1995). https://doi.org/10.1007/3-540-59451-5_4
13. Peyton Jones, S.: Haskell 98 Language and Libraries: The Revised Report. Cambridge University Press, Cambridge (2003)
14. Kleene, S.C.: Introduction to Metamathematics. Van Nostrand, New York (1968)
15. Martin-Löf, P., Sambin, G.: Intuitionistic Type Theory. Bibliopolis, Naples (1984)
16. McBride, C., Paterson, R.: Applicative programming with effects. J. Funct. Program. $18(1)$, 1–13 (2008)
17. Monroe, C., et al.: Programmable quantum simulations of spin systems with trapped ions (2019). https://arxiv.org/abs/1912.07845
18. Mosca, M., Roetteler, M., Selinger, P.: Quantum programming languages (Dagstuhl Seminar 18381). Technical report, Schloss Dagstuhl, Leibniz-Zentrum für Informatik (2019)
19. Nielsen, M.A., Chuang, I.L.: Quantum Computation and Quantum Information. Cambridge University Press, Cambridge (2002)
20. Paykin, J., Rand, R., Zdancewic, S.: QWIRE: a core language for quantum circuits. In: Proceedings of the 44th ACM SIGPLAN Symposium on Principles of Programming Languages, vol. 52(1), pp. 846–858. ACM (2017)
21. Peng, F., Kohei, K., Peter, S.: Linear dependent type theory for quantum programming languages. In: Proceedings of the 35th Annual ACM/IEEE Symposium on Logic in Computer Science. ACM (2020, to appear)
22. Qiskit. https://qiskit.org/. Accessed 01 Feb 2020
23. Rios, F., Selinger, P.: A categorical model for a quantum circuit description language. Extended abstract. In: Proceedings of the 14th International Workshop on Quantum Physics and Logic, QPL 2017, Nijmegen. Electronic Proceedings in Theoretical Computer Science, vol. 266, pp. 164–178 (2018)
24. Ross, N.J.: Algebraic and logical methods in quantum computation. Ph. D. thesis, Department of Mathematics and Statistics, Dalhousie University (2015). https://arxiv.org/abs/1510.02198
25. Peter, S., Benoît, V.: A lambda calculus for quantum computation with classical control. Math. Struct. Comput. Sci. $16(3)$, 527–552 (2006)
26. Steiger, D.S., Häner, T., Troyer, M.: ProjectQ: an open source software framework for quantum computing (2016). https://arxiv.org/abs/1612.08091
27. Svore, K., et al.: Q#: Enabling scalable quantum computing and development with a high-level DSL. In: Proceedings of the Real World Domain Specific Languages Workshop, RWDSL 2018. Association for Computing Machinery (2018)
28. Wadler, P.: Linear types can change the world. In: Broy, M., Jones, C. (eds.) TC 2 Working Conference on Programming Concepts and Methods, pp. 546–566 (1990)
29. Wadler, P., Blott, S.: How to make ad-hoc polymorphism less ad hoc. In: Proceedings of the 16th ACM SIGPLAN-SIGACT Symposium on Principles of Programming Languages, pp. 60–76. ACM (1989)

Fractional Types

Expressive and Safe Space Management for Ancilla Bits

Chao-Hong Chen[1]📷, Vikraman Choudhury[1]📷, Jacques Carette[2]📷,
and Amr Sabry[1(✉)]📷

[1] Indiana University, Bloomington, Bloomington, IN, USA
{chen464,vikraman,sabry}@indiana.edu
[2] McMaster University, Hamilton, ON, Canada
carette@mcmaster.ca

Abstract. In reversible computing, the management of space is subject
to two broad classes of constraints. First, as with general-purpose computation, every allocation must be paired with a matching de-allocation.
Second, space can only be safely de-allocated if its contents are restored
to their initial value from allocation time. Generally speaking, the state of
the art provides limited partial solutions, either leaving both constraints
to programmers' assertions or imposing a stack discipline to address
the first constraint and leaving the second constraint to programmers'
assertions.

We propose a novel approach based on the idea of *fractional types*. As
a simple intuitive example, allocation of a new boolean value initialized
to false also creates a value 1/false that can be thought of as a garbage
collection (GC) process specialized to reclaim, and only reclaim, storage
containing the value false. This GC process is a first-class entity that can
be manipulated, decomposed into smaller processes and combined with
other GC processes.

We formalize this idea in the context of a reversible language founded
on type isomorphisms, prove its fundamental correctness properties, and
illustrate its expressiveness using a wide variety of examples. The development is backed by a fully-formalized Agda implementation (https://
github.com/DreamLinuxer/FracAncilla).

Keywords: Reversible computing · Monoidal categories · Type
isomorphisms · Pointed types · Program extraction · Agda

1 Introduction

We solve the ancilla problem in reversible computation using a novel concept:
fractional types. In the next section, we introduce the problem of ancilla management, motivate its importance, and explain the limitations of current approaches.

Although the concept of fractional types could potentially be integrated with
general-purpose languages, its natural technical definition exploits symmetries
present in the categorical model of type isomorphisms. To that end, we first

© Springer Nature Switzerland AG 2020
I. Lanese and M. Rawski (Eds.): RC 2020, LNCS 12227, pp. 169–186, 2020.
https://doi.org/10.1007/978-3-030-52482-1_10

review in Sect. 3 our previous work [7,8,13,14] on a reversible programming language built using type isomorphisms. In Sect. 4, we introduce a simple version of fractional types that allows allocation and de-allocation of ancilla bits in patterns beyond the scoped model but, like existing stack-based solutions, still requires a runtime check to verify the safety of de-allocation. In Sect. 5 we show how to remove this runtime check, by lifting programs to a richer type system with pointed types, expressing the proofs of safety in that setting, and then, from the proofs, extracting programs with guaranteed safe de-allocations and no runtime checks. The last section concludes with a summary of our results.

2   Ancilla Bits: Review and a Type-Based Approach

Restricting a reversible circuit to use no ancilla bits is like restricting a Turing machine to use no memory other than the n bits used to represent the input [1]. Since such a restriction disallows countless computations for trivial reasons, reversible models of computation have, since their inception, included management for scratch storage in the form of ancilla bits [25] with the fundamental restriction that such bits must be returned to their initial states before being safely reused or de-allocated.

2.1   Review

Reversible programming languages adopt different approaches to the management of ancilla bits, which we review below.

Quipper [12]. The language provides a scoped mechanism to manage ancilla bits via:

```
with_ancilla :: (Qubit -> Circ a) -> Circ a
```

The operator takes a block of gates parameterized by an ancilla value, allocates a new ancilla value of type Qubit initialized to $|0\rangle$, and runs the given block of gates. At the end of its execution, the block is expected to return the ancilla value to the state $|0\rangle$ at which point it is de-allocated. The expectation that the ancilla value is in the state $|0\rangle$ is enforced via a runtime check.

Quipper also provides primitives qinit and qterm, which allow programmers to manage ancilla bits manually without scoping constraints. This management is not supported by the type system, however. For example, the following statically-valid expression allocates an ancilla bit using qinit but neither it nor its caller are required by the type system to de-allocate it:

```
ex :: Qubit -> Circ (Qubit,Qubit)
ex x = do
  y <- qinit 0
  y <- qnot y 'controlled' x
  x <- qnot x 'controlled' y
  return (x,y)
```

rFun [23,26]. This language similarly allows expressions to freely allocate constant values:

```
data Bool = True | False

ex :: Bool <-> (Bool,Bool)
ex b = (b , False)
```

Using such expressions, it is possible to define expressions that behave like `qinit` and `qterm` in Quipper:

```
initF :: () <-> Bool
initF () = False

termF :: Bool <-> ()
termF False = ()
```

At run-time `termF` might fail with an incomplete pattern-matching exception but, statically, the type system neither enforces that `termF` is called nor that it is called with only the value `False`.

Ricercar [24]. This language uses a scoped way to manage ancilla bits. The expression $\alpha x.A$ allocates an ancilla wire x for the gate A requiring that x is set to 0 after the evaluation of A.

Janus [27]. This is a reversible imperative programming language that is not based on the circuit model but as Rose [20] explains, its treatment is essentially similar to above:

> All variables in original Janus are global, but in the University of Copenhagen interpreter you can allocate local variables with the local statement. The inverse of the local statement is the delocal statement, which performs deallocation. When inverted, the deallocation becomes the allocation and vice versa. In order to invert deallocation, the value of the variable at deallocation time must be known, so the syntax is delocal <variable> = <value>. Again the onus is on the programmer to ensure that the equality actually holds.

2.2   A Type-Based Approach

The approaches above are pragmatic but limited in two ways: non-scoped approaches do not enforce de-allocation and scoped ones do not enforce that the de-allocated bit has the correct value. To understand these points more vividly, consider the following analogy: allocating an ancilla bit by creating a new wire in the circuit is like borrowing some money from a global external entity (the memory manager); the computation has access to a new resource temporarily. De-allocating the ancilla bit is like returning the borrowed money to the global entity; the computation no longer has access to that resource. It would however be unreasonably restrictive to insist that the person (function) borrowing the money must be the same person (function) returning it. Indeed, as far as reversible computation is concerned, the only important invariant is that information is conserved, i.e., that money is conserved. The identities of bits are not observable as they are all interchangeable in the same way that particular bills with different serial numbers are interchangeable in financial transactions. Thus the only invariant is that the net flow of money between the computation and the global entity is zero. This observation allows us to go even further than just switching the identities of borrowers. It is even possible for one person to borrow $10, and have three different persons collectively collaborate to pay back the debt with one person paying $5, another $2, and a third $3, or the opposite situation of gradually borrowing $10 and returning it all at once.

Computationally, this extra generality is not a gratuitous concern: since scope is a *static property* of programs, it does not allow the flexibility of heap allocation in which the lifetime of resources is dynamically determined. Furthermore, limiting ancilla bits to static scope does not help in solving the fundamental problem of ensuring that their value is properly restored to their initial value before de-allocation.

We demonstrate that both problems can be solved with a typing discipline. The main idea is simple: we introduce a type representing "processes specialized to garbage-collect specific values." The infrastructure of reversible computing will ensure that the information inherent in this process will never be duplicated or erased, enforcing that proper, safe, de-allocation must happen in a complete program. Furthermore, since reversible computation focuses on conservation of *information* rather than syntactic entities, this approach will permit fascinating mechanisms in which allocations and de-allocations can be sliced and diced, decomposed and recomposed, run forwards and backwards, in arbitrary ways as long as the net balance is 0.

3   Preliminaries: Π

The syntax of the language Π [8] consists of several sorts:

$$
\begin{array}{ll}
\textit{Value types} & \tau ::= 0 \mid 1 \mid \tau + \tau \mid \tau \times \tau \\
\textit{Values} & v ::= \mathsf{tt} \mid inj_1(v) \mid inj_2(v) \mid (v, v) \\
\textit{Program types} & \tau \leftrightarrow \tau \\
\textit{Programs} & c ::= (\text{See Fig. 1})
\end{array}
$$

Focusing on finite types, the building blocks of the type theory are: the empty type (0), the unit type (1, where $\mathsf{tt} : 1$ is the only inhabitant), the sum type (+), and the product (×) type. One may view each type τ as a collection of physical wires that can transmit $|\tau|$ distinct values where $|\tau|$ is a natural number that indicates the size of a type, computed as: $|0| = 0$; $|1| = 1$; $|\tau_1 + \tau_2| = |\tau_1| + |\tau_2|$; and $|\tau_1 \times \tau_2| = |\tau_1| * |\tau_2|$. Thus the type $\mathbb{B} = 1 + 1$ corresponds to a wire that can transmit one of two values, i.e., bits, with the convention that $inj_1(\mathsf{tt})$ represents $\mathbb{F}$ and $inj_2(\mathsf{tt})$ represents $\mathbb{T}$. The type $\mathbb{B} \times \mathbb{B} \times \mathbb{B}$ corresponds to a collection of

$$id_{\leftrightarrow}: \qquad\qquad \tau \leftrightarrow \tau \qquad\qquad\qquad : id_{\leftrightarrow}$$

$$unite_{+}l : \qquad\qquad 0 + \tau \leftrightarrow \tau \qquad\qquad\quad : uniti_{+}l$$
$$swap_{+} : \qquad\quad \tau_1 + \tau_2 \leftrightarrow \tau_2 + \tau_1 \qquad\quad : swap_{+}$$
$$assocl_{+} : \tau_1 + (\tau_2 + \tau_3) \leftrightarrow (\tau_1 + \tau_2) + \tau_3 \quad : assocr_{+}$$

$$unite_{*}l : \qquad\qquad 1 \times \tau \leftrightarrow \tau \qquad\qquad\quad : uniti_{*}l$$
$$swap_{*} : \qquad\quad \tau_1 \times \tau_2 \leftrightarrow \tau_2 \times \tau_1 \qquad\quad : swap_{*}$$
$$assocl_{*} : \tau_1 \times (\tau_2 \times \tau_3) \leftrightarrow (\tau_1 \times \tau_2) \times \tau_3 \quad : assocr_{*}$$

$$absorbr : \qquad\qquad 0 \times \tau \leftrightarrow 0 \qquad\qquad\quad : factorzl$$
$$dist : (\tau_1 + \tau_2) \times \tau_3 \leftrightarrow (\tau_1 \times \tau_3) + (\tau_2 \times \tau_3) : factor$$

$$\frac{\vdash c_1 : \tau_1 \leftrightarrow \tau_2 \quad \vdash c_2 : \tau_2 \leftrightarrow \tau_3}{\vdash c_1 \,\mathbin{;}\, c_2 : \tau_1 \leftrightarrow \tau_3} \qquad \frac{\vdash c_1 : \tau_1 \leftrightarrow \tau_2 \quad \vdash c_2 : \tau_3 \leftrightarrow \tau_4}{\vdash c_1 \oplus c_2 : \tau_1 + \tau_3 \leftrightarrow \tau_2 + \tau_4} \qquad \frac{\vdash c_1 : \tau_1 \leftrightarrow \tau_2 \quad \vdash c_2 : \tau_3 \leftrightarrow \tau_4}{\vdash c_1 \otimes c_2 : \tau_1 \times \tau_3 \leftrightarrow \tau_2 \times \tau_4}$$

Fig. 1. Π-terms and combinators.

wires that can transmit three bits. From that perspective, a type isomorphism between types τ_1 and τ_2 (such that $|\tau_1| = |\tau_2| = n$) models a *reversible* combinational circuit that *permutes* the n different values. These type isomorphisms are collected in Fig. 1. It is known that these type isomorphisms are sound and complete for all permutations on finite types [9,10] and hence that they are *complete* for expressing combinational circuits [11,13,25]. Algebraically, these types and combinators form a *commutative semiring* (up to type isomorphism). Logically they form a superstructural logic capturing space-time tradeoffs [21]. Categorically, they form a *distributive bimonoidal category* [17].

Below, we show code, in our Agda formalization, that defines types corresponding to bits (booleans), two-bits, and three-bits. We then define an operator ctrl that builds a controlled version of a given combinator c. This controlled version takes an additional "control" bit and only applies c if the control bit is true. The code then iterates the control operation several times starting from boolean negation building up to Toffoli.

```
data U : Set where
  0    : U
  1    : U
  _+u_ : U → U → U
  _×u_ : U → U → U

⟦_⟧ : (A : U) → Set
⟦ 0 ⟧ = ⊥
⟦ 1 ⟧ = ⊤
⟦ t₁ +u t₂ ⟧ = ⟦ t₁ ⟧ ⊎ ⟦ t₂ ⟧
⟦ t₁ ×u t₂ ⟧ = ⟦ t₁ ⟧ × ⟦ t₂ ⟧

data _↔_ : U → U → Set where
  unite*l : {t : U} → 1 ×u t ↔ t
```

```
uniti∗l : {t : U} → t ↔ 1 ×ᵤ t
-- elided

pattern F = inj₁ tt
pattern T = inj₂ tt

B B² B³ : U
B  = 1 +ᵤ 1
B² = B ×ᵤ B
B³ = B ×ᵤ B²

ctrl : {A : U} → (A ↔ A) → B ×ᵤ A ↔ B ×ᵤ A
ctrl c = dist ⨾ (id↔ ⊕ (id↔ ⊗ c)) ⨾ factor

NOT : B ↔ B
NOT = swap₊

CNOT : B² ↔ B²
CNOT = ctrl NOT

TOFFOLI : B³ ↔ B³
TOFFOLI = ctrl (ctrl NOT)
```

Although austere, this combinator-based language has the advantage of being more amenable to formal analysis for at least two reasons: (i) it is conceptually simple and small, and (ii) it has direct and evident connections to type theory and category theory. Indeed our solution for managing ancillae is inspired by the construction of *compact closed categories* [2,3,15]. These categories extend the monoidal categories [4,5,18] which are used to model many resource-aware (e.g., based on linear types) programming languages [6,16] (including Π) with a new type constructor that creates duals or inverses to existing types. This dual will be our fractional type.

4   First-Class Garbage Collectors

The main idea is to extend the Π terms with two combinators η and ϵ witnessing the isomorphism $A * 1/A = 1$. The names and types of these operations are inspired by compact closed categories which are extensions of the monoidal categories that model Π. Intuitively, η allows one, from "no information," to create a pair of a value of type A and a value of type $1/A$. We interpret the latter value as a GC process specialized to collect the created value. Dually, ϵ applies the GC process to the appropriate value annihilating both.[1]

To make this idea work, several technical issues need to be dealt with. Most notably, we must exclude the empty type from this creation and annihilation process. Otherwise, we would be able to prove that:

$$
\begin{aligned}
1 &= 0 \times 1/0 & \text{by } \eta \\
  &= 0 & \text{by } absorbr
\end{aligned}
$$

---

[1] Another interesting interpretation is that these operations correspond to creation and annihilation of entangled particle/antiparticle pairs in quantum physics [19].

The second important issue is to ensure that the GC process is specialized to collect a particular value. We therefore exploit ideas from dependent type theory to treat individual values as singleton types. More precisely, we extend the syntax of core Π in Sect. 3 as follows:

$$
\begin{array}{lll}
\textit{Value types} & \tau ::= \cdots \mid 1/v \\
\textit{Values} & v ::= \cdots \mid \circlearrowleft \\
\textit{Program types} & \tau \leftrightarrow \tau \\
\textit{Programs} & c ::= \cdots \mid \eta_{v:\tau} : 1 \leftrightarrow (\tau \times 1/v) \quad \mid \epsilon_{v:\tau} : (\tau \times 1/v) \leftrightarrow 1
\end{array}
$$

For now, the core Π language is simply extended with a new type $1/v$ which represents a GC process specialized to collect the value v. Since all relevant information is present in the type, at runtime, this GC process is represented using a trivial value denoted by $\circlearrowleft$. The combinators η and ϵ are parameterized by the value v (and its type τ) which serves two purposes. First it guarantees that the combinators operate on non-empty types, and second it fixes the type of the GC process. At this point, however, although the language guarantees that the GC process can only collect a particular value, the type system does not track the value created by η, nor does it predict the value that reaches ϵ. In other words, it is possible to write programs in which ϵ expects one value but is instead applied to another value. In this section, we will deal with such situations by including a runtime check in the formal semantics, and show how to remove it, via a safety proof, in the next section.

Our Agda formalization clarifies our semantics, with the new type as:

$$1/\_ : \{t : \mathsf{U}\} \to [\![\, t\,]\!] \to \mathsf{U}$$

The new combinators are defined as follows:

$$
\begin{array}{l}
\eta : \{t : \mathsf{U}\}\ (v : [\![\, t\,]\!]) \to 1 \leftrightarrow t \times_u (1/\, v) \\
\epsilon : \{t : \mathsf{U}\}\ (v : [\![\, t\,]\!]) \to t \times_u (1/\, v) \leftrightarrow 1
\end{array}
$$

The most relevant excerpt of the formal semantics is given below:

```
interp : {t₁ t₂ : U} → (t₁ ↔ t₂) → [[ t₁ ]] → Maybe [[ t₂ ]]
interp swap* (v₁ , v₂) = just (v₂ , v₁)
interp (c₁ ⨾ c₂) v = interp c₁ v >>= interp c₂
-- (elided)
interp (η v) tt = just (v , ○)
interp (ε v) (v' , ○) with v ≟ᵤ v'
... — yes _ = just tt
... — no _ = nothing
```

The interpreter either returns a proper value (just ...) or throws an exception nothing. The semantics of the core Π combinators performs the appropriate isomorphism and returns a proper value. At η, the v that parameterizes the combinator is used to create a new value v and a GC process specialized to collect it. By the time evaluation reaches ϵ, the value created by η may have undergone arbitrary transformations and is not guaranteed to be the value expected by the GC process. A runtime check is performed: if the value is the expected one, it is annihilated together with the GC process; otherwise an exception is thrown which is demonstrated in the following example which returns normally if given $\mathbb{F}$ and otherwise throws an exception:

$$\mathsf{Ex} : \mathbb{B} \leftrightarrow \mathbb{B}$$
$$\mathsf{Ex} = \mathsf{uniti}_*\mathsf{r} \ ; \ (\mathsf{id}{\leftrightarrow} \otimes \eta \ \mathbb{F}) \ ;$$
$$\mathsf{assocl}_* \ ; \ (\mathsf{CNOT} \otimes \mathsf{id}{\leftrightarrow}) \ ; \ \mathsf{assocr}_* \ ;$$
$$(\mathsf{id}{\leftrightarrow} \otimes \epsilon \ \mathbb{F}) \ ; \ \mathsf{unite}_*\mathsf{r}$$

$$\mathsf{ExTest}_1 : \mathsf{interp} \ \mathsf{Ex} \ \mathbb{F} \equiv \mathsf{just} \ \mathbb{F}$$
$$\mathsf{ExTest}_1 = \mathsf{refl}$$

$$\mathsf{ExTest}_2 : \mathsf{interp} \ \mathsf{Ex} \ \mathbb{T} \equiv \mathsf{nothing}$$
$$\mathsf{ExTest}_2 = \mathsf{refl}$$

Changing the value used to instantiate η will force a corresponding change for ϵ:

$$\mathsf{Ex}' : \mathbb{B} \leftrightarrow \mathbb{B}$$
$$\mathsf{Ex}' = \mathsf{uniti}_*\mathsf{r} \ ; \ (\mathsf{id}{\leftrightarrow} \otimes \eta \ \mathbb{T}) \ ;$$
$$\mathsf{assocl}_* \ ; \ (\mathsf{CNOT} \otimes \mathsf{id}{\leftrightarrow}) \ ; \ \mathsf{assocr}_* \ ;$$
$$(\mathsf{id}{\leftrightarrow} \otimes \epsilon \ \mathbb{T}) \ ; \ \mathsf{unite}_*\mathsf{r}$$

$$\mathsf{Ex'Test}_1 : \mathsf{interp} \ \mathsf{Ex}' \ \mathbb{F} \equiv \mathsf{just} \ \mathbb{F}$$
$$\mathsf{Ex'Test}_1 = \mathsf{refl}$$

$$\mathsf{Ex'Test}_2 : \mathsf{interp} \ \mathsf{Ex}' \ \mathbb{T} \equiv \mathsf{nothing}$$
$$\mathsf{Ex'Test}_2 = \mathsf{refl}$$

For future reference, we will call this language Π/D for the fractional extension of Π with a dynamic check. We illustrate the expressiveness of the language with two small examples. The Agda code for the examples is written in a style that reveals the intermediate steps for expository purposes.

The first circuit has one input and one output. Immediately after receiving the input, the circuit generates an ancilla wire and its corresponding GC process (first two steps in the Agda definition). The original input and the ancilla wire interact using two CNOT gates, after which the ancilla wire is redirected to the output (next three steps in the Agda code). Finally the original input is GC'ed (last two steps in the Agda code). The entire circuit is extensionally equivalent to the identity function but it does highlight an important functionality beyond scoped ancilla management: the allocated ancilla bit is redirected to the output and a completely different bit (with the proper default value) is collected instead.

$$\mathsf{id}' : \mathbb{B} \leftrightarrow \mathbb{B}$$
$$\mathsf{id}' = \mathbb{B}$$
$$\qquad \mathbb{B} \times_u 1 \qquad\qquad \leftrightarrow\langle \ \mathsf{uniti}_*\mathsf{r} \ \rangle$$
$$\qquad \mathbb{B} \times_u (\mathbb{B} \times_u 1/\ \mathbb{F}) \leftrightarrow\langle \ \mathsf{id}{\leftrightarrow} \otimes \eta \ \mathbb{F} \ \rangle$$
$$\qquad (\mathbb{B} \times_u \mathbb{B}) \times_u 1/\ \mathbb{F} \leftrightarrow\langle \ \mathsf{assocl}_* \ \rangle$$
$$\qquad (\mathbb{B} \times_u \mathbb{B}) \times_u 1/\ \mathbb{F} \leftrightarrow\langle \ (\mathsf{CNOT} \ ; \ \mathsf{CNOT}' \ ; \ \mathsf{swap}_*) \otimes \mathsf{id}{\leftrightarrow} \ \rangle$$
$$\qquad (\mathbb{B} \times_u \mathbb{B}) \times_u 1/\ \mathbb{F} \leftrightarrow\langle \ \mathsf{assocr}_* \ \rangle$$
$$\qquad \mathbb{B} \times_u (\mathbb{B} \times_u 1/\ \mathbb{F}) \leftrightarrow\langle \ \mathsf{id}{\leftrightarrow} \otimes \epsilon \ \mathbb{F} \ \rangle$$
$$\qquad \mathbb{B} \times_u 1 \qquad\qquad \leftrightarrow\langle \ \mathsf{unite}_*\mathsf{r} \ \rangle$$
$$\qquad \mathbb{B} \ \square$$

The second example illustrates the manipulation of GC processes. A process for collecting a pair of values can be decomposed into two processes each collecting one of the values (and vice-versa):

$$\text{rev}\times \; : \{A\;B:\mathbb{U}\} \to (a:[\![\,A\,]\!])\,(b:[\![\,B\,]\!])$$
$$\to 1/\,(a\,,\,b) \leftrightarrow 1/\,a\times_u 1/\,b$$
$$\text{rev}\times \;\{A\}\,\{B\}\;a\;b =$$

$1/\,(a\,,\,b)$	$\leftrightarrow\langle$ uniti$_*$l $\,\mathring{,}\,$ uniti$_*$l $\,\mathring{,}\,$ assocl$_*$ $\rangle$
$(1\times_u 1)\times_u 1/\,(a\,,\,b)$	$\leftrightarrow\langle\,(\eta\;a\otimes\eta\;b)\otimes\text{id}\leftrightarrow\rangle$
$((A\times_u 1/\,a)\times_u (B\times_u 1/\,b))\times_u 1/\,(a\,,\,b)$	$\leftrightarrow\langle\,(\text{shuffle}\otimes\text{id}\leftrightarrow)\,\mathring{,}\,\text{assocr}_*\,\rangle$
$(1/\,a\times_u 1/\,b)\times_u ((A\times_u B)\times_u 1/\,(a\,,\,b))$	$\leftrightarrow\langle\,\text{id}\leftrightarrow\otimes\,\epsilon\,(a\,,\,b)\,\rangle$
$(1/\,a\times_u 1/\,b)\times_u 1$	$\leftrightarrow\langle\,\text{unite}_*\text{r}\,\rangle$
$1/\,a\times_u 1/\,b\;\Box$	

    where

      shuffle $: \{A\;B\;C\;D:\mathbb{U}\}\to (A\times_u B)\times_u (C\times_u D)\leftrightarrow (B\times_u D)\times_u (A\times_u C)$

      shuffle $= (\text{swap}_*\otimes\text{swap}_*)\,\mathring{,}\,\text{assocr}_*\,\mathring{,}\,$
           $(\text{id}\leftrightarrow\otimes\,(\text{assocl}_*\,\mathring{,}\,(\text{swap}_*\otimes\text{id}\leftrightarrow)\,\mathring{,}\,\text{assocr}_*))\,\mathring{,}\,$
           assocl_*

5   Dependently-Typed Garbage Collectors

By lifting the scoping restriction, the development in the previous sections is already more general than the state of the art in ancilla management. It still shares the same limitation of needing a runtime check to ensure ancilla values are properly restored to their allocation value [12, 24]. We now address this limitation using a combination of pointed types, singleton types, monads, and comonads.

5.1   Lifting Evaluation to the Type System

Before giving all the (rather involved) technical details, we highlight the main idea using the toy language below:

```
data T : Set where
    N : T
    B : T

[_] : T → Set
[ N ] = ℕ
[ B ] = Bool

data Fun : T → T → Set where
    square   : Fun N N
    isZero   : Fun N B
    compose : {a b c : T} → Fun b c → Fun a b → Fun a c

eval : {a b : T} → Fun a b → [ a ] → [ b ]
eval square n = n * n
eval isZero 0 = true
eval isZero (suc _) = false
eval (compose g f) v = eval g (eval f v)
```

The toy language has two types (natural numbers and booleans) and two functions square and isZero and their compositions. Say we wanted to prove that compose isZero square always returns false when applied to a non-zero natural number. We can certainly do this proof in Agda (i.e., in the meta-language of our formalization) but we would like to do the proof within the toy language itself. The most important reason is that it can then be used within the language to optimize programs (or, for the case of Π/D, to remove a runtime check).

The strategy we adopt is to create a lifted version of the toy language with *pointed types* [22], i.e., types paired with a value of the type. In the lifted language, the evaluation function has an interesting type: it keeps track of the result of evaluation within the type:

```
data T• : Set where
    _#_ : (a : T) → (v : ⟦ a ⟧) → T•

⟦_⟧• : T• → Σ[ A ∈ Set ] A
⟦ T # v ⟧• = ⟦ T ⟧ , v

data Fun• : T• → T• → Set where
    lift : {a b : T} {v : ⟦ a ⟧} → (f : Fun a b) → Fun• (a # v) (b # (eval f v))
```

This allows various properties of compose isZero square to be derived within the extended type system. For example:

```
test1 : Fun• (N # 3) (B # false)
test1 = lift (compose isZero square)

test2 : Fun• (N # 0) (B # true)
test2 = lift (compose isZero square)

test3 : ∀ {n} → Fun• (N # (suc n)) (B # false)
test3 = lift (compose isZero square)
```

The first two tests show that the type system can track exact concrete values. More interestingly, test3 shows a property that holds for all natural numbers n; its proof uses "symbolic" evaluation within the type system. In more detail, from the definition of eval, we see that eval square (suc n) produces (suc n) * (suc n); by definition of multiplication, this is an expression with a leading suc constructor which is enough to determine that evaluating isZero on it yields false. This form of partial evaluation is quite expressive, and sufficient to allow to keep track of ancilla values throughout complex programs.

After proving properties about a program in T•, we can extract a T program that still satisfies those properties.

```
getT : T• → T
getT (t # _) = t

extract : ∀ {t₁ t₂} → Fun• t₁ t₂ → Fun (getT t₁) (getT t₂)
extract (lift f) = f

test3' : Fun N B
test3' = extract (test3 {0})
```

Note that, since the property of test3 holds for all ℕ, it does not matter which value we use to instantiate it. And it indeed satisfies the property:

$$\text{test4 : eval test3' (suc 8)} \equiv \text{false}$$
$$\text{test4 = refl}$$

However, there are no such guarantees in the case not covered by the property:

$$\text{test5 : } \neg \text{ (eval test3' 0} \equiv \text{false)}$$
$$\text{test5 ()}$$

5.2   Pointed and Singleton Types: $\Pi/\bullet$

We now use the above idea to create a version of the Π language, which we call $\Pi/\bullet$, in which all types are pointed, i.e., for each type t some value v of type t is "in focus" $t\#v$. As the goal of the language is to keep track of fractional types, it is sufficient to inherit the multiplicative structure of Π. We also need a special kind of pointed type that includes just one value, a singleton type. The singleton types will allow the type system to track the flow of one particular value (the ancilla value), which is exactly what is needed to prove the safety of deallocation. We present the relevant definitions from our formalization and explain each:

```
Singleton : (A : Set) → (v : A) → Set
Singleton A v = ∃ (λ • → v ≡ •)

Recip : (A : Set) → (v : A) → Set
Recip A v = Singleton A v → ⊤

data •𝕌 : Set where
  _#_  : (t : 𝕌) → (v : ⟦ t ⟧) → •𝕌
  _•×ᵤ_ : •𝕌 → •𝕌 → •𝕌
  (|_|) : •𝕌 → •𝕌
  •1/_  : •𝕌 → •𝕌

•⟦_⟧ : •𝕌 → Σ[ A ∈ Set ] A
•⟦ t # v ⟧     = ⟦ t ⟧ , v
•⟦ T₁ •×ᵤ T₂ ⟧ = let (t₁ , v₁) = •⟦ T₁ ⟧
                     (t₂ , v₂) = •⟦ T₂ ⟧
                 in (t₁ × t₂) , (v₁ , v₂)
•⟦ (| T |) ⟧    = let (t , v) = •⟦ T ⟧ in Singleton t v , (v , refl)
•⟦ •1/ T ⟧      = let (t , v) = •⟦ T ⟧ in Recip t v , λ _ → tt
```

Given a set A with an element v, the singleton set containing v is the subset of A whose elements are equal to v. In Agda's type theory, this is encoded using the Singleton type. For a given type A, and a value v of type A, the type Singleton A v is inhabited by a choice of point $\bullet$ in A, along with a proof that v is equal to $\bullet$. In other words, it is possible to refer to a singleton value v using several distinct syntactic expressions that all evaluate to v. Put differently, any claim that a value belongs to the singleton type must come with a proof that this value is equal to v. The reciprocal type Recip A v consumes exactly this singleton value. The universe of pointed types $\bullet\mathsf{U}$ contains plain Π types together with a selection of a value in focus; products of pointed types; singleton types; and reciprocal types. Note that the actual value in focus for reciprocals, i.e., the runtime value of a GC process, is a function that disregards its argument returning the constant value of the unit type. As we show, this is safe, as the type system prevents the GC process being applied to anything but the particular singleton value in question.

The combinators in the lifted language $\Pi/\bullet$ consist of all the combinators in the core Π language together with their multiplicative structure. The types for η and ϵ are now specialized to guarantee safety of de-allocation as follows. When applying η at a pointed type, the current witness value is put in focus in a singleton type and a GC process for that particular singleton type is created. To apply this process using ϵ the very same singleton value must be the current one.

```
data _o—o_ : •U → •U → Set where
   -- lifting from plain Π
•c      : {t₁ t₂ : U} {v : [[ t₁ ]]} → (c : t₁ ↔ t₂) → t₁ # v o—o t₂ # (eval c v)
•times# : {t₁ t₂ : U} {v₁ : [[ t₁ ]]} {v₂ : [[ t₂ ]]}
          → ((t₁ ×ᵤ t₂) # (v₁ , v₂)) o—o ((t₁ # v₁) •×ᵤ (t₂ # v₂))
•#times : {t₁ t₂ : U} {v₁ : [[ t₁ ]]} {v₂ : [[ t₂ ]]}
          → ((t₁ # v₁) •×ᵤ (t₂ # v₂)) o—o ((t₁ ×ᵤ t₂) # (v₁ , v₂))
   -- multiplicative structure (omitted)
   -- monad / comonad
return  : {T : •U} → T o—o (| T |)
extract : {T : •U} → (| T |) o—o T
   -- eta/epsilon
η : (T : •U) → •1 o—o (| T |) •×ᵤ •1/ T
ε : (T : •U) → (| T |) •×ᵤ •1/ T o—o •1
```

The mediation between general pointed types and singleton types is done via return and extract, which form a dual monad/comonad pair, from which many structural properties can be derived: specifically a pair of singleton types is a singleton of the pair of underlying types, and a singleton of a singleton is the same singleton.

Proposition 1. $(|\cdot|)$ *is both an idempotent strong monad and an idempotent costrong comonad over pointed types.*

Proof. The main insight needed is to define the functor $\bullet\mathsf{Sing}_u$, the tensor/cotensor, and the join/cojoin (duplicate):

•Sing$_u$: $\{T_1\ T_2 : \bullet U\} \to (T_1 \multimap T_2) \to (T_1) \multimap (T_2)$
•Sing$_u$ $\{T_1\}$ $\{T_2\}$ $c = $ extract $\bullet\,;\ c\ \bullet\,;$ return

tensor : $\{T_1\ T_2 : \bullet U\} \to (T_1) \bullet\times_u (T_2) \multimap (T_1 \bullet\times_u T_2)$
tensor $\{T_1\}$ $\{T_2\}$ $=$ (extract $\bullet\otimes$ extract) $\bullet\,;$ return

cotensor : $\{T_1\ T_2 : \bullet U\} \to (T_1 \bullet\times_u T_2) \multimap (T_1) \bullet\times_u (T_2)$
cotensor $\{T_1\}$ $\{T_2\}$ $=$ extract $\bullet\,;$ (return $\bullet\otimes$ return)

join : $\{T_1 : \bullet U\} \to ((T_1)) \multimap (T_1)$
join $\{T_1\}$ $=$ extract

duplicate : $\{T_1 : \bullet U\} \to (T_1) \multimap ((T_1))$
duplicate $\{T_1\}$ $=$ return

Like for the toy language, evaluation is reflected in the type system, and in this case we have the additional property that evaluation is reversible:

•eval : $\{T_1\ T_2 : \bullet U\} \to (C : T_1 \multimap T_2) \to$
$\qquad$ let $(t_1\ ,\ v_1) = \bullet[\![\ T_1\ ]\!]$; $(t_2\ ,\ v_2) = \bullet[\![\ T_2\ ]\!]$
$\qquad$ in $\Sigma\ (t_1 \to t_2)\ (\lambda\ f \to f\ v_1 \equiv v_2)$

!•_ : $\{A\ B : \bullet U\} \to A \multimap B \to B \multimap A$

The type of evaluation now states that given a combinator mapping pointed type T_1 to pointed type T_2 where T_i consists of an underlying type t_i and value v_i, evaluation succeeds if applying the combinator to v_1 produces v_2. In other words, the result of evaluation is completely determined by the type system:

Ex : $\Sigma\ ((x : [\![\ \mathbb{B}\ ]\!]) \to [\![\ \mathbb{B}\ ]\!])\ (\lambda\ f \to f\,\mathbb{F} \equiv \mathbb{T})$
Ex $= $ •eval (•c NOT)

To summarize, if a combinator expects a singleton type, then it would only typecheck in the lifted language, if it is given the unique value it expects. A particularly intriguing instance of that situation is the following program:

revrev : $\{A : \bullet U\} \to \bullet 1/\ (\bullet 1/\ A) \multimap (A)$
revrev $\{A\} = $ •uniti$_*$l $\bullet\,;$
$\qquad$ ($\eta\ A \bullet\otimes$ •id$\leftrightarrow$) $\bullet\,;$
$\qquad$ ((•id$\leftrightarrow$ $\bullet\otimes$ return) $\bullet\otimes$ •id$\leftrightarrow$) $\bullet\,;$
$\qquad$ •assocr$_*$ $\bullet\,;$
$\qquad$ •id$\leftrightarrow$ $\bullet\otimes$ ϵ (•1/ A) $\bullet\,;$
$\qquad$ •unite$_*$r

The program takes a value of type $\bullet 1/\ (\bullet 1/\ A)$. This would be a GC process specialized to collect another GC process! By collecting this process, the corresponding singleton value is "rematerialized." At runtime, there would be no information other than the functions that ignore their argument but the type system provides enough guarantees to ensure that this process is well-defined and safe.

5.3 Extraction of Safe Programs

By lifting programs and their evaluation to the type level, we can naturally leverage the typechecking process to verify properties of interest, including the safe de-allocation of ancillae. One "could" just forget about Π/D and instead use $\Pi/\bullet$ as *the* programming language for ancilla management. Indeed the dual nature of proofs and programs is more and more exploited in languages like the one used to formalize this paper (Agda).

However, it is also often the case that constructive proofs are further processed to extract native efficient programs that eschew the overhead of maintaining information needed just for proof invariants. In our case, the question is whether we can extract from a $\Pi/\bullet$ program, a program in Π/D that uses a simpler type system, a simpler runtime representation, and yet is guaranteed to be safe and hence can run without the runtime checks associated with de-allocation sites. In this section, we show that this indeed the case.

We demonstrate this by constructing an extraction map from the syntax of $\Pi/\bullet$ to Π/D. This is fully implemented in the underlying Agda formalization, but we present the most significant highlights. There are three important functions whose signatures are given below:

$$\mathsf{ExtU} : \bullet\mathbb{U} \to \varSigma[\ t \in \mathsf{Pi/D.U}\ ]\ \mathsf{Pi/D.}[\![\ t\ ]\!]$$

$$\mathsf{Ext}\mathord{\circ}\mathord{-}\mathord{\circ} : \forall\ \{t_1\ t_2\} \to t_1 \mathrel{\circ\!\!-\!\!\circ} t_2 \to \mathsf{let}\ (s_1\ ,\ w_1) = \mathsf{ExtU}\ t_1$$
$$(s_2\ ,\ w_2) = \mathsf{ExtU}\ t_2$$
$$\mathsf{in}\ s_1\ \mathsf{Pi/D.}\mathord{\leftrightarrow}\ s_2$$

$$\mathsf{Ext}\equiv : \forall\ \{t_1\ t_2\} \to (c : t_1 \mathrel{\circ\!\!-\!\!\circ} t_2)$$
$$\to \mathsf{interp}\ (\mathsf{Ext}\mathord{\circ}\mathord{-}\mathord{\circ}\ c)\ (\mathsf{proj}_2\ (\mathsf{ExtU}\ t_1)) \equiv \mathsf{just}\ (\mathsf{proj}_2\ (\mathsf{ExtU}\ t_2))$$

The function ExtU maps a $\Pi/\bullet$ type to a Π/D type and a value in the type. The function $\mathsf{Ext}\mathord{\circ}\mathord{-}\mathord{\circ}$ maps a $\Pi/\bullet$ combinator to a Π/D combinator, whose types are fixed by ExtU. And finally, the function $\mathsf{Ext}\equiv$ asserts that the extracted code cannot throw an exception (it must return a just value).

Each of these functions has one or two enlightening cases which we explain below. In Π/D the fractional type expresses that it expects a particular value but lacks any mechanisms to enforce this requirement. Thus we have no choice when mapping a fractional type from $\Pi/\bullet$ to Π/D but to use the $\mathbb{1}/\ v$ type with the trivial value:

$$\mathsf{ExtU}\ (\bullet\mathbb{1}/\ T) = \mathsf{let}\ (t\ ,\ v) = \mathsf{ExtU}\ T$$
$$\mathsf{in}\ \mathbb{1}/\ v\ ,\ \circlearrowleft$$

When mapping $\Pi/\bullet$ combinators to Π/D combinators, the main interesting cases are for η and ϵ. In each of those, we use the values from the pointed type as choices for the ancilla value, and the expectation for the GC process respectively:

$$\mathsf{Ext}\mathord{\circ}\mathord{-}\mathord{\circ}\ (\eta\ T) = \eta\ (\mathsf{proj}_2\ (\mathsf{ExtU}\ T))$$
$$\mathsf{Ext}\mathord{\circ}\mathord{-}\mathord{\circ}\ (\epsilon\ T) = \epsilon\ (\mathsf{proj}_2\ (\mathsf{ExtU}\ T))$$

Finally we can prove the correctness of extraction. The punchline is in the following case:

Ext≡ (ϵ T) with (proj$_2$ (Ext$\mathbb{U}$ T) $\overset{?}{=}_u$ proj$_2$ (Ext$\mathbb{U}$ T))
... — yes p = refl
... — no $\neg p$ = $\bot$-elim ($\neg p$ refl)

Here, the singleton type in $\Pi/\bullet$ guarantees that the runtime check cannot fail!

5.4   Example

This new language not only allows us to *verify* circuits but also allows us to merge verification with programming. To clarify this idea, we show how to implement a 4-bit Toffoli gate using proper ancilla management while at the same time proving its correctness.

We start with verification of the Toffoli gate implementation we have in Sect. 3 in $\Pi/\bullet$ using pattern matching:

$\bullet$times#^{3} : $\forall$ $\{t_1\ t_2\ t_3\ v_1\ v_2\ v_3\}$
$\quad\quad \rightarrow ((t_1\ \times_u (t_2\ \times_u\ t_3))\ \#\ (v_1\ ,\ v_2\ ,\ v_3))$
$\quad\quad \multimap ((t_1\ \#\ v_1)\ \bullet\times_u (t_2\ \#\ v_2)\ \bullet\times_u (t_3\ \#\ v_3))$
$\bullet$times#^{3} = $\bullet$times# $\bullet$; $\bullet$id$\leftrightarrow$ $\bullet\otimes$ $\bullet$times#

$\bullet$#times^3 : $\forall$ $\{t_1\ t_2\ t_3\ v_1\ v_2\ v_3\}$
$\quad\quad \rightarrow ((t_1\ \#\ v_1)\ \bullet\times_u (t_2\ \#\ v_2)\ \bullet\times_u (t_3\ \#\ v_3))$
$\quad\quad \multimap ((t_1\ \times_u (t_2\ \times_u\ t_3))\ \#\ (v_1\ ,\ v_2\ ,\ v_3))$
$\bullet$#times^3 = $\bullet$id$\leftrightarrow$ $\bullet\otimes$ $\bullet$#times $\bullet$; $\bullet$#times

$\bullet$TOFFOLI : $\forall$ $\{a\ b\ c\}$ $\rightarrow$ ($\mathbb{B}\ \#\ a\ \bullet\times_u \mathbb{B}\ \#\ b\ \bullet\times_u \mathbb{B}\ \#\ c$)
$\quad\quad\quad\quad\quad\quad \multimap (\mathbb{B}\ \#\ a\ \bullet\times_u \mathbb{B}\ \#\ b\ \bullet\times_u \mathbb{B}\ \#\ ((a\ \&\ b)\ \hat{}\ c))$
$\bullet$TOFFOLI = $\bullet$#times^3 $\bullet$; TOFFOLI' $\bullet$; $\bullet$times#^{3}
  where
    TOFFOLI' : $\forall$ $\{a\ b\ c\}$ $\rightarrow$ ($\mathbb{B}^3\ \#\ (a\ ,\ b\ ,\ c)$) $\multimap$ ($\mathbb{B}^3\ \#\ (a\ ,\ b\ ,\ ((a\ \&\ b)\ \hat{}\ c))$)
    TOFFOLI' $\{\mathbb{F}\}$ $\{\mathbb{F}\}$ $\{c\}$ = $\bullet$c TOFFOLI
    TOFFOLI' $\{\mathbb{F}\}$ $\{\mathbb{T}\}$ $\{c\}$ = $\bullet$c TOFFOLI
    TOFFOLI' $\{\mathbb{T}\}$ $\{\mathbb{F}\}$ $\{c\}$ = $\bullet$c TOFFOLI
    TOFFOLI' $\{\mathbb{T}\}$ $\{\mathbb{T}\}$ $\{\mathbb{F}\}$ = $\bullet$c TOFFOLI
    TOFFOLI' $\{\mathbb{T}\}$ $\{\mathbb{T}\}$ $\{\mathbb{T}\}$ = $\bullet$c TOFFOLI

Since we use the same implementation in all the cases, it does not matter which value we use to instantiate extraction:

ExtEq : Ext$\multimap$ ($\bullet$TOFFOLI $\{\mathbb{F}\}$ $\{\mathbb{F}\}$ $\{\mathbb{F}\}$) $\equiv$ Ext$\multimap$ ($\bullet$TOFFOLI $\{\mathbb{T}\}$ $\{\mathbb{T}\}$ $\{\mathbb{T}\}$)
ExtEq = refl

Using this as the building block, we can use Toffoli's construction [25] to construct a 4-bit Toffoli gate using an additional ancilla bit:

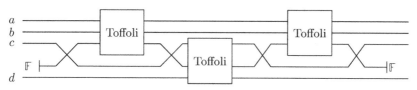

The code is written in a conventional Π/D style except for the pervasive lifting to pointed types:

•TOFFOLI$_4$: ∀ $\{a\ b\ c\ d\}$ →
$$(\mathbb{B}\ \#\ a\ \bullet\times_u\ \mathbb{B}\ \#\ b\ \bullet\times_u\ \mathbb{B}\ \#\ c\ \bullet\times_u\ \mathbb{B}\ \#\ d)\ \circ\!-\!\circ$$
$$(\mathbb{B}\ \#\ a\ \bullet\times_u\ \mathbb{B}\ \#\ b\ \bullet\times_u\ \mathbb{B}\ \#\ c\ \bullet\times_u\ \mathbb{B}\ \#\ (((a\ \&\ b)\ \&\ c)\ \char`^\ d))$$

•TOFFOLI$_4$ =
  •assocl$_*$ •$_9^o$
  ((•uniti$_*$r •$_9^o$ (•id↔ •⊗ (η ($\mathbb{B}$ # $\mathbb{F}$) •$_9^o$ (extract •⊗ •id↔)))) •⊗ •id↔) •$_9^o$
  ((•assocl$_*$ •$_9^o$ ((•assocr$_*$ •$_9^o$ •TOFFOLI) •⊗ •id↔) •$_9^o$ shuffle) •⊗ •id↔) •$_9^o$
  (•assocr$_*$ •$_9^o$ (•id↔ •⊗ •TOFFOLI) •$_9^o$ •assocl$_*$)   •$_9^o$
  ((shuffle •$_9^o$ ((•TOFFOLI •$_9^o$ •assocl$_*$) •⊗ •id↔) •$_9^o$ •assocr$_*$) •⊗ •id↔) •$_9^o$
  (((•id↔ •⊗ ((return •⊗ •id↔) •$_9^o$ ϵ ($\mathbb{B}$ # $\mathbb{F}$))) •$_9^o$ •unite$_*$r) •⊗ •id↔) •$_9^o$
  •assocr$_*$
  where
    shuffle : ∀ $\{A\ B\ C\ D\}$ →
               $(A\ \bullet\times_u\ B\ \bullet\times_u\ C)\ \bullet\times_u\ D\ \circ\!-\!\circ\ (A\ \bullet\times_u\ B\ \bullet\times_u\ D)\ \bullet\times_u\ C$
    shuffle = •assocr$_*$ •$_9^o$ (•id↔ •⊗ (•assocr$_*$ •$_9^o$ (•id↔ •⊗ •swap$_*$))) •$_9^o$
              (•id↔ •⊗ •assocl$_*$) •$_9^o$ •assocl$_*$

With this construction however, we can verify that the circuit satisfies the specification of 4-bit Toffoli gate and the ancilla bit is correctly garbage collected without pattern matching. And using the extraction mechanism, we obtain a fully verified 4-bit Toffoli gate in Π/D:

TOFFOLI$_4$: $\mathbb{B}^4$ ↔ $\mathbb{B}^4$
TOFFOLI$_4$ = Ext$\circ\!-\!\circ$ (•TOFFOLI$_4$ $\{\mathbb{F}\}$ $\{\mathbb{F}\}$ $\{\mathbb{F}\}$ $\{\mathbb{F}\}$)

Note that, the type above has shown that our implementation is independent of any input, so it does not matter which value we use to instantiate the extraction:

TOFFOLI$_4$Test$_1$: interp TOFFOLI$_4$ ($\mathbb{F}$, $\mathbb{F}$, $\mathbb{F}$, $\mathbb{F}$) ≡ just ($\mathbb{F}$, $\mathbb{F}$, $\mathbb{F}$, $\mathbb{F}$)
TOFFOLI$_4$Test$_1$ = refl

TOFFOLI$_4$Test$_2$: interp TOFFOLI$_4$ ($\mathbb{T}$, $\mathbb{T}$, $\mathbb{T}$, $\mathbb{F}$) ≡ just ($\mathbb{T}$, $\mathbb{T}$, $\mathbb{T}$, $\mathbb{T}$)
TOFFOLI$_4$Test$_2$ = refl

6   Conclusion

We have introduced, in the context of reversible languages, the concept of fractional types as descriptions of specialized GC processes. Although the basic idea is rather simple and intuitive, the technical details needed to reason about individual values are somewhat intricate. The use of fractional types, however, enables a complete elegant type-based solution to the management of ancilla values in reversible programming languages.

Acknowledgments. We thank the reviewers for their extensive comments and corrections. This material is based upon work supported by the National Science Foundation under Grant No. OMA-1936353 and by an EAR grant from the Office of the Vice Provost for Research at Indiana University.

References

1. Aaronson, S., Grier, D., Schaeffer, L.: The classification of reversible bit operations. In: Papadimitriou, C.H. (ed.) 8th Innovations in Theoretical Computer Science Conference (ITCS 2017). Leibniz International Proceedings in Informatics (LIPIcs), vol. 67, pp. 23:1–23:34. Schloss Dagstuhl-Leibniz-Zentrum fuer Informatik, Dagstuhl (2017)
2. Abramsky, S.: A structural approach to reversible computation. Theor. Comput. Sci. **347**(3), 441–464 (2005). https://doi.org/10.1016/j.tcs.2005.07.002
3. Abramsky, S., Haghverdi, E., Scott, P.J.: Geometry of interaction and linear combinatory algebras. Math. Struct. Comput. Sci. **12**(5), 625–665 (2002). https://doi.org/10.1017/S0960129502003730
4. Bénabou, J.: Catégories avec multiplication. C. R. de l'Académie des Sciences de Paris **256**(9), 1887–1890 (1963)
5. Bénabou, J.: Algèbre élémentaire dans les catégories avec multiplication. C. R. Acad. Sci. Paris **258**(9), 771–774 (1964)
6. Benton, P.N.: A mixed linear and non-linear logic: proofs, terms and models. In: Pacholski, L., Tiuryn, J. (eds.) CSL 1994. LNCS, vol. 933, pp. 121–135. Springer, Heidelberg (1995). https://doi.org/10.1007/BFb0022251
7. Bowman, W.J., James, R.P., Sabry, A.: Dagger traced symmetric monoidal categories and reversible programming. In: RC (2011)
8. Carette, J., Sabry, A.: Computing with semirings and weak rig groupoids. In: Thiemann, P. (ed.) ESOP 2016. LNCS, vol. 9632, pp. 123–148. Springer, Heidelberg (2016). https://doi.org/10.1007/978-3-662-49498-1_6
9. Fiore, M.P., Di Cosmo, R., Balat, V.: Remarks on isomorphisms in typed calculi with empty and sum types. Ann. Pure Appl. Logic **141**(1–2), 35–50 (2006)
10. Fiore, M.: Isomorphisms of generic recursive polynomial types. In: POPL, pp. 77–88. ACM (2004)
11. Fredkin, E., Toffoli, T.: Conservative logic. Int. J. Theor. Phys. **21**(3), 219–253 (1982)
12. Green, A.S., Lumsdaine, P.L., Ross, N.J., Selinger, P., Valiron, B.: Quipper: a scalable quantum programming language. In: Proceedings of the 34th ACM SIGPLAN Conference on Programming Language Design and Implementation, PLDI 2013, pp. 333–342. ACM, New York (2013)
13. James, R.P., Sabry, A.: Information effects. In: POPL, pp. 73–84. ACM (2012)
14. James, R.P., Sabry, A.: Isomorphic interpreters from logically reversible abstract machines. In: Glück, R., Yokoyama, T. (eds.) RC 2012. LNCS, vol. 7581, pp. 57–71. Springer, Heidelberg (2013). https://doi.org/10.1007/978-3-642-36315-3_5
15. Kelly, G.M.: Many-variable functorial calculus. I. In: Kelly, G.M., Laplaza, M., Lewis, G., Mac Lane, S. (eds.) Coherence in Categories. LNM, vol. 281, pp. 66–105. Springer, Heidelberg (1972). https://doi.org/10.1007/BFb0059556
16. Krishnaswami, N.R., Pradic, P., Benton, N.: Integrating dependent and linear types. In: POPL 2015 (2015)
17. Laplaza, M.L.: Coherence for distributivity. In: Kelly, G.M., Laplaza, M., Lewis, G., Mac Lane, S. (eds.) Coherence in Categories. LNM, vol. 281, pp. 29–65. Springer, Heidelberg (1972). https://doi.org/10.1007/BFb0059555
18. MacLane, S.: Natural associativity and commutativity. Rice Inst. Pamphlet Rice Univ. Stud. **49**(4), 28–46 (1963)

19. Panangaden, P., Paquette, É.: A categorical presentation of quantum computation with anyons. In: Coecke, B. (ed.) New Structures for Physics. Lecture Notes in Physics, vol. 813, pp. 983–1025. Springer, Heidelberg (2010). https://doi.org/10.1007/978-3-642-12821-9_15

20. Rose, E.: Arrow: A Modern Reversible Programming Language. Oberlin College (2015). https://books.google.com/books?id=sX1vnQAACAAJ

21. Sparks, Z., Sabry, A.: Superstructural reversible logic. In: 3rd International Workshop on Linearity (2014)

22. The Univalent Foundations Program: Homotopy Type Theory: Univalent Foundations of Mathematics. Institute for Advanced Study (2013). http://homotopytypetheory.org/book

23. Thomsen, M.K., Axelsen, H.B.: Interpretation and programming of the reversible functional language RFUN. In: Proceedings of the 27th Symposium on the Implementation and Application of Functional Programming Languages, IFL 2015. Association for Computing Machinery, New York (2015). https://doi.org/10.1145/2897336.2897345

24. Thomsen, M.K., Kaarsgaard, R., Soeken, M.: Ricercar: a language for describing and rewriting reversible circuits with ancillae and its permutation semantics. In: Krivine, J., Stefani, J.-B. (eds.) RC 2015. LNCS, vol. 9138, pp. 200–215. Springer, Cham (2015). https://doi.org/10.1007/978-3-319-20860-2_13

25. Toffoli, T.: Reversible computing. In: de Bakker, J., van Leeuwen, J. (eds.) ICALP 1980. LNCS, vol. 85, pp. 632–644. Springer, Heidelberg (1980). https://doi.org/10.1007/3-540-10003-2_104

26. Yokoyama, T., Axelsen, H.B., Glück, R.: Towards a reversible functional language. In: De Vos, A., Wille, R. (eds.) RC 2011. LNCS, vol. 7165, pp. 14–29. Springer, Heidelberg (2012). https://doi.org/10.1007/978-3-642-29517-1_2

27. Yokoyama, T., Glück, R.: A reversible programming language and its invertible self-interpreter. In: PEPM, pp. 144–153. ACM (2007)

Circuit Synthesis

Quantum CNOT Circuits Synthesis for NISQ Architectures Using the Syndrome Decoding Problem

Timothée Goubault de Brugière[1,3]([✉]), Marc Baboulin[1], Benoît Valiron[2], Simon Martiel[3], and Cyril Allouche[3]

[1] Université Paris-Saclay, CNRS, Laboratoire de Recherche en Informatique,
91405 Orsay, France
`timothee.goubault@lri.fr`
[2] Université Paris-Saclay, CNRS, CentraleSupélec, Laboratoire de Recherche en
Informatique, 91405 Orsay, France
[3] Atos Quantum Lab, Les Clayes-sous-Bois, France

Abstract. Current proposals for quantum compilers involve the synthesis and optimization of linear reversible circuits and among them CNOT circuits. This class of circuits represents a significant part of the cost of running an entire quantum circuit and therefore we aim at reducing the size of CNOT circuits. In this paper we present a new algorithm for the synthesis of CNOT circuits based on the solution of the syndrome decoding problem. Our method addresses the case of ideal hardware with an all-to-all qubit connectivity and the case of near-term quantum devices with restricted connectivity. Benchmarks show that our algorithm outperforms existing algorithms in both cases of partial and full connectivity.

Keywords: Quantum circuit synthesis · CNOT circuits · Syndrome decoding · Reversible computation · Noisy Intermediate Scaled Quantum Computers (NISQ)

1 Introduction

Quantum compilers transform a quantum algorithm into an optimized sequence of instructions (elementary gates) directly executable by the hardware. The most common universal set of gates for this task is the Clifford+T gate set, used in many quantum architectures [7]. With this setup two resources have to be optimized in priority: the T gate and the CNOT gate. The T gate is considered to be the most costly gate to implement and many efforts have been made to reduce their number in quantum circuits [1,13,18]. Yet, when implementing complex quantum algorithms, e.g, reversible functions, it is estimated that the total number of CNOT gates increases much more rapidly with the number of qubits than the number of T gates, and it is likely that the CNOT cost will not be negligible on medium sized registers [13,21].

© Springer Nature Switzerland AG 2020
I. Lanese and M. Rawski (Eds.): RC 2020, LNCS 12227, pp. 189–205, 2020.
https://doi.org/10.1007/978-3-030-52482-1_11

Circuits consisting solely of CNOT gates, also called linear reversible circuits, represent a class of quantum circuits playing a fundamental role in quantum compilation. They are part of the so-called Clifford circuits and the CNOT+T circuits, two classes of circuits that have shown crucial utility in the design of efficient quantum compilers [1,13] and error correcting codes [6,12]. For instance the Tpar optimizer [1] takes a Clifford+T circuit as input and decomposes it into a series of CNOT+T circuits separated by Hadamard gates. Then each CNOT+T circuit is optimized and re-synthesized by successive syntheses of CNOT circuits and applications of T gates.

Hence the synthesis of CNOT circuits naturally occurs in general quantum compilers and giving efficient algorithms for optimizing CNOT circuits will then be of uttermost importance.

With the current near term quantum devices, also called Noisy Intermediate Scaled Quantum Computers (NISQ) [26], the synthesis of circuits is subject to constraints on the elementary operations available. In this situation, a physical qubit on the hardware can only interact with its neighbors, restricting the 2-qubit gates —such as CNOT— one can apply. Taking into account these constraints is a crucial and difficult task for the design of quantum algorithms and the optimization of the corresponding quantum circuits. In particular, in the literature several works present post-processing techniques to convert with minimum overhead a circuit designed for an ideal hardware to a circuit designed for a specific architecture [8].

Contribution and Outline of the Paper. In this paper we focus on the size optimization of linear reversible circuits. We present a new method for the synthesis of CNOT circuits relying on solving a well-known cryptographic problem: the syndrome decoding problem. Our algorithm transforms the synthesis problem into a series of syndrome decoding problems and we propose several methods to solve this particular subproblem. This method, initially designed for a full qubit connectivity, is robust enough to be extended to partial connectivity.

The outline of the paper is the following: in Sect. 2 we present the basic notions and the state of the art in the synthesis of linear reversible circuits. We first present our algorithm in the case of an all-to-all connectivity in Sect. 3. Then we extend it to the case of restricted connectivity in Sect. 4. Benchmarks are given at the end of Sects. 3 and 4.

2   Background and State of the Art

Synthesis of a Linear Reversible Function. Let $\mathbb{F}_2$ be the Galois field of two elements. A linear reversible function f on n qubits applies a linear Boolean function on the inputs to each qubit. Given $x \in \mathbb{F}_2^n$ as inputs, the output of qubit i is

$$f_i(x) = \alpha^i \cdot x = \alpha_1^i x_1 \oplus \alpha_2^i x_2 \oplus ... \oplus \alpha_n^i x_n$$

where $\oplus$ is the bitwise XOR operation and the α^i's are Boolean vectors also called *parities*. The action of f can be represented as an $n \times n$ binary matrix A with $A[i,:] = \alpha^i$ (using Matlab notation for row selection) and $f(x) = Ax$. In other words each row of A corresponds to the parity held by the corresponding qubit after application of A. By reversibility of f, A is also invertible in $\mathbb{F}_2$. The application of two successive operators A and B is equivalent to the application of the operator product BA.

We are interested in synthesizing general linear reversible Boolean functions into reversible circuits i.e series of elementary reversible gates that can be executed on a suitable hardware. To that end we use the CNOT gate, it performs the following 2-qubit operation:

$$\text{CNOT}(x_1, x_2) = (x_1, x_1 \oplus x_2).$$

where x_1, resp. x_2, is the parity held by the control qubit, resp. the target qubit. If applied after an operator A, the total operator $(A + \text{CNOT})$ is given from A by adding the row of the control qubit to the row of the target qubit. Such row operations are enough to reduce any invertible Boolean matrix to the identity matrix, so the CNOT gate can be solely used to implement any linear reversible operator. Overall, a CNOT-based circuit can be simulated polynomially: starting from $A = I$ the identity operator, we read sequentially the gates in the circuit and apply the corresponding row operation to A.

We use the size of the circuit, i.e, the number of CNOT gates in it, to evaluate the quality of our synthesis. The size of the circuit gives the total number of instructions the hardware has to perform during its execution. Due to the presence of noise when executing every logical gate, it is of interest to have the shortest circuit possible.

Connectivity Constraints. At the current time, for superconducting technologies, full connectivity between the qubits cannot be achieved. The connections between the qubits are given by a connectivity graph, i.e, an undirected, unweighted graph where 2-qubit operations, such as the CNOT gate, can be performed only between neighbors in the graph. Examples of connectivity graphs from current physical architectures are given on Fig. 1.

LU Decomposition. Given the matrix representation A of a generic linear reversible operator, we can always perform an LU decomposition [11] such that there exists an upper (resp. lower) triangular matrix U (resp. L) and a permutation matrix P such that $A = PLU$. The invertibility of A ensures that the diagonal elements of L and U are all equal to 1. In the remainder of this paper, the term "triangular operator" stands for an operator whose corresponding matrix is either upper or lower triangular. The LU decomposition is at the core of our synthesis of general linear reversible Boolean operators: synthesizing U, L, P and concatenating the circuits gives an implementation of A.

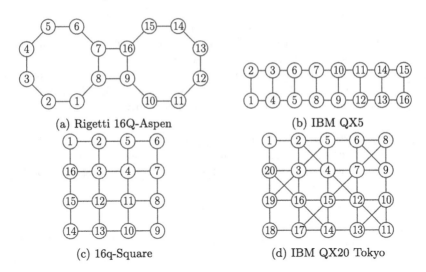

Fig. 1. Example of qubit connectivity graphs from existing architectures

State of the Art. In the unrestricted case the best algorithm reaching an asymptotic optimum is [23, Algo. 1] and produces circuits of size $\mathcal{O}(n^2/\log_2(n))$. This algorithm is for instance used in the Tpar and Gray-Synth algorithms [1,2] so any improvement over [23, Algo. 1] will also improve any quantum compiler that relies on it. In the restricted case the first proposed approach has been to transform the circuits given by an unrestricted algorithm with swap insertion algorithms to match the connectivity constraints [20,24,28]. To produce more efficient circuits, two concomitant papers proposed a modification of the Gaussian elimination algorithm [17,22]. They synthesize the operator column by column similarly to the Gaussian Elimination algorithm but they use Steiner trees to compute the shortest sequence of CNOT gates for the synthesis of one column. In [17] the authors compare their method based on Steiner trees against two compilers: Rigetti Computing's QuilC and Cambridge Quantum Computing's t|ket⟩ that both produced state of the art results on benchmarks published by IBM [9]. The benchmarks show a consequent savings in the total number of CNOT gates in favor of the Steiner tree method, so we consider that the work in [17] is state-of-the-art and we will compare solely to their algorithm.

3   Algorithm for an All-to-All Connectivity

In this section we present our algorithm in the case of a complete connectivity between the qubits. We focus on the synthesis of a lower triangular operator $L \in F_2^{n \times n}$. What follows can be straightforwardly extended to the case of upper triangular operators and to general operators using the LU decomposition. With an all-to-all connectivity one can avoid to apply the permutation P by doing a post-processing of the circuit that would transfer the permutation operation directly at the end of the total circuit. This can be done without any overhead in the number of gates.

A circuit implementing L can solely consist of "oriented" CNOTs, whose controlled qubit i and target qubit j satisfy $i < j$. The circuit given by the Gaussian elimination algorithm is an example. For this particular kind of circuits, a CNOT applied to a qubit k does not have any influence on the operations performed on the first $k-1$ qubits: removing such a CNOT will not modify the result of the synthesis of the first $k-1$ parities. We use this property to design a new algorithm where we synthesize L parity by parity and where we reuse all the information acquired during the synthesis of the first k parities to synthesize parity $k+1$.

Given $L_{n-1} = L[1{:}n-1, 1{:}n-1]$ (again using Matlab notation), a circuit C implementing the operator $\left(\begin{smallmatrix} L_{n-1} & 0 \\ 0 & 1 \end{smallmatrix} \right)$ and considering that we want to synthesize the operator $L = \left(\begin{smallmatrix} L_{n-1} & 0 \\ s & 1 \end{smallmatrix} \right)$ the core of our algorithm consists in adding a sequence of CNOTs to C such that we also synthesize the parity s of the n-th qubit. During the execution of C, applying a CNOT $i \rightarrow n$ will add the parity currently held by qubit i to the parity of qubit n without impacting the synthesis of the first $n-1$ parities. In other words, if we store in memory all the parities that appeared on all $n-1$ qubits during the execution of the circuit C, we want to find the smallest subset of parities such that their sum is equal to s. Then when a parity belonging to this subset appears during the execution of C, on qubit i for instance, we insert in C a CNOT $i \rightarrow n$. We ultimately have a new circuit C' that implements L.

The problem of finding the smallest subset of parities whose sum equals s can be recast as a classical cryptographic problem. Assuming that $H \in F_2^{n-1 \times m}$ is a Boolean matrix whose columns correspond to the m available parities, any Boolean vector x satisfying $Hx = s^T$ gives a solution to our problem and the Hamming weight of x, $wt(x)$, gives the number of parities to add, i.e, the number of CNOTs to add to C. We are therefore interested in an optimal solution of the problem

$$\begin{array}{cc} \underset{x \in F_2^m}{\text{minimize}} & wt(x) \\ \text{such that} & Hx = s^T. \end{array} \tag{1}$$

Problem 1 is an instance of the *syndrome decoding problem*, a well-known problem in cryptography. The link between CNOT circuit synthesis and the syndrome decoding problem has already been established in [2], yet it was used in a different problem for proving complexity results (under the name of Maximum Likelihood Decoding problem) and the authors did not pursue the optimization. The syndrome decoding problem is presented in more details in Sect. 3.1.

To summarize, we propose the following algorithm to synthesize a triangular operator L. Starting from an empty circuit C, for i from 1 to n perform the three following steps:

1. scan circuit C to compute all the parities available on a single matrix H,
2. solve the syndrome decoding problem $Hx = s$ with s the parity of qubit i,
3. add the relevant CNOT gates to C depending on the solution obtained.

Provided that the size of C remains polynomial in n, which will be the case, then steps 1 and 3 can be performed in polynomial time and in practice in a very short amount of time. The core of the algorithm, both in terms of computational complexity and final circuit complexity, lies in Step 2.

3.1   Syndrome Decoding Problem

In its general form, the syndrome decoding problem is known to be NP-Hard [4] and cannot be approximated by a constant factor [3]. A good overview of how difficult the problem is can be found in [27].

We give two methods for solving the syndrome decoding problem. The first one is an optimal one and uses integer programming solvers. The second one is a greedy heuristic for providing sub-optimal results in a short amount of time.

Integer Programming Formulation. The equality $Hx = s$ is a Boolean equality of n lines. For instance the first line corresponds to

$$H_{1,1}x_1 \oplus H_{1,2}x_2 \oplus \ldots \oplus H_{1,m}x_m = s_1.$$

We transform it into an "integer-like" equality constraint. A standard way to do it is to add an integer variable t and to create the constraint

$$H_{1,1}x_1 + H_{1,2}x_2 + \ldots + H_{1,m}x_m - 2t = s_1.$$

If we write $c = (1, ..., 1, 0, ..., 0)^T \in \mathbb{N}^{m+n}$ and $A = [H|-2I_n]$ then the syndrome decoding problem is equivalent to the integer linear programming problem

$$\min_{x \in F_2^m, t \in \mathbb{N}^n} \quad c^T \cdot [x; t] \tag{2}$$
$$\text{such that} \quad A[x; t] = s.$$

A Cost Minimization Heuristic. Although the integer programming approach gives optimal results, it is very unlikely that it will scale up to a large number of qubits. Moreover, to our knowledge the other existing algorithms proposed in the literature give exact results, they are complex to implement and their time complexity remains exponential with the size of the problem. We therefore have to consider heuristics to compute an approximate solution in a much shorter amount of time.

We use a simple cost minimization approach: starting with the parity s we choose at each iteration the parity v in H that minimizes the Hamming weight of $v \oplus s$ and we pursue the algorithm with the new parity $v \oplus s$. The presence of the canonical vectors in H (as we start with the identity operator) is essential because they ensure that this method will ultimately converge to a solution.

A simple way to improve our heuristic is to mimic path finding algorithms like Real-Time A* [19]. Instead of directly choosing the parity that minimizes the Hamming weight, we look up to a certain horizon and we make one step in the direction of the most promising path. To control the combinatorial explosion of the number of paths to browse, we only expand the most promising parities at each level. We set the maximum width to m and the depth to k so that it represents at most m^k paths to explore. With suitable values of m and k we can control the total complexity of the algorithm. A limitation of such a simple approach is that we can store the same path but with different parities order: we decided to ignore this limitation in order to keep a simple implementation.

Lastly, we introduce some randomness by change of basis and we solve the problem $PHx = Ps$ for several change of basis matrices P. Repeating this several times for one syndrome decoding problem increases the chance to find an efficient solution. This technique has been proven to be efficient for a class of cryptographic algorithms called Information Set Decoding [25], even though the complexity of these algorithms remains exponential.

3.2 Benchmarks

All the code is written in Julia and executed on the QLM (Quantum Learning Machine) located at ATOS/BULL. We generate random operators by generating random circuits with randomly placed CNOT gates. When the number of input gates is sufficiently large we empirically note that the operators generated represent the worst case scenario.

We first generate an average complexity for different problem sizes: for $n = 1..200$ we generated 20 random operators on n qubits with more than n^2 gates to reach with high probability the worst cases. We run our algorithms on this set of operators in the following cases:

- with the integer programming solver (Coin-or branch and cut solver),
- with the cost minimization heuristic with unlimited width and depth 1,
- with the cost minimization heuristic with width 60 and depth 2,
- with the cost minimization heuristic with width 15 and depth 3,
- with the cost minimization heuristic (width=Inf, depth=1) and 50 random changes of basis, the "ISD" case.

In the case of the ISD experiment, due to its probabilistic nature, one can hope that repeating the complete synthesis several times and keeping the shortest circuit would improve the results. Yet the experiments show that it has a minor influence on the final result.

The results are given on Fig. 2. For clarity, instead of plotting the size of the circuits we plot the ratio between the size of the circuits given by our algorithms and the state of the art algorithm [23, Algo. 1]. We stopped the calculations when the running time was too large for producing benchmarks in several hours.

Overall, for the considered range of qubits and for all versions of our algorithm we outperform [23, Algo. 1]. The integer programming solver gives the best results with a maximum gain of more than 40% but its scalability is limited: beyond 50 qubits it requires too much computational time. Using commercial softwares for reaching larger problem sizes would be interesting to confirm the tendency toward an increasing gain.

Concerning the cost minimization heuristic, it seems better to increase the depth of search than the width. With depth 3 and width 15 we have the best results for the range 70–125 with 30% of gain. Surprisingly the ISD based method with 50 random changes of basis works well until 60/70 qubits with more than 35% of gain. Then it seems that the number of random changes is not enough to search efficiently an optimal solution and ultimately after 150 qubits the random changes have no effect at all compared to the simpler heuristic with one try. It is possible to increase this number of random changes but this comes at the price of a longer computational time and the ISD method cannot compete with the other versions of the cost minimization heuristic.

As the number of qubits increases our method performs worse. We ran a few computations for much larger problems and the results are that [23, Algo. 1] produces shorter circuits whenever n goes approximately beyond 400. This raises the question of whether it is due to the method in itself or to the solution of the syndrome decoding that becomes less and less optimal as the problem size increases. We leave this question as future work.

We now look at the performance of the algorithms on a specific number of qubits, here $n = 60$, but for different input circuit sizes. This experiment reveals how close to optimal our algorithm is when we synthesize an operator for which we expect a small output circuit. The results are given on Fig. 3. As the ISD method produces the best results for this size of problem we only plot the results for this method. We also plot the line $y = x$ that shows how far we still are from the optimal solution. Again we outperform the best algorithm in the literature even for small input circuits with more than 50% of savings when the input circuit is of size 100–300 gates, with a maximum saving of 60% for 200 gates.

4   Extension to an Arbitrary Connectivity

In this section we extend the algorithm to the case where the connectivity is not complete. First we present how to adapt our algorithm based on syndrome decoding for the synthesis of triangular operators, then we extend our method to the synthesis of any general operator.

4.1   Synthesis of a Triangular Operator

Let G be a qubit connectivity graph and L the lower triangular operator to synthesize. We require an ordering on the nodes of G such that the subgraphs containing only the first k nodes, for $k = 1..n$, are connected. As we need to synthesize both L and U we need in fact this property to be true for an ordering of the qubits and the reverse ordering. An Hamiltonian path in G is enough to have this property so for simplicity we assume that the ordering follows an Hamiltonian path in G.

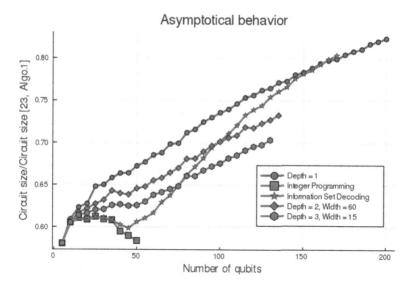

Fig. 2. Average performance of the Syndrome Decoding based algorithms versus the state of the art [23, Algo. 1].

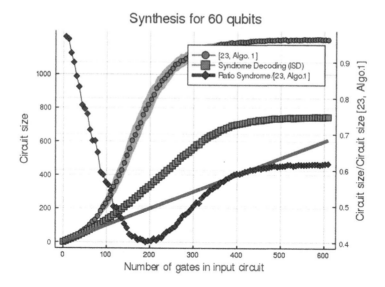

Fig. 3. Performance of Syndrome Decoding based algorithms versus [23, Algo. 1] on 60 qubits for different input circuit sizes.

Even though the native CNOTs in the hardware are CNOTs between neighbor qubits in the connectivity graph, it is possible to perform an arbitrary CNOT gate but this requires more local CNOT gates. Given a target qubit q_t and a qubit control q_c and assuming we have a path $(q_c, q_1, ..., q_k, q_t)$ in the graph connecting the two nodes (such path always exists with the assumption we made above), it is possible to perform the CNOT $q_c \to q_t$ with $\max(1, 4k)$ CNOTs. An example for 4 qubits (with $k = 2$) is given Fig. 4.

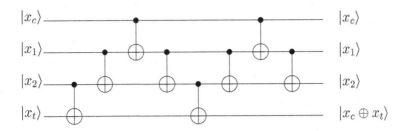

Fig. 4. CNOT in LNN architecture

Hence, it is still possible to perform the synthesis parity by parity but we have to be more careful in the setting and in the solution of the syndrome decoding problem. Not all parities have the same cost, depending on the qubit holding the parity and its position on the hardware. Therefore we have to solve a weighted version of the syndrome decoding problem. Namely once we have a set of parities in a matrix H and a cost vector $c \in \mathbb{N}^m$, we look for the solution of the optimization problem

$$\underset{x \in F_2^m}{\text{minimize}} \quad c^T \cdot x \tag{3}$$
$$\text{such that} \quad Hx = s^T.$$

Problem 3 can be recasted again as an integer linear programming problem: we only have to change the value of c. We also propose a greedy heuristic for solving quickly and approximately the problem: we define the "basis cost" of implementing s as the sum of the costs of each canonical vector whose component in s is nonzero. Let $\mathrm{bc}(s)$ be this cost. Our greedy approach consists in finding among the parities of H the parity v (column i of H) that minimizes the cost

$$c[i] + \mathrm{bc}(s \oplus v).$$

This approach gives a good trade-off between zeroing the most costly components of s and applying parities at a very high cost. Again we can repeat the algorithm with random changes of basis to find a better solution. Especially we focused on computing bases for which the canonical vectors have the lowest possible costs.

Nonetheless, compared to the all-to-all case, solving the weighted syndrome decoding problem is not the only computational core for controlling both the quality of the solution and the computational time. Another key task lies in the enumeration of the available parities. As we will see, it is possible to generate more parities for one syndrome decoding problem instance and this increases the chances to get a low-cost solution.

Listing the Parities Available. Until now we set the weighted syndrome decoding instances by computing the parities appearing during the synthesis and by using the template in Fig. 4 to estimate their costs. This is in fact inefficient because it ignores some specificities of the problem:

– It is possible to add multiple parities in one shot using the template in Fig. 4.
– There is not necessarily one unique path in G between the control qubit and the target qubit.

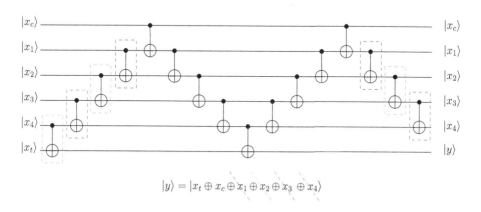

$$|y\rangle = |x_t \oplus x_c \oplus x_1 \oplus x_2 \oplus x_3 \oplus x_4\rangle$$

Fig. 5. Fan in CNOT in LNN architecture

More precisely, the template shown in Fig. 4 is the best to our knowledge, in terms of size, to apply solely the parity on qubit q_c to qubit q_t. However it is possible to apply any parity

$$q_t \leftarrow q_t \oplus q_c \oplus_{i=1}^{k} \alpha_i q_i$$

with $\alpha_i \in \{0, 1\}$ using less CNOTs than required for applying only q_c. In fact the less costly linear combination of parities is the complete combination $q_c \oplus q_1 \oplus ... \oplus q_k$, showing that $2k + 1$ CNOTs are enough. Removing any parity from this combination requires 2 additional CNOTs per parity except for the qubit q_k that needs only one extra CNOT. An explanatory template on 6 qubits ($k = 4$) is given on Fig. 5. For any parity at a distance k of the target qubit, there is at most 2^{k-1} different linear combinations possible and just as many new parities to consider. Moreover the path between the control qubit and the target qubit matters as a different path will result in different linear combinations of parities. A slight modification of the A* algorithm is enough to compute all the shortest paths between two nodes in a graph.

Even for a small number of qubits the number of parities becomes quickly intractable. The number of linear combinations along a path increases exponentially with the length of the path as the number of paths for most of the architectures—a grid for instance. In practice we control the total number of parities by favoring paths over the choices in the linear combinations. This option is empirically justified but a more detailed analysis could be made. For one path we only consider the less costly linear combination, i.e, the one that adds all the parities on the way. On the other hand if possible we go through all the shortest paths between one control qubit and one target qubit. We introduce a parameter $P_{\max}$ equal to the maximum number of shortest paths we consider between two qubits.

4.2 Synthesis of a General Operator

The extension of the synthesis from triangular to general operator is not as straightforward as in the all-to-all connectivity case. We cannot simply write $A = PLU$ and concatenate the circuits synthesizing L and U and ultimately permuting the qubits. If we want to use this algorithm as a sub-task of a global circuit optimizer for NISQ architectures we cannot afford to swap the qubits because it could break the optimizations done in the rest of the circuit.

To avoid the permutation of the qubits we have to transform the matrix A by applying a pre-circuit C such that $CA = LU$. Then the concatenation of C^{-1} and the circuits synthesizing L and U gives a valid implementation of A.

Computation of C. If A is invertible, which is always the case, then it admits an LU factorization if and only if all its leading principal minors are nonzero. We propose an algorithm for computing C exploiting this property while trying to optimize the final size of C. We successively transform A such that every submatrix $A[1{:}i, 1{:}i]$ is invertible. By construction when trying to make $A[1 : k, 1 : k]$ invertible for some k we have $A[1{:}k-1, 1{:}k-1]$ invertible. If $A[1 : k, 1 : k]$ is invertible then we do nothing, otherwise we look in the parities $A[k+1{:}n,1{:}k]$ those who, added to $A[k, 1 : k]$, make $A[1 : k, 1 : k]$ invertible. By assumption A is invertible so there is at least one such row that verifies this property. Then among the valid parities we choose the closest one to qubit k in G. We can add all the parities along the path because by assumption they belong to the span of the first $k-1$ rows of $A[1 : k, 1 : k]$ so it has no effect on the rank of $A[1 : k, 1 : k]$.

Choice of the Qubit Ordering. A last optimization can be performed by changing the qubits ordering. The algorithm we have presented for synthesizing a triangular operator is still valid up to row and column permutations. Thus, given a permutation P of the qubits, one can synthesize $P^{-1}LP$ by applying our algorithm with the order given by P. Then, instead of computing a circuit C such that $CA = LU$ we search for a circuit C satisfying $P^{-1}CAP = LU$ and

$$CA = PLP^{-1}PUP^{-1} = L'U'$$

where L' and U' can be synthesized using our algorithm. Searching for such C can be done using our algorithm on $A[P, P]$ (in Matlab notation, i.e. the reordering of A along the vector P).

This means that we can choose P such that the synthesis of L and U will yield shorter circuits. Empirically we noticed that when synthesizing the kth parity of L it is preferable to have access to the parities appearing on qubits $k-1, k-2$ etc. in priority for two reasons: first because they can modify more bits on the kth parity and secondly because it is likely that there will be much more parities available, increasing the chance to have an inexpensive solution to the weighted syndrome decoding problem. Intuitively we want the ordering of the qubits to follow at least an Hamiltonian path in $G = (V, E)$ which would match the previous restriction on the ordering we formulated at the beginning of the section. We formulate the best ordering $\pi : V \rightarrow [\![1, n]\!]$ as a solution of the Minimum Linear Arrangement problem

$$\underset{\pi}{\text{minimize}} \sum_{(u,v)\in E} w_{uv} \, |\pi(u) - \pi(v)| \tag{4}$$

where w_{uv} is the weight of the edge connecting u and v in the graph. Here we want to give priority to neighbors in the hardware: the nodes must be as close as possible in the hardware if their "numbers" are also close. A way to do so is to solve the MinLA problem, not in the hardware graph, but in the complete graph with suitable weights. Namely w_{ij} must be large when i, j are neighbors in the hardware and w_{ij} must be smaller if i, j are at distance 2 etc. The MinLA problem has already been used for qubit routing [24] and the problem is in general NP-Hard [10]. In our case we did not use any heuristic for solving this problem: all the architectures chosen to test our method have Hamiltonian paths and we simply chose manually a suitable ordering of the qubits. Figure 1 features the choices we made for some architectures: nodes are labeled with their position in the linear arrangement. We leave as a future work the inclusion of the solution of the MinLA problem in our algorithm.

4.3   Benchmarks

We compare our method against the best algorithm in the literature [17] whose source code is available on the PyZX Github repository [16]. For each architecture considered in their implementation we generate a set of 100 random operators and perform the synthesis using the Steiner trees. Their algorithm provides an optimization using genetic algorithms but this implements the circuit up to a permutation of the qubits. As we focus on implementing exactly the operator we considered their algorithm without this extra optimization.

Our own algorithm is implemented in Julia. The experiments have been carried out on one node of the QLM (Quantum Learning Machine) located at ATOS/BULL. We set a time limit of 10 min for the synthesis of an operator. We recall that P_{max} is the maximum number of shortest paths considered between two qubits. We also set $N_{\text{iter\_syndrome}}$ to be the number of iterations for the solution of a decoding syndrome and N_{iter} the number of times that the synthesis has been repeated. The values of the parameters for the different problem sizes are the following:

- $n < 36$, $P_{\max} = \text{Inf}$, $N_{\text{iter}} = 100$ and $N_{\text{iter\_syndrome}} = 1$,
- $n = 36$, $P_{\max} = \text{Inf}$, $N_{\text{iter}} = 20$ and $N_{\text{iter\_syndrome}} = 1$,
- $n = 49$, $P_{\max} = 10$, $N_{\text{iter}} = 100$ and $N_{\text{iter\_syndrome}} = 1$,
- $n > 49$, $P_{\max} = 1$, $N_{\text{iter}} = 100$ and $N_{\text{iter\_syndrome}} = 1$.

Table 1. Performance of our Syndrome Decoding based algorithm vs Steiner trees algorithm [17] for several architectures

Architecture	#	Steiner [17]	Syndrome	Saving				t_{St} (s)	t_{Sy} (s)
				Mean	Min.	Max.	Positive		
9q Square	9	60	56	6%	−25.5%	40.6%	66%	0.01	0.16
Rigetti 16q	16	272	245	10%	−6%	23.1%	97%	0.022	1.6
IBM QX 5	16	245	195	20.2%	10%	28.7%	100%	0.019	2
16q Square	16	205	183	10.7%	−7.1%	33%	93%	0.02	1.6
19q Line	19	455	470	−6.7%	−19.4%	7.9%	6%	0.045	4.5
IBM Q20 Tokyo	20	292	239	18.1%	8.7%	26.9%	100%	0.025	1.8
25q Square	25	512	458	10.6%	3.5%	19.1%	100%	0.04	19
25q Sq. + diag	25	410	324	21%	10.7%	28.3%	100%	0.035	8
36q Square	36	1067	891	16.5%	11%	22.4%	100%	0.1	67
36q Sq. + diag	36	861	667	22.5%	18.2%	26.6%	100%	0.09	22
49q Square	49	1981	1662	16%	11.9%	20.7%	100%	0.2	420
49q Sq. + diag	49	1607	1246	22.4%	19%	25.2%	100%	0.19	114
64q Square	64	3374	2812	16.6%	13.9%	18.9%	100%	0.54	79
81q Square	81	5363	4447	17%	14.4%	19.2%	100%	1.04	192
100q Square	100	8148	6666	18.2%	16.8%	19.8%	100%	2.1	449

The results are summarized in Table 1. Columns 3 and 4 give the average size of the generated circuits for the method using Steiner trees in [17] and our algorithm based on syndrome decoding. The next columns detail the savings: the mean saving, the minimum saving (negative saving means that our algorithm performs worse), the maximum saving and the proportion of operators for which our circuit is actually shorter than the one provided by the state-of-the-art method. The last two columns give the average time required to perform the synthesis of one operator (all iterations included for our algorithm).

We can expect our algorithm to behave better if there are more connections between the qubits. When the connectivity is as limited as possible, for instance with an LNN architecture, our algorithm does not outperform the algorithm based on Steiner trees. Except for 6% of the operators where we have a slight gain (less than 8%) we provide circuits with more gates, up to 19%. For other architectures the results are more promising. In the case of the 9-qubit square there is a lot of variance in the results: depending on the operator we can have a gain of 40% or a loss of 25%. Overall we still manage to produce a shorter circuit 66% of the time. For larger square architectures, we outperform the state-of-the-art algorithm consistently with increasing savings, between 10% for the 25 qubits square to 18% for the 100 qubits square. When adding diagonal connections in the square architectures the results are even better. This shows that improving just slightly the connectivity can improve consistently the results of our algorithm compared to the state of the art method. Finally on specific architectures we also provide better results. The results for Rigetti's chip are not as good as for IBM's chips essentially because the connectivity is still close to a straight line, otherwise we manage to have a saving of around 20% for both IBM-QX5 and IBM-Tokyo chips.

5   Conclusion

We have presented a new framework for the synthesis of linear reversible circuits. We exploit the specific structure of triangular operators to transform the synthesis into a series of syndrome decoding problems, which are well-known problems in cryptography. Using an LU decomposition we can synthesize any quantum operator in the case of an all-to-all connectivity. Benchmarks show that we outperform a state-of-the-art algorithm for intermediate sized problems ($n < 400$). Our heuristics for solving the syndrome decoding problem are efficient but could be still improved, both in circuit size and computational time. For instance, some quantum algorithms have been proposed for solving the syndrome decoding problem via the Information Set Decoding algorithm [5,14,15], which gives the possibility of designing a hybrid quantum/classical compiler for this particular synthesis problem.

Then we have highlighted the robustness of our framework by extending it to an arbitrary connectivity graph having a Hamiltonian path. With a suitable pre-processing of the matrix we transform the problem into a series of weighted syndrome decoding problems. Except for the LNN architecture whose connectivity is too sparse, we consistently outperform existing algorithms by a percentage that increases with the number of qubits. As a future work, we can study how to extend our method to the case where the connectivity graph does not have a Hamiltonian path, similarly to [17].

Acknowledgment. This work was supported in part by the French National Research Agency (ANR) under the research project SoftQPRO ANR-17-CE25-0009-02, and by the DGE of the French Ministry of Industry under the research project PIA-GDN/QuantEx P163746-484124. We thank Bertrand Marchand for comments on the manuscript.

References

1. Amy, M., Maslov, D., Mosca, M.: Polynomial-time T-depth optimization of Clifford+T circuits via matroid partitioning. IEEE Trans. Comput. Aided Des. Integr. Circuits Syst. **33**(10), 1476–1489 (2014)
2. Amy, M., Azimzadeh, P., Mosca, M.: On the controlled-NOT complexity of controlled-NOT-phase circuits. Quantum Sci. Technol. **4**(1), 015002 (2018)
3. Arora, S., Babai, L., Stern, J., Sweedyk, Z.: The hardness of approximate optima in lattices, codes, and systems of linear equations. J. Comput. Syst. Sci. **54**(2), 317–331 (1997)

4. Berlekamp, E., McEliece, R., Van Tilborg, H.: On the inherent intractability of certain coding problems. IEEE Trans. Inf. Theory **24**(3), 384–386 (1978)
5. Bernstein, D.J.: Grover vs. McEliece. In: Sendrier, N. (ed.) PQCrypto 2010. LNCS, vol. 6061, pp. 73–80. Springer, Heidelberg (2010). https://doi.org/10.1007/978-3-642-12929-2_6
6. Campbell, E.T., Anwar, H., Browne, D.E.: Magic-state distillation in all prime dimensions using quantum Reed-Muller codes. Phys. Rev. X **2**(4), 041021 (2012)
7. Campbell, E.T., Terhal, B.M., Vuillot, C.: Roads towards fault-tolerant universal quantum computation. Nature **549**(7671), 172–179 (2017)
8. Childs, A.M., Schoute, E., Unsal, C.M.: Circuit transformations for quantum architectures. In: 14th Conference on the Theory of Quantum Computation, Communication and Cryptography (TQC 2019). LIPIcs, vol. 135, pp. 3:1–3:24 (2019)
9. Cowtan, A., Dilkes, S., Duncan, R., Krajenbrink, A., Simmons, W., Sivarajah, S.: On the qubit routing problem. In: 14th Conference on the Theory of Quantum Computation, Communication and Cryptography (TQC 2019). LIPIcs, vol. 135, pp. 5:1–5:32 (2019)
10. Garey, M.R., Johnson, D.S.: Computers and Intractability: A Guide to the Theory of NP-Completeness. W. H. Freeman & Co (1979)
11. Golub, G.H., Van Loan, C.F.: Matrix Computations, 3rd edn. The Johns Hopkins University Press, Baltimore (1996)
12. Gottesman, D.: Stabilizer Codes and Quantum Error Correction. Ph.D. thesis, Caltech (1997)
13. Heyfron, L.E., Campbell, E.T.: An efficient quantum compiler that reduces T count. Quantum Sci. Technol. **4**(1), 015004 (2019)
14. Kachigar, G., Tillich, J.-P.: Quantum information set decoding algorithms. In: Lange, T., Takagi, T. (eds.) PQCrypto 2017. LNCS, vol. 10346, pp. 69–89. Springer, Cham (2017). https://doi.org/10.1007/978-3-319-59879-6_5
15. Kirshanova, E.: Improved quantum information set decoding. In: Lange, T., Steinwandt, R. (eds.) PQCrypto 2018. LNCS, vol. 10786, pp. 507–527. Springer, Cham (2018). https://doi.org/10.1007/978-3-319-79063-3_24
16. Kissinger, A.: PyZX. https://github.com/Quantomatic/pyzx
17. Kissinger, A., van de Griend, A.M.: CNOT circuit extraction for topologically-constrained quantum memories (2019). arXiv:1904.00633
18. Kissinger, A., van de Wetering, J.: Reducing T-count with the ZX-calculus (2019), draft available as arXiv:1903.10477
19. Korf, R.E.: Real-time heuristic search. Artif. Intell. **42**(2–3), 189–211 (1990)
20. Li, G., Ding, Y., Xie, Y.: Tackling the qubit mapping problem for NISQ-era quantum devices. In: International Conference on Architectural Support for Programming Languages and Operating Systems, pp. 1001–1014 (2019)
21. Maslov, D.: Optimal and asymptotically optimal NCT reversible circuits by the gate types. Quantum Inf. Comput. **16**(13–14), 1096–1112 (2016)
22. Nash, B., Gheorghiu, V., Mosca, M.: Quantum circuit optimizations for NISQ architectures (2019). arXiv:1904.01972
23. Patel, K.N., Markov, I.L., Hayes, J.P.: Optimal synthesis of linear reversible circuits. Quantum Inf. Comput. **8**(3), 282–294 (2008)
24. Pedram, M., Shafaei, A.: Layout optimization for quantum circuits with linear nearest neighbor architectures. IEEE Circuits Syst. Mag. **16**(2), 62–74 (2016)
25. Prange, E.: The use of information sets in decoding cyclic codes. IRE Trans. Inf. Theor. **8**(5), 5–9 (1962)
26. Preskill, J.: Quantum computing in the NISQ era and beyond. Quantum **2**, 79 (2018)

27. Vardy, A.: Algorithmic complexity in coding theory and the minimum distance problem. In: Symposium on Theory of Computing, pp. 92–109. ACM (1997)
28. Wille, R., Keszocze, O., Walter, M., Rohrs, P., Chattopadhyay, A., Drechsler, R.: Look-ahead schemes for nearest neighbor optimization of 1D and 2D quantum circuits. In: Asia and South Pacific Design Automation Conference, pp. 292–297. IEEE (2016)

Maximality of Reversible Gate Sets

Tim Boykett[1,2,3]([⊠]) [iD]

[1] Institute for Algebra, Johannes-Kepler University, Linz, Austria
tim.boykett@jku.at, tim@timesup.org
[2] Time's Up Research, Linz, Austria
[3] University for Applied Arts, Vienna, Austria

Abstract. We investigate collections of reversible gates closed under parallel and serial composition. In order to better understand the structure of these collections of reversible gates, we investigate the lattice of closed sets and the maximal members of this lattice, that is, collections that are not all gates, but the addition of a single new gate will allow us to construct all gates. We find the maximal closed sets over a finite alphabet.

We then extend to ancilla and borrow closure for reversible gates. Here we find some structural results, including some examples.

Keywords: Reversible gates · Maximal closed classes · Permutation groups

1 Introduction

For a given finite set A, we investigate the collections of reversible gates, or bijections of A^k for all k. The work derived from Tomasso Toffoli's work [14] and as such we call closed systems of bijections reversible Toffoli Algebras (RTAs). We also consider ancilla and borrow closure, where an extra input and output is allowed; an *ancilla* is provided and returned in a particular state, whereas a *borrowed* bit is provided and returned in an arbitrary state.

The work also relates to permutation group theory, as an RTA C is a $\mathbb{N}$-indexed collection of permutations groups, $C^{[i]} \leq Sym(A^i)$.

In previous papers, Aaronson, Grier and Schaeffer have determined all ancilla closed gates on a set of order 2 [1], and the author, together with Jarkko Kari and Ville Salo, has investigated generating sets [2,3] and other themes.

In this paper, we determine the possible maximal closed systems, relying strongly on Liebeck, Praeger and Saxl's work [11], and determine some properties of maximal borrow and ancilla closed RTAs.

We show that the maximal RTAs are defined by an index that defines the single arity at which the RTA is not the full set of bijections. We then show that for different indices and orders of A, only certain possibilities can arise. For

The research has been supported by Austrian Science Fund (FWF) research projects AR561 and P29931.

I. Lanese and M. Rawski (Eds.): RC 2020, LNCS 12227, pp. 206–217, 2020.
https://doi.org/10.1007/978-3-030-52482-1_12

ancilla and borrow closed RTAs we find that there is similarly an index below which the maximal RTAs are full symmetry groups and above which they are never full.

We start by introducing the background properties of RTAs and some permutation group theory. The next section is an investigation of maximality, with the main result, Theorem 4, taking up the main body of this section. We then investigate properties of borrow and ancilla closed RTAs.

2 Background

In this section we will introduce the necessary terminology.

Let A be a finite set. $Sym(A) = S_A$ is the set of permutations or bijections of A, $Alt(A)$ the set of permutations of even parity. If $A = \{1, \ldots, n\}$ we will write S_n and A_n. We write permutations in cycle notation and act from the right. We write the action of a permutation $g \in G \leq Sym(A)$ on an element $a \in A$ as a^g. A subgroup $G \leq S_A$ is *transitive* if for all $a, b \in A$ there is a $g \in G$ such that $a^g = b$. We also say that G acts *transitively* on A. If for all distinct $a_1, \ldots, a_n \in A$ and $b_1, \ldots, b_n \in A$ there is a $g \in G$ such that $a_i^g = b_i$ for all i, then we say G is n-transitive on A. A subgroup G of S_A acts *imprimitively* if there is a nontrivial equivalence relation ρ on A such that for all $a, b \in A$, for all $g \in G$, $a \rho b \Rightarrow a^g \rho b^g$. If there is no such equivalence relation, then G acts *primitively* on A.

Let G be a group of permutations of a set A. Let $n \in \mathbb{N}$. Then the *wreath product* $G wr S_n$ is a group of permutations acting on A^n. The elements of $G wr S_n$ are $\{(g_1, \ldots, g_n, \alpha) \mid g_i \in G, \alpha \in S_n\}$ with action defined as follows: for $(a_1, \ldots, a_n) \in A^n$, $(a_1, \ldots, a_n)^{(g_1, \ldots, g_n, \alpha)} = (a_{\alpha^{-1}1}^{g_1}, \ldots, a_{\alpha^{-1}n}^{g_n})$.

Let $B_n(A) = Sym(A^n)$ and $B(A) = \bigcup_{n \in \mathbb{N}} B_n(A)$. We call $B_n(A)$ the set of n-*ary reversible gates* on A, $B(A)$ the set of *reversible gates*. For $\alpha \in S_n$, let $\pi_\alpha \in B_n(A)$ be defined by $\pi_\alpha(x_1, \ldots, x_n) = (x_{\alpha^{-1}(1)}, \ldots, x_{\alpha^{-1}(n)})$. We call this a *wire permutation*. Let $\Pi = \{\pi_\alpha | \alpha \in S_n, n \in \mathbb{N}\}$. In the case that α is the identity, we write $i_n = \pi_\alpha$, the n-ary identity. Let $f \in B_n(A)$, $g \in B_m(A)$. Define the *parallel composition* as $f \oplus g \in B_{n+m}(A)$ with $(f \oplus g)(x_1, \ldots, x_{n+m}) = (f_1(x_1, \ldots, x_n), \ldots, f_n(x_1, \ldots, x_n), g_1(x_{n+1}, \ldots, x_{n+m}), \ldots, g_m(x_{n+1}, \ldots, x_{n+m}))$. For $f, g \in B_n(A)$ we can compose $f \bullet g$ in $Sym(A^n)$. If they have distinct arities we "pad" them with identity, for instance $f \in B_n(A)$ and $g \in B_m(A)$, $n < m$, then define $f \bullet g = (f \oplus i_{m-n}) \bullet g$ and we can thus serially compose all elements of $B(A)$.

We call a subset $C \subseteq B(A)$ that includes Π and is closed under $\oplus$ and $\bullet$ a *reversible Toffoli algebra* (RTA) based upon Toffoli's original work [14]. These have also been investigated as *permutation clones* [8], with ideas from category theory [9] and as *memoryless computation* [6]. If we do not insist upon the inclusion of Π, then we have *reversible iterative algebras* [3] in reference to Malcev and Post's iterative algebras. For a set $F \subseteq B(A)$ we write $\langle F \rangle$ as the smallest RTA that includes F, the RTA *generated* by F.

Let C be an RTA. We write $C^{[n]} = C \cap B_n(A)$ for the elements of C of arity n. We will occasionally write $(a_1, \ldots, a_n) \in A^n$ as $a_1 a_2 \ldots a_n$ for clarity.

In any RTA C, the unary part $C^{[1]}$ is found as a wreath product in all other parts, $C^{[1]}wrS_n \leq C^{[n]}$ because the wire permutations give us the right hand factor while $f_1 \oplus \cdots \oplus f_n$ for $f_i \in C^{[1]}$ gives us the left hand side.

Let q be a prime power, $GF(q)$ the field of order q, $AGL_n(q)$ the collection of affine invertible maps of $GF(q)^n$ to itself. We note that for all $m \in \mathbb{N}$, $AGL_n(q^m) \leq AGL_{nm}(q)$. For a prime p, let $\mathrm{Aff}(p^m) = \bigcup_{n \in \mathbb{N}} AGL_{nm}(p)$ be the RTA of affine maps over $A = GF(p)^m$.

We say that an RTA $C \leq B(A)$ is *borrow closed* if for all $f \in B(A)$, $f \oplus i_1 \in C$ implies that $f \in C$. We say that an RTA $C \leq B(A)$ is *ancilla closed* if for all $f \in B_n(A)$, $g \in C^{[n+1]}$ with some $a \in A$ such that for all $x_1, \ldots, x_n \in A$, for all $i \in \{1, \ldots, n\}$, $f_i(x_1, \ldots, x_n) = g_i(x_1, \ldots, x_n, a)$ and $g_{n+1}(x_1, \ldots, x_n, a) = a$ implies that $f \in C$. If an RTA is ancilla closed then it is borrow closed. For any prime power q, $\mathrm{Aff}(q)$ is borrow and ancilla closed.

3 Maximality in Permutation Groups

In this section we introduce some results from permutation group theory that will be of use. The maximal subgroups of permutation groups have been determined.

Theorem 1 ([11]). *Let $n \in \mathbb{N}$. Then the maximal subgroups of S_n are conjugate to one of the following G.*

1. *(alternating) $G = A_n$*
2. *(intransitive) $G = S_k \times S_m$ where $k + m = n$ and $k \neq m$*
3. *(imprimitive) $G = S_m wr S_k$ where $n = mk$, $m, k > 1$*
4. *(affine) $G = AGL_k(p)$ where $n = p^k$, p a prime*
5. *(diagonal) $G = T^k.(Out(T) \times S_k)$ where T is a nonabelian simple group, $k > 1$ and $n = |T|^{(k-1)}$*
6. *(wreath) $G = S_m wr S_k$ with $n = m^k$, $m \geq 5$, $k > 1$*
7. *(almost simple) $T \triangleleft G \leq Aut(T)$, $T \neq A_n$ a nonabelian simple group, G acting primitively on A*

Moreover, all subgroups of these types are maximal when they do not lie in A_n, except for a list of known exceptions.

It is worth noting that in the imprimitive case, A is a disjoint sum of k sets of order m, giving an equivalence relation with k equivalence classes of order m, the wreath product acts by reordering the equivalence classes as S_k, then acting as S_m on each equivalence class. In the wreath case, the set A is a direct product of k copies of a set of order m, the wreath product acts by permuting indices by S_k then acting as S_m on each index.

Lemma 1. *Let A be a set of even order and $n \geq 3$. Then $S_A wr S_n \leq Alt(A^n)$.*

Proof. $S_A wr S_n$ is generated by S_A acting on the first coordinate of A^n and S_n acting on coordinates.

The action of S_A on A^n is even because for each cycle in the first coordinate, the remaining $n-1$ coordinates are untouched. Every cycle occurs $|A|^{n-1}$ times, which is even, so the action of S_A lies in $Alt(A^n)$.

S_n is generated by S_{n-1} and the involution $(n-1\ n)$. By the same argument, each cycle of the action occurs an even number of times, so the action of S_{n-1} and the involution $((n-1)\ n)$ on A^n lies in $Alt(A^n)$ so we are done.   □

We have a similar inclusion for affineness.

Lemma 2. *For $n \geq 3$, $AGL_n(2) \leq Alt(2^n)$.*

Proof. $AGL_n(2)$ is generated by the permutation matrices $\{\pi_{(1,i)} \mid i = 2, \ldots, n\}$ and the matrix $\begin{bmatrix} 1 & 1 \\ 0 & 1 \end{bmatrix} \oplus i_{n-2}$. These bijections are even parity because they only act on two entries, thus have parity divisible by 2^{n-2} modulo 2 which is 0.   □

Lemma 3. *Let A be even order. Then $S_A wr S_2 \leq Alt(A^2)$ iff 4 divides $|A|$.*

Proof. The same argument as above applies for S_A. The action of S_2 swaps $\frac{|A|(|A|-1)}{2}$ pairs. This is even iff 4 divides $|A|$.   □

4   Maximality in RTAs

In this section, we will determine the maximal RTAs on a finite set A.

We have some generation results from other papers that will be useful.

Theorem 2 ([2] Theorem 5.9]). *Let A be odd. If $B_1(A), B_2(A) \subseteq C \subseteq B(A)$, then $C = B(A)$.*

Theorem 3 ([3] Theorem 20]). *If $Alt(A^4) \subseteq C \subseteq B(A)$ then $Alt(A^k) \subseteq C$ for all $k \geq 5$.*

Lemma 4. *Let $|A| \geq 3$, then $\langle B_1(A), B_2(A) \rangle$ is 3-transitive on A^3.*

Proof. Let $A = \{1, 2, 3, \ldots\}$. Let $a, b, c \in A^3$ be distinct. We show that we can map these to $111, 112, 113 \in A^3$. There are three cases. See Fig. 1.

Case 1: Suppose a_3, b_3, c_3 all distinct. Let $\alpha = (a_1a_3\ 1a_3)(b_1b_3\ 1b_3)(c_1c_3\ 1c_3) \in B_2(A)$. Let $\beta = (a_2a_3\ 11)(b_2b_3\ 12)(c_2c_3\ 13) \in B_2(A)$. Then $\gamma = (\pi_{(23)} \bullet (\alpha \oplus i_1) \bullet \pi_{(23)}) \bullet (i_1 \oplus \beta)$ satisfies the requirements.

Case 2: Suppose a_3, b_3, c_3 contains two values, wlog suppose $a_3 = b_3$. Let $d \in A - \{a_3, c_3\}$. Let $\delta = (a_1a_3\ a_1d) \in B_2(A)$. Let $\lambda = \pi_{(23)} \bullet (\delta \oplus i_1) \bullet \pi_{(23)}$. Then λ will map a, b, c to the situation in the first case.

Case 3: Suppose $a_3 = b_3 = c_3$. Then one of a_1, b_1, c_1 or a_2, b_2, c_2 must contain at least two values, wlog let a_1, b_1, c_1 be so. Then $\pi_{(13)}$ will give us the Case 1 if a_1, b_1, c_1 contains three values, Case 2 if a_1, b_1, c_1 contains two values.   □

The two following results are only relevant for even A.

Fig. 1. Cases 1 and 2 in Lemma 4

Lemma 5. *Let* $|A| \geq 4$, $B_1(A), B_2(A) \subset C \leq B(A)$. *Then* $Alt(A^3) \subseteq C^{[3]}$.

Proof. For $|A| = 4$, the result is shown by calculation in GAP [7] that $\langle B_1(A) \oplus i_2 \cup B_2(A) \oplus i_1 \cup \Pi^{[3]} \rangle$ as a subgroup of $B_3(A)$ is $Alt(A^3)$.

For $|A| = 5$ the result follows from Theorem 2.

Suppose $|A| \geq 6$ Since $B_2(A) \subseteq C$, we have all 1-controlled permutations of A in C. By [3] Lemma 18, with $P \subset Alt(A)$ the set of all 3-cycles, we have all 2-controlled 3-cycles in C. Thus $(111\ 112\ 113) \in C$. $B_1(A) \cup B_2(A)$ is 3-transitive on A^3 by Lemma 4, so we have all 3-cycles in C, so $Alt(A^3) \subseteq C$.   □

We know that this is not true for A of order 2, where $B_2(A)$ generates a group of order 1344 in $B_3(A)$, which is of index 15 in $Alt(A^3)$ and is included in no other subgroup of $B_3(A)$. However we find the following.

Lemma 6. *Let* $|A|$ *be even,* $B_1(A), B_2(A), B_3(A) \subset C \leq B(A)$. *Then* $Alt(A^4) \subseteq C^{[4]}$.

Proof. For A of order 4 or more, we use the same techniques as in Lemma 5.

For A of order 2, we calculate. We look at $C^{[4]}$ as a subgroup of S_{16}. The wire permutations $\Pi^{[4]}$ are generated by $(2,9,5,3)(4,10,13,7)(6,11)(8,12,14,15)$ and $(5,9)(6,10)(7,11)(8,12)$. Then $i_1 \oplus B_3(A)$ is a subgroup of $B_4(A)$ acting on the indices $\{2,3,4\}$, generated by $(1,2,3,4,5,6,7,8)(9,10,11,12,13,14,15,16)$ and $(1,2)(9,10)$. It is a simple calculation to determine that this group is the entire alternating group A_{16}, so $Alt(A^4) \subseteq C^{[4]}$.   □

We can now state our main theorem.

Theorem 4. *Let* A *be a finite set. Let* M *be a maximal sub RTA of* $B(A)$. *Then* $M^{[i]} \neq B_i(A)$ *for exactly one* i *and* M *belongs to the following classes:*

1. $i = 1$ *and* $M^{[1]}$ *is one of the classes in Theorem 1.*
2. $i = 2$, $|A| = 3$, *and* $M^{[2]} = AGL_2(3)$ *(up to conjugacy)*
3. $i = 2$, $|A| \geq 5$ *is odd and* $M^{[2]} = S_A wr S_2$
4. $i = 2$, $|A| \equiv 2 \mod 4$ *and* $M^{[2]} = S_A wr S_2$
5. $i = 2$, $|A| \equiv 0 \mod 4$ *and* $M^{[2]} = Alt(A^2)$
6. $i = 2$, $|A| \equiv 0 \mod 4$ *and* $M^{[2]} = T^{(3)}.(Out(T) \times S_3)$ *where* T *is a finite nonabelian simple group, with* $|A| = |T|$ *(up to conjugacy)*
7. $i = 2$, $|A| \equiv 0 \mod 4$ *and* $M^{[2]}$ *is an almost simple group (up to conjugacy)*
8. $i \geq 3$, $|A|$ *is even and* $M^{[i]} = Alt(A^i)$

Proof. Suppose $M < B(A)$ with $i \neq j$ natural numbers such that $M^{[i]} \neq B_i(A)$ and $M^{[j]} \neq B_j(A)$. Wlog, $i < j$, let $N = \langle M \cup B_j(A) \rangle$. Remember that compositions of mappings of arity at least j will also be of arity at least j, so $N^{[k]} = M^{[k]}$ for all $k < j$. Then $M < N$ because N contains all of $B_j(A)$ and $N < B(A)$ because $N^{[i]} = M^{[i]} \neq B_i(A)$. Thus M was not maximal, proving our first claim.

For the rest of the proof, take M maximal with $M^{[i]} \neq B_i(A)$. Then $M^{[i]}$ is a maximal subgroup of $B_i(A)$.

Suppose $i = 1$. Then $B_1(A) = S_A$ and we are interested in the maximal subgroups of S_A. From Theorem 1 we know that these are in one of the 7 classes.

Suppose $i \geq 2$. Then $S_A^i \leq M^{[i]}$ so $M^{[i]}$ is transitive on A^i. As $\Pi^{[i]} \leq M^{[i]}$ we also know that $S_A wr S_i \leq M^{[i]}$. Assume $M^{[i]}$ acts imprimitively on A^i with equivalence relation ρ. Let $a, b \in A^i$, $a \rho b$ with $a_i \neq b_i$. By the action of S_A acting on the ith coordinate we obtain $a' \rho b'$ with $a_j = a'_j$ and $b_j = b'_j$ for all $j \neq i$. By the action of S_i on coordinates we can move this inequality to any index. Thus by transitivity we can show that $\rho = (A^n)^2$ and is thus trivial, so our action cannot be imprimitive.

We now consider the cases of A odd and even separately.

Suppose $i \geq 2$ and $|A|$ is odd. If $i \geq 3$ then $M^{[1]} = B_1(A)$ and $M^{[2]} = B_2(A)$, so by Theorem 2 we have all of $B(A)$ and thus M is not maximal, a contradiction. Thus we have $i = 2$. $M^{[1]} = B_1(A) = S_A$ and $\pi_{(1\,2)} \in M$ so M contains $S_A wr S_2$. If $|A| \geq 5$ then by Theorem 1 this is maximal in $Sym(A^2)$ so $M^{[2]}$ must be precisely this. So the case of A order 3 is left. We want to know which maximal subgroups of $Sym(A^2)$ contain $S_A wr S_2$. There are 7 classes of maximal subgroups, we deal with them in turn.

- Since $\pi_{(1\,2)} \in M$ is odd on A^2, $M^{[2]} \nsubseteq Alt(A^2)$.
- From the discussion above we know that $M^{[2]}$ is transitive and primitive on A^2, so the second and third cases do not apply.
- The permutations in S_3 can be written as affine maps in $\mathbb{Z}_3$ and $\pi_{(1\,2)}$ can be written as $\begin{bmatrix} 0 & 1 \\ 1 & 0 \end{bmatrix}$, the off diagonal 2×2 matrix over $\mathbb{Z}_3$, so $S_3 wr S_2$ embeds in the affine general linear group. Thus $M^{[2]} = AGL_2(3)$ is one possibility.
- The diagonal case requires $|T|^{k-1} = 9$ for some nonabelian finite simple group T, a contradiction.
- The wreath case requires $9 \geq 5^2$, a contradiction.
- By [4] all G acting primitively on A^2 with subgroups that are nonabelian finite simple groups are subgroups of $Alt(A^2)$, and we have odd elements in M, so this is a contradiction.

Thus the only maximal subgroup is $M^{[2]} = AGL_2(3)$.

Suppose $i \geq 2$ and $|A|$ is even. We know from Theorem 3 that for $i > 4$ we can get all of $Alt(A^i)$ from $\cup_{1 \leq j < i} B_j(A)$. $Alt(A^i)$ is maximal in $Sym(A^i)$ so we are done.

Thus we are left with 3 cases, $i = 2, 3, 4$.

From Lemma 6 we know that for $i = 4$, $M^{[4]} = Alt(A^4)$ is the only possibility.

From Lemma 5 we know that for $i = 3$ and $|A| \neq 2$, $M^{[3]} = Alt(A^3)$ is the only possibility. For $|A| = 2$ we find that $B_2(A)$ generates a subgroup of $B_3(A)$ that is only included in $Alt(A^3)$, so again $M^{[3]} = Alt(A^3)$ is the only possibility.

Thus we are left with the case $i = 2$. From the above we know that the intransitive and imperfect cases cannot arise. Thus we need to consider the wreath, affine, diagonal and almost simple cases.

- $|A| = 2$: $S_A wr S_2$ has order 8, $B_2(2)$ has order 24, so $M^{[2]} = S_A wr S_2$ is maximal and we are done.
- Case $6 \leq |A| \equiv 2 \mod 4$: Lemma 3 above says that $S_A wr S_2 \not\leq Alt(A^2)$ so it is maximal by Theorem 1.
- Case $|A| = 4$: Alternating is possible by inclusion. The affine case $AGL_4(2)$ lies in A_{16} by Lemma 2. Diagonal not possible by order. Almost simple not possible because all primitive groups of degree 16 lie in the alternating group A_{16} [4] .
- Case $8 \leq |A| \equiv 0 \mod 4$: Alternating is always possible. If $A = 2^m$ for some m, then $AGL_m(2)$ might be possible, but lies in $Alt(A^2)$ by Lemma 2. Diagonal, almost simple might be possible, if $S_A wr S_2 \leq M^{[2]}$.

$\square$

4.1   The Existence of Maximal RTAs

It is not immediately clear that all the classes of maximal RTAs can actually exist. So let us investigate a few small examples.

Let us take A of order 2. For $i = 1$ we find no nontrivial subgroups, so the maximal is $M^{[1]}$ of order 1. For $i = 2$ case 4 gives us $S_2 wr S_2$ of order 8 as a maximal subgroup. We note that $B_2(A) = AGL_2(2)$, i.e. all binary bijections are affine maps. For $i \geq 3$ we have $M^{[i]}$ alternating as the only example, as we know from Toffoli [14] and others that the alternating bijections of arity i are generated by the collection of all permutations of arity less than i.

Taking A of order 3, we obtain a few more examples. For $i = 1$ we write $A = \{1, 2, 3\}$ and we know that S_3 has maximal subgroups A_3 as well as $\langle (1\,2) \rangle$, $\langle (1\,3) \rangle$, $\langle (2\,3) \rangle$. These correspond in Theorem 1 to the alternating case and intransitive cases. For $i = 2$ we write $A = Z_3$ and note that the unary maps are all affine, that is, the set of affine maps $\{x \mapsto ax + b | a, b \in \mathbb{Z}_3, a \neq 0\}$ is identical to the permutations $S_3 = B_1(A)$. The binary affine maps $AGL_2(3)$ include all sums of unary affine maps and the wire permutation $\begin{bmatrix} 0 & 1 \\ 1 & 0 \end{bmatrix}$. With the inclusion of the linear map $(x, y) \mapsto (x + y, y) = \begin{bmatrix} 1 & 1 \\ 0 & 1 \end{bmatrix}$ we obtain all affine maps. From Theorem 1 above we know this is maximal as a subgroup of $B_2(A)$. For $i \geq 3$ we know that $B_1(A), B_2(A)$ generate all of $B(A)$ so we are done.

For A of order 4 things get a touch more complex. For $i = 1$ we get a number of maximal subgroups. A_4 is maximal. By fixing one element we obtain 4 maximal subgroups isomorphic to S_3 as intransitive subgroups. By imposing an equivalance relation with two classes of two elements each ($1,2 \mid 3,4$ or $1,3 \mid 2,4$ or $1,3 \mid 2,3$) we obtain subgroups isomorphic to $S_2 wr S_2$ that act imprimitively on A. $AGL_2(2)$ is of order 24, same as S_4, we see that the affine maps are precisely the permutations, not maximal. There is no nonabelian simple group to allow a diagonal maximal subgroup. The wreath product also fails by order, and no nonabelian simple group of order less than 24 exists, so the almost simple case cannot arise. For $i \geq 2$ we find $M^{[2]} = Alt(A^2)$ a maximal subgroup. For $i = 2$ we see that there are no nonabelian finite simple groups of order 16, so case 6 cannot arise. It can be shown by investigation of [4] that $M^{[2]}$ cannot be an almost simple group.

For orders 5 and above, we know that the maximal RTAs for $i = 1$ can be obtained by permutation group analysis directly. For A of odd order we have the wreath case $S_A wr S_2$ maximal in $B_2(A)$ and none others. For A even we have the alternating and wreath cases easily constructible. We are left with the question whether, for A of order a multiple of 4, the diagonal or almost simple cases can actually arise.

The possibilities for the diagonal case with A of order equal to the order of a finite simple nonabelian group start with A of order 60. The other possibility is that $|A|^2 = |T|$ for some finite simple nonabelian group T. The only known result in this direction is in [13] where they show that symplectic groups $Sp(4, p)$ where p is a certain type of prime, now known as NSW primes, have square order. The first of these groups is of order $(2^4 \cdot 3 \cdot 5 \cdot 7^2)^2$ corresponding to A of order $(2^4 \cdot 3 \cdot 5 \cdot 7^2) = 11760$. We note that the sporadic simple groups have order that always contains a prime to the power one, so they are not of square order. We know that the Alternating group can never have order that is a square, as the highest prime less than n will occur exactly once in the order of the group. It might be possible that there are other finite simple groups of square order. As far as we are aware, there have been no further results in this direction.

Each of these possibilities is far beyond the expected useful arities for computational processes.

The other case is to look at almost simple groups. Let A be of order $4k$, then we are looking for an almost simple action of degree $16k^2$. In [4] we saw that all primitive actions of degree 16 are alternating, that is, they are subgroups of A_{16}. In order to find an example, we can hope to use results about primitive permutation groups of prime power [5] and product of two prime power [10] degrees, so we would be able to investigate A of order $4k$ for $k \leq 14$. Once again this would include all examples of arities expected to be useful for computational processes.

5   Maximality with Borrow and Ancilla Closure

The strength of Theorem 4 is partially due to the fact that there is no effect of the existence of mappings of a certain arity in a given RTA on the size of the lower arity part, as there are no operators to lower the arity of a mapping. This does not apply with ancilla and borrow closure. In this section we collect some results about maximal ancilla and borrow closed RTAs. The following result reflects the first part of Theorem 4.

Lemma 7. *Let $M \leq B(A)$ be a maximal borrow or ancilla closed RTA. Then there exists some $k \in \mathbb{N}$ such that for all $i < k$, $M^{[i]} = B_i(A)$ and for all $i \geq k$, $M^{[i]} \neq B_i(A)$.*

Proof. Suppose $M^{[k]} = B_k(A)$. Then for all $f \in B_m(A)$, $m < k$, $f \oplus i_{k-m} \in M$ so by borrow closure $f \in M$, so $M^{[m]} = B_m(A)$ for all $m \leq k$. As M is maximal, there must be a largest k for which $M^{[k]} = B_k(A)$, since otherwise $M = B(A)$. □

We will call k the *index* of the maximal ancilla closed or borrow closed RTA. From Theorem 2 we then note the following.

Lemma 8. *Let $|A|$ be odd. Then M maximal with index $k = 1, 2$ are the only options.*

In this case, we can say a bit more for index 2. If A is of order 3, then by the argument in Theorem 4 above, we find that $M = \text{Aff}(A)$, the affine maps over a field of order 3. Otherwise A is at least 5 and $B_1(A)$ is no longer affine. See Lemma 11 below.

Similarly, we obtain the following, but see Corollary 1 below for a stronger result.

Lemma 9. *Let $|A| \geq 4$ be even. Then M maximal with index $k = 1, 2, 3$ are the only options and for $i > k$, $M^{[i]} \neq Alt(A^i)$.*

Proof. We start by noting that for even $|A|$, for all $f \in B_i(A)$, $f \oplus i_1 \in Alt(A^{i+1})$. Thus if $M^{[i]} = Alt(A^i)$ for some $i > k$, then $M^{[i-1]} = B_{i-1}(A)$ which is a contradiction, which shows the second part of the result.

Suppose $k \geq 4$, so $B_1(A), B_2(A), B_3(A) \subseteq M$. Then by Lemma 6 $Alt(A^4) \subseteq M$, so by Theorem 3 $Alt(A^j) \subseteq M$ for all $j \geq 5$. But we know that by borrow closure, this implies that $B_{j-1}(A) \subseteq M$ so M is in fact $B(A)$. This is a contradiction, so $k < 4$. □

Using similar arguments, we obtain the following.

Lemma 10. *Let $|A| = 2$. Then M maximal with index $k = 1, 2, 3$ are the only options and for $i > k$, $M^{[i]} \neq Alt(A^i)$.*

Proof. Suppose M is maximal with $k \geq 5$. Then by Theorem 3 we obtain $M^{[i]} = Alt(A^i)$ for all $i \geq 5$, which by the first argument in the previous Lemma, implies that M is not maximal.

Suppose M is maximal with $k = 4$. We know that $M^{[3]} = B_3(A)$. Then by Lemma 6 we find that $M^{[4]} = Alt(A^4)$, by Theorem 3 we obtain all of $Alt(A^5)$ so by borrow closure all of $B_4(A)$ and thus M is not maximal. □

We obtain some examples of maximal borrow and ancilla closed RTA. The expression *degenerate* to describe maps where each output index depends only upon one input comes from [1].

Lemma 11. *For $|A| \geq 5$, the degenerate RTA $Deg(A)$ generated by $B_1(A)$ is a maximal borrow closed RTA and maximal ancilla closed RTA.*

Proof. Let $Deg(A)$ be generated by $B_1(A) = S_A$. Then $Deg(A)^{[i]} = S_A wr S_i$ for all $i \geq 2$ which is maximal in $B_i(A)$ by Theorem 1. Thus any RTA N properly containing $Deg(A)$ will have $N^{[i]} = B_i(A)$ for some $i \geq 2$ and thus $N^{[2]} = B_2(A)$ by Lemma 7. Let $f \in N^{[2]} - Deg(A)^{[2]}$, then $f \oplus f \in N[4] - Deg(A)^{[4]}$ so $N^{[4]} = B_4(A)$ and by Lemmas 8 and 9, $N = B(A)$, so $Deg(A)$ is maximal. □

For $|A| < 5$, $B_1(A)$ consists of affine maps, so $Deg(A) < \mathrm{Aff}(A)$ and thus cannot be maximal.

Corollary 1. *Let $|A| \geq 4$ be even. Then M maximal with index $k = 1, 2$ are the only options.*

Proof. From Lemma 9 we know $k = 1, 2, 3$ are possible. Suppose M is maximal in B(A) with $k = 3$.

Suppose $|A| = 4$. $B_2(A)$ can be embedded in $B_4(A)$ represented on S_{256} with the tuples in A^4 represented by the integers $1, \ldots, 256$, generated by the permutations

$$(1, 2, 3, 4, 5, 6, 7, 8, 9, 10, 11, 12, 13, 14, 15, 16)$$
$$(17, 18, 19, 20, 21, 22, 23, 24, 25, 26, 27, 28, 29, 30, 31, 32) \ldots$$
$$\ldots (241, 242, 243, 244, 245, 246, 247, 248, 249, 250, 251, 252, 253, 254, 255, 256)$$

and $(1, 2)(17, 18) \ldots (241, 242)$. With the wire permutations we obtain a subgroup of S_{256} that is the alternating group, so $M^{[4]} = Alt(A^4)$ and by Theorem 3 we then get $M^{[5]} = Alt(A^5)$ and thus M is not maximal.

Suppose A is even with more than 6 elements. The degenerate RTA $Deg(A) \leq M$ because $M^{[1]} = B_1(A)$, but because $Deg(A)$ is maximal and $M^{[2]}$ is a supergroup of $Deg(A)^{[2]}$, M is all of $B(A)$ and is not maximal. □

Lemma 12. *Let A be of prime power order. Then $\mathrm{Aff}(A)$ is a maximal borrow closed RTA and a maximal ancilla closed RTA.*

Proof. Let $M = \mathrm{Aff}(A)$. Suppose M is not maximal, so $M < N < B(A)$.

Let A be of odd order. For every i, except $i = 1$ with A of order 3, $M^{[i]}$ is maximal in $B_i(A)$ by Theorem 1. Let $f \in B_n(A)$, $f \in N - M$. Then $N^{[n]} = B_n(A)$ by subgroup maximality, so for all $i < n$, $N^{[i]} = B_i(A)$. For all $j \in \mathbb{N}$, $f \oplus i_j \in (N - M)^{[n+j]}$ so similarly $N^{[n+j]} = B_{n+j}(A)$ so $N = B(A)$ and M is maximal.

Let A be of even order, so a power of 2. Let $f \in B_n(A)$, $f \in N - M$. We know from Lemma 2 above that $M^{[n]} \leq Alt(A^n)$ is not maximal, so the odd order argument above does not hold. By [12] we know that $N^{[n]} = B_n(A)$ or $N^{[n]} = Alt(A^n)$. For all $j \in \mathbb{N}$, $f \oplus i_j \in (N - M)^{[n+j]}$ so $N^{[n+j]} = B_{n+j}(A)$ or $N^{[n+j]} = Alt(A^{n+j})$. In both cases this means that $N^{[n+j-1]} = B_{n+j-1}(A)$, as for all $g \in B_{n+j-1}(A)$ $g \oplus i_1 \in Alt(A^{n+j})f$, so $N = B(A)$ and M was maximal.

Because $\mathrm{Aff}(A)$ is ancilla closed and maximal as borrow closed, there can be no ancilla closed RTA between $\mathrm{Aff}(A)$ and $B(A)$ so $\mathrm{Aff}(A)$ is a maximal ancilla closed RTA. □

We look at a few concrete examples.

By [1] we know that for A of order 2, we have the following maximal ancilla closed RTAs.

- The affine mappings,
- The parity respecting mappings, which either preserve the number of 1s mod 2, or invert it,
- The odd prime-conservative mappings, that preserve the number of 1s mod p, an odd prime.

The affine mappings have index 3, the parity respecting index 2 and the odd prime-conservative mappings have index 1.

It remains an open problem whether these are the borrow closed maximal RTAs over A of order 2.

For A of order 3, we know that the affine maps $\mathrm{Aff}(3)$ is an index 2 maximal borrow closed RTA and a maximal ancilla closed RTA.

For A of order 4, we can say the following about index 2 maximals. There are the following inclusions, $S_4 wr S_2 < ASp < AGL_4(2) < Alt(4^2)$ where ASp is a group of order 11520 that consists of the affine maps where the linear part is a symplectic linear map in $Sp(4,2)$. If $M^{[2]} = Alt(4^2)$ then M includes the affine maps properly. We know that the affine maps are maximal, a contradiction. $M^{[2]} = AGL_4(2)$ for the affine maps that we know form a maximal borrow and ancilla closed RTA. It is possible that $M^{[2]} = S_4 wr S_2$ or $M^{[2]} = ASp$ for some maximal M.

For A of order 5 or more, we know that index 2 arises only for the degenerate RTA $Deg(A)$.

6   Conclusion and Further Work

We have determined the maximal RTAs, using results from permutation group theory and some generation results.

As we have not been able to construct explicitly an example of a maximal RTA with $i = 2$ and $M^{[i]}$ of diagonal or almost simple type, the conjecture remains that these are not, in fact, possible. We note however that if such examples exist, they will arise for A of order 8 or more, so will probably not be relevant for any practical reversible computation implementation.

In future work we aim to determine the weight functions as described by [8] for maximal RTAs, in order to determine whether they hold some interesting insights.

The results for borrow and ancilla closed RTAs are not as comprehensive. We hope to determine these in the foreseeable future. We note interestingly that for a state set of order 5 or more, Lemma 11 indicates that if we can implement all permutations of the state set, we need only have one non-degenerate gate in order to implement all gates under borrow or ancilla closure. Similarly we see that once we can implement all affine maps on a state set of prime power order, then only one nonaffine gate is needed to implement all gates. For the ancilla case, many of the techniques of [1] will prove useful. In the ancilla case, we know all maximal RTA with index 2 except for A of order 4.

Acknowledgements. Michael Guidici has helped extensively with understanding primitive permutations groups, for which I thank him greatly.

References

1. Aaronson, S., Grier, D., Schaeffer, L.: The classification of reversible bit operations. Electron. Colloquium Comput. Complexity (66) (2015). https://eccc.weizmann.ac.il//report/2015/066/
2. Boykett, T.: Closed systems of invertible maps. J. Multiple-Valued Logic Soft Comput. **32**(5–6), 565–605 (2019)
3. Boykett, T., Kari, J., Salo, V.: Finite generating sets for reversible gate sets under general conservation laws. Theor. Comput. Sci. **701**(C), 27–39 (2017). https://doi.org/10.1016/j.tcs.2016.12.032
4. Buekenhout, F., Leemans, D.: On the list of finite primitive permutation groups of degree ≤ 50. J. Symb. Comput. **22**(2), 215–225 (1996). https://doi.org/10.1006/jsco.1996.0049
5. Cai, Q., Zhang, H.: A note on primitive permutation groups of prime power degree. J. Discrete Math. **2**, 191–192 (2015)
6. Gadouleau, M., Riis, S.: Memoryless computation: new results, constructions, and extensions. Theoret. Comput. Sci. **562**, 129–145 (2015). https://doi.org/10.1016/j.tcs.2014.09.040
7. The GAP Group: GAP - Groups, Algorithms, and Programming, Version 4.10.2 (2019). https://www.gap-system.org
8. Jeřábek, E.: Galois connection for multiple-output operations. Algebra Universalis **79**(2), 1–37 (2018). https://doi.org/10.1007/s00012-018-0499-7
9. LaFont, Y.: Towards an algebraic theory of Boolean circuits. J. Pure Appl. Algebra **184**, 257–310 (2003)
10. Li, C.H., Li, X.: On permutation groups of degree a product of two prime-powers. Commun. Algebra **42**(11), 4722–4743 (2014). https://doi.org/10.1080/00927872.2013.823500
11. Liebeck, M.W., Praeger, C.E., Saxl, J.: A classification of the maximal subgroups of the finite alternating and symmetric groups. J. Algebra **111**(2), 365–383 (1987). https://doi.org/10.1016/0021-8693(87)90223-7
12. Mortimer, B.: Permutation groups containing affine groups of the same degree. J. Lond. Math. Soc. **2**(3), 445–455 (1977). https://doi.org/10.1112/jlms/s2-15.3.445
13. Newman, M., Shanks, D., Williams, H.C.: Simple groups of square order and an interesting sequence of primes. Acta Arith. **38**(2), 129–140 (1980)
14. Toffoli, T.: Reversible computing. In: de Bakker, J., van Leeuwen, J. (eds.) ICALP 1980. LNCS, vol. 85, pp. 632–644. Springer, Heidelberg (1980). https://doi.org/10.1007/3-540-10003-2_104

Search-Based Transformation Synthesis for 3-Valued Reversible Circuits

D. Michael Miller[1(✉)] and Gerhard W. Dueck[2]

[1] University of Victoria, Victoria, Canada
mmiller@uvic.ca
[2] University of New Brunswick, Fredericton, Canada
gdueck@unb.ca

Abstract. A novel bounded search transformation-based synthesis approach is presented that finds a reversible circuit implementation for a given reversible function. Methods for simplifying the circuit post-synthesis are presented. Quantum implementation constraints are also considered. Experimental results for all 2-input 3-valued functions show the effectiveness of the new approaches compared to earlier transformation-based synthesis approaches. Other examples are given to show both the effectiveness and limitations of the new approach which point to a number of key areas for further research.

1 Introduction

An r-valued n-variable reversible logic function maps each of the r^n input patters to a unique output pattern. Hence the function has n outputs. The synthesis problem is to realize a reversible function by a cascade of basic reversible gates. In this paper we present a novel bounded search method for this synthesis problem as well as systematic approaches to circuit simplification. Quantum circuit implementation is considered with respect to a variety of practical constraints.

Reversible functions and circuits have the interesting property that if one has a circuit for a function f, reversing the order of the gates and replacing each by the gate implementing the inverse operation yields a circuit realizing f^{-1}. Consequently, one can synthesize a circuit for f and a second circuit for f^{-1} and choose the better circuit as the basis to realize f.

Transformation-based synthesis was introduced in [4] for Boolean reversible functions and extended to MVL functions in [3,5]. A study of the MVL reversible logic synthesis including the transformation-based approach appears in [1]. The method introduced here employs a bounded recursive search to more extensively explore alternative circuits. It employs the basic pattern transform operation of earlier transformation-based synthesis approaches. The bound is based on the best circuit found to date.

Empirical results for 3-valued functions show the new search method produces significantly better circuits. Since the new method is a search, significantly more CPU time is required but this is justified by the improvement in the synthesized circuits. Limitations of the approach are discussed and issues for further research are identified.

I. Lanese and M. Rawski (Eds.): RC 2020, LNCS 12227, pp. 218–236, 2020.
https://doi.org/10.1007/978-3-030-52482-1_13

2 Background

2.1 Reversible Functions, Gates and Circuits

Definition 1. *An n-input, n-output, (written $n \times n$) totally-specified r-valued function is* reversible *if it maps each input assignment to a unique output assignment. We use $x_0, x_1, ..., x_{n-1}$ to denote the function inputs and $x_0^+, x_1^+, ..., x_{n-1}^+$ to denote the corresponding outputs. A reversible function defines a permutation of the input patterns. There are $r^n!$ r-valued, $n \times n$ reversible functions.* □

An r-valued $n \times n$ reversible function can be specified as a list F with r^n entries $F_0, F_1, ..., F_{r^n-1}$ where the n digit r-valued expansion of each F_i specifies the output pattern corresponding to the input pattern which is the n digit r-valued expansion of i. The specification list for the identity function has the ith entry equal to i for all i.

Definition 2. *For a given f with specification F, the* distance *between f and the identity function is given by*

$$\triangle(f) = \sum_{j=0}^{r^n-1} d(j, F_j) \quad d(a, b) = \sum_{k=0}^{n-1} |a_k - b_k|$$

where a_k and b_k denote the kth digit in the r-valued expansion of a and b, respectively. □

Definition 3. *A reversible gate has p inputs and p outputs and realizes a $p \times p$ reversible function.* □

In this work, we employ 3-valued reversible gates given by the following definition:

Definition 4. *A 3-valued $p \times p$ controlled unary reversible gate passes $p - 1$ control lines through unchanged, and applies a specified unary operator to the pth line, the target line, if the control lines assume particular specified values. Otherwise the target line is passed through unaltered. The permitted unary operators are the five listed in Table 1. Note that a gate must have a single target and the case of 0 controls $(p = 1)$ is permitted in which case the gate is said to be* uncontrolled. □

Definition 5. *A reversible circuit realizing an $n \times n$ reversible function is a cascade of reversible gates with no fanout or feedback [7]. The circuit has n inputs and n outputs and is thus identified as $n \times n$.* □

The synthesis problem considered here is how to realize a given reversible function specification as a circuit using a basic set of reversible gates. The presentation focuses on 3-valued functions and circuits but the methods can be readily extended to a higher radix.

We will use circuit diagrams where targets are boxes labeled by the appropriate unary operation and controls are shown as circles containing the control value for reversible circuits and as • for quantum circuits.

Table 1. 3-valued unary operators

x	$C_1[x]$	$C_2[x]$	$N[x]$	$D[x]$	$E[x]$
0	1	2	2	0	1
1	2	0	1	2	0
2	0	1	0	1	2

Consider the operators in Table 1. C_1 and C_2 are inverses of each other. D, E and N are each self-inverse. The following readily verified identities are used in the circuit simplification techniques discussed later in this paper.

$$C_2[C_2[x]] = C_1[x] \tag{1}$$
$$C_1[C_1[x]] = C_2[x] \tag{2}$$
$$D[x] = E[C_1[x]] = N[C_2[x]] \tag{3}$$
$$E[x] = D[C_2[x]] = N[C_1[x]] \tag{4}$$
$$N[x] = D[C_1[x]] = E[C_2[x]] \tag{5}$$

2.2 Quantum Circuits

Reversible circuits may be implemented in a variety of technologies. Here we are interested in potential quantum circuit implementations [6–8,10]. The objective is to map a reversible circuit composed of reversible gates as defined in Definition 4 to a circuit composed of gates directly implementable in a given quantum technology.

Muthukrishnan and Stroud [6] introduced a family of elementary ternary quantum gates (MS gates) widely used in the quantum MVL circuit literature which for the ternary case can be defined as follows:

Definition 6. *A Muthukrishnan and Stroud (MS) gate is a gate as defined in Definition 4 with at most one control.*

Muthukrishnan and Stroud considered ion trap technology for implementing these gates and for the ternary case required that all control values be 2. Here, we do not assume a particular underlying technology and consider a number of possible scenarios. In particular, we consider situations where only a subset of the MS gates are physically available since in some technologies certain MS gates are readily implemented while others are more costly or may not be implementable. In addition, we require that all controls in a quantum circuit have the same *global control value* (*cv*). We will consider cases with $cv = 1$ or 2.

It is clear from equations (1) to (5) that a single cycle gate, C_1 or C_2, and at least one of D, E or N, is sufficient as the other gates can be implemented by suitable gate pairings. In this work, we distinguish between the gates that are *logically* available during circuit synthesis and the gates that are *physically* available for the quantum circuit with the assumption that all physically available gates are available for use during the synthesis process. We also assume that both C_1 and C_2 are physically, and therefore logically, available as a cycle gate is implemented as a rotation the difference between C_1 and C_2 being the direction of rotation. A technology that supports one type of cycle can reasonably be expected to support the other.

Given a set of physically available MS gates, we next consider how to implement reversible gates with more than 1 control. A realization for 2 controls as given in [2] is shown in Fig. 1[1]. α can be any of C_1, C_2, D, E or N that are physically available. h is a helper line which is initialized to 0. Given that, a gate with three controls can be implemented as shown in Fig. 2. Two helper lines, h_1 and h_2 are required and must both be initialized to 0. Gates with more controls can be implemented following a similar strategy.

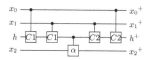

Fig. 1. Implementation for $\alpha[x_2, x_1 = 2, x_0 = 2]$ with helper line h

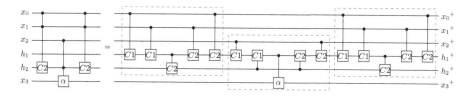

Fig. 2. Implementation for $\alpha[x_3, x_2 = 2, x_1 = 2, x_0 = 2]$ with helper lines h_1 and h_2

The 2 control case requires 5 MS gates whereas the 3 control case requires 15. We have shown the circuits where the control values are 2. These are readily changed to 1, but recall that we assume all controls in a quantum circuit have the same global value. If a control line to a gate g is required to have a different value, a simple solution is to place uncontrolled gates on that line before and after gate g. This leads to the following definition of quantum cost.

Definition 7. *A gate which applies $\alpha \in \{C_1, C_2, D, E, N\}$ with 0, 1, 2, 3 controls has a base cost of 1, 1, 5, 15, respectively. In general, the base cost for a k-control gate, $k > 2$, is $5 + 2 \times$ the cost of a gate with $k-1$ controls. If the gate type α is not physically available as a single MS gate a pair of gates is required and the cost increases by 1. The cost increases by 2, for each control that does not have the global control value.*

Adding uncontrolled gates before and after each control not equal to the global control value can obviously be very costly. A more efficient approach will be introduced in Sect. 5.

---

[1] The gate notation is *type*[*target, controls*].

Table 2. Transition options

Transition	Options	Transition	Options
$0 \to 1$	$C_1 \ E$	$0 \to 2$	$C_2 \ N$
$1 \to 0$	$C_2 \ E$	$1 \to 2$	D
$2 \to 0$	$C_1 \ N$	$2 \to 1$	D

3   Transformation-Based Synthesis

Transformation-based synthesis was introduced by the current authors and D. Maslov in [4] for Boolean functions and in [3,5] for MVL, specifically 3-valued, functions. The core operation, TRANSFORM(a, b), is the identification of an ordered list of reversible gates to map an n digit pattern a to an n digit pattern b where $a > b$. The gates are chosen so they will not affect any pattern $< b$. We here describe TRANSFORM(a, b) for the 3-valued case. Note that we use $\leftarrow$ to denote assignment, **break** to indicate exiting the current loop and **continue** to indicate going back to the top of the current loop.

```
 1: procedure TRANSFORM(a, b)
 2:     list ← φ
 3:     for i=0, 1, ..., n − 1 do
 4:         if aᵢ=bᵢ then
 5:             continue
 6:         end if
 7:         create a new gate G with target xᵢ
 8:         use aᵢ → bᵢ to get the type for G using Table 2
 9:             there may be a choice in which case both are recorded
10:         c ← a and then set cᵢ ← 0
11:         for j=0, 1, ..., n − 1 do
12:             if setting cⱼ to 0 results in c < b then
13:                 break
14:             else
15:                 cⱼ ← 0
16:             end if
17:         end for
18:         the nonzero digits in c identify the controls for G
19:         append G to the end of list
20:         aᵢ ← bᵢ
21:     end for
22:     return list
23: end procedure
```

TRANSFORM generates a gate for each i such that $a_i \neq b_i$. The gates generated use only control values 1 and 2. 0 controls are generated by an optimization discussed in Sect. 5. The for j loop in 11–17 reduces the number of controls for the gate while ensuring the gate will not affect any pattern $< b$. TRANSFORM is readily extended to other radices by revising the options in Table 2.

As noted, TRANSFORM can generate a choice of gate depending on the transition required and also of course which gates are available to be used in a particular synthesis. Our approach to resolving a choice is to choose the one that when applied moves the function closest to the identity. Note that D gates are specified as single choices in the table for transitions $1 \rightarrow 2$ and $2 \rightarrow 1$. C_1 and C_2 cannot be used alone for those two cases as they would always affect an entry earlier in the specification.

The basic bidirectional transformation-based synthesis approach [5] is shown as METHOD1. TRANSFORM is as just described. INVERSE computes the specification of the inverse of a reversible function which by definition must always exist. Applying a gate to a function specification F means to apply the gate to update each of the entries in F.

```
 1: procedure METHOD1(F)
 2:     set gate lists C_in ← C_out ← φ
 3:     FI ← INVERSE(F)
 4:     for i=0, 1, ..., r^n − 2 do
 5:         if F_i ≠ i then
 6:             T_out ←TRANSFORM(F_i, i)
 7:             apply the gates in T_out to update F
 8:             T_in ←TRANSFORM(FI_i, i)
 9:             apply the gates in T_in to update FI
10:             if |T_out| < |T_in| or
11:                 |T_out|=|T_in| and △F < △FI then
12:                 append the gates in T_out to the end of C_out
13:                 FI ← INVERSE(F)
14:             else
15:                 append the gates in T_in to the end of C_in
16:                 F ← INVERSE(FI)
17:             end if
18:         end if
19:     end for
20:     reverse the order of the gates in C_out
21:     replace each gate in C_out by its inverse
22:     form the circuit by appending C_out to the end of C_in
23:     return circuit
24: end procedure
```

The operation of METHOD1 is straightforward. The basic idea is to find a circuit that will map F to the identity. The inverse circuit will of course map the identity to the desired F. For each i starting at 0, the method determines the output-side gates that will map the ith output side entry to i. Separately, it finds the input-side gates that will map the appropriate input pattern to match the output pattern i. The latter is expressed in terms of FI, the inverse of F, so that lines 6–7 and 8–9 are similar and can be implemented with common code which is more efficient that treating the output and input sides of F separately. Recall, that TRANSFORM is such that the gates chosen will not alter an entry $F_j, j < i$. Also note that entry $i = r^n - 1$ need not be considered since as the last entry aligning all previous entries to the identity means it is also mapped to the identity.

For each i, the method chooses to use the output-side or input-side transformation based on the number of gates required and if those factors are the same based on which choice leads to a specification closest to the identity using the $\triangle$ operator. In the event of a tie, the output-side transform is used. A more fulsome description of this algorithm can be found in [5].

METHOD1 uses either all input or all output gates for each iteration as it only considers two possibilities. An extension to this approach, developed in [9] for the 2-valued case, is to for each i, consider all $j, i \leq j \leq r^n - 1$ and for each apply TRANSFORM(F_j, i) to find output-side gates and TRANSFORM(FI_j, i) to find input-side gates. From the results for each j, the one is chosen that requires the fewest gates (input plus output) and if there is a tie the lowest j resulting in an F closest to the identity is used. We call this approach METHOD2. A full description can be found in [9]. The bounded search transformation-based synthesis method introduced in the next section is derived from this approach.

4   Bounded Search Transformation-Based Synthesis

METHOD3 is the new bounded search approach introduced in this paper. The basic idea is to search through the options to transform each entry of F in order $0, 1, ..., r^n - 1$ in a recursive manner. A bounded search is performed where the bound is based on the best circuit found to that point in the search. Any search path where the circuit to that point has a higher cost than the best circuit found so far is abandoned.

A key question is how to set the initial bound. One could use a cost of ∞ but that can lead to excessive searching. The approach we adopt is to apply METHOD1 to find an initial circuit and to use it as the initial best circuit which is retained in a global called *BestCircuit*. The invocation of METHOD1 to set the initial bound is made prior to calling METHOD3 to initiate the search. In the initial call to METHOD3 a value of 0 should be provided for parameter k and an empty list for parameter *circuit*.

COST is a function that computes the cost of a circuit which can be selected to be either (a) the number of gates in the circuit, or (b) the sum of the quantum costs of the gates in the circuit as specified in Definition 7.

SIMPLIFY is a procedure that applies the post-synthesis simplifications process described in Sect. 5.

Function MAP used in METHOD3 orders the alternatives to be considered in a special way. If $j = k$ it returns k. If $j = k + 1$, it returns the value p such that $F_p = k$. Those two cases are considered first since the first one only requires output side gates and the second only requires input side gates. Those cases quite often have the cheapest incremental costs. For $j > k + 1$ in order, function MAP returns the other choices from k to $R^n - 1$ in ascending order.

```
 1: procedure METHOD3(F, k, circuit)
 2:     if k=r^n − 1 then
 3:         SIMPLIFY(circuit)
 4:         if COST(circuit) <COST(BestCircuit) then
 5:             BestCircuit ← circuit
 6:         end if
 7:         return
 8:     end if
 9:     for j=k, k + 1, ..., r^n − 1 do
10:         i ← MAP(j, k)
11:         copy F into FC
12:         T_out ←TRANSFORM(F_i, k)
13:         apply the gates in T_out to update FC
14:         T_in ←TRANSFORM(i, k)
15:         if |T_in| + |T_out| + |circuit| ≥ |BestCircuit| then
16:             return
17:         end if
18:         FIC ← INVERSE(FC)
19:         apply the gates in T_in to update FIC
20:         FC ← INVERSE(FIC)
21:         append gates in T_out reversed and inverted
22:                         to the end of circuit
23:         prepend gates in T_in to the front of circuit
24:         METHOD3(FC, k + 1, circuit)
25:         remove gates in T_in and T_out from circuit
26:     end for
27:     return
28: end procedure
```

Lines 2–8 in METHOD3 is the terminal case for the recursive search. The current circuit is compared to the best circuit found so far and replaces it if it is cheaper. Lines 15–17 implement the bound on the search by comparing the number of gates in the circuit being built to the number of gates in the best circuit found so far. This bound is used as it has been found to better bound the search in terms of computational time than using the quantum cost. Line 24 is the recursive call to move to the next entry in F and line 25 removes the gates generated for one alternative before iterating to consider the next.

5   Post-synthesis Circuit Simplification

Suggestions for circuit simplification were made in [5] with a hand-worked example. Here we present two procedures for circuit simplification of 3-valued circuits. The first, REDUCE, accepts an ordered list of gates $G = G_0 G_1 ... G_{ngates−1}$ and returns a modified list of gates. The following four definitions are employed.

Definition 8. *Two gates are inverses of each other if they have the same target, the same control variables and control values and either they are both D, E or N gates, or one is a C_1 gate and the other is a C_2 gate.* □

Definition 9. *Two C_k gates are* mergeable *if they have the same target, the same control variables and control values. The merge into a single gate has the given target, control variables and control values and is of type C_{3-k}.*   □

Definition 10. *Two gates G_i and G_j are* control reducible *if they are of the same type, have the same target and controls and matching control values except for one control x_k. The gates can be modified by removing x_k from G_i and setting the control value for x_k for G_j to $3 - s$ where s is the sum of the original x_k control values for the two gates. If the gates are C gates, G_j is replaced by its inverse.*   □

The commonly used rule [4] for whether two adjacent gates G_i and G_{i+1} can be interchanged is to check that the target for G_i is not a control for G_{i+1} and the target for G_{i+1} is not a control for G_i. Here we introduce a more flexible definition which permits more optimization possibilities.

Definition 11. *Two adjacent gates G_i and G_{i+1} can be* interchanged *unless:*

1. *The two gates have the same target but the gates are not both of the same type (C, D, E or N);*
2. *If G_i has type $t \in \{C, D, E, N\}$, the target of G_i is a control for G_{i+1} with control value v and $t = C$, or $t = D, E, N$ and $v \neq 0, 2, 1$ respectively; or*
3. *If G_{i+1} has type $t \in \{C, D, E, N\}$, the target of G_{i+1} is a control for G_i with control value v and $t = C$ or $t = D, E, N$ and $v \neq 0, 2, 1$ respectively.*   □

(1) in the above definition states two gates cannot be interchanged if they have the same target but potentially conflicting gate operations. (2) and (3) state two gates cannot be interchanged if the target for one gate is a control for the second gate and the target operation could affect the corresponding control value. This allows more gate movement than the simple blocking rule [4].

REDUCE, Fig. 3, implements our gate simplification strategy. It should be noted that the procedure looks for two gates G_i and G_j that could be moved to be adjacent but does not actually move them. Lines 8–9, 18–19 and 30–31 follow the removal or modification of G_i and start the reduction search over to look for simplifications that may have been previously blocked.

Our second simplification procedure, *insert_C*, Fig. 4, accepts G, an ordered list of gates and a global control value $cv = 1$ or 2, and inserts uncontrolled C_1 and C_2 gates so that all control values in the circuit will be cv. Effort is made to reduce the number of gates inserted, *i.e.* it does not insert a gate before and after every control that differs from the global value.

Post-synthesis circuit simplification used in this work involves four steps:

1. apply *reduce* to the circuit produced by the chosen synthesis method;
2. if the target is a quantum circuit, apply *insert_C* to add the required uncontrolled C gates to map all gate control values to the desired value;
3. perform any logical gate substitutions for D, E or N gates depending on which types of gate substitution have been specified for the current synthesis.
4. if step 2 and/or step 3 has been applied, apply *reduce* a second time to identify any possible reductions arising from steps 2 and 3.

```
 1: procedure REDUCE(G)
 2:     i ← 0
 3:     while i < ngates − 1 do
 4:         j ← i + 1
 5:         while j < ngates do
 6:             if G_i and G_j are inverses of each other then
 7:                 remove G_i and G_j from G
 8:                 i ← −1
 9:                 break
10:             end if
11:             if G_i are G_j are mergeable C gates then
12:                 remove G_i from G
13:                 if G_j is a C_1 then
14:                     change G_j to a C_2
15:                 else
16:                     change G_j to a C_1
17:                 end if
18:                 i ← −1
19:                 break
20:             end if
21:             if G_i and G_j are control reducible gates then
22:                 let x_k be the control difference variable
23:                 set the control value for x_k for G_j to
24:                     the value unused for control x_k
25:                     by G_i and G_j
26:                 remove x_k from the controls for G_i
27:                 if the gates are type C then
28:                     replace G_j by its inverse
29:                 end if
30:                 i ← −1
31:                 break
32:             end if
33:             if G_i and G_j cannot be interchanged then
34:                 break
35:             end if
36:             j ← j + 1
37:         end while
38:         i ← i + 1
39:     end while
40: end procedure
```

Fig. 3. Gate reduction procedure

Step 3 requires some explanation. If a D, E or N gates is logically available, *i.e.* available during synthesis, but not physically available for the final circuit, it must be substituted by other gates. Step 3 is a *logical* substitution where the gate is replaced during the simplification process at which point the substituted gates become candidates for reduction. The alternative is to do a physical gate substitution in the final quantum circuit as suggested in Definition 7.

```
 1: procedure INSERT_C(G, cv)
 2:    if cv = 1 then
 3:        p ← 2, q ← 1
 4:    else
 5:        p ← 1, q ← 2
 6:    end if
 7:    for i=0,1,...,n-1 do
 8:        aᵢ ← cv
 9:    end for
10:    i ← 0
11:    while i<ngates do
12:        if gᵢ is a D, E or N gate and aₖ ≠ cv where xₖ is
13:                        the target for Gᵢ then
14:            if aₖ=0 then
15:                insert a Cₚ[xₖ] gate before Gᵢ
16:            else
17:                insert a C_q[xₖ] gate before Gᵢ
18:            end if
19:            aₖ ← 1
20:            for each control xₖ for Gᵢ do
21:                c ← control value for xₖ in Gᵢ
22:                if c ≠ aₖ then
23:                    v = (aₖ + 2 × c)mod3
24:                    insert a C_v[xₖ] gate before Gᵢ
25:                    j ← j + 1
26:                end if
27:                set control value for xₖ for Gᵢ to cv
28:            end for
29:            j ← j + 1
30:        end if
31:    end while
32:    for i=0,1,...,n-1 do
33:        if aᵢ ≠ cv then
34:            if aᵢ=0 then
35:                append a Cₚ[xᵢ] to the end of G
36:            else
37:                append a C_q[xᵢ] to the end of G
38:            end if
39:        end if
40:    end for
41: end procedure
```

Fig. 4. Insertion of uncontrolled C gates

6   Experimental Results

We have implemented the above techniques in C using the gcc compiler with optimization level -O3. Experiments were run on a computer with an Intel i5 650 CPU @ 3.20 GHz and 3 GB of RAM.

Our first experiment generated reversible circuits for the $9! = 362,880$ 2-variable 3-valued reversible functions. Table 3 shows the results for methods 1, 2 and 3 with and without applying REDUCE. Since the target is reversible circuits, INSERT_C is not applied and gate count is used for circuit cost.

To make the results comparable to [5], D gates are used as individual gates, *i.e.* without substitution, and E gates are not used. In each case, results are shown for synthesizing the function alone and synthesizing the function and its inverse and choosing the better circuit. The table shows the average gate count and total CPU time in seconds for each scenario. The CPU time, here and for the other experiments, includes the time required to verify the circuits. The table shows that METHOD2 provides quite small improvement over METHOD1.

METHOD3 yields substantial improvement but at a high increase in computational cost. For each METHOD3 scenario, the table shows the average number of circuits examined per function which is a good indicator of where the computational cost comes from. For example, for the gate reduction using f and f^{-1} scenario, a total of 21,798,180 circuits were generated in finding solutions for the 362,880 functions an average of 60.07.

As an aside, noted by one of the referees, the METHOD1 search considering f and f^{-1} with no gate reduction took 5.31 CPU sec. whereas the same search in 2004 [3] took several CPU minutes on a then modern desktop computer. An interesting illustration of the tremendously increased computing power that is now available.

Table 3. 2-variable 3-valued functions: average gate count

Method	No gate reduction					
	f			f and f^{-1}		
	Avg. Gates	CPU Sec.	Avg. Circ. per Func.	Avg. Gates	CPU Sec.	Avg. Circ. per Func.
1	7.160	2.51		6.957	5.31	
2	7.078	12.67		6.860	25.28	
3	6.125	86.42	21.727	6.083	171.63	43.450
impr. 3 vs 1	14.46%			12.56%		
Method	Gate reduction					
	f			f and f^{-1}		
	Avg. Gates	CPU Sec.	Avg. Circ. per Func.	Avg. Gates	CPU Sec.	Avg. Circ. per Func.
1	7.077	2.67		6.855	5.51	
2	6.989	12.73		6.753	25.65	
3	5.983	103.45	30.030	5.919	209.25	60.070
impr. 3 vs 1	15.46%			13.65%		

Our second experiment again considers all 2-variable 3-valued functions. The results are shown in Table 4. Each row of the table represents a particular scenario regarding the use of D, E and N gates and choice for the global control value cv. Recall that C_1 and C_2 are assumed to be physically, and therefore logically, available in all the scenarios. In every case, the best circuit found by considering f and f^{-1} is used. The table is ordered by ascending cost for METHOD3 with $cv = 2$ which most often yields the best results.

Column Synth. identifies which of D, E and N are available during the synthesis process. As noted above, D must always be available. Column Sub. identifies what gate substitutions are performed. A 1 denotes logical substitution during the synthesis process $i.e.$ gate substitution during the circuit simplification step. A 2 denotes physical substitution in the final circuit. Results are shown for the three methods with cv, the circuit wide control value, equal 1 and 2. Each trial for METHOD1 required 5–6 CPU sec. For METHOD2 and METHOD3 the CPU usage per trial is around 35–40 s and 3–3.5 min, respectively.

As before, METHOD3 shows very significant improvement over the other methods at a rather high computational cost. It is interesting that, as one would tend to expect, the best performance (shown in bold) for all methods, except for METHOD3 with $cv = 2$, is for the scenario where D, E and N are available during synthesis with no logical or physical substitution, $i.e.$ all three gate types are available with lowest cost. For the case of METHOD3 with $cv = 2$, the best result is when only D and N are available for synthesis and direct implementation. This is reflective of the fact our methods are heuristic and even the search based method relies on heuristic choices as to which gates are best to use at each step of the synthesis.

In all cases for METHOD1 and METHOD2 a cv value of 2 leads to lower average quantum cost than does a cv value of 1. For METHOD3, there are some exceptions (shown in italics). In those cases the differences are rather small. This effect arises from the fundamental property that the transformation-based synthesis methods process the specification in a fixed order and tend to produce more gate control values of 2 than 1. Consequently, fewer uncontrolled C gates need to be inserted to map all control values in the circuit to 2 than to 1.

The results also strongly suggest that logical substitution for D, E and N is more effective than physical substitution. This is because for logical substitution, the substituted gates are considered during the circuit simplification process.

To further illustrate the effectiveness of the circuit reductions performed by procedure REDUCE, consider the best result in Table 4 – the scenario using METHOD3 with D and N gates with no gate substitution, $cv = 2$, and considering f and f^{-1}. If one turns off reductions but leaves insertion of uncontrolled C gates on, the average quantum cost rises from 7.837 to 8.771 an increase of 11.9%.

Our third experiment considers a 3-valued full adder which is an irreversible function with three inputs, here identified as x_0, x_1, x_2 and two outputs sum and $carry$. To make it reversible, requires an additional input and two additional outputs. As noted in [3], experience with a reversible binary full adder is helpful and leads to the following specification which behaves as a full adder when

$x_3 = 0$.

$$x_0^+ = sum[x_0, x_1, x_2) \quad x_1^+ = x_1 \oplus x_2 \quad x_2^+ = x_2 \quad x_3^+ = carry[x_0, x_1, x_2) \oplus x_3 \quad (6)$$

Figure 5 shows the reversible adder circuit found using METHOD1 forward synthesis with circuit reduction but no gate substitutions. This circuit has 17

Table 4. 2 variable 3-valued functions: average quantum cost

Synth.	Sub.			METHOD1		METHOD2		METHOD3	
	D	E	N	CV = 2	CV = 1	CV = 2	CV = 1	CV = 2	CV = 1
D N				9.950	11.667	9.896	11.279	**7.837**	8.488
D E N				**9.701**	**10.884**	**9.623**	**10.553**	7.963	**8.048**
D				10.193	11.995	10.143	11.617	8.057	8.684
D E				10.001	11.301	9.917	10.935	8.163	*8.154*
D N			1	10.416	12.224	10.355	11.823	8.275	8.934
D E N	1			10.386	11.713	10.307	11.404	8.327	8.730
D E N			1	10.244	11.409	10.157	11.063	8.477	*8.345*
D N			2	10.614	12.328	10.546	11.923	8.486	9.082
D E N	2			10.543	11.772	10.464	11.459	8.502	8.800
D E N			2	10.338	11.513	10.245	11.164	8.545	8.507
D E	1			10.653	11.988	10.591	11.674	8.566	8.786
D E	2			10.762	12.109	10.697	11.783	8.722	8.978
D E N	1			11.489	12.215	11.345	11.876	8.799	*8.670*
D E N		1	1	10.898	12.212	10.813	11.892	8.859	9.085
D E N	2			11.627	12.769	11.479	12.346	8.879	*8.809*
D N	1			12.208	13.355	12.086	12.975	8.887	9.237
D E N		2	1	11.003	12.326	10.916	11.996	8.977	9.251
D E N		1	2	11.075	12.289	10.982	11.968	9.045	9.185
D N	2			12.484	14.180	12.37	13.723	9.130	9.643
D E N		2	2	11.181	12.403	11.086	12.072	9.175	9.357
D E	1			12.077	13.132	11.892	12.701	9.197	*8.979*
D E N	1		1	12.211	13.072	12.071	12.755	9.285	9.475
D E N	2		1	12.350	13.626	12.204	13.227	9.386	9.640
D E	2			12.316	13.575	12.13	13.083	9.406	*9.189*
D E N	1		1	12.040	12.992	11.886	12.598	9.443	*9.135*
D E N	1	2		12.365	13.129	12.225	12.807	9.478	9.548
D E N	1		2	12.133	13.093	11.973	12.697	9.518	*9.305*
D E N	2		1	12.179	13.304	12.023	12.867	9.519	*9.219*
D E N	2	2		12.507	13.685	12.362	13.282	9.586	9.718
D E N	2		2	12.274	13.408	12.112	12.968	9.597	*9.393*

gates. D and E gates were allowed. METHOD2 finds the same circuit. Figure 6 shows the reversible adder circuit found using METHOD3 forward synthesis. This circuit has 10 gates.

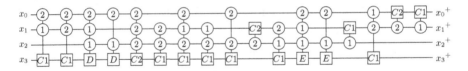

Fig. 5. METHOD1 forward synthesis: 17 gate reversible adder circuit

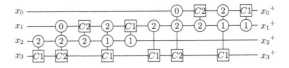

Fig. 6. METHOD3 forward synthesis: 10 gate reversible adder circuit

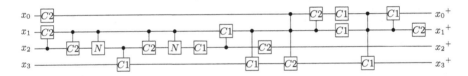

Fig. 7. METHOD3 forward synthesis with simplification: 18 gate full adder quantum circuit, cost 26, $cv = 2$

Table 5 shows our full experimental results for the full adder. Uncontrolled C gates were inserted for a global control of 2 and logical substitution of D and E gates was employed. The top half of the table shows the results for the reversible full adder and the bottom half shows the results for the inverse function. Here the new search method (METHOD3) significantly outperforms the basic transformation-based synthesis methods. Note that METHOD3 is quite quick for the full adder but takes significantly longer for the inverse case.

It is interesting to contrast the results in the top half of Table 5 to the discussion in [5] where an initial 16 gate solution was hand optimized to a circuit with 23 gates with a quantum cost of 96. that circuit contains four 3-control C gates which are quite expensive in terms of elementary quantum operations. In particular, METHOD3 forward synthesis followed by circuit simplification as described in Sect. 5 produces the circuit in Fig. 7 which has 18 gates and a quantum cost of 26. There are only two 2-control gates (shown in bold) in this circuit, the rest having 1 or 0 controls.

Table 5. Ternary full adder

Method	No E Gates			E Gates		
	Gates	Cost	CPU	Gates	Cost	CPU
Forward synthesis						
1	30	106	0.047	37	157	0.047
2	30	106	0.062	37	157	0.078
3	18	26	0.438	18	26	0.703
impr. 3 vs. 1		75.5%			83.4%	
Reverse synthesis						
1	44	180	0.063	59	289	0.078
2	44	180	0.094	59	289	0.125
3	18	34	379.8	18	34	593.7
impr. 3 vs. 1		81.1%			88.2%	

Next we consider a 5-variable function with inputs $x_4, x_3, ..., x_0$ which acts as a controlled counter. The 4-digit 3-valued number represented by x_3, x_2, x_1, x_0 is incremented by the value of x_4 and that result is taken modulo 3^4. In specifying F for this problem x_4 is treated as the most significant variable and x_0 as the least significant. The results are shown in Table 6. Note that the same circuits are found regardless of whether E gates are used. The synthesis scenario and circuit simplification used are as described for the adder.

The results are significantly better for METHOD3 compared to the other methods but once again at a high computation cost. The 11 gate quantum cost 29 circuit is shown in Fig. 8.

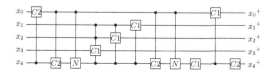

Fig. 8. METHOD3 Forward synthesis: 11 gate quantum counter circuit, cost 29, $cv = 2$

The previous two examples, the adder and counter, are arithmetic functions. It is constructive to consider a different type of example. We consider a reversible function with four inputs x_3, x_2, x_1, x_0 which rotates the order of x_2, x_1, x_0 based on the value of x_3. Specifically, the output is x_3, x_2, x_1, x_0 if $x_3 = 0$, x_3, x_1, x_0, x_2 if $x_3 = 1$, and x_3, x_0, x_2, x_1 if $x_3 = 2$.

Applying METHOD1 using N, D and E gates with D and E gate logical substitution and the simplification procedure outlined above yields a reversible circuit with 76 gates and a quantum cost of 358. Applying the same approach to the inverse function yields a circuit with 75 gates and quantum cost 358.

Table 6. Controlled counter

Method	No E Gates			E Gates		
	Gates	Cost	CPU	Gates	Cost	CPU
Forward synthesis						
1	15	137	0.03	15	137	0.05
2	15	137	0.11	15	137	0.13
3	11	29	182.17	11	29	290.64
impr. 3 vs. 1		78.8%			78.8%	
Reverse synthesis						
1	17	137	0.03	17	137	0.03
2	17	137	0.11	17	137	0.13
3	11	29	210.96	11	29	272.52
impr. 3 vs. 1		78.8%			78.8%	

The same results are found if METHOD2 is used. About 0.125 CPU seconds is required for each synthesis.

Applying METHOD3 directly to this function is problematic. Unlike the previous examples, the search takes a truly inordinate amount of time. We have implemented two changes to METHOD3 to make it a bit more reasonable for this problem: (1) A check is inserted between lines 8 and 9 to test if $F_k = k$ and if it does to accept that 0 gate case without exploring all other alternatives i.e. $j = k + 1...r^n - 1$. (2) The search is aborted if a preset circuit cost is reached.

Applying the modified METHOD3 with a cost limit of 170 to the inverse of the rotation function a circuit was found with 50 gates and quantum cost 170 – a bit less than half the cost found using METHOD1. The search took 3.8 CPU hours and considered 1,551 circuits. The question is whether this is a good result.

Consider a gate $swap[x_i, x_j]$ that interchanges the values of the two inputs and assume that controls can be applied to such a gate. This is a generalization of the well-known binary Fredkin gate [7]. Given such a gate, the input rotation function as described above can be realized as shown in (7) which can be simplified by applying control reduction to the first and third swaps, which is possible because swaps two and three can be reordered, yielding the circuit in (8).

$$swap[x_0, x_2, x_3 = 1] \, swap[x_1, x_2, x_3 = 1] \, swap[x_0, x_2, x_3 = 2] \, swap[x_0, x_1, x_3 = 2] \quad (7)$$
$$swap[x_0, x_2] \, swap[x_0, x_2, x_3 = 0] \, swap[x_1, x_2, x_3 = 1] \, swap[x_0, x_1, x_3 = 2] \quad (8)$$

Using $method3$ with quantum cost as the cost metric and without post-synthesis simplification yields the circuit in Fig. 9(a) for the uncontrolled swap of x_i and x_j. Substituting this circuit for each of the swaps in (8) with x_3 control added appropriately we find the circuit in Fig. 9(b) where the lines separate the swap gate implementations. Note that the inverse circuit has been used for the third swap so that the two D gates in red are brought together. This is possible since the swap operation is self-inverse.

Applying the circuit simplification procedures from Sect. 5 yields the circuit in Fig. 9(c). That circuit has 50 gates and quantum cost 122 which is a reduction of 28.2% from the 170 found by applying METHOD3 directly to the rotation function specification.

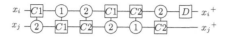

(a) METHOD3 no simplification: uncontrolled swap of x_i and x_j

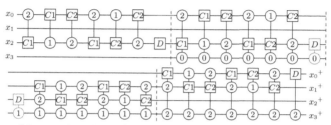

(b) reversible rotation circuit by substituting swap circuit in (a) into eqn. 8

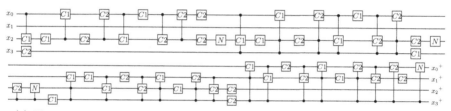

(c) 50 gate quantum rotation circuit found by simplification of the circuit in (b), quantum cost 122, $cv = 2$

Fig. 9. Rotation circuit derived from 4 swap gate circuit

7   Conclusions and Future Work

This paper has presented a novel bounded search transformation-based synthesis method as well as circuit simplification and quantum mapping procedures. The discussion of the rotation function example shows the limitation of the search based approach on its own but also the potential to use it within a broader approach using alternative gates and decomposition techniques. It is an issue for further study why METHOD3 takes so much longer for the rotation function compared to the adder and counter.

Our implementation accepts and handles F, the specification of a reversible function, in tabular form. Other researchers [9] have explored alternative more compact representations in the Boolean case. It would be interesting to consider how those approaches might be used in our search based synthesis approach.

The search based approach has been described in terms of r-valued functions, but our implementation concentrates on 3-valued functions. The procedure TRANSFORM and the circuit simplification techniques need to be extended if MVL functions with $r > 3$ are to be considered.

We have considered various circuit simplification techniques but not the optimization of the final quantum circuit after substitution of the realizations of gates with more than one control. That is an interesting area for further research.

Lastly, we have developed the new methods for the MVL case. It would be interesting to adapt them to the Boolean case, which is simpler, and see how they compare to other Boolean reversible circuit synthesis approaches.

Acknowledgement. The authors gratefully acknowledge the comments and suggestions by the reviewers, particularly the suggestion that we better clarify issues regarding quantum circuits which has led to inclusion of much broader experimental results.

References

1. Barbieri, C., Moraga, C.: A complexity analysis of the cycles-based synthesis of ternary reversible circuits. In: 13th International Workshop on Boolean Problems (2018)
2. Kole, A., Rani, P.M.N., Datta, K., Sengupta, I., Drechsler, R.: Exact synthesis of ternary reversible functions using ternary toffoli gates. In: Proceedings of the International Symposium on Multiple-Valued Logic, pp. 179–184 (2017)
3. Miller, D.M., Dueck, G.W., Maslov, D.: A synthesis method for MVL reversible logic. In: Proceedings of the International Symposium on Multiple-Valued Logic, pp. 74–80 (2004)
4. Miller, D.M., Maslov, D., Dueck, G.W.: A transformation-based algorithm for reversible logic synthesis. In: Proceedings of the IEEE/ACM Design Automation Conference (DAC), pp. 318–323 (2003)
5. Miller, D.M., Maslov, D., Dueck, G.: Synthesis of quantum multiple-valued circuits. J. Multiple-Valued Logic Soft Comput. **12**(5–6), 431–450 (2006)
6. Muthukrishnan, A., Stroud, C.R.: Multivalued logic gates for quantum computation. Phys. Rev. A **62**, 052309 (2000)
7. Nielsen, M., Chuang, I.: Quantum Computation and Quantum Information. Cambridge University Press, Cambridge (2000)
8. Resch, S., Karpuzcu, U.R.: Quantum computing: An overview across the system stack. arXiv:1905.07240v3 [quant-ph] (2019)
9. Soeken, M., Dueck, G.W., Rahman, M.M., Miller, D.M.: An extension of transformation-based reversible and quantum circuit synthesis. In: Proceedings of the International Symposium on Circuits and Systems, pp. 2290–2293 (2016)
10. Töormä, P.: Realizations of quantum computing using optical manipulations of atoms. Nat. Comput. **1**, 199–209 (2002)

Tools and Applications

ReverCSP: Time-Travelling in CSP Computations

Carlos Galindo[1] , Naoki Nishida[2] , Josep Silva[1(✉)] ,
and Salvador Tamarit[1]

[1] Departament de Sistemes Informàtics i Computació, Universitat Politècnica de
València, Camino de Vera sn, 46022 Valencia, Spain
jsilva@dsic.upv.es
[2] Graduate School of Informatics, Nagoya University, Furo-cho, Chikusa-ku,
Nagoya 464-8603, Japan

Abstract. This paper presents *reverCSP*, a tool to animate both forward and backward CSP computations. This ability to reverse computations can be done step by step or backtracking to a given desired state of interest. *reverCSP* allows us to reverse computations exactly in the same order in which they happened, or also in a causally-consistent way. Therefore, *reverCSP* is a tool that can be especially useful to comprehend, analyze, and debug computations. *reverCSP* is an open-source project publicly available for the community. We describe the tool and its functionality, and we provide implementation details so that it can be reimplemented for other languages.

Keywords: Reversible computations · CSP · Tracing

1 Introduction

The Communicating Sequential Processes (CSP) is nowadays one of the must used process algebras [16]. The analysis of CSP computations has traditionally been based on the so-called *CSP traces*. Roughly, CSP traces are a representation to specify all possible computations that may occur in a system, and they are represented with sequences of events. Among the different analyses defined over traces we have security analysis [6], livelock analysis [3], and deadlock analysis [7,17].

Unfortunately, CSP traces are not very appropriate for debugging because they do not relate the computations with the source code. For this reason, a data structure called CSP track [12] was defined to overcome that problem. CSP tracks were originally conceived for program comprehension and debugging because they can represent forward CSP computations with the advantage that every single step of the operational semantics is associated with the positions in the source code (i.e., initial and final line and column) of the literals of the specification participating in that step. This means that, with a CSP track, one can see directly in the source code the parts that are being executed.

© Springer Nature Switzerland AG 2020
I. Lanese and M. Rawski (Eds.): RC 2020, LNCS 12227, pp. 239–245, 2020.
https://doi.org/10.1007/978-3-030-52482-1_14

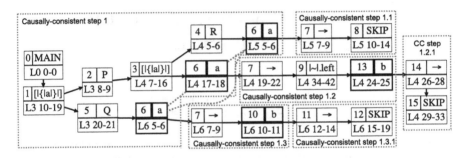

Fig. 1. Extended track of the computation produced by the trace ⟨abb⟩ in *reverCSP*.

Example 1. Consider the following CSP specification:[1]

```
channel a,b

MAIN = P  ||  Q
          {a}

P = R  ||  a → (b → SKIP ⊓ Q)
      {a}

R = a → SKIP

Q = a → b → SKIP
```

The only possible traces of this specification are: $\{\langle\rangle, \langle a\rangle, \langle ab\rangle, \langle abb\rangle\}$

If we consider the trace ⟨abb⟩, it can be produced by two different computations due to the non-deterministic evaluation order of the processes. While the first event (a) is deterministic, the b events are not (they could correspond to either process P or Q). Therefore, a trace ⟨abb⟩ does not give information about what parts of the computation have been executed and in what order.

In contrast, if we observe the track in Fig. 1, we can see that it represents the source code literals inside nodes (at the top right); each node is labelled with its associated timestamp (at the top left) and they contain pairs line-column to uniquely identify the literals in the CSP specification. Synchronizations are represented with a dashed edge. For the time being the reader can ignore the green text and lines.

In this paper we present a new tool called *reverCSP* that uses an extension of CSP tracks to animate and reverse computations. We explain how to download and install the tool, and we explain its functionality and architecture.

---

[1] Those readers non familiar with the CSP syntax are referred to [16], where all CSP syntax constructs are explained.

2   Recording the History of a CSP Computation

According to the Landauer's embedding principle [8] a record of a computation can make that computation reversible. In order to record CSP computations we have defined an extension of CSP tracks [12] so that they also store the exact time when each literal in the track was executed. This gives us the ability to know exactly in what order where the literals executed and, thus, to reverse computations. Observe in Fig. 1 that each node has a label with a timestamp that represents the instant where this node was generated. Therefore, synchronized events have the same timestamp.

With the timestamp we can serialize the program. For instance, if we only focus on event nodes (those in bold) then it is trivial to generate the associated trace ⟨abb⟩ following the sequence: $(6,a) \rightarrow (10,b) \rightarrow (13,b)$. Timestamps together with synchronizations also allow us to define a causally-consistent relation between nodes. This relation allows us to perform (forward and backward) causally-consistent steps. These steps group a set of nodes that must happen before a given action (a visible event or the end of the computation represented with SKIP or STOP) and after another action that already happened.

Example 2. Consider again the track in Fig. 1. Those nodes that belong to the same causally-consistent step have been grouped inside an area marked with a dotted green line. The causal relation is represented by the identifier of the causally-consistent steps. Step X.Y cannot be undone until any suffix of X.Y has been undone. This means that steps 1.1, 1.2, and 1.3 must be undone (in any order) before undoing step 1. Similarly, step 1.2.1 must be undone before undoing step 1.2. Steps 1.2.1 and 1.3.1 can be undone in any order. All this information is automatically computed by *reverCSP* and used to control that steps are (un)done (and offered to the user) in the correct order.

3   The System *reverCSP*

3.1   Downloading and Installation

The *reverCSP* system is open-source and free. It can be downloaded from: https://github.com/tamarit/reverCSP. The system can be run either on Linux or in a Docker container. The later is the simplest, as the user only needs to install docker and run the following commands:

```
$ git clone --recursive https://github.com/tamarit/reverCSP
$ docker build -t reverCSP .
$ docker run -it -v $PWD/examples:/reverCSP/examples \
    -v $PWD/output:/reverCSP/output --rm reverCSP
```

Then, from within the shell inside the docker container, the user can run the script reverCSP, accompanied by the path to a CSP specification file, as can be seen in Fig. 2. The two volumes exposed to docker (the -v option) allow

```
$ ./reverCSP examples/rc2020.csp        Current expression:
[...]                                   MAIN
Current expression:                      | MAIN
MAIN                                    (P [|{|a|}|] Q)
                                         | Q
These are the available options:       (P [|{|a|}|] a->b->SKIP)
1 .- MAIN                                | P
2 .- Random choice.                    (R [|{|a|}|] a->(b->SKIP |~| Q) [|{|a|}|] a->b->SKIP)
3 .- Random forward-reverse choice.      | Reverse evaluation
4 .- See current trace.                  | Q
5 .- Print current track.              (R [|{|a|}|] a->(b->SKIP |~| Q) [|{|a|}|] Q)
6 .- Reverse evaluation.                 | P
7 .- Undo.                             (P [||a||] Q)
8 .- Roll back.
0 .- Finish evaluation.
What do you want to do?
[1/2/3/4/5/6/7/8/0]: 1
```

Fig. 2. Main menu (left) and a series of user actions and the resulting states (right). (Color figure online)

the user to view the generated PDF files in the output folder and to add new specifications to be analyzed.

The system uses the Erlang/OTP framework[2] to animate CSP specifications, and it (optionally) uses Graphviz[3] to produce PDF outputs of the tracks. Otherwise, only DOT files will be produced. Both systems are also freely available under open-source licenses.

3.2 Main Functionality

reverCSP implements in Erlang a reversible CSP interpreter with two phases:

Generation of tracks. Tracks can be generated using a random number of steps (a random execution) or following the computation steps defined by the user (user-directed execution). This means that, at any point of the computation, the user can choose how to proceed and the associated track is dynamically generated. For instance, a user can perform, say, 50 random steps, then go backward, say 20 steps, and then go forward again but selecting a different rule to be applied. Thus, a different computation (and track) is produced.

Exploration of tracks. Provided that we have a track generated, it can be traversed backward. The traversal is done with computation steps that can be deterministic (using the Undo option) or causally-consistent (using the Reverse evaluation option). After each step, the system shows the current expression and it gives the option to output the trace and the track. Figure 2 shows the menu displayed during a computation (left), followed by the computation steps selected by the user (right). The states reached are in black, the user actions are in blue and the changes in the state produced by the last action selected are in red.

---

[2] https://www.erlang.org/.

[3] https://www.graphviz.org/.

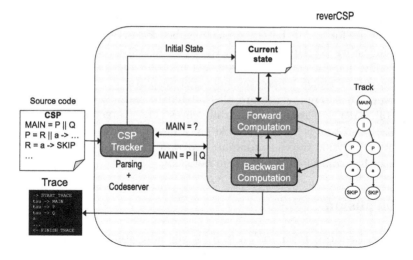

Fig. 3. *reverCSP* architecture.

3.3   Architecture and Implementation Details

Figure 3 shows the architecture of *reverCSP*. The source code is parsed by module CSP tracker to produce an initial state (of the operational semantics). This state is used by module Forward Computation to perform a forward step and generate the associated track. If we want to reverse the computation, then module Backward Computation can update the state with the information of the track. When required, module CSP tracker serves the parsed code to the other modules and performs semantic steps from a given state. The interface interacts with the user and continuously displays the trace of the computation.

4   Related Work

There exist different works that propose techniques for rollback-recovery [5] and for reversibility in sequential systems [15] and concurrent systems [11]. Our system, *reverCSP*, is a replay debugger that uses tracks to record the execution. In the core of our tool we use a library called CSP-tracker [13] that can be invoked to produce tracks. One interesting tool that is related to our work is CauDEr [10]. It can also causal-consistently reverse computations, but in this case for Erlang and using a different notion of track. The idea of reversing computations in a causally-consistent manner was introduced in [4] for CCS. Since then, different approaches have emerged. A survey that very nicely describes some of those approaches is [9].

There are other systems such as [1,2] and [11] that are somehow related to our tool. The work in [1] proposes a modular framework that can be used to define causal-consistent reversible extensions of different concurrent models and languages. The extension of tracks that we defined was inspired by that work.

Another interesting work that also proposes a tool that can reverse computations, this time for a CSP-based language embedded in Scala, was presented by Brown and Sabry [2]. Unfortunately, the implementation is not publicly available. Finally, Lanese et al. [11] proposed a novel approach called *controlled causal-consistent replay* where the debugger displays all and only the causes of an error. These approaches are also related to causally-consistent dynamic slicing [14], but there are important differences: They target pi calculus and we target CSP. Our tool is based on tracks to reverse computations, while dynamic slicing uses execution traces to compute program slices that contain the parts of the source that could influence a given behavior.

5   Conclusions

This paper described *reverCSP*, a tool for the animation and analysis of CSP specifications. On the practical side, *reverCSP* can be seen as a CSP animator with the ability to replay and reverse computations. This ability is provided by the fact that *reverCSP* records every execution step of the computation in a graph-like data structure called track.

We have extended the original definition of track to incorporate timestamps that make explicit the order in which the components of the specification were executed; and this order allows us to reverse the computation. *reverCSP* implements different functionalities such as step-by-step forward and backward execution, random (multiple) steps, undo, and rollback. Besides, it allows to perform both deterministic and causally-consistent reversible steps.

Because *reverCSP* (re)generates the corresponding part of the track with every computation step, the complete track is available to perform different post-mortem analyses. One of them is program slicing, which was already implemented in a tool called CSP-tracker. As future work we plan to adapt our analyses to also implement a causally-consistent dynamic program slicer based on tracks for CSP.

Acknowledgements. This work has been partially supported by the EU (FEDER) and the Spanish MCI/AEI under grants TIN2016-76843-C4-1-R and PID2019-104735RB-C41, and by the *Generalitat Valenciana* under grant Prometeo/2019/098 (DeepTrust).

References

1. Bernadet, A., Lanese, I.: A modular formalization of reversibility for concurrent models and languages. In: Proceedings of ICE 2016, EPTCS (2016)
2. Brown, G., Sabry, A.: Reversible communicating processes. Electron. Proc. Theor. Comput. Sci. **203**, 45–59 (2016)
3. Conserva Filhoa, M., Oliveira, M., Sampaio, A., Cavalcanti, A.: Compositional and local livelock analysis for CSP. Inf. Process. Lett **133**, 21–25 (2018)

4. Danos, V., Krivine, J.: Reversible communicating systems. In: Gardner, P., Yoshida, N. (eds.) CONCUR 2004. LNCS, vol. 3170, pp. 292–307. Springer, Heidelberg (2004). https://doi.org/10.1007/978-3-540-28644-8_19

5. Elnozahy, E.N.M., Alvisi, L., Wang, Y.-M., Johnson, D.B.: A survey of rollback-recovery protocols in message-passing systems. ACM Comput. Surv. **34**(3), 375–408 (2002)

6. Fang, Y., Zhu, H., Zeyda, F., Fei, Y.: Modeling and analysis of the disruptor framework in csp. In: Proceedings of CCWC 2018. IEEE Computer Society (2018)

7. Ladkin, P.B., Simons, B.B.: Static deadlock analysis for CSP-type communications. In: Fussell, D.S., Malek, M. (eds.) Responsive Computer Systems: Steps Toward Fault-Tolerant Real-Time Systems. The Springer International Series in Engineering and Computer Science, vol. 297, pp. 89–102. Springer, Boston (1995). https://doi.org/10.1007/978-1-4615-2271-3_5

8. Landauer, R.: Irreversibility and heat generation in the computing process. IBM J. Res. Dev. **5**, 183–191 (1961)

9. Lanese, I., Antares Mezzina, C., Tiezzi, F.: Causal-consistent reversibility. Bull. EATCS **114**, 17 (2014)

10. Lanese, I., Nishida, N., Palacios, A., Vidal, G.: CauDEr: a causal-consistent reversible debugger for erlang. In: Gallagher, J.P., Sulzmann, M. (eds.) FLOPS 2018. LNCS, vol. 10818, pp. 247–263. Springer, Cham (2018). https://doi.org/10.1007/978-3-319-90686-7_16

11. Lanese, I., Palacios, A., Vidal, G.: Causal-consistent replay debugging for message passing programs. In: Pérez, J.A., Yoshida, N. (eds.) FORTE 2019. LNCS, vol. 11535, pp. 167–184. Springer, Cham (2019). https://doi.org/10.1007/978-3-030-21759-4_10

12. Llorens, M., Oliver, J., Silva, J., Tamarit, S.: Dynamic slicing of concurrent specification languages. Parallel Comput. **53**, 1–22 (2016)

13. Llorens, M., Oliver, J., Silva, J., Tamarit, S.: Tracking CSP computations. J. Log. Algebr. Meth. Program. **102**, 138–175 (2019)

14. Perera, R., Garg, D., Cheney, J.: Causally consistent dynamic slicing. In Proceedings of CONCUR 2016, LIPIcs, vol. 59, pp. 18:1–18:15 (2016)

15. Phillips, I., Ulidowski, I., Yuen, S.: A reversible process calculus and the modelling of the ERK signalling pathway. In: Glück, R., Yokoyama, T. (eds.) RC 2012. LNCS, vol. 7581, pp. 218–232. Springer, Heidelberg (2013). https://doi.org/10.1007/978-3-642-36315-3_18

16. Roscoe, A.W.: The Theory and Practice of Concurrency. Prentice Hall PTR, Upper Saddle River (1997)

17. Zhao, H., Zhu, H., Yucheng, F., Xiao, L.: Modeling and verifying storm using CSP. In: Proceedings of HASE 2019. IEEE Computer Society (2019)

Reversible Computations in Logic Programming

Germán Vidal[✉]

MiST, VRAIN, Universitat Politècnica de València, Valencia, Spain
gvidal@dsic.upv.es

Abstract. In this work, we say that a computation is *reversible* if one can find a procedure to undo the steps of a standard (or forward) computation in a deterministic way. While logic programs are often *invertible* (e.g., one can use the same predicate for adding and for subtracting natural numbers), computations are not reversible in the above sense. In this paper, we present a so-called *Landauer embedding* for SLD resolution, the operational principle of logic programs, so that it becomes reversible. A proof-of-concept implementation of a reversible debugger for Prolog that follows the ideas in this paper has been developed and is publicly available.

1 Introduction

In this work, we say that a semantics is *reversible* if there exists a deterministic procedure to undo the steps of any computation (often called *backward determinism*). The ability to explore the steps of a computation back and forth is particularly useful in the context of program debugging, as witnessed by several previous tools like Undo [8], rr [6] or CauDEr [4], to name a few.

In this paper, we present a reversible version of SLD resolution [5], the operational semantics of logic programs, that may constitute the basis of a reversible debugger for Prolog. As is well known, logic programming is already *invertible*, i.e., one can exchange the input and output arguments of a predicate so that, e.g., the same predicate is used both for addition and for subtraction of natural numbers. However, SLD resolution is in principle irreversible according to the definition above. Nevertheless, given an irreversible semantics, one can always define an instrumented version which is reversible (this process is often called *reversibilization*) by defining an appropriate Landauer embedding [3], i.e., by adding a "history" to each state with enough information to undo the steps of a computation. However, defining a non-trivial Landauer embedding for SLD resolution is particularly challenging due to *non-determinism* and *unification*.

This work is partially supported by the EU (FEDER) and the Spanish MCI/AEI under grants TIN2016-76843-C4-1-R/PID2019-104735RB-C41, by the *Generalitat Valenciana* under grant Prometeo/2019/098 (DeepTrust), and by the COST Action IC1405 on Reversible Computation - extending horizons of computing.

I. Lanese and M. Rawski (Eds.): RC 2020, LNCS 12227, pp. 246–254, 2020.
https://doi.org/10.1007/978-3-030-52482-1_15

Let us first briefly recall some basic notions from logic programming (see, e.g., [1,5] for more details). A *query* is a finite conjunction of atoms which is denoted by a sequence of the form $A_1, \dots, A_n$, where the *empty query* is denoted by *true*. A *clause* has the form $H \leftarrow B_1, \dots, B_n$, where H (the *head*) and $B_1, \dots, B_n$ (the *body*) are atoms, $n \geq 0$ (thus we only consider *definite* logic programs, i.e., logic programs without negated atoms in the body of the clauses). Clauses with an empty body, $H \leftarrow true$, are called *facts*, and are typically denoted by H.

In the following, atoms are ranged over by $A, B, C, H, \dots$ while queries (possibly empty sequences of atoms) are ranged over by $\mathcal{A}, \mathcal{B}, \dots$ Substitutions and their operations are defined as usual; they are ranged over by $\sigma, \theta, \dots$ In particular, the application of a substitution θ to a syntactic object o is denoted by juxtaposition, i.e., we write $o\theta$ rather than $\theta(o)$. We denote by $\sigma \circ \theta$ the composition of substitutions σ and θ. Moreover, *id* denotes the identity substitution A *variable renaming* is a substitution that is a bijection on the domain of variables. A substitution θ is a unifier of two atoms A and B iff $A\theta = B\theta$; furthermore, θ is the *most general unifier* of A and B, denoted by $\mathsf{mgu}(A, B)$ if, for every other unifier σ of A and B, we have that θ is more general than σ.

A logic *program* is a finite sequence of clauses. Given a program P, we say that $A, \mathcal{B}' \leadsto_{P,\sigma} (\mathcal{B}, \mathcal{B}')\sigma$ is an *SLD resolution step*[1] if $H \leftarrow \mathcal{B}$ is a renamed apart clause (i.e., with fresh variables) of program P, in symbols, $H \leftarrow \mathcal{B} \ll P$, and $\sigma = \mathsf{mgu}(A, H)$. The subscript P will often be omitted when the program is clear from the context. An *SLD derivation* is a (finite or infinite) sequence of SLD resolution steps. A *terminating* SLD derivation can be either *successful*, if it ends with the query *true*, or *failed*, if it ends in a query where the leftmost atom does not unify with the head of any clause. SLD derivations are represented by a (possibly infinite) finitely branching tree, which is called *SLD tree*, where *choice points* (queries with more than one child) correspond to queries where the leftmost atom unifies with the head of more than one program clause.

Consider, for instance, the following simple logic program:

$$p(b, b, Y) \leftarrow q(Y), r(Y, Y).$$
$$q(b).$$
$$r(b, b).$$

Given the query $p(X, b, b), r(b, X)$, we have the following SLD derivation:

$$p(X, b, b), r(b, X) \leadsto_\theta q(b), r(b, b), r(b, b) \leadsto r(b, b), r(b, b) \leadsto \dots$$

with $\theta = \{X/b, Y/b\}$. In order to undo, e.g., the first step in this derivation, we face several problems:

– First, one needs to know the applied rule, since there exist several possibilities; for instance, one can always consider undoing the application of a fact by

---

[1] In this paper, we only consider Prolog's *computation rule*, so that the selected atom in a query is always the leftmost one.

adding a call to this predicate to the left of the current query. E.g., one could go backwards from $q(b), r(b, b), r(b, b)$ to $q(b), q(b), r(b, b), r(b, b)$, which is not the desired backward step.

- Second, we need to "unapply" the computed substitution in this step (which is applied to all the atoms of the query). Unfortunately, there is no deterministic way to do that. E.g., given the last atom $r(b, b)$ in the second query, we can undo the application of θ and get $r(b, X)$ but also $r(X, b)$ or $r(X, X)$.
- Finally, we have no deterministic way to obtain the selected call in the previous goal, even if we know the applied rule and the computed unifier (this is also related to the previous point and the fact that there is no deterministic way to undo the application of a substitution).

Of course, one could define a *trivial* Landauer embedding where all queries in a derivation are stored, e.g.,

$$\langle p(X, b, b), r(b, X); [\,] \rangle \rightsquigarrow_\theta \langle q(b), r(b, b), r(b, b); [p(X, b, b), r(b, X)] \rangle$$
$$\rightsquigarrow \langle r(b, b), r(b, b); [q(b), r(b, b), r(b, b); p(X, b, b), r(b, X)] \rangle$$
$$\rightsquigarrow \ldots$$

but the overhead would be very high since we would need to store the entire derivation. In the next section, we present a more efficient approach.

2 A Reversible Semantics for Logic Programs

In this section, we present a reversible version of SLD resolution. In principle, in order to avoid the nondeterminism when undoing the application of a substitution, one could consider some non-standard queries where computed substitutions (mgu's) are not applied to the atoms of the query but stored in a list. For instance, one could redefine SLD resolution as follows:

$$\langle A, \mathcal{B}'; [\theta_n, \ldots, \theta_1] \rangle \rightsquigarrow_{P, \theta_{n+1}} \langle \mathcal{B}, \mathcal{B}'; [\theta_{n+1}, \theta_n, \ldots, \theta_1] \rangle$$

if $H \leftarrow \mathcal{B} \ll P$ and $\mathsf{mgu}(A\theta_1 \ldots \theta_n, H) = \theta_{n+1}$. An initial query $\mathcal{A}$ would now have the form $\langle \mathcal{A}; [\,] \rangle$. Of course, this definition introduces some additional (possibly unavoidable) overhead since the computed substitutions must be composed and applied at each resolution step.

However, this is not enough to make SLD resolution reversible. Additionally, one would also need to store the selected call of the previous query, since it cannot be obtained even if we know the applied rule and keep the computed substitutions in a list. Furthermore, we need to know how many (leftmost) atoms should be discarded when performing a backward step (i.e., we need to store the number of atoms in the body of the applied clause).

In summary, we define our (forward) reversible SLD resolution semantics (denoted by $\rightarrow$) as shown in Fig. 1, where the auxiliary function subst is used to compute the (partial) answer computed so far from the current history (this notion is formalized below). In this semantics, *reversible* queries have the form $\langle \mathcal{B}; \mathcal{H} \rangle$, where $\mathcal{B}$ is a standard query (a sequence of atoms) and $\mathcal{H}$, the *history*, is a list of elements of the form $\mathsf{fail}(\mathcal{A})$ or $\mathsf{unf}(A, H, m)$. The first one, $\mathsf{fail}(\mathcal{A})$, is used to denote that $\mathcal{A}$ is the last query of a failing derivation (i.e., the leftmost atom in $\mathcal{A}$ unifies with the head of no clause). The second one, $\mathsf{unf}(A, H, m)$, is used for unfolding steps, where A is the selected call of the query (the leftmost atom), H is the head of the applied clause, and m is the number of atoms in the body of this clause. This is enough to make SLD resolution reversible.

It is worthwhile to note that we have chosen to store elements of the form $\mathsf{unf}(A, H, m)$ instead of $\mathsf{unf}(A, \theta, m)$ as observed above. This decision might introduce some additional overhead since we should not only compose and apply the computed substitutions at each step, but we must also recompute the mgu's of all considered pairs of atoms (A, H) once per forward step. Nevertheless, storing pairs (A, H) instead of the corresponding mgu's is rather convenient since we do not need to implement (expensive) operations like substitution composition and application, but rely on Prolog's native unification and propagation of variable bindings. There are, however, several possible optimizations that can be applied to improve performance, like storing mgu's as lists of pairs *Variable = value* (as suggested by one of the reviewers of this paper). This is left as future work.

In the following, we use Haskell's notation for lists so that $E : \mathcal{H}$ denotes a history where E is the first element and $\mathcal{H}$ contains the remaining elements of the list; the empty history is denoted by an empty list $[\,]$. Moreover, we also use Haskell's list concatenation operator, $++$, so that $\mathcal{H}++[E]$ denotes a history that begins with the elements of list $\mathcal{H}$ and ends with element E.

(success)	$\dfrac{\mathsf{subst}(\mathcal{H}) = \sigma}{\langle \mathsf{true}; \mathcal{H} \rangle \rightharpoonup \langle \mathrm{SUCCESS}(\sigma); \mathcal{H} \rangle}$
(failure)	$\dfrac{\mathsf{subst}(\mathcal{H}) = \sigma \wedge \; \not\exists H \leftarrow B_1, \ldots, B_m \ll P \text{ such that } \mathsf{mgu}(A\sigma, H) \neq \mathsf{fail}}{\langle A, \mathcal{B}; \mathcal{H} \rangle \rightharpoonup \langle \mathrm{FAIL}; \mathsf{fail}(A, \mathcal{B}) : \mathcal{H} \rangle}$
(unfold)	$\dfrac{\mathsf{subst}(\mathcal{H}) = \sigma \wedge \exists H \leftarrow B_1, \ldots, B_m \ll P \text{ such that } \mathsf{mgu}(A\sigma, H) \neq \mathsf{fail}}{\langle A, \mathcal{B}; \mathcal{H} \rangle \rightharpoonup \langle B_1, \ldots, B_m, \mathcal{B}; \mathsf{unf}(A, H, m) : \mathcal{H} \rangle}$

Fig. 1. Reversible SLD resolution: forward semantics.

Let us briefly explain the rules of the reversible forward semantics in Fig. 1:

- Rule success is used to denote the end of a successful derivation. Here, σ denotes the computed answer substitution of the derivation (typically restricted to the variables of the initial goal), where the auxiliary function subst is defined as follows:

$$\mathsf{subst}(\mathcal{H}) = \begin{cases} \mathsf{mgu}(A, H) \circ \mathsf{subst}(\mathcal{H}') & \text{if } \mathcal{H} = \mathcal{H}'++[\mathsf{unf}(A, H, m)] \\ id & \text{if } \mathcal{H} = [\,] \end{cases}$$

Intuitively speaking, subst($\mathcal{H}$) computes the substitution encoded by the elements in $\mathcal{H}$. In this rule, we add nothing to the current history since the step is trivially reversible.

- Rule failure is used to denote the end of a failing derivation. Essentially, a query fails when the (instantiated) leftmost atom, $A\sigma$, does not unify with the head of any program clause, where σ is the substitution encoded by the current history. In this case, we store an element fail($A, \mathcal{B}$) since the current goal is needed to undo the step.

- Finally, rule unfold performs an unfolding step. In this case, we add an element unf(A, H, m) to the history, where A is the selected atom (the leftmost atom of the query), H is the head of the considered (renamed apart) clause, and m is the number of atoms in the body of this clause.

Consider again the program from Sect. 1 and the initial query $p(X, b, b), r(b, X)$. An (incomplete) reversible SLD derivation is then as follows:

$$\langle p(X, b, b), r(b, X); [\,]\rangle$$
$$\rightharpoonup \ \langle q(Y), r(Y, Y), r(b, X); [\mathsf{unf}(p(X, b, b), p(b, b, Y), 2)]\rangle$$
$$\rightharpoonup \ \langle r(Y, Y), r(b, X); [\mathsf{unf}(q(Y), q(b), 0), \mathsf{unf}(p(X, b, b), p(b, b, Y), 2)]\rangle$$

Now, we have enough information in each query in order to deterministically undo a step. The corresponding backward semantics (denoted by $\leftharpoonup$) is shown in Fig. 2, where each forward rule (e.g., unfold) has a counterpart in the backward semantics (e.g., $\overline{\mathsf{unfold}}$). The rules are self-explanatory. Note that H is not needed in rule $\overline{\mathsf{unfold}}$; it was only stored in order to be able to compute the mgu's of the derivation for the next steps of the forward computation.

($\overline{\mathsf{success}}$) $\langle \mathrm{SUCCESS}(\sigma); \mathcal{H}\rangle \ \leftharpoonup \ \langle \mathsf{true}; \mathcal{H}\rangle$

($\overline{\mathsf{failure}}$) $\langle \mathrm{FAIL}; \mathsf{fail}(A, \mathcal{B}) : \mathcal{H}\rangle \ \leftharpoonup \ \langle A, \mathcal{B}; \mathcal{H}\rangle$

($\overline{\mathsf{unfold}}$) $\langle B_1, \ldots, B_m, \mathcal{B}; \mathsf{unf}(A, H, m) : \mathcal{H}\rangle \ \leftharpoonup \ \langle A, \mathcal{B}; \mathcal{H}\rangle$

Fig. 2. Reversible SLD resolution: backward semantics.

We note that extending our developments to SLD resolution with an arbitrary computation rule (i.e., different from Prolog's rule, which always selects the leftmost atom) is not difficult. Basically, one only needs to extend the unf elements as follows: unf(A, H, i, m), where i is the position of the selected atom, and m is the number of atoms in the body of the applied clause (as before).

The following result states the correctness of our reversible semantics (it can be proved by a simple induction on the length of the considered derivation):

Theorem 1. *Let P be a logic program and $\mathcal{A}$ a query. Given a forward deriva-tion $\langle \mathcal{A}_1, \mathcal{H}_1 \rangle \rightharpoonup \ldots \rightharpoonup \langle \mathcal{A}_n, \mathcal{H}_n \rangle$, there exists a unique (deterministic) backward derivation of the form $\langle \mathcal{A}_n, \mathcal{H}_n \rangle \leftharpoondown \ldots \leftharpoondown \langle \mathcal{A}_1, \mathcal{H}_1 \rangle$. Moreover, both derivations perform exactly the same number of steps.*

For instance, given the previous (incomplete) forward derivation, we can produce the following backward derivation:

$$\langle r(Y,Y), r(b,X); [\mathsf{unf}(q(Y), q(b), 0), \mathsf{unf}(p(X,b,b), p(b,b,Y), 2)] \rangle$$
$$\leftharpoondown \langle q(Y), r(Y,Y), r(b,X); [\mathsf{unf}(p(X,b,b), p(b,b,Y), 2)] \rangle$$
$$\leftharpoondown \langle p(X,b,b), r(b,X); [\,] \rangle$$

3   Discussion

To the best of our knowledge, no other reversible debugger for Prolog has been defined. Typical Prolog debuggers are based on the so called "box model", where every predicate call or atom, A, has four associated events: call, the initial call to A; exit, when unification of A with the head of a program clause succeeds; redo, when A is tried again after backtracking; and fail, when A does not unify with any other head clause. Typically, debuggers can only proceed forward in the computation or redo the current goal. The closer approach we are aware of is that of Opium [2], which introduces a trace query language for inspecting and analyzing trace histories. In this tool, the trace history of the considered execution is stored in a database, which is then used for trace querying. Several analysis can then be defined in Prolog itself by using a set of given primitives to explore the trace elements.

A proof-of-concept implementation of a Prolog reversible debugger that fol-lows the ideas in this paper has been developed. It is publicly available from https://github.com/mistupv/Prolog-reversible-debugger. The main features of our debugger are the following:

- It implements both the (nondeterministic) forward semantics and the (deter-ministic) backward semantics presented in the previous section. Some addi-tional extensions include dealing with built-in's, using colors and other visual improvements, etc. Essentially, the debugger shows a trace including every call and whether it succeeds (exit) or fails. Calls that unify with the head of more than one clause (*choice points*) are distinguished in bold. In contrast to traditional Prolog debuggers, we show the entire goal and underline the selected atom, rather than showing only the selected atom.
- The SLD tree of a query can be explored step by step using the cursor arrows: down (next step), up (previous step), left/right (considering alter-native clauses for choice points). When a derivation ends with failure, press-ing the down arrow will jump to the next pending choice (backtracking). In particular, we follow Prolog's *search strategy*, where clauses are considered in their textual order (from top to bottom) and the SLD tree is explored using

a depth-first strategy with backtracking (despite the fact that this strategy is incomplete [1]). However, the debugger cannot undo a backtracking step. If we press the up arrow after a backtracking step jumps to the next alternative of a choice point, the debugger will show the previous goal in this derivation (the parent of this node) rather than the failing leaf that caused backtracking. This was a design decision to ease the exploration of a given computation (following the ideas in this paper). Finally, if a derivation ends with an empty query (a successful derivation), the computed answer is shown. Alternative derivations (if any) can be explored by typing ";" (as in Prolog).

– We have also implemented a "continuous" mode (pressing "s", a shorthand for "skip"), where the entire trace up to a leaf of the SLD tree (either a failure or a success) is shown.

Consider, for instance, the following example:

```
p(X,Y)  :- q(X),  r(X,Y).
q(a).
q(f(X))  :- X is 2+1.
q(c).
r(f(X),f(X)).
```

where the built-in is/2 evaluates the expression in the second argument and unifies it with the first argument. A typical session looks as follows:

```
Call : p(A, B)
Exit : p(A, B)          [↓]
Call : q(A), r(A, B)
Exit : q(a), r(a, A)    [↓]
Call : r(a, A)
Fail : r(a, A)
```

so our first derivation is a failing one. Now, if we press the up arrow once, we get back to

```
Call : p(A, B)
Exit : p(A, B)
Call : q(A), r(A, B)
Exit : q(a), r(a, A)
```

and we can consider the next choice (pressing the right arrow), ending up with the following successful derivation:

```
Call : p(A, B)
Exit : p(A, B)                                    [↓]
Call : q(A), r(A, B)
Exit : q(f(A)), r(f(A), B)                        [↓]
Call : A is 2 + 1, r(f(A), B)
Exit : 3 is 2 + 1, r(f(3), A)                     [↓]
Call : r(f(3), A)
Exit : r(f(3), f(3))
**Solution [p(A,B)]:A = f(3), B = f(3)
```

Our reversible debugger can be a useful tool both for program understanding and for locating the source of a misbehaviour.

The development of a reversible debugger is an ongoing work, so several extensions are planned. In particular, we would like to consider more Prolog features (e.g., deal with exceptions, so that one can explore a computation backwards from a runtime error) as well as introducing a technique for *record and replay*. Often, one is not interested in exploring all the SLD tree but just a single root-to-leaf derivation (the one that led to the misbehaviour). Here, being able to produce a log of the considered computation and use this log to replay only this particular derivation in our reversible debugger might be useful.

As for the overhead, we consider several possibilities: first, we can consider a more efficient representation by storing pairs *Variable = value* instead of atoms, as discussed in Sect. 2; moreover, we could *simplify* the stored unification problems (the pairs A, H) when they cannot affect the current query (e.g., when they are ground or the bindings do not affect to other atoms); also, one might consider the introduction of "spy points" (as in the standard debugger for Prolog) so that the reversible mode is restricted to some computations rather than the entire SLD tree. Finally, we also plan to explore the definition of a reversible *linear* semantics for Prolog, analogous to that of [7]. This approach might be useful to undo backtracking steps.

Acknowledgements. The author gratefully acknowledges the anonymous referees for their useful comments and suggestions.

References

1. Apt, K.: From Logic Programming to Prolog. Prentice Hall, Upper Saddle River (1997)
2. Ducassé, M.: Opium: an extendable trace analyzer for prolog. J. Log. Program. **39**(1–3), 177–223 (1999). https://doi.org/10.1016/S0743-1066(98)10036-5
3. Landauer, R.: Irreversibility and heat generation in the computing process. IBM J. Res. Dev. **5**, 183–191 (1961)
4. Lanese, I., Palacios, A., Vidal, G.: Causal-consistent replay debugging for message passing programs. In: Pérez, J.A., Yoshida, N. (eds.) FORTE 2019. LNCS, vol. 11535, pp. 167–184. Springer, Cham (2019). https://doi.org/10.1007/978-3-030-21759-4_10

5. Lloyd, J.: Foundations of Logic Programming, 2nd edn. Springer, Berlin (1987). https://doi.org/10.1007/978-3-642-83189-8
6. O'Callahan, R., Jones, C., Froyd, N., Huey, K., Noll, A., Partush, N.: Engineering record and replay for deployability: Extended technical report (2017). CoRR abs/1705.05937, http://arxiv.org/abs/1705.05937
7. Ströder, T., Emmes, F., Schneider-Kamp, P., Giesl, J., Fuhs, C.: A linear operational semantics for termination and complexity analysis of ISO prolog. In: Vidal, G. (ed.) LOPSTR 2011. LNCS, vol. 7225, pp. 237–252. Springer, Heidelberg (2012). https://doi.org/10.1007/978-3-642-32211-2_16
8. Undo Software: Increasing software development productivity with reversible debugging (2014). https://undo.io/media/uploads/files/Undo_ReversibleDebugging_Whitepaper.pdf

Towards a Formal Account for Software Transactional Memory

Doriana Medić[1]([⊠]), Claudio Antares Mezzina[2], Iain Phillips[3],
and Nobuko Yoshida[3]

[1] Focus Team/University of Bologna, Inria, Sophia Antipolis, France
doriana.medic@gmail.com
[2] Dipartimento di Scienze Pure e Applicate, Università di Urbino, Urbino, Italy
[3] Imperial College London, London, UK

Abstract. Software transactional memory (STM) is a concurrency control mechanism for shared memory systems. It is opposite to the lock based mechanism, as it allows multiple processes to access the same set of variables in a concurrent way. Then according to the used policy, the effect of accessing to shared variables can be committed (hence, made permanent) or undone. In this paper, we define a formal framework for describing STMs and show how with a minor variation of the rules it is possible to model two common policies for STM: reader preference and writer preference.

Keywords: STM · Transactions · Concurrency

1 Introduction

Starting from the 1960s, reversible computing has been studied in several contexts ranging from quantum computing [6], biochemical modelling [7], programming [8,9], and program debugging [10,15]. Distributed reversible actions can be seen as defeasible partial agreements: the building blocks for different transactional models and recovery techniques. The work of Danos and Krivine on reversible CCS (RCCS) [1] provides a good example: they show how notions of reversible and irreversible actions in a process calculus can model a primitive form of transaction, an abstraction that has been found useful, in different guises, in reliable concurrent and distributed programming. Since the seminal work of [1], other works have investigated the interplay between transactions and reversibility [2,11] in the area of message passing systems. On the shared memory side, we just recall the work of [12] where a CCS endowed with a mechanism for software transactional memories (STMs) is presented. Another work

This work has been partially supported by French ANR project DCore ANR-18-CE25-0007 and by the Italian INdAM – GNCS project 2020 *Reversible Concurrent Systems: from Models to Languages*. We also acknowledge partial support from the following projects: EPSRC EP/K011715/1, EP/K034413/1, EP/L00058X/1, EP/N027833, EP/N028201/1, and EP/T006544/1.

I. Lanese and M. Rawski (Eds.): RC 2020, LNCS 12227, pp. 255–263, 2020.
https://doi.org/10.1007/978-3-030-52482-1_16

about reversibility and a high-level abstraction of shared memory (tuple spaces) is presented in [16].

Software Transactional Memory [3,4] is an elegant way to address the problem of concurrent programming, by relieving the programmer from the burden of dealing with locks. The lock-based approach is error prone and usually leads to deadlocks when the complexity of the system grows. Opposite to the lock-based approach, STM uses transactions. A transaction is a block of code accessing shared data which is meant to be executed *atomically* with an "all or nothing" policy: that is either all the effects of a transaction have to be visible when it commits, or none of them has to be visible in case of abortion. This abstraction allows for multiple transactions to be executed "at the same time". The programmer just needs to specify the sequences of operations to be enclosed in transactions, while the system is in charge of the interleaving between the concurrent transactions. A transaction can either *commit* and update the system permanently or *abort* and discard all the changes done by its execution.

In this work, we are interested in the interplay between reversible computing and the STM approach to control the concurrent executions. Therefore, we present a formal framework for describing STMs in a simple shared memory context. In particular, when a transaction aborts, it is necessary to discard all the updates that it made and we need to bring the system back to the state before the execution of the transaction. To accomplish the behaviour above, we implement a rollback operator following the approach given in [13]. A transaction can access a shared variable either in read or in write mode. Given this, different policies can be used to regulate the transactions which are accessing the same value in the shared memory. According to the implemented policy, some transactions will succeed and some will be aborted. We will show how it is possible to model *writer* and *reader preference* [5] in our framework. Consider the following C-like code where two functions/threads access the same shared variables:

int x = 0;
int y = 5;
int z = 0;
	void t1 ()
	{z = y+x; }
	void t2 ()
	{ x = z+1; }
		t1 ; t2
		z = 5
		x = 6
			t2 ; t1
			z = 6
			x = 1
				t1 | t2
				z = 5
				x = 1

All the possible executions of the two functions are reported above: either the two functions are executed sequentially or are interleaved (leading to an unwanted state). If we wrap the two functions into two atomic blocks then the third behaviour would be automatically ruled out by the system as one of the two transactions will be aborted depending on the implemented policy.

2   Syntax

In this section we give the syntax of our calculus. Let us assume the existence of the mutually disjoint sets $\mathcal{V}$ (a set of variables) and $\mathcal{I}$ (a set of transaction identifiers), ranged over by x, y, z and t, h, respectively.

$$\text{(Actions)} \quad \alpha, \beta \quad ::= \mathbf{wr}(x) \mid \mathbf{rd}(x)$$

$$\text{(Processes)} \quad A, B \quad ::= \mathbf{0} \mid \sum_i \alpha_i.A_i$$

$$\text{(Expressions)} \quad X, Y \quad ::= B \mid \alpha.X \mid X; Y \mid (X \mid Y) \mid t : [\![A]\!]_\Gamma$$

$$\text{(Configuration)} \quad C \quad ::= X \parallel M$$

$$\text{(Shared Memory)} \quad M \quad ::= \langle x, W, R \rangle \parallel M$$

Fig. 1. Syntax

The syntax of the calculus is given in Fig. 1. *Write* and *read* access to the variable x are represented with actions $\mathbf{wr}(x)$ and $\mathbf{rd}(x)$. The sequential execution of the actions $\mathbf{wr}(x)$ and $\mathbf{rd}(x)$ together with the choice operator + build the *processes*, given with A, B productions. The term $t : [\![A]\!]_\Gamma$ represents a *transaction*, where t is a unique identifier, A is the body of the transaction and Γ is the set recording the identifiers of the transactions which have the write access to the variable that transaction t has to read. The idea behind the set Γ is to allow transaction t to have read access to any variable, but to record the write access to them. In this way if the transaction that writes on the variable fails, the transaction that reads the same variable has to fail too. More explanations will be given in Sect. 3.

Transactions, together with processes, build *expressions*. An expression can be prefixed with the actions $\mathbf{wr}(x)$ and $\mathbf{rd}(x)$ and we denote it as $\alpha.X$. Two expressions X and Y can be executed in parallel, $X \mid Y$, or in sequential order $X; Y$. We can note that the expression X can be the process that is not inside of the transaction, and that operation ; allows us to have a transaction followed by an action (for example $t : [\![A]\!]_\Gamma; \mathbf{wr}(x)$). The whole system, called *configuration*, is denoted with C and it represents the expressions together with the *shared memory*. The shared memory M is made of triples of the form $\langle x, W, R \rangle$ for every variable in the system. In $\langle x, W, R \rangle$, x is the variable name, W and R are the sets recording transactions which had write and read access to x, respectively. Let us note that we abstract away from the value contained by variables, since this is not relevant for our framework. We just need to record whether a variable is read (a transaction reads its value) or modified (a transaction changes its value).

In order to write expressions in a more compact way, we define the notion of *history* context. For instance, having a transaction $t : [\![\mathbf{wr}(x).\mathbf{rd}(x_1)\mathbf{rd}(y).A + B]\!]_\Gamma$ we can write it as $t : [\![\mathtt{H}[\mathbf{rd}(x_1)\mathbf{rd}(y).A]]\!]_\Gamma$ where $\mathtt{H} = \mathbf{wr}(x).\bullet + B$. Formally:

Definition 1 (History context). *A history context* $\mathtt{H}$ *is a process with a hole* $\bullet$, *defined by the following grammar:* $\mathtt{H} ::= \bullet \mid \alpha. \bullet + A$.

3   Semantics

The semantics of our calculus is presented in two steps. First, we give the basic rules of the framework (common to all the policies) and then, we present the extra rules, necessary to model *reader* or *writer preference*. With *reader preference*, we intend that reading the value of a variable is always possible, i.e. no read access should be suspended, unless the write access already took place. *Writer preference*, on the other side, allows the write access to the value of a variable x even if some read access already took place. In this case, all the executing transactions with the read access to a value x need to be aborted and brought back to their initial state.

In what follows we provide the auxiliary functions necessary for the semantics of the calculus: the function which computes the set of the transaction identifiers of a given expression and the operation which removes transaction identifiers from the system.

Definition 2 (Set of the transaction identifiers). *The set of the transaction identifiers of a given expression* X, *written* $\mathtt{id}(X)$, *is inductively defined as:*

$$\mathtt{id}(Y|Y') = \mathtt{id}(Y) \cup \mathtt{id}(Y') \qquad \mathtt{id}(\alpha.Y) = \mathtt{id}(Y) \qquad \mathtt{id}(A) = \emptyset$$
$$\mathtt{id}(Y;Y') = \mathtt{id}(Y) \cup \mathtt{id}(Y') \qquad \mathtt{id}(t : [\![A]\!]_\Gamma) = \{t\}$$

Definition 3 (Removing of identifiers). *The operation of deleting transaction identifier* t *from the configuration* C, *denoted as* $C_{@t}$, *is defined as follows:*

$$(X \parallel M)_{@t} = X_{@t} \parallel M_{@t} \qquad (\alpha.X)_{@t} = \alpha.(X_{@t})$$
$$(X|Y)_{@t} = X_{@t}|Y_{@t} \qquad (t' : [\![A]\!]_\Gamma)_{@t} = t' : [\![A]\!]_{\Gamma \setminus t}$$
$$(X;Y)_{@t} = X_{@t};Y_{@t} \qquad (\langle x, W, R \rangle \parallel M)_{@t} = \langle x, W \setminus t, R \setminus t \rangle \parallel M_{@t}$$

When a transaction fails, the effects of the internal computation are undone and the entire transaction is restarted, that is, brought back to its initial state. As a consequence, the transactions depending on it are also rolled back. Dependency between transactions changes with the chosen preference. We shall see more information about the preferences by the end of this section.

To be able to identify the state of the internal computation of a transaction, we mark it with symbol $^\wedge$. For instance, if we consider transaction $t : [\![\mathtt{rd}(x).\mathtt{rd}(y).^\wedge\mathtt{wr}(z).\mathtt{wr}(x')]\!]_\Gamma$, the actions $\mathtt{rd}(x)$ and $\mathtt{rd}(y)$ represent the past of the transaction and the action $\mathtt{wr}(z)$ is the next action to be executed.

Now we define our rollback operator which brings a transaction back to its initial state i.e. the symbol $^\wedge$ is placed in the beginning of the transaction and its set Γ is empty. For instance, if we roll back transaction t : $[\![\mathtt{rd}(x).\mathtt{rd}(y).^\wedge\mathtt{wr}(z).\mathtt{wr}(x')]\!]_\Gamma$, we obtain t : $[\![^\wedge\mathtt{rd}(x).\mathtt{rd}(y).\mathtt{wr}(z).\mathtt{wr}(x')]\!]_\emptyset$. Formally, we have:

Definition 4 (Rollback operator). *The rollback operator on the transaction* $t : [\![A]\!]_\Gamma$, *written* $\mathbf{roll}(t)$, *is defined as:* $\mathbf{roll}(t) = t : [\![^\wedge A]\!]_\emptyset$.

$$(\text{WriteP}) \;\; \texttt{wr}(x).A + B \;\|\; \langle x, \emptyset, \emptyset \rangle \;\to\; A \;\|\; \langle x, \emptyset, \emptyset \rangle$$

$$(\text{ReadP}) \;\; \texttt{rd}(x).A + B \;\|\; \langle x, \emptyset, \emptyset \rangle \;\to\; A \;\|\; \langle x, \emptyset, \emptyset \rangle$$

$$(\text{Write}) \;\; \frac{(W \subseteq \{t\} \wedge R \subseteq \{t\})}{t : [\![\texttt{H}[^{\wedge}\texttt{wr}(x).A + B]]\!]_{\Gamma} \;\|\; \langle x, W, R \rangle \;\|\; M \;\to\; t : [\![\texttt{H}[\texttt{wr}(x).{}^{\wedge}A + B]]\!]_{\Gamma} \;\|\; \langle x, W \cup t, R \rangle \;\|\; M}$$

$$(\text{Read}) \;\; t : [\![\texttt{H}[^{\wedge}\texttt{rd}(x).A + B]]\!]_{\Gamma} \;\|\; \langle x, W, R \rangle \;\|\; M \;\to\; t : [\![\texttt{H}[\texttt{rd}(x).{}^{\wedge}A + B]]\!]_{\Gamma \cup (W \setminus t)} \;\|\; \langle x, W, R \cup t \rangle \;\|\; M$$

$$(\text{Par}) \;\; \frac{X \;\|\; M \to X' \;\|\; M' \quad \texttt{id}(X) \cap \texttt{id}(Y) = \emptyset}{X \mid Y \;\|\; M \to X' \mid Y \;\|\; M'}$$

$$(\text{Commit}) \;\; \frac{t : [\![A^{\wedge}]\!]_{\Gamma}; Y \mid X \;\|\; M \quad \wedge \quad \Gamma = \emptyset}{t : [\![A^{\wedge}]\!]_{\Gamma}; Y \mid X \;\|\; M \to Y \mid X_{@t} \;\|\; M_{@t}}$$

$$(\text{RollR}) \;\; \frac{t : [\![A]\!]_{\Gamma} \;\|\; M \to \textbf{roll}(t) \;\|\; M_{@t} \quad \forall t_i \; t_i : [\![A_i]\!]_{\Gamma_i \cup \{t\}}}{t : [\![A]\!]_{\Gamma} \mid \prod_i t_i : [\![A_i]\!]_{\Gamma_i} \;\|\; M \to \textbf{roll}(t) \mid \prod_i \textbf{roll}(t_i) \;\|\; (M_{@t})_{@t_i}}$$

Fig. 2. Common rules for both models

In what follows, we give the semantics of our calculus. We shall start by introducing semantics rules representing the base of our framework (rules that are common for both models) and then we show the additional rules for each preference.

The common rules are given in Fig. 2. An action executed outside a transaction can be seen as an atomic step in which the action is discarded after the execution (rules WriteP and ReadP). Therefore, there is no need to keep track of its access to the variable. The only constraint is that they cannot access the variable while some transaction has read or write access to it.

Rule Write describes when a transaction can modify the content of a variable. To do so, there should not be another transaction which has already accessed the variable in either writing or reading mode. After the execution, the identifier t is added to the write access set W of the variable x and the symbol $^{\wedge}$ is moved to the next computational step. Rule Read allows the transaction t to execute the action $\texttt{rd}(x)$ at any moment. Then the identifier t is added to the set R of the variable x and the set $W \setminus t$ is added to the set Γ (if write and read access to the variable x are in the same transaction t, then it is not necessary to save the identifier t into a set Γ).

To have a better intuition about these two rules, we give a simple example. Consider the transaction t with a corresponding shared memory

$$t : [\![^{\wedge}\texttt{wr}(x).\texttt{rd}(y)]\!]_{\emptyset} \;\|\; \langle x, \emptyset, \emptyset \rangle \;\|\; \langle y, \emptyset, \emptyset \rangle$$

After executing the write access to the variable x, we obtain the system

$$t : [\![\texttt{wr}(x).{}^{\wedge}\texttt{rd}(y)]\!]_{\emptyset} \;\|\; \langle x, \{t\}, \emptyset \rangle \;\|\; \langle y, \emptyset, \emptyset \rangle$$

where the pointer $^{\wedge}$ is moved to the next action and the identifier t is added to the write set of the variable x. Now we can perform the read access to variable

y and we have:

$$t : [\![\mathtt{wr}(x).\mathtt{rd}(y)^\wedge]\!]_\emptyset \parallel \langle x, \{t\}, \emptyset\rangle \parallel \langle y, \emptyset, \{t\}\rangle$$

where the identifier t is added to the read set of the variable y. The set Γ of the transaction t remains empty since there is no transaction which had write access to variable y.

Rule PAR allows expressions to execute in parallel (in an interleaving fashion) ensuring the uniqueness of the identifier t. By executing its last action, the transaction t can commit if the set Γ is empty, by applying the rule COMMIT. After it commits, the execution proceeds with the continuation Y and the identifier t is deleted from the remaining system. The intuition is that transaction t can commit if the other transactions, having a write access to the variables that transaction t read, have been committed. The rollback of the transaction t can be done with the rule ROLLR. It will force every transaction in parallel having the identifier t in their set Γ to roll back too. The intuition is that when the transaction with $\mathtt{wr}(x)$ rolls back, every transaction which has read access to x should roll back as well. For instance, let us consider the system containing following transactions:

$$t : [\![A]\!]_\Gamma \mid t_1 : [\![A_1]\!]_{\{t\}} \mid t_2 : [\![A_2]\!]_{\Gamma_2} \qquad \text{such that } \mathtt{rd}(x) \in A_1 \text{ and } t \notin \Gamma_2$$

and that transaction t needs to be rolled back. Then, by applying the rule ROLLR, we obtain the system:

$$\mathbf{roll}(t) \mid \mathbf{roll}(t_1) \mid t_2 : [\![A_2]\!]_{\Gamma_2}$$

in which transaction t_1 is rolled back too since $t \in \Gamma_1$ while t_2 remains the same.

Now we can give the rules necessary to model *reader* and *writer* preference. To give a better intuition about the differences between the two models, we use the example from the introduction as a running example.

Reader Preference. To model the reader preference we use the rules from Fig. 2 and the rule given below.

$$(\text{R-ROLLW}) \; \frac{(W \not\subseteq \{t\} \vee R \not\subseteq \{t\})}{t : [\![\mathtt{H}[^\wedge\mathtt{wr}(x).A]]\!]_\Gamma \parallel \langle x, W, R\rangle \parallel M \to \mathbf{roll}(t) \parallel \langle x, W, R\rangle_{@t} \parallel M_{@t}}$$

The rollback operator is triggered when the transaction t cannot write on the variable x (this happens when $W \not\subseteq \{t\}$ or $R \not\subseteq \{t\}$). With the rule R-ROLLW the transaction t goes to the state $\mathbf{roll}(t)$, i.e. the initial state of the transaction. Additionally, the identifier t is removed from every triple of the shared memory.

To illustrate it, we use the example from the introduction, abstracting away from the read and write values contained in variables and representing accesses of two threads to the shared memory in our framework with transactions t_1 and t_2. Transaction t_1 has read accesses to variables y and x and then writes on variable z, while t_2 has read access to variables z and then writes on x. We have the following system

$$t_1 : [\![^\wedge \mathtt{rd}(y).\mathtt{rd}(x).\mathtt{wr}(z)]\!]_\emptyset \,|\, t_2 : [\![^\wedge \mathtt{rd}(z).\mathtt{wr}(x)]\!]_\emptyset \,\|\, \langle x, \emptyset, \emptyset \rangle \,\|\, \langle y, \emptyset, \emptyset \rangle \,\|\, \langle z, \emptyset, \emptyset \rangle$$

We assume that read accesses are executed in parallel and the obtained system is

$$t_1 : [\![\mathtt{rd}(y).\mathtt{rd}(x).^\wedge \mathtt{wr}(z)]\!]_\emptyset \,|\, t_2 : [\![\mathtt{rd}(z).^\wedge \mathtt{wr}(x)]\!]_\emptyset \,\|\, \langle x, \emptyset, \{t_1\} \rangle \,\|\, \langle y, \emptyset, \{t_1\} \rangle \,\|\, \langle z, \emptyset, \{t_2\} \rangle$$

Now transaction t_1 is executing write access to variable z but since in the memory for variable z we have $R \not\subseteq \{t_1\}$ ($R = \{t_2\}$), the transaction t_1 needs to roll back according to the rule R-ROLLW, and we have

$$\mathbf{roll}(t_1) \,|\, t_2 : [\![\mathtt{rd}(z).^\wedge \mathtt{wr}(x)]\!]_\emptyset \,\|\, \langle x, \emptyset, \emptyset \rangle \,\|\, \langle y, \emptyset, \emptyset \rangle \,\|\, \langle z, \emptyset, \{t_2\} \rangle$$

where $\mathbf{roll}(t_1) = t_1 : [\![^\wedge \mathtt{rd}(y).\mathtt{rd}(x).\mathtt{wr}(z)]\!]_\emptyset$.

Writer Preference. To model the writer preference we use the rules from Fig. 2 and the rules given below.

$$(\text{W-PREF}) \; \dfrac{W \subseteq \{t\} \quad \wedge \quad R \not\subseteq \{t\} \quad \wedge \quad R' = R \setminus t}{\begin{array}{c} t : [\![\mathtt{H}[^\wedge \mathtt{wr}(x).A + B]]\!]_\Gamma \,|\, \displaystyle\prod_{t_i \in R'} t_i : [\![A_i]\!]_{\Gamma_i} \,\|\, \langle x, W, R \rangle \,\|\, M \;\rightarrow\; t : [\![\mathtt{H}[\mathtt{wr}(x).^\wedge A + B]]\!]_\Gamma \,| \\[2mm] \displaystyle\prod_{t_i \in R'} \mathbf{roll}(t_i) \,\|\, \langle x, W \cup t, R \rangle_{@t_i} \,\|\, M_{@t_i} \end{array}}$$

$$(\text{W-ROLLW}) \; \dfrac{(W \not\subseteq \{t\})}{t : [\![\mathtt{H}[^\wedge \mathtt{wr}(x).A]]\!]_\Gamma \,\|\, \langle x, W, R \rangle \,\|\, M \;\rightarrow\; \mathbf{roll}(t) \,\|\, \langle x, W, R \rangle_{@t} \,\|\, M_{@t}}$$

The rollback is triggered by the writer only in the case when another transaction has write access to the same variable. Therefore the condition on the rule W-ROLLW is simply $W \not\subseteq \{t\}$. The additional rule, with respect to the reader preference is the rule W-PREF. It allows a transaction to modify the value of a variable x if other transactions have read access to it. At the same time, all transactions executing in parallel whose identifiers belong to the set R, are requested to roll back.

To illustrate it, we use the same example as for the reader preference where read accesses are executed already. Therefore, we have the system

$$t_1 : [\![\mathtt{rd}(y).\mathtt{rd}(x).^\wedge \mathtt{wr}(z)]\!]_\emptyset \,|\, t_2 : [\![\mathtt{rd}(z).^\wedge \mathtt{wr}(x)]\!]_\emptyset \,\|\, \langle x, \emptyset, \{t_1\} \rangle \,\|\, \langle y, \emptyset, \{t_1\} \rangle \,\|\, \langle z, \emptyset, \{t_2\} \rangle$$

Now we can execute the write access to variable z, since in the rule W-PREF the condition for the read set R allows a transaction to perform the write access, and in that case all transactions in parallel having read access to variable z need to be rolled back. Therefore, transaction t_1 executes write access, while t_2 will be rolled back, and we have:

$$t_1 : [\![\mathtt{rd}(y).\mathtt{rd}(x).\mathtt{wr}(z)^\wedge]\!]_\emptyset \,|\, \mathbf{roll}(t_2) \,\|\, \langle x, \emptyset, \{t_1\} \rangle \,\|\, \langle y, \emptyset, \{t_1\} \rangle \,\|\, \langle z, \{t_1\}, \emptyset \rangle$$

where $\mathbf{roll}(t_2) = t_2 : [\![^\wedge \mathtt{rd}(z).\mathtt{wr}(x)]\!]_\emptyset$.

4   Conclusion and Future Work

We have presented a framework to express the STM mechanism in a simple shared memory context. The framework is able to model two different policies for the execution of the concurrent transactions: writer and reader preference. Our intention is to start from a simple calculus and then to add in a modular way: nested transactions, data structures (e.g., C structures) and more complex scheduling policies. Nested transactions will require to record for each transaction a list of its *children* transactions. These children inherit the access of the parent transaction. There exist different policies to deal with nested transactions: *closed* nested transactions [17] and *open* nested transactions [18]. The difference is that in the first case the parent does not execute till all the children have committed, while in the second case the parent can commit even before its children. This may lead to inconsistencies which have to be dealt with compensations.

Our ultimate goal is then to prove that the modular framework satisfies the *opacity* [14] property, that is, all the execution traces of our semantics, where the transactional bodies are interleaved, are equivalent to executions in which transactional blocks are executed as a whole (in a lock-based fashion) without being interleaved with other transactions.

References

1. Danos, V., Krivine, J.: Transactions in RCCS. In: Abadi, M., de Alfaro, L. (eds.) CONCUR 2005. LNCS, vol. 3653, pp. 398–412. Springer, Heidelberg (2005). https://doi.org/10.1007/11539452_31
2. Lanese, I., Lienhardt, M., Mezzina, C.A., Schmitt, A., Stefani, J.-B.: Concurrent flexible reversibility. In: Felleisen, M., Gardner, P. (eds.) ESOP 2013. LNCS, vol. 7792, pp. 370–390. Springer, Heidelberg (2013). https://doi.org/10.1007/978-3-642-37036-6_21
3. Herlihy, M., Moss, J.E.B.: Transactional memory: architectural support for lock-free data structures. In: Annual International Symposium on Computer Architecture, pp. 289–300. ACM, San Diego (1993)
4. Shavit, N., Touitou, D.: Software transactional memory. In: PODC, pp. 204–213. ACM, New York (1995)
5. Courtois, P.-J., Heymans, F., Parnas, D.L.: Concurrent control with "readers" and "writers". Commun. ACM **14**, 667–668 (1971)
6. Grattage, J.: A functional quantum programming language. In: LICS 2005, pp. 249–258. IEEE Computer Society, Washington (2005)
7. Phillips, I., Ulidowski, I., Yuen, S.: A reversible process calculus and the modelling of the ERK signalling pathway. In: Glück, R., Yokoyama, T. (eds.) RC 2012. LNCS, vol. 7581, pp. 218–232. Springer, Heidelberg (2013). https://doi.org/10.1007/978-3-642-36315-3_18
8. Lutz, C.: Janus: a time-reversible language. Letter to R. Landauer (1986)
9. Yokoyama, T., Axelsen, H.B., Glück, R.: Principles of a reversible programming language. In: Conference on Computing Frontiers, Italy, pp. 43–54. ACM (2008)
10. Lanese, I., Nishida, N., Palacios, A., Vidal, G.: CauDEr: a causal-consistent reversible Debugger for Erlang. In: Gallagher, J.P., Sulzmann, M. (eds.) FLOPS 2018. LNCS, vol. 10818, pp. 247–263. Springer, Cham (2018). https://doi.org/10.1007/978-3-319-90686-7_16

11. de Vries, E., Koutavas, V., Hennessy, M.: Communicating transactions. In: Gastin, P., Laroussinie, F. (eds.) CONCUR 2010. LNCS, vol. 6269, pp. 569–583. Springer, Heidelberg (2010). https://doi.org/10.1007/978-3-642-15375-4_39
12. Acciai, L., Boreale, M., Dal Zilio, S.: A concurrent calculus with atomic transactions. In: De Nicola, R. (ed.) ESOP 2007. LNCS, vol. 4421, pp. 48–63. Springer, Heidelberg (2007). https://doi.org/10.1007/978-3-540-71316-6_5
13. Lanese, I., Mezzina, C.A., Schmitt, A., Stefani, J.-B.: Controlling reversibility in higher-order pi. In: Katoen, J.-P., König, B. (eds.) CONCUR 2011. LNCS, vol. 6901, pp. 297–311. Springer, Heidelberg (2011). https://doi.org/10.1007/978-3-642-23217-6_20
14. Guerraoui, R., Kapalka, M.: On the correctness of transactional memory. In: PPOPP, pp. 175–184. ACM, New York (2008)
15. Giachino, E., Lanese, I., Mezzina, C.A.: Causal-consistent reversible debugging. In: Gnesi, S., Rensink, A. (eds.) FASE 2014. LNCS, vol. 8411, pp. 370–384. Springer, Heidelberg (2014). https://doi.org/10.1007/978-3-642-54804-8_26
16. Giachino, E., Lanese, I., Mezzina, C.A., Tiezzi, F.: Causal-consistent rollback in a tuple-based language. JLAMP **88**, 99–120 (2017)
17. Gray, J., Reuter, A.: Transaction Processing: Concepts and Techniques (1993)
18. Moss, J.E.B.: Open Nested Transactions: Semantics and Support (2006)

Encoding Reversing Petri Nets in Answer Set Programming

Yannis Dimopoulos, Eleftheria Kouppari, Anna Philippou$^{(\boxtimes)}$, and Kyriaki Psara

Department of Computer Science, University of Cyprus, Nicosia, Cyprus
{yannis,ekoupp02,annap,kpsara01}@cs.ucy.ac.cy

Abstract. Reversing Petri nets (RPNs) have been proposed as a reversible approach to Petri nets, which allows the transitions of a net to be reversed. This work presents an approach towards an implementation of RPNs to support their simulation and analysis. Specifically, we define how to model RPNs in Answer Set Programming (ASP), a declarative programming framework with competitive solvers. We highlight how the methodology can be used to reason about the behavior of RPN models.

1 Introduction

Reversibility is a phenomenon referring to the ability of a system to execute its actions in both the forward and the reverse directions. It occurs in a variety of systems (e.g., quantum computation and biochemical systems) and can be exploited in many others (e.g., robotics, manufacturing systems, distributed systems, and logical circuits). Recently, its study has been receiving increased attention. Among the developments, a variety of formal frameworks of modeling reversible systems have been defined, contributing towards an improved understanding of the basic principles of reversibility. A natural next step for this work is the development of techniques for the automatic analysis of reversible models.

In this paper we consider reversing Petri nets (RPNs) [8], a recently-proposed Petri-net framework that allows transitions to be carried out in both the forward and the reverse directions in or out of causal order. Specifically, we present work in progress towards a framework for simulation and analysis of RPN models via an encoding into Answer Set Programming (ASP) [5,7] a declarative programming framework with competitive solvers that may be used to model a system as well as a query about the system via a logic program, such that models of the program provide the answers to the set query. ASP has proved to be a promising approach towards reasoning about Petri nets with encodings to ASP having been defined for a number of Petri net subclasses, e.g. [1–3,6]. In this paper we provide a systematic way of modelling RPNs and their causal reversibility semantics in ASP. Our long term goal is the development of an ASP-based framework for reasoning about RPN models.

I. Lanese and M. Rawski (Eds.): RC 2020, LNCS 12227, pp. 264–271, 2020.
https://doi.org/10.1007/978-3-030-52482-1_17

2   Reversing Petri Nets

In this section we briefly recall RPNs and we refer the reader to [8,9] for the full exposition. Following [9], RPNs are cyclic structures defined as follows:

Definition 1. A *reversing Petri net* (RPN) is a tuple (A, P, B, T, F) where:

1. A is a finite set of *bases* or *tokens* ranged over by a, b, …. We write $\overline{A} = \{\overline{a} \mid a \in A\}$ and $\mathcal{A} = A \cup \overline{A}$.
2. P is a finite set of *places* and T a finite set of *transitions*.
3. $B \subseteq A \times A$ is a set of undirected *bonds* ranged over by β, γ, …. We write $a{-}b$ for a bond $(a, b) \in B$, $\overline{B} = \{\overline{\beta} \mid \beta \in B\}$, and $\mathcal{B} = B \cup \overline{B}$.
4. $F : (P \times T \cup T \times P) \to 2^{\mathcal{A} \cup \mathcal{B}}$ defines a set of directed *arcs*.

RPNs are built on the basis of a set of *bases* or *tokens* each having a unique name. Tokens may occur as stand-alone elements or merge together to form *bonds*. *Places* and *transitions* have the standard meaning. Directed arcs connect places to transitions and vice versa and are labelled by a subset of $\mathcal{A} \cup \mathcal{B}$ where $\overline{A}$ and $\overline{B}$ are the sets of "negative" tokens and bonds, expressing token and bond absence, respectively. For a label $\ell = F(x, t)$ or $\ell = F(t, x)$, we assume that each token a can appear in ℓ at most once, either as a or as $\overline{a}$, and that if $(a, b) \in \ell$ then $a, b \in \ell$. Furthermore, for $\ell = F(t, x)$ it must be that $\ell \cap (\overline{A} \cup \overline{B}) = \emptyset$. $F(x, y) = \emptyset$ implies that there is no arc between x and y. Finally, we assume that F is defined so that transitions (1) do not erase tokens, (2) do not destroy bonds, and (3) do not clone tokens/bonds into more than one outgoing place.

We write $\circ t = \{x \in P \mid F(x, t) \neq \emptyset\}$ and $t\circ = \{x \in P \mid F(t, x) \neq \emptyset\}$, $\mathsf{pre}(t) = \bigcup_{x \in P} F(x, t)$ and $\mathsf{post}(t) = \bigcup_{x \in P} F(t, x)$, and define the *effect* of a transition as $\mathsf{eff}(t) = \mathsf{post}(t) - \mathsf{pre}(t)$. Furthermore, we employ the notion of a *marking* defined as a distribution of tokens and bonds across places, $M : P \to 2^{\mathcal{A} \cup \mathcal{B}}$. In addition, a *history* assigns a memory to each transition, $H : T \to 2^{\mathbb{N}}$, where $H(t) = \emptyset$ captures that transition t has not taken place, or it has been reversed, and $H(t) = \{k_1, \ldots, k_n\}$ captures that t was executed and not reversed n times where the k_i indicate the order of the execution instances. A pair $\langle M, H \rangle$ describes a *state* of a RPN. Finally, we write $\mathsf{con}(a, C)$, where $a \in C$ and $C \subseteq A \cup B$, for the connected component of token a in the graph described by C.

We proceed to define forward execution for RPNs.

Definition 2. Consider a RPN (A, P, B, T, F), a transition $t \in T$, and a state $\langle M, H \rangle$. We say that t is *forward enabled* in $\langle M, H \rangle$ if:

1. if $a \in F(x, t)$ (resp. $\beta \in F(x, t)$), for some $x \in \circ t$, then $a \in M(x)$ (resp. $\beta \in M(x)$), and if $\overline{a} \in F(x, t)$ (resp. $\overline{\beta} \in F(x, t)$) for some $x \in \circ t$, then $a \notin M(x)$ (resp. $\beta \notin M(x)$),
2. if $a \in F(t, y_1)$, $b \in F(t, y_2)$, $y_1 \neq y_2$, then $b \notin \mathsf{con}(a, M(x))$ for all $x \in \circ t$,
3. if $\beta \in F(t, x)$ for some $x \in t\circ$ and $\beta \in M(y)$ for some $y \in \circ t$, then $\beta \in F(y, t)$.

Definition 3. Given a RPN (A, P, B, T, F), a state $\langle M, H \rangle$, and a transition t forward enabled in $\langle M, H \rangle$, we write $\langle M, H \rangle \xrightarrow{t} \langle M', H' \rangle$ where:

$$M'(x) = \begin{cases} M(x) - \bigcup_{a \in F(x,t)} \mathsf{con}(a, M(x)) & \text{if } x \in \mathsf{o}t \\ M(x) \cup F(t,x) \cup \bigcup_{a \in F(t,x) \cap F(y,t)} \mathsf{con}(a, M(y)) & \text{if } x \in t\mathsf{o} \\ M(x), & \text{otherwise} \end{cases}$$

$$H'(t') = \begin{cases} H(t') \cup \{\max(\{0\} \cup \{k \mid k \in H(t''), t'' \in T\}) + 1\}, & \text{if } t' = t \\ H(t'), & \text{otherwise} \end{cases}$$

Thus, when a transition is executed all tokens and bonds on its incoming arcs are relocated from its input to its output places with their connected components.

According to causal-order reversibility, a transition may be reversed only if all transitions causally dependent on it have either been reversed or not executed:

Definition 4. Consider a RPN (A, P, B, T, F), a state $\langle M, H \rangle$, and a transition $t \in T$. Then t is co-enabled in $\langle M, H \rangle$ if $H(t) \neq \emptyset$ and, for all $a \in F(t,x)$, if $a \in M(y)$ for some y and $\mathsf{con}(a, M(y)) \cap \mathsf{pre}(t') \neq \emptyset$ for some t' then either $H(t') = \emptyset$ or there is $k \in H(t)$ such that $k > k'$ for all $k \in H(t')$.

When a transition is reversed in a causal fashion, all tokens and bonds in the postcondition of the transition and their connected components are transferred to the incoming places of the transition and any created bonds are broken.

Definition 5. Given a RPN (A, P, B, T, F), a state $\langle M, H \rangle$, and a transition t co-enabled in $\langle M, H \rangle$, we write $\langle M, H \rangle \xrightarrow{t}_c \langle M', H' \rangle$ where

$$M'(x) = \begin{cases} M(x) \cup \bigcup_{y \in t\mathsf{o}, a \in F(x,t) \cap F(t,y)} \mathsf{con}(a, M(y) - \mathsf{eff}(t)), & \text{if } x \in \mathsf{o}t \\ M(x) - \bigcup_{a \in F(t,x)} \mathsf{con}(a, M(x)), & \text{if } x \in t\mathsf{o} \\ M(x) & \text{otherwise} \end{cases}$$

$$H'(t') = \begin{cases} H(t') - \{k\}, & \text{if } t' = t, k = \max(H(t)) \\ \{k' \mid k' \in H(t'), k' < k\} \cup \{k' - 1 \mid k' \in H(t'), k' > k\}, & \text{otherwise} \end{cases}$$

An example of a reversing Petri net can be seen in Fig. 1 simulating the assembly of a three-component product. A principal process during the remanufacturing of worn-out or malfunctioning products is disassembly that enables the dumping, cleaning, repair or replacement of components as desired. Therefore, reversible computation can be used as means of modelling the disassembly process while considering the product topology, mating relations, and precedence relations. Here we have three tokens a, b, and c representing the three components of an assembly line. Token d represents the machine required in order to assemble the components into the final product. The system consists of two independent transitions, t_2 and t_3 causally following transition t_1, and transition t_4 causally following t_2. This structure gives the ability to the machine to directly bond component a with c by executing t_3 or to indirectly bond a with c through component b. The ability to reverse every transition in

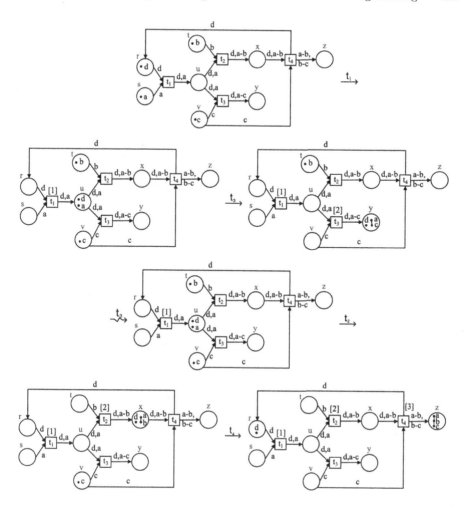

Fig. 1. Causal-order example

the context of manufacturing task planning, can be used in order to recover from failures during the assembly process. In the figure, we observe the execution of transition sequence $t_1; t_3; \underline{t_3}; t_2; t_4$, demonstrating a causally-ordered reversal of transition t_3 (denoted by $\underline{t_3}$) in order to accommodate the manufacturing of a product consisting of $a-b-c$. Note that a non-empty history of transitions is presented as a list over the transitions.

3   Translating RPNs into ASP

Answer Set Programming (ASP) [5,7] is an extension of logic programming with negation as failure under the *stable model* or *answer set* semantics. An Answer

Set Program is a set of rules of the form

$$A_0 \leftarrow A_1, A_2, \ldots A_m, not\ A_{m+1}, not\ A_{m+2}, \ldots not\ A_n$$

with the intuitive reading that if all atoms $A_1, A_2, \ldots, A_m$ are true and none of $A_{m+1}, A_{m+2}, \ldots, A_n$ is true, then A_0 must be true. Most ASP systems, such as clingo (https://potassco.org/clingo/) that we use for our encoding, extend the basic language with additional constructs such as *choice rules* of the form $\{A_0^1, \ldots, A_0^k\} \leftarrow A_1, \ldots, A_m, not\ A_{m+1}, \ldots not\ A_n$, with the meaning that if the right hand side of the rule holds, then some subset of the atoms $\{A_0^1, \ldots, A_0^k\}$ must hold true, which introduces a form of non-determinism that is useful when modeling combinatorial problems. ASP systems, such as clingo, couple a highly expressive language that provides constructs from various fields, such as database systems and constraint programming, with powerful solvers. Therefore, these systems can be successfully applied to a large number of application domains and they have shown the potential of solving problems with thousands of variables and hundreds of thousands of rules in seconds or minutes.

In the following we discuss a translation of reversing Petri nets under the causal reversibility semantics into ASP for a simulation length that is encoded by the last argument TS of the predicates of our model. The basic predicates that represent the input network are trans(T), token(Q), and place(P), that correspond to the transitions, tokens and places, respectively, whereas predicates ptarc(P,T,Q) declare that $Q \in F(P,T)$ (similarly for tparc(T,P,Q)) and ptarcbond(P,T,Q1,Q2) refer to bonds, i.e. $Q1-Q2 \in F(P,T)$. The markings of a RPN are captured by predicates holds for tokens and holdsbonds for bonds. That is, holdsbonds(P,Q1,Q2,TS) means $Q1-Q2 \in M_{TS}(P)$, where M_{TS} refers to the marking at step TS of the simulation.

In the following we discuss some excerpts of the RPN to ASP translation that has been implemented in the clingo system.

Forward-enableness of Definition 2 is captured via notenabled(T,TS), which assumes the value true if transition T cannot be enabled at step TS. Some of the rules for this predicate are depicted in Listing 3.1. The first rule refers to the case $Q \in F(P,T)$ and $Q \notin M_{TS}(P)$, and the second to the similar case for bonds. The rule in lines 5–6 corresponds to the second item of Definition 2, i.e. $Q1 \in F(P1,T)$, $Q2 \in F(P2,T)$ and $Q2 \in con(Q1, M_{TS}(P))$, where predicate connected defines the set $con(a, C)$. The third case of Definition 2 corresponds to the rule in lines 7–9.

If none of the conditions that disable a transition holds, the transition is enabled, as encoded by the rule in line 11. The *choice rule* of line 12, allows clingo to assign any of the values true or false to atom fires(T,TS), i.e. choose whether transition T executes or not.

Lines 15–22 of Listing 3.1 are the rules for bond addition and deletion that result from forward transition execution. The rule in line 15 says that $Q1-Q2 \in M(TP_{TS+1})$ for $Q1-Q2 \in F(T,TP)$ if transition T fires at time TS. The rule in lines 16–18 enforces that $Q1-Q2 \in M(TP_{TS+1})$ for $Q1-Q2 \in M(PT_{TS})$, $Q1-Q2 \in con(Q, M(PT_{TS})$, $Q \in F(PT,T) \cap F(T,TP)$, and transition T that fires at time TS. Lines 20–22 implement bond deletion in a similar way. The encoding also contains rules for token addition and deletion.

Listing 3.1. Forward enabledness and execution

```
1   notenabled(T,TS):-ptarc(P,T,Q),not holds(P,Q,TS).
2   notenabled(T,TS):-ptarcbond(P,T,Q1,Q2),
3                      not holdsbonds(P,Q1,Q2,TS).
4
5   notenabled(T,TS):-tparc(T,P1,Q1),tparc(T,P2,Q2),P1!=P2,
6                      connected(P,Q1,Q2,TS),ptarc(P,T,_).
7   notenabled(T,TS):-tparcbond(T,TP,Q1,Q2),ptarc(PT,T,_),
8                      holdsbonds(PT,Q1,Q2,TS),
9                      not ptarcbond(PT,T,Q1,Q2).
10
11  enabled(T,TS):-not notenabled(T,TS).
12  {fires(T,TS)}:-enabled(T,TS).
13
14
15  addBond(TP,Q1,Q2,TS+1):-fires(T,TS),tparcbond(T,TP,Q1,Q2).
16  addBond(TP,Q1,Q2,TS+1):-fires(T,TS),tparc(T,TP,Q),
17                      ptarc(PT,T,Q),connected(PT,Q,Q1,TS),
18                      holdsbonds(PT,Q1,Q2,TS).
19
20  delBond(PT,Q1,Q2,TS+1):-fires(T,TS),ptarcbond(PT,T,Q1,Q2).
21  delBond(PT,Q1,Q2,TS+1):-fires(T,TS),ptarc(PT,T,Q),
22                      connected(PT,Q,Q1,TS),holdsbonds(PT,Q1,Q2,TS).
```

Listing 3.2. Co-enabledness

```
1   dependent(T2,T1,TS):-tparc(T1,_,Q),ptarc(_,T2,Q),
2                      H2=#max{H:transHistory(T2,H,TS),history(H)},
3                      H1=#max{H:transHistory(T1,H,TS),history(H)},
4                      H2>H1,H1>0.
5   dependent(T2,T1,TS):-tparc(T1,_,Q),ptarc(_,T2,Q1),
6                      connected(_,Q,Q1,TS),
7                      H2=#max{H:transHistory(T2,H,TS),history(H)},
8                      H1=#max{H:transHistory(T1,H,TS),history(H)},
9                      H2>H1,H1>0.
10
11  notenabledC(T,TS):-dependent(T1,T,TS).
12  enabledC(T,TS):-not notenabledC(T,TS),transHistory(T,H,TS),H>0.
13  {reversesC(T,TS)}:-enabledC(T,TS).
```

Lines 1–9 of Listing 3.2 define predicate `dependent(T2,T1,TS)`, which is true if the execution of transition `T2` depends on the execution of transition `T1`. The rule in lines 1–4 requires that this is the case if $max(H(\mathtt{T2})) > max(H(\mathtt{T1}))$ and there is `Q` such that $\mathtt{Q} \in F(\mathtt{T1}, x)$ and $\mathtt{Q} \in F(y, \mathtt{T2})$. The rule in lines 5–9 covers the similar case where $\mathtt{Q} \in F(\mathtt{T1}, x)$, $\mathtt{Q1} \in F(y, \mathtt{T2})$, and $\mathtt{Q1} \in \mathrm{con}(\mathtt{Q}, M_{TS}(\mathtt{P}))$. Lines 11 and 12 encode coenableness, whereas the rule in line 13 encodes the choice of reversing a transition or not.

The ASP encoding can be used to tackle complex reasoning tasks about RPNs. Consider for instance the network of Fig. 1 and its ASP representation in Listing 3.3. Lines 1–6 define the places, transitions and tokens of the network, whereas lines 8–24 list all arcs (both incoming and outgoing) associated with each transition. For instance, lines 11–14 define all arcs related to transition t2. Finally, line 26 represents the initial marking.

Listing 3.3. ASP representation of network of Fig. 1

```
1  place(r).    place(s).    place(t).    place(u).    place(v).
2  place(x).    place(y).    place(z).
3
4  trans(t1).   trans(t2).   trans(t3).   trans(t4).
5
6  token(a).    token(b).    token(c).    token(d).
7
8  ptarc(r,t1,d).    ptarc(s,t1,a).
9  tparc(t1,u,a).    tparc(t1,u,d).
10
11 ptarc(t,t2,b).    ptarc(u,t2,a).
12 ptarc(u,t2,d).
13 tparc(t2,x,a).    tparc(t2,x,b).    tparc(t2,x,d).
14 tparcbond(t2,x,a,b).
15
16 ptarc(v,t3,c).    ptarc(u,t3,a).    ptarc(u,t3,d).
17 tparc(t3,y,a).    tparc(t3,y,c).    tparc(t3,y,d).
18 tparcbond(t3,y,a,c).
19
20 ptarc(v,t4,c).    ptarc(x,t4,a).    ptarc(x,t4,b).
21 ptarc(x,t4,d).    ptarcbond(x,t4,a,b).
22 tparc(t4,z,a).    tparc(t4,z,b).    tparc(t4,z,c).
23 tparc(t4,z,d).
24 tparcbond(t4,z,a,b).   tparcbond(t4,z,b,c).
25
26 holds(r,d,0).   holds(s,a,0).   holds(t,b,0).   holds(v,c,0).
```

Then, query

```
goal:- connected(P,a,c,T),place(P),time(T).
:- not goal.
```

asks for a reachable state where there is a place P s.t. $a - c \in M(\texttt{P})$. The ASP encoding returns the answer `fires(t1,0) fires(t3,1)`. For query

```
goal:-C>1,C=#count{K2:connected(P,K1,K2,T),token(K2)},holds(P,K1,T).
:- not goal.
```

where a state is sought where some place holds a bond with at least three tokens, clingo finds the solution `fires(t1,0) fires(t2,1) fires(t4,2)`. We can arbitrarily increase the complexity of the analysis, by combining aggregates such as #count in conjunctive or disjunctive queries such as

```
goal1(T):- C>1,C=#count{K2:connected(P,K1,K2,T),token(K2)},
           holds(P,K1,T).
goal2(T):- connected(P,a,c,T), not connected(P,a,b,T),time(T).
goal:- goal1(T1),goal2(T2),T2>T1,time(T1),time(T2).
:- not goal.
```

where we search for a sequence of transitions that first create a bond with at least three tokens, and then a bond with a and c but without b. The answer computed now is `fires(t1,0) fires(t2,1) fires(t4,2) reversesC(t4,3) reversesC(t2,4) fires(t3,5)`.

4   Conclusions

We have presented work in progress towards a methodology for analysing reversible systems modeled as RPNs based on ASP. We argue that ASP allows an expressive and flexible methodology for defining models and their properties, which can handle difficult queries on complex models efficiently. As future work, we plan to extend our translation to out-of-causal reversibility, to capture a variety of RPN properties, and to apply the framework on realistic systems. We remark that a complementary approach which we are also exploring is the possibility to exploit existing model-checking Petri net tools (CPN tools [10]) for analysing RPN models through a translation of RPNs to coloured Petri nets [4]. CPN tools is a graphical tool for the simulation of Reversing Petri nets. However, it does not pursue more than one simulation and it breaks transition choice ties randomly. Its effectiveness is still to be verified as the approach is characterized by a blow-up in the state space during the translation to coloured Petri nets.

References

1. Anwar, S., Baral, C., Inoue, K.: Encoding higher level extensions of petri nets in answer set programming. In: Cabalar, P., Son, T.C. (eds.) LPNMR 2013. LNCS (LNAI), vol. 8148, pp. 116–121. Springer, Heidelberg (2013). https://doi.org/10.1007/978-3-642-40564-8_12
2. Anwar, S., Baral, C., Inoue, K.: Encoding Petri nets in answer set programming for simulation based reasoning. TPLP, 13(4-5-Online-Supplement) (2013)
3. Anwar, S., Baral, C., Inoue, K.: Simulation-based reasoning about biological pathways using Petri nets and ASP. Logical Modeling of Biological Systems, pp. 207–243 (2014)
4. Barylska, K., Gogolinska, A., Mikulski, L., Philippou, A., Piatkowski, M., Psara, K.: Reversing computations modelled by coloured Petri nets. In: Proceedings of ATAED 2018, CEUR Workshop, vol. 2115, pp. 91–111 (2018)
5. Gebser, M., Kaminski, R., Kaufmann, B., Schaub, T.: Answer Set Solving in Practice. Morgan Claypool Publishers, San Rafael (2012)
6. Heljanko, K., Niemelä, I.: Bounded LTL model checking with stable models. TPLP 3(4–5), 519–550 (2003)
7. Lifschitz, V.: Answer Set Programming. Springer, Berlin (2019)
8. Philippou, A., Psara, K.: Reversible computation in petri nets. In: Kari, J., Ulidowski, I. (eds.) RC 2018. LNCS, vol. 11106, pp. 84–101. Springer, Cham (2018). https://doi.org/10.1007/978-3-319-99498-7_6
9. Philippou, A., Psara, K., Siljak, H.: Controlling reversibility in reversing petri nets with application to wireless communications. In: Thomsen, M.K., Soeken, M. (eds.) RC 2019. LNCS, vol. 11497, pp. 238–245. Springer, Cham (2019). https://doi.org/10.1007/978-3-030-21500-2_15
10. Ratzer, A.V., et al.: CPN tools for editing, simulating, and analysing coloured petri nets. In: van der Aalst, W.M.P., Best, E. (eds.) ICATPN 2003. LNCS, vol. 2679, pp. 450–462. Springer, Heidelberg (2003). https://doi.org/10.1007/3-540-44919-1_28

A Reversible Runtime Environment for Parallel Programs

Takashi Ikeda and Shoji Yuen[✉]

Graduate School of Informatics, Nagoya University,
Furo-cho, Chikusa-ku, Nagoya 464-8601, Japan
{tikeda,yuen}@sqlab.jp

Abstract. We present a reversible runtime environment for simple parallel programs and its experimental implementation. We aim at a lightweight implementation of the *backtrack reversibility* by the *state-saving* mechanism using stacks. We translate a program to a sequence of simple commands of an executable intermediate representation for reversible stack machines. The parallel composition is implemented using the multiprocessing feature of Python. While executing the commands, the stack machines collect the information for the backward execution in the auxiliary stacks for the update history of the variables and the history of jumps. The commands for the backward execution is obtained by reversing the commands for the forward execution by replacing each command with the corresponding reversed command. In the purpose of behaviour analysis with reversibility such as debugging, our runtime is more portable than the source-to-source translation of a high-level programming language.

Keywords: Reversible computation · Imparative parallel programs · Stack machine · Python multiprocessing

1 Introduction

Reverse execution of programs has been investigated based on the reversible computing recently. Undoing the effect of an execution of a program till returning to the initial state is useful in analysing the finer-grained behavioural property of the program. In general, the execution of a parallel program depends on the environment such as the scheduler and I/O channels. Replaying the program may not reach the same states as the previous run. This makes behavioural analysis difficult to work out the cause of the defect for debugging.

Reversible programming languages such as Janus [4,7] and RFUN [6] are designed for the reversed execution at the level of the design of programming languages. For example, Janus needs the extra-control structure at the end of the conditional branch in order to know which branch is executed to reverse the conditional statement. For this approach, the state-saving mechanism is not needed

© Springer Nature Switzerland AG 2020
I. Lanese and M. Rawski (Eds.): RC 2020, LNCS 12227, pp. 272–279, 2020.
https://doi.org/10.1007/978-3-030-52482-1_18

since the computation is fully reversed. However, introducing parallel composition becomes difficult since the runtime environment is not directly described in programs.

We present a reverse execution mechanism that the runtime collects the information in stacks at a forward execution. At the reverse execution, the runtime executes the program simply in the reversed order using the information stored in the stacks. A source program is compiled to a sequence of simple commands executed by the stack machine. Each process in the parallel composition is dispatched to each stack machine forked from the initial stack machine. We implement the backtrack reversibility with the multiprocessing feature of Python. In the reverse execution, multiple stack machines are invoked, but they are controlled by the stacks to follow back the forward execution.

The report is structured as follows. Section 2 gives the syntax of the programs, Sect. 3 presents the stack machine design and Sect. 4 states the concluding remarks.

2 Programming Language with Parallel Composition

Our parallel programming language is defined as follows where $()^+$ and $()^*$ denotes the repetition of one or more times and zero or more times respectively:

$$
\begin{aligned}
P &::= DQR \mid DQ \text{ par } \{Q\}(\{Q\})^+ R \\
D &::= (\text{var } X;)^* \\
R &::= (\text{remove } X;)^* \\
Q &::= (S;)^* S \\
S &::= \text{skip} \mid X{=}E \mid \text{if } C \text{ then } Q \text{ else } Q \text{ fi} \mid \text{while } C \text{ do } Q \text{ od} \\
E &::= X \mid n \mid E \text{ op } E \mid (E) \\
C &::= B \mid C \text{ \&\& } C \mid \text{not } C \mid (C) \\
B &::= E \text{ == } E \mid E < E
\end{aligned}
$$

The language is a simplified version of that in [2,3]. par denotes the parallel composition of sequential procedures. For simplicity, we remove the nested block structure and procedures. remove statements at the end of a program correspond to the variables declared at the beginning of the program, where the order of declarations is supposed to be reversed. For example, if variables are declared as var X; var Y, the variables are removed as remove Y; remove X. This ensures the correspondence between the variable and the entry of the symbol table.

3 Reversible Execution of Stack Machine Code

3.1 Reversible Stack Machine

For simplicity, a parallel program in this report is limited in the form that an initial stack machine runs first followed by parallel blocks. For values, we consider the integers $\mathbb{Z}$. $\mathbb{A}$ is the set of *address* $\mathbb{A}$ as the locations of commands in a stack machine code. Here an address is a positive natural number. $\mathbb{P}$ is the set of stack machine identifiers (SMid). An SMid is a natural number. We assume the initial stack machine has the SMid of 0. Other stack machines have id's in a row from 1 to N where N is the number of parallel blocks.

The stack machine configuration is $(PC, PC', w, \rho, \xi)_\sigma$ where PC is the program counter, PC' holds the previous PC value, $w \in \mathbb{Z}^*$ is a local stack, $\rho \in (\mathbb{A} \times \mathbb{P})^*$ is a label stack, and $\xi \in (\mathbb{Z} \times \mathbb{P})^*$ is a value stack. σ is a symbol table that maps a variable to its value. $\sigma(v)$ presents the value of v. For the local stack w and $z \in \mathbb{Z}$, zw is the concatenation of z and w.

Each stack machine is identified by (p, N) with p is a process identifier and N is a number of all parallel blocks in a program. The behaviour of a stack machine $SM_{(p,N)}$ for command c is specified by $\xrightarrow{c}_{(p,N)}$ as follows:

nop: $(PC_p, PC'_p, w_p, \rho, \xi)_\sigma \xrightarrow{\langle \text{nop } 0 \rangle}_{(p,N)} (PC_p + 1, PC_p, w_p, \rho, \xi)_\sigma$
$\langle \text{nop } 0 \rangle$ does nothing but increasing the program counter.

ipush: $(PC_p, PC'_p, w_p, \rho, \xi)_\sigma \xrightarrow{\langle \text{ipush } z \rangle}_{(p,N)} (PC_p + 1, PC_p, zw_p, \rho, \xi)_\sigma$
$\langle \text{ipush } z \rangle$ pushes an immediate value of z to the local stack.

load: $(PC_p, PC'_p, w_p, \rho, \xi)_\sigma \xrightarrow{\langle \text{load } v \rangle}_{(p,N)} (PC_p + 1, PC_p, \sigma(v)w_p, \rho, \xi)_\sigma$
$\langle \text{load } v \rangle$ puts a value of v on the top of the local stack.

store: $(PC_p, PC'_p, zw_p, \rho, \xi)_\sigma \xrightarrow{\langle \text{store } v \rangle}_{(p,N)} (PC_p + 1, PC_p, w_p, \rho, \langle \sigma(v), p \rangle \xi)_{\sigma[v \mapsto z]}$
$\langle \text{store } v \rangle$ pops a value from the local stack and store the value z to the local storage σ *after* saving the previous value $\sigma(v)$ to the value stack along with the process number.

jpc: $(PC_p, PC'_p, zw_p, \rho, \xi)_\sigma \xrightarrow{\langle \text{jpc } a \rangle}_{(p,N)} \begin{cases} (a, PC_p, w_p, \rho, \xi)_\sigma & \text{if } z \neq 0 \\ (PC_p + 1, PC_p, w_p, \rho, \xi)_\sigma & \text{if } z = 0 \end{cases}$
$\langle \text{jpc } a \rangle$ jumps to a when the stack top is 0. Otherwise, it moves to the next instruction by increasing the program counter.

jmp: $(PC_p, PC'_p, w_p, \rho, \xi)_\sigma \xrightarrow{\langle \text{jmp } a \rangle}_{(p,N)} (a, PC_p, w_p, \rho, \xi)_\sigma$
$\langle \text{jmp } a \rangle$ jumps to a unconditionally.

op: $(PC_p, PC'_p, z_1 z_2 w_p, \rho, \xi)_\sigma \xrightarrow{\langle \text{op } k \rangle}_{(p,N)} (PC_p + 1, PC_p, \text{op}_k(z_1, z_2)w_p, \rho, \xi)_\sigma$
where $\text{op}_1 \equiv +, \text{op}_2 \equiv \times, \text{op}_3 \equiv -, \text{op}_4 \equiv <, \text{op}_5 \equiv ==$.
$z_1 < z_2$ and $z_1 == z_2$ are 1 when the relations hold and 0 otherwise.
$\langle \text{op } k \rangle$ applies the operation specified by k. Depending on k, it pops two or one from the local stack and pushes the result on the local stack. When $\langle \text{op } k \rangle$ is a relation, it pushes 1 when the relation holds and pushes 0 otherwise.

label: $(PC_p, PC'_p, w_p, \rho, \xi)_\sigma \xrightarrow{\langle \text{label } n \rangle} (PC_p + 1, PC_p, w_p, \langle n + 1 - PC'_p, p \rangle \rho, \xi)$
$\langle \text{label } n \rangle$ pushes the address for backward execution to the label stack where n is the number of all instructions. **label** is the only instruction that uses PC'_p.

rjmp: $(PC_p, PC'_p, w_p, \langle a, N + 1 - i \rangle \rho, \xi)_\sigma \xrightarrow{\langle \text{rjmp } 0 \rangle}_{(p,N)} (a, PC_p, w_p, \rho, \xi)_\sigma$
$\langle \text{rjmp } 0 \rangle$ is a reverse jump that pops an address and a stack machine number from the label stack and jump back to the address on that process with the number.

restore: $(PC_p, PC'_p, w_p, \rho, \langle z, N + 1 - i \rangle \xi)_\sigma \xrightarrow{\langle \text{restore } v \rangle}_{(p,N)} (PC_p + 1, PC_p, zw_p, \rho, \xi)_{\sigma[v \mapsto z]}$
$\langle \text{restore } v \rangle$ pops the value of v and the stack machine number from the value stack on the specified stack machine.

alloc: $(PC_p, PC'_p, w_p, \rho, \xi)_\sigma \xrightarrow{\langle \text{alloc } v \rangle}_{(p,N)} (PC_p + 1, PC_p, w_p, \rho, \xi)_{\sigma[v \mapsto 0]}$
$\langle \text{alloc } v \rangle$ adds v to the environment σ and initialises v.

free: $(PC_p, PC'_p, w_p, \rho, \xi)_\sigma \xrightarrow{\langle \text{free } v \rangle}_{(p,N)} (PC_p + 1, PC_p, w_p, \rho, \xi)_{\sigma \setminus v}$
$\langle \text{free } v \rangle$ removes v from the environment σ.

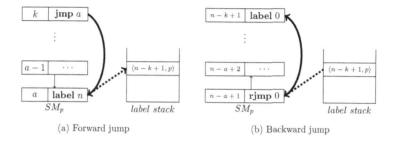

(a) Forward jump   (b) Backward jump

Fig. 1. Reversing jump instructions

store and **label** collect the information in a forward execution. **store** updates σ and ξ. In ξ, it records the value is stored by p. But in the backward execution, the process number is also reversed, and it stores $N + 1 - p$ as the backward process number. **label** records from which address the control reach this place.

rjmp and **restore** restore the information for a backward execution. **rjmp** corresponds to **label** and pops the location from ρ and jump back to the location where the forward execution came from. And **restore** puts back the previous value from the value stack. In both cases, the stack machine must be identified where the SMid is inverted since the order of the parallel blocks is reversed[1].

Figure 1 shows the mechanism of **label** and **rjmp**. **label** is a destination of **jpc** and **jmp**. If **label** is executed, it pushes the source address of that jump to the label stack. In the backward execution, **label** is substituted by **rjmp**. By popping the label stack, one of the stack machines executes **rjmp** and jumps back to the source address.

alloc allocates a variable slot on the stack and updates the symbol table. **free** removes a variable slot. $\sigma\backslash v$ removes v from the domain of σ. In current target codes, **alloc** and **free** are executed only by the initial stack machine with id 0.

3.2   Inverting Stack Machine Code

We do not present the detailed translation from a source program to the stack machine code here. The translator is implemented using Javacc. In the translation, **label** is inserted at a target of **jmp** and **jpc**. The argument of **label** is the length of the generated code. Since this is not known until the whole translation is done, it can be specified by back-patching. **par** 0 and **par** 1 are inserted for a parallel block.

From a forward stack machine code s, the backward code $\mathtt{i}(s)$ is obtained:

$$\mathtt{i}(s) = \begin{cases} \varepsilon & s = \varepsilon \\ \mathtt{i}(s')\mathtt{inv}(c) & s = cs' \end{cases}$$

---

[1] Since an address of command is uniquely assigned to a unique stack machine, it is not essential to record p in ρ. Without p in ρ, another table is necessary.

where inv_n for each command is defined as below where n is the :

$$
\begin{aligned}
\text{inv}(\langle\text{store } v\rangle) &= \langle\text{restore } v\rangle, & \text{inv}(\langle\text{jpc } a\rangle) &= \langle\text{label } 0\rangle, \\
\text{inv}(\langle\text{jmp } a\rangle) &= \langle\text{label } 0\rangle, & \text{inv}(\langle\text{label } n\rangle) &= \langle\text{rjmp } 0\rangle, \\
\text{inv}(\langle\text{par } 0\rangle) &= \langle\text{par } 1\rangle, & \text{inv}(\langle\text{par } 1\rangle) &= \langle\text{par } 0\rangle, \\
\text{inv}(\langle\text{alloc } v\rangle) &= \langle\text{free } v\rangle, & \text{inv}(\langle\text{free } v\rangle) &= \langle\text{alloc } v\rangle
\end{aligned}
$$

For other command c, $\text{inv}(\langle c \ n\rangle) = \langle\text{nop } 0\rangle$.

3.3   Execution from the Initial Stack Machine

Let s be the forward stack machine code. From the construction of a program, s is partitioned to:

$$s_I s_0 \langle\text{par } 0\rangle s_1 \langle\text{par } 1\rangle \cdots \langle\text{par } 0\rangle s_N \langle\text{par } 1\rangle s_F$$

where M is the length of the code and $SM_{(0,N)}$ executes s_I, s_0, and s_F where s_I and s_F are **alloc** and **free** for variables. s_0 is the sequential code for SM_0 to initiase the variables followed by the parallel composition. $SM_{(p,N)}$ executes s_p in parallel for $1 \le p \le N$.

Figure 2 shows the overview of executing a program. The code starts on the initial stack machine SM_0. After reaching the parallel composition starting with **par** 0, the N stack machines run in parallel. When all the executions of parallel processes terminate, it passes the control to the initial stack machine, freeing the variable at the end. The environment σ, the label stack ρ, and the value stack ξ are shared by all stack machines.

Let ρ and ξ be the label stack and the value stack. $\langle\text{Exec}_s(PC, PC', w), \rho, \xi\rangle$ is a configuration of code s with the initial SM. For the forward execution, the initial configuration is $\langle\text{Exec}_s(1, 0, \varepsilon), \varepsilon, \varepsilon\rangle$ and the final configuration is $\langle\text{Exec}_s(M+1, M, \varepsilon), \rho_F, \xi_F\rangle$. The corresponding backward execution starts with $\langle\text{Exec}_{i(s)}(1, 0, \varepsilon), \rho_F, \xi_F\rangle$ and ends with $\langle\text{Exec}_{i(s)}(M+1, M, \varepsilon), \varepsilon, \varepsilon\rangle$. While the parallel blocks are executed, the configuration is in the form:

$$\langle\text{Exec}_s^1(PC_1, PC_1', w_1)\| \cdots \|\text{Exec}_s^N(PC_N, PC_N', \varepsilon), \sigma, \rho, \xi\rangle$$

We define the execution of s as the transition relation between configurations shown in Fig. 3. In the rules above, $PC \in s$ denotes that PC points a code in s. $s(PC)$ is the code pointed by PC and $loc(s_i)$ is the address of s_i in the stack machine code.

- Init defines the behaviour before and after the parallel composition. ℓ is the number of variables. SM_0 constructs the symbol table by s_I and executes the initial sequential code s_0.
- Fork dispatches the development of the parallel blocks once it reaches the first **par** 0. The program counter of stack machine SM_i is set to $loc(s_i)$.
- Par defines the interleaving behaviour of the parallel composition.
- Merge goes back to the initial stack machine and sets the PC to $loc(s_F)$ once all SM_p reaches **par** 0. The execution continues with Init.

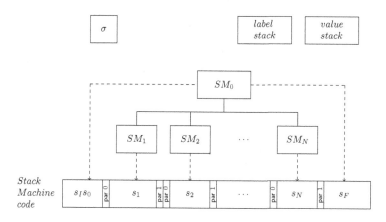

Fig. 2. Execution by stack machines

$$\frac{PC^1 \in s_0, s_I, s_F, (PC^1, PC'^1, w^1, \rho^1, \xi^1)_{\sigma^1} \xrightarrow{s(PC^1)}_{(0,N)} (PC^2, PC'^2, \rho^2, \xi^2)_{\sigma^2}}{\langle \mathsf{Exec}_s(PC^1, PC'^1, w^1), \rho^1, \xi^1 \rangle \rightarrow \langle \mathsf{Exec}_s(PC^2, PC'^2, w^2), \rho^2, \xi^2 \rangle} \;[\mathsf{Init}]$$

$$\frac{s(PC_0) = \langle \mathbf{par}\ 0 \rangle}{\langle \mathsf{Exec}_s(PC_0, PC_0', w_0), \rho_0, \xi_0 \rangle \rightarrow \atop \langle \mathsf{Exec}_s^1(loc(s_1), PC_0, \varepsilon) \| \cdots \| \mathsf{Exec}_s^N(loc(s_N), PC_0, \varepsilon), \sigma, \rho_0, \xi_0 \rangle} \;[\mathsf{Fork}]$$

$$\frac{(PC_p^1, PC_p'^1, w_p, \rho, \xi)_\sigma \xrightarrow{s(PC_p^1)}_{(p,N)} (PC_p^2, PC_p'^2, w_p', \rho', \xi')_{\sigma'}, PC_p^1 \in s_p}{\langle \mathsf{Exec}_s^1(PC_1, PC_1', w_1) \| \cdots \| \mathsf{Exec}_s^p(PC_p^1, PC_p'^1, w_p) \| \cdots \| \mathsf{Exec}_s^N(PC_N, PC_N', w_N), \sigma, \rho, \xi \rangle \atop \rightarrow \langle \mathsf{Exec}_s^1(PC_1, PC_1', w_1) \| \cdots \| \mathsf{Exec}_s^p(PC_p^2, PC_p'^2, w_p') \| \cdots \| \mathsf{Exec}_s^N(PC_N, PC_N', w_N), \sigma', \rho', \xi' \rangle} \;[\mathsf{Par}]$$

$$\frac{\wedge_p s(PC_p) = \langle \mathbf{par}\ 1 \rangle}{\langle \mathsf{Exec}_s^1(PC_1, PC_1', w_1) \| \cdots \| \mathsf{Exec}_s^N(PC_N, PC_N', w_N), \sigma, \rho, \xi \rangle \rightarrow \langle \mathsf{Exec}_s(loc(s_F), 0, \varepsilon), \sigma, \rho, \xi' \rangle} \;[\mathsf{Merge}]$$

Fig. 3. Execution for code s

In order to implement the operational semantics, it is necessary to scan the whole stack machine code before executing the code to identify N, $loc(s_i)$ and $loc(s_F)$.

4   Concluding Remarks

We present a reversible runtime environment for simple parallel programs and its experimental implementation by Python. The reversibility mechanism is *state-saving* and the environment performs the *back-track* reversibility. The runtime environment is a set of reversible stack machines. The stack machines that execute the parallel blocks share the stacks for value-updates and jumps. Since we focus on the reversibility of states, we do not precisely reverse the forward computation. We replace the commands for computing values with **nop** in the backward code. This eases the concurrency control in the backward execution since it has no effect for states. We regard this is enough for behavioural analysis such as debugging. The approach of forward and backward executions is fundamentally similar to that of [2]. Our approach is finer-grained than [2]. This eases the implementation with the existing runtime since the runtime is often less controlled. As the result, in our approach a backward execution does not precisely undo the forward execution at the level of stack machine code. By sharing the variable environment, the label stack, and the value stack, we manage the consistency of variable updates among the stack machines running in parallel.

As related work, our stack machine is close to the basic architecture of [1] in jumping mechanism although only a sequential execution is considered. The label stack maintains the control of jumps across the parallel composition. [5] presents the reversible semantics in the functional programming style at the abstract machine level with communications and concurrency. [5] gives the operational semantics for backward execution, while our approach translates the abstract machine instructions for backwards within the single operational semantics. Our language has no built-in communication mechanism.

For future work, we need to prove the correctness of our translation by strictly formalising the behaviour of the concurrent execution of a program. The programming language in Sect. 2 limits the class of programs although the stack machine operations have more capability. Adding the nested structure of blocks and procedure is possible by extending the reference mechanism for variables. Adding recursion with the parallel composition make the number of parallel processes dynamic. We need to extend the numbering scheme for identifying the sequential processes executed in parallel and how to choose the next available process in the backward execution.

Acknowledgement. The authors thank Dr. I. Ulidowski and Dr. J. Hoey for the valuable suggestions and discussion. This work was supported by JSPS KAKENHI Grant Numbers JP17H01722 and JP17K19969.

A   Runtime Environment by Python

The concrete examples and our implementation by Python are shown at https:// github.com/syuen1/RevRunTimeEnv.

A source program is compiled to the forward stack machine code.

```
% java Parser "source program"
```

The forward stack machine code is stored in `code.txt`. To run the code forward,

```
% Python vm.py code.txt f v
```

Then, we get `stack.txt`,`rstack.txt`, and `lstack.txt` as the stack for variable values and the stack for labels[2]

---

[2] The last v shows the verbose mode to show all the steps. No intermediate result is shown when q is specified.

To invert the forward code,

```
% Python inv.py code.txt invcode.txt
```

And run the backward code,

```
% Python vm.py invcode.txt b v
```

In the backward, `vm.py` reads the stack files. The result for the airline ticket example is shown in the appendix.

A.1 Controlling Parallel Blocks

The runtime can be executed step-by-step choosing which parallel block is executed in the next step in both directions. The execution of the parallel blocks is controlled by the process that is running the initial stack machine. By entering the process number, the program executes one step in the forward and backward execution showing the stacks.

References

1. Axelsen, H.B., Glück, R., Yokoyama, T.: Reversible machine code and its abstract processor architecture. In: Diekert, V., Volkov, M.V., Voronkov, A. (eds.) CSR 2007. LNCS, vol. 4649, pp. 56–69. Springer, Heidelberg (2007). https://doi.org/10.1007/978-3-540-74510-5_9
2. Hoey, J., Ulidowski, I.: Reversible imperative parallel programs and debugging. In: Thomsen, M.K., Soeken, M. (eds.) RC 2019. LNCS, vol. 11497, pp. 108–127. Springer, Cham (2019). https://doi.org/10.1007/978-3-030-21500-2_7
3. Hoey, J., Ulidowski, I., Yuen, S.: Reversing parallel programs with blocks and procedures. In: EXPRESS/SOS 2018, Beijing, China, 3 September 2018, EPTCS, vol. 276, pp. 69–86 (2018)
4. Levin, R.Y., Sherman, A.T.: A note on Bennett's time-space tradeoff for reversible computation. SIAM J. Comput. **19**(4), 673–677 (1990)
5. Lienhardt, M., Lanese, I., Mezzina, C.A., Stefani, J.-B.: A reversible abstract machine and its space overhead. In: Giese, H., Rosu, G. (eds.) FMOODS/FORTE -2012. LNCS, vol. 7273, pp. 1–17. Springer, Heidelberg (2012). https://doi.org/10.1007/978-3-642-30793-5_1
6. Thomsen, M.K., Axelsen, H.B.: Interpretation and programming of the reversible functional language RFUN. In: IFL 2015, Koblenz, Germany, 14–16 September 2015, pp. 8:1–8:13. ACM (2015)
7. Yokoyama, T., Glück, R.: A reversible programming language and its invertible self-interpreter. In: PEPM 2007, pp. 144–153. ACM (2007)

Author Index

Printed in the United States
By Bookmasters